COMPETITION LAW *in* INDIA

COMPETITION LAW *in* INDIA

Policy, Issues, and Developments

REVISED AND UPDATED
THIRD EDITION

T. RAMAPPA

Oxford University Press is a department of the University of Oxford.
It furthers the University's objective of excellence in research, scholarship,
and education by publishing worldwide. Oxford is a registered trademark of
Oxford University Press in the UK and in certain other countries

Published in India by
Oxford University Press
22 Workspace, 2nd Floor, 1/22 Asaf Ali Road, New Delhi 110002, India

© Oxford University Press 2006

The moral rights of the author have been asserted

First Edition published in 2006
Oxford India Paperbacks (Second Edition) published in 2009
Third Revised Edition published in 2014
22nd impression 2023

All rights reserved. No part of this publication may be reproduced, stored in
a retrieval system, or transmitted, in any form or by any means, without the
prior permission in writing of Oxford University Press, or as expressly
permitted by law, by licence or under terms agreed with the appropriate
reprographics rights organization. Enquiries concerning reproduction outside
the scope of the above should be sent to the Right Department, Oxford
University Press, at the address above

You must not circulate this book in any other form
and you must impose this same condition on any acquirer

ISBN 13: 978-0-19-809727-3
ISBN 10: 0-19-809727-1

Typeset in Adobe Garamond Pro 10.5/12.5
by TheG raphics Solution, New Delhi 110 092
Printed in India by Manipal Technologies Limited, Manipal

To
*the enterprising spirit of those intrepid merchants of the Indus Valley
who engaged in international commerce centuries ago*

Contents

Preface to the Third Edition   xv
Preface to the Second Edition   xix
Preface to the First Edition   xxv
Acknowledgements   xxvii

1. An Introduction and Overview   1

The Competition Act, 2002	1
Antitrust Issues	2
Coverage of the Act—The New Regulatory System	4
Anti-competitive Agreements	5
Abuse of a Dominant Position	6
Combination/Acquisition	6
The Background Setting Leading to the Act	7
The Committee's Assessment	8
WTO Obligations	10
GATS	10
TRIPS	12
WTO Agreements and the Act	12
The New Competition Law—Repealing the MRTP Act	13
Fair Criticism?	14
The Scheme of the MRTP Act	15
The Material Provisions of the Law	15
Concentration of Economic Power	15
Monopolistic Trade Practices	16
Restrictive Trade Practice	17

Registrable Agreements Relating to Restrictive Trade Practices	18
Unfair Trade Practices	18
Enforcement Authorities	18
Implementation of the MRTP Act	19
The Competition Act—An Overview	21
The Law Relating to Competition	21
Anti-competitive Agreements	21
Cartels	23
Abuse of a Dominant Position	25
Combinations	25
Enforcement	26
Authorities Enforcing the Competition Act, 2002	26
Competition Advocacy	35
Draft National Competition Policy	36
Power to Make Rules, Regulations—Sections 63, 64	37
Power of the Commission to Make Regulations—Section 64	37
Some Issues in Enforcement	42
Penalties under the Act	43
Potential for Conflict	44
Areas Needing Further Consideration	49
Telecommunications	49
Competition Issues in Telecommunication Services	50
The Telecom Regulatory Authority of India Act (TRAI), 1997	51
The Functions of TRAI—Aligning with the Competition Commission	51
Professional Services	53
Multidisciplinary Partnerships	54
Competition in Professional Services	57
'Report on Competition in Professional Services' (European Commission)	57
Acts of Persons from Abroad Affecting Competition in India	58
The Future	61

2. ANTI-COMPETITIVE AGREEMENTS — 67
- The Terms Used — 68
- Section 3—Substance — 73
- Comparative Law — 75
  - Competition Law of the EEC — 75
  - Modernizing Legislation—EEC — 76
  - The Competition Act, 1998, UK — 77
  - Competition Law of the US — 77
- Section 3—The Elements — 78
  - Section 3(1)—Appreciable Adverse Effect on Competition within India — 78
  - Evaluating Appreciable Adverse Effect on Competition within India — 89
  - Rules for Determining Effect on Competition — 93
  - The Two Rules Under the Competition Act — 94
  - Causing Entry Barriers — 99
  - Eliminating Competition — 99
  - Benefits that may Flow from an Agreement — 102
- Section 3(2) — 104
- Section 3(3) Cartels and Similar Groups — 104
  - What is a Cartel? — 104
- Section 3(4) — 120
  - Vertical Restraints — 120
- Section 3(5)—Exercise of Intellectual Property Rights and Competition — 131
  - Patents — 132
  - Adequacy of Section 3(5) — 136
  - Obligation under TRIPS — 137
  - Evaluating Technology Transfer Agreements Under Competition Law — 138
  - US — 138
  - EU — 138
  - Need to Review Section 3(5) — 140
- Enforcement Provisions — 141
  - Orders that may be Passed by the Competition Commission — 141
  - Enforcement against Those not Carrying on Business in India—Section 32 — 144

Contents

3. ABUSE OF A DOMINANT POSITION	157
Section 4—Dominant Position Abuse	157
Amendments to Section 4	158
Acts in Bonafide Competition Excepted	159
Dominant Position—Definition	159
Predatory Price	160
Dominant Position—Elaboration	160
Abuse of a Dominant Position	161
Comparative Law	162
The Competition Act, 1998, UK	163
Ascertaining the Dominant Position—Statutory Guides under the Competition Act, 2002	164
Dominant Position—Relevant Market	165
Factors to be Considered in Determining the Geographic and Product Market	167
Abuse of a Dominant Position	167
Precedents	169
Assessing Dominant Position	169
Collective Dominance—Sharing the Market on a Geographical Basis	171
Subsidiary's Conduct Attributed to Holding Company	172
Abusive Conduct Outside the Dominated Market	173
Unfair Trading Conditions	176
Abuse by Holder of Exclusive Right Conferred by State	177
Discriminatory Pricing	178
Selling at a Lower Price	179
Predatory Pricing	180
Conspiracy to Sell at Predatory Prices	182
Volume Rebates	183
EC Position	185
Predatory Pricing—Internet Access Services	188
Legitimate Competition	188
Restriction of Territory of Sale, Persons, etc.	189
Entry Barriers	190
Refusal to Supply	191
Discontinuing Sale of Raw Material	192

Refusal to Licence Copyright Material	193
The Process of Dealing with Abuse of a Dominant Position	195
Orders that the Commission may Pass	195
Section 27	196
Discontinuance of Abuse/Penalties	196
Compensation	196
Division of the Enterprise	197
Interim Orders—Section 33	197

4. COMBINATION — 201

The MRTP Act	201
Acquisition of Shares	202
The Companies Act, 1956	202
The Securities and Exchange Board of India (SEBI)	202
Mergers—the Companies Act, 1956	203
Why a Merger	204
The Courts' Approach	205
The Need for Control of Mergers and Acquisitions	207
Combination—the Legal Framework	208
Acquisition/Merger	208
Regulations Setting Out the Procedure Applicable to Combinations	214
Comparative Law	214
The Clayton Act—USA	214
The EC Merger Regulation	215
The Enterprise Act, 2002—UK	217
Regulation of Combinations—Section 6	218
Definitions under the Competition Act, 2002	219
Combination	219
Acquisition	222
Assets	224
Control	225
Enterprise	229
Group	229
Merger or Amalgamation	229
Turnover	229
Control of Anti-competitive Combinations	230

Appreciable Adverse Effect on Competition	230
Evaluating a Combination	231
Guidelines for Evaluating Effects of a Merger on Competition	235
US	235
UK	235
The 2002 Act	236
Acquisition	236
Causing Another Company to Become a Subsidiary	237
Concentrated Industry	241
Vertical Integration	241
Acquisition of Assets	244
Acquiring Machinery for Standardization	245
Shares in a Competing Company	246
Joint Ventures	247
Agreement Among Joint Venture Partners	248
Potential Competition—Section 7 of the Clayton Act	249
Merger	251
Joint Control—Shareholding and Restructuring Agreement	251
Merger Eliminating a Competitor	252
Product Market, End-uses	254
Telecommunication Services	255
Internet Access Services	256
Regulation of Combinations Under the Competition Act	258
The Process	258
Section 31—Orders of the Commission on Certain Combinations	259
Reliefs	260
Multijurisdiction Mergers	261
5. ENFORCEMENT	**275**
Authorities Enforcing the Competition Act, 2002 as Amended by the 2007 Act	275
Duties, Powers, and Functions of the Commission	275
Anti-competitive Agreements and Abuse of Dominance	276

Orders which may be Passed by the Commission after Inquiry into Anti-competitive Agreements or Abuse of a Dominant Position	281
Inquiry into a Combination—The Procedure	283
Investigation of a Combination—The Procedure	284
Orders of the Commission on Certain Combinations—Section 31	286
Acts Taking Place Outside India but having an Effect on Competition in India—Section 32	287
Duties of Director-General—Section 41	292
Penalties	293
Power to Award Compensation	294
The Competition Appellate Tribunal	298
Adjudication on Claims for Compensation	299
Awarding Compensation—Section 53N	300
The Procedure for Adjudicating a Claim for Compensation	302
Provision for Representative Actions	303
Comparative Law	304
The Competition Commission, UK	308
US—Enforcement	312
Cross-border Issues and Competition	317
Cooperation Agreements Among States—Bilateral Agreements	321
Epilogue	336
Appendix	339
Bibliography	341
Case Index	345
General Index	349
About the Author	357

Preface to the Third Edition

The Competition Act, 2002 ('the Act'), received the assent of the President of India on 13 January 2003. Consequent on the challenge in the Supreme Court of India in *Brahm Dutt* v. *Union of India*, and the order on that petition, a number of amendments to the Act were made in 2007 by the Competition (Amendment) Act, 2007 (Act No. 39 of 2007), which received the assent of the President on 24 September 2007. The Competition (Amendment) Act, 2007, was brought into force on 12 October 2007. The principal amendments of the 2007 Act related to: the composition of the Competition Commission, selection committee for chairperson and members of the Commission, appointment of the secretary, experts, and officers and other employees of the Commission, a provision requiring a mandatory notice to be given to the Commission by any person or enterprise proposing to enter into a combination to which the Act applied, whereas previously this notice was optional; the establishment of the Competition Appellate Tribunal, its composition, the mechanism for selection of the chairperson and members of the Competition Appellate Tribunal, procedure for appeals to it, power to award compensation, a provision for an appeal to the Supreme Court of India against the orders of the Competition Appellate Tribunal, the repeal of the Monopolies and Restrictive Trade Practices Act, 1969 ('the MRTP Act'), and the dissolution of the MRTP Commission.

One of the key amendments of 2007 was that the Competition Commission was to act only as a market regulator, an expert body performing advisory and regulatory functions. Its adjudicatory powers were taken away and vested in the Competition Appellate Tribunal. The functions of the Appellate Tribunal are to hear and dispose of appeals against any direction issued or decision made or order passed by the

Competition Commission under certain specific provisions of the Act and to adjudicate on claims for compensation that may arise from the findings or orders of the Competition Commission or any order of the Appellate Tribunal itself in any appeal and also to pass orders for the recovery of compensation.

Section 66 of the original Act as passed in 2002, provided for the repeal of the MRTP Act, the dissolution of the MRTP Commission and for the transfer, on such dissolution, of cases pending before the MRTP Commission, under the MRTP Act, to the Competition Commission and the National Commission constituted under the Consumer Protection Act, 1986.

Section 66 has been amended twice, first in 2007 and then in 2009. As provided in the original Act of 2002, the MRTP Commission could not be dissolved on the coming into force of section 66, as the Competition Commission had not then been established, and cases pending before the MRTP Commission, on its dissolution, could not be transferred to the Competition Commission as directed by the original section 66. The 2007 amendment provided that the MRTP Commission was authorized to continue to exercise jurisdiction and power under the repealed Act for a period of two years from the date of the commencement of the 2007 Act, and section 66 was not brought into force. Section 66 of the Act was brought into force on 1 September 2009. The 2009 amendment of section 66 provides, among other matters, for the transfer of pending cases and investigations, on the commencement of the Competition Amendment Act, 2009, to the specified authorities under the Competition Act, 2002, as amended.

The amendments of 2007 and 2009 and other related provisions are discussed in the body of the text at the relevant places. The list of sections amended in 2007 and in 2009 is given as an appendix at the end of the book.

Pursuant to the 2007 amendments, the chairman and members of the Competition Commission and the chairperson and members of the Appellate Tribunal were appointed and the machinery for the administration of the Act was established. The Competition Commission has decided a number of cases under the Act, issued directions, regulations, etc. A view of the position after the 2007 and the 2009 amendments needs to be shown in a revised edition in a consolidated form and hence this third edition.

Throughout the book, the Competition Act, 2002, thus amended, will be referred to as the Competition Act, 2002, or the Act. The law is stated as on 1 June 2013.

Needless to add, no advice of any kind, legal or otherwise, is to be considered as given to the reader by the author, or for that matter, the publishers, on any of the issues covered by this book.

Chennai
June 2013

T. RAMAPPA

Preface to the Second Edition

The history of the Competition Act, 2002 ('the Act'), is a good example of the proverb that the road to hell is paved with good intentions. True, the Act was late compared to the legislation of many countries, but it was unexceptionable in terms of the key issues it was intended to deal with. Its aim was to preserve competition in the market, principally through control of anti-competitive acts, agreements, abuse of dominant position, and mergers that would impair or eliminate competition in a particular market. It was introduced at a time when large multinational companies, taking advantage of India's liberalized economic policy, permitting greater participation of overseas companies in economic activities in India established their businesses here. The Act received the assent of the President of India on 13 January 2003. Most of the sections were brought into force through notifications in the Gazette, but key sections relating to prohibition of anti-competitive agreements [section 3], abuse of dominant position [section 4], combinations [section 5], and regulation of combinations [section 6] were not.

The progress of the Act was stymied by a successful challenge, in the Supreme Court of India, in *Brahm Dutt* v. *Union of India*,[1] to the adequacy of the legal basis on which the constitution, by the Central Government, of the Competition Commission rested. Section 7 of the Act authorized the Central Government to appoint for the purposes of the Act, a commission to be called the 'Competition Commission of India'. Section 8 specified the number of members of the Commission, but it is not clear why the proviso to sub-section (1) gave the right to the Central Government to appoint the chairperson and a member during the first year of the establishment of the Commission. Sub-section (2) prescribed the qualifications for the chairperson and the other members of the Commission. It required that he shall be a person of ability, integrity and standing and who, has been, or is qualified to be, a judge of a High Court; or, has special knowledge of, and professional experience of not less than fifteen years in international trade, economics, business, commerce, law, finance, accountancy, management, industry, public affairs, administration or in any other matter which, in the opinion of the Central Government, may be useful to the Commission.

After this statement, section 9 left the selection of the chairperson and members of the Commission to be in the manner as may be prescribed, which meant that it had to await the rules that would be made under the Act. The result was that the Act was incomplete as regards the manner of selection of the chairperson and the members of the Competition Commission. On 4 April 2003, the Central Government notified the Competition Commission of India (Selection of Chairperson and Other Members of the Commission) Rules, 2003. Rule 3 empowered the Central Government to constitute a committee for the selection of the chairperson and other members of the Commission. The committee for selection was to consist of (1) a retired judge of the Supreme Court or a high court or a retired chairperson of a tribunal established or constituted under an Act of Parliament or a distinguished jurist or a senior advocate for five years standing or more; (2) a person with special knowledge of, and professional experience of twenty-five years or more in international trade, economics, business, commerce or industry; (3) a person with special knowledge of, and professional experience of twenty-five years or more in accountancy, management, finance, public affairs or administration, all to be nominated by the Central Government. The Central Government was to nominate one of the members of the committee to act as the chairperson of the committee. On the recommendation of this committee, the Central Government appointed a civil servant as chairman of the Competition Commission and another person as a member of the Commission.

The Act and Rule 3 were challenged in the Supreme Court of India, in *Brahm Dutt* v. *Union of India*, by a writ petition, pleading that Rule 3 of the Competition Commission of India (Selection of Chairperson and Other Members of the Commission) Rules, 2003, may be struck down and for other consequential reliefs, including the issue of a writ of mandamus directing the Union of India to appoint a person who may be at the time or had been, the Chief Justice of a high court or a senior judge of a high court in India to be the head of the selection committee.

The objection was on the ground that the Competition Commission envisaged by the Act was more of a judicial body having adjudicatory powers and in the background of the doctrine of separation of powers recognized by the Indian Constitution, the right to appoint the judicial members of the Commission should rest with the Chief Justice of India or his nominee. Further, it was argued that the chairman of the commission had necessarily to be a retired Chief Justice or judge of the Supreme Court or of the high court, to be nominated by the Chief Justice of India or by a committee presided over by the Chief Justice of India. In other words, the appointment of a civil servant, without reference to the head of the judiciary, was argued as being undesirable in law, considering the purposes of the Act and the functions to be discharged by the Competition Commission. Before the Supreme Court, the Central Government represented that the Central Government intended to make certain amendments to the Act and also to Rule 3 of 'the Rules', to carry into effect the selection of the chairman and the members of the Commission by a committee presided over by the Chief Justice of India or his nominee. It was also submitted that the chairman of the Commission would be an expert in the field and that it was not necessary for him to be a judge or a retired judge of the high court or the Supreme Court. The Supreme Court was satisfied with that as a basic position, and that the establishment of an appellate authority to be constituted, by an amendment of the Act, which would be an adjudicatory body, would conform to the concept of separation of judicial powers and closed the writ application without pronouncing on the issues raised. It left open all questions regarding the validity of the enactment including the validity of Rule 3 of the Rules, to be decided after the amendment of the Act as held out, if there were any challenges to the amended Act.

In the light of the order of the Supreme Court, the Central Government introduced in Parliament, the Competition (Amendment) Bill, 2006. The Bill was referred to the Parliamentary Standing Committee on Finance (2006–7), hereafter referred to as 'the Standing Committee' and after taking into account its recommendations, the Competition (Amendment) Bill, 2007, was introduced in Parliament and after approval by both Houses, the Competition (Amendment) Act, 2007 (Act No. 39 of 2007) received the assent of the President on 24 September 2007. Section 1 of the Amendment Act, that is, the Competition (Amendment) Act, 2007 was brought into force on 12 October 2007 by the Notification dated 12 October 2007 by the Central Government.[2] Certain other sections of the 2007 Act were also brought into force on the same day by a different notification issued on that day. The notes in the relevant pages will show the sections that have so far been notified as having been brought into force.

The principal amendments relate to: the composition of the Competition Commission, Selection Committee for chairperson and members of the Commission, appointment of the secretary, experts and officers and other employees of the Commission, a provision requiring a mandatory notice to be given to the Commission by any person or enterprise proposing to enter into a combination to which the Act applies, whereas previously this notice was optional; the establishment of the Competition Appellate Tribunal, its composition, the mechanism for selection of the chairperson and members of the Competition Appellate Tribunal, procedure for appeals to it, power to award compensation, a provision for an appeal to the Supreme Court of India against the orders of the Competition Appellate Tribunal, the repeal of the MRTP Act, and the dissolution of the MRTP Commission.

Under the amended Act, the Competition Commission will only function as a market regulator, an expert body performing advisory and regulatory functions. The new section 8, relating to the composition of the Competition Commission, which has replaced the original section 8, has made two important changes. One is that the qualification for one to be a member of the Commission, that he or she should be one who has been, or is qualified to be, a judge of a high court, has been omitted. The other is that under the new section 8, one of the conditions for eligibility for appointment as a member of the Commission, which includes that of the chairperson, is that the person to be considered for appointment should have special knowledge and professional experience in competition matters, including competition law and policy.

The amendment has introduced a new section 9 in the place of the original one providing for the composition of a Selection Committee for Chairperson and Members of the Commission. The chairperson of this Committee will be the Chief Justice of India or his nominee. Section 53A to section 53U of the newly introduced Chapter VIIIA provide for the establishment of the Competition Appellate Tribunal and related matters. The Competition Appellate Tribunal would be a three-member quasi-judicial body, headed by a person who is or has been a judge of the Supreme Court or the Chief Justice of a high court, performing adjudicatory functions. This structure would satisfy the doctrine of separation of powers. There are also a number of consequential amendments.

The 2007 amendments, made in each chapter of the Act, are discussed in sequence, in the Addendum to this second edition. The updated contents page and the revised index to the book including the material in the Addendum, it is expected, will enable the reader to understand the Act as amended in context. The proper way of referring to the 2002 Act incorporating these amendments is to call it the Competition Act, 2002 (as amended in 2007) and it will hereafter be referred to only as the Act. The Competition Act, 2002 as amended by the 2007 Act, may be browsed at the website of the Competition Commission www.cci.gov.in.

The response to the book published in 2006 and the legislative changes in 2007 have rendered updating the book necessary.

Chennai T. RAMAPPA
May 2009

Notes

[1] [2005] 64 CLA 214 SC.
[2] Notification No. SO 1746[E] dated 12 October 2007.

Preface to the First Edition

The need for evolving and stating the competition policy of India can hardly be overemphasized. In fact, it has long been overdue. What has pushed it to the forefront by the government now is the entry of multinational industries which have significant positions in international markets and which should be expected to use this to their advantage. Indian industry, used to protection, has belatedly recognized the gross inequality between them, and the multinationals, in terms of size and experience, and now expects the government to lay out what is customary called a 'level playing field', to borrow a cliché from the language relating to sports, a field not compatible with the spirit in which commerce should usually be expected to be carried on.

What seems to have been overlooked in all this discussion on what the government should do is the position of the consumer of the goods and services for whose benefit all this toil is exercised. There ought to be a greater emphasis on subserving the interests of the consumer, through a supply of the necessary range of goods and services, meaning eschewing miniscule product differentiation of no commercial significance, at reasonable prices.

After allowing suppliers of goods and services the freedom to choose their form and mode of activity, consistent with domestic law, a mechanism should be provided to ensure that in providing such supply they do not do anything in the way of upsetting the balance among the needs of the consumers, the suppliers of goods and services themselves and the economic and social concerns of the society in which the industries operate. In simple terms, this means that the task of the government will only be to ensure that there are no attempts, direct or indirect, to tinker with the market.

The experience of industrially advanced countries, the US, for example, shows that direct intervention of the government in the running of industries through controls is inappropriate as a means to speed up industrial progress. The government's role is best limited to laying the basic rules for operating in the country, and providing the means for preserving the freedom of both sellers and buyers, so that there is the minimum of 'a working competition'.

That takes us to the question of appropriate machinery for enforcing such a competition policy. This again is determined by the structure of the country's market and is to be one suited to deal with its special problems.

One certain criterion for evaluating the usefulness of any mechanism is its effectiveness in achieving the purposes for which it has been set up. For a number of reasons, the Monopolies and Restrictive Trade Practices Act ('the MRTP Act'), by all accounts did not achieve, in a coherent and cogent manner, the regulation of anti-competitive conduct, even though that Act contained some provisions to do it in a noticeable manner. It is clear that a specific law for preserving competition is necessary in the wake of the influx of large multinational companies, on the opening up of the economy of the country and, the enlargement of the range of goods and services offered to the consumer.

Obviously, in meeting such a challenge, each country will have to evolve its own model, though consideration of the experience of other countries, which have their own unique social and economic setting, will be a useful guide.

The Competition Act, 2002, received the assent of the President of India on 13 January 2003, and many of the provisions have, over a period of time, been brought into force. The key sections 3 to 6 regulating anti-competitive conduct can only be made operational on the constitution of the Competition Commission of India and filling up of the positions, which will follow after amendments are made to the Act, to make the Competition Commission an expert body. The other proposed amendments relate to the creation of an appellate body to hear appeals from the decisions of the Commission and to provide that the Commission's orders be executed by courts lower than the high courts and not the high courts as at present.

The law is stated as on 1 December 2005.

Needless to add, no advice of any kind, legal or otherwise is deemed to be given to the readers by the author, or for that matter, the publishers, on any of the issues covered by this book.

Chennai
December 2005

T. RAMAPPA

Acknowledgements

I would like to express my grateful thanks to all the institutions, organizations, and governmental and other bodies abroad who have given me access through their web pages to much of the information relevant to the subject covered by this book. Reference to the source of information thus obtained has been made in all cases in the text of the book.

I sincerely thank the Government of the UK, which has permitted the use of the material made available on their website, subject to the condition that Crown copyright in the material is acknowledged and the source of the material indicated. I acknowledge Crown copyright in all the material of the Government of the UK thus obtained and used in this book, the major ones being the Competition Act, 1998, the Enterprise Act, 2002, and many of the publications of the Office of Fair Trading (OFT), from which, extracts, to a reasonable extent, have been used as necessary. The names of all these publications, and that they are OFT publications, are stated in the text at the appropriate places.

I am also deeply grateful to the European Union (EU) for permitting use of material collected from their websites, the requirement being that the source is indicated. Most of the material used by me in this book was collected through their main site http://europa.int/lex-eur. The titles, dates, etc., of the directives and recommendations and, the references to decisions of the European Commission and the European Court have been given in the text at places where the references to them are made.

In a subject such as that the book attempts to cover, without the information provided by key agencies like the Federal Trade Commission (FTC), the Department of Justice, the Department of Commerce and other departments of the Government of the US, the text would lack balance. I thank them for giving access to their major reports and other public documents on antitrust. The use of such material taken from published reports of public bodies has been appropriate to the purpose. At all places of references to them in the book, the source of the material is indicated. The Sherman Act, Clayton Act, and other related statutes have been taken from the website of the Department of Justice. Most of the decisions of the US Supreme Court were obtained from *findlaw* and some from the Legal Information Institute of Cornell University. I thank them for making the information available.

I also thank the WTO for giving access to many of their public documents needed for reference in writing this book.

Chennai
June 2013

T. RAMAPPA

1

An Introduction and Overview

THE COMPETITION ACT, 2002

The Competition Act, 2002, 'the Act', received the assent of the President on 13 January 2003, subsequent to which various sections have been brought into force from time to time. The object of the Act, set out in the Preamble, is to provide for the establishment of a Competition Commission, '…to prevent practices having adverse effect on competition, to promote and sustain competition in markets, to protect the interests of consumers and to ensure freedom of trade carried on by other participants in markets, in India….' and for incidental matters. The basic objective is to provide a law relating to competition among enterprises that will ensure that the process of competition is left free without stronger trading enterprises manipulating the market to their advantage and following from that, to the disadvantage of consumers. The key provisions include section 3, which deals with anti-competitive agreements, section 4, which discusses abuse of a dominant position, and section 5, which deals with combinations. Section 6 deals with the regulation of combinations. A combination may be an acquisition or a merger.

Under the Act as originally enacted, the Competition Commission was the authority to deal with competition issues arising out of market conditions and complaints of violations of the Act. In *Brahm Dutt* v. *Union of India*[1] it was successfully challenged that the Competition Commission could not combine in itself the roles of a market regulator and an adjudicatory body. This led to a large number of amendments to the Act in 2007, the principal ones being the basic nature of the functions of the Competition Commission in that the Competition Commission will only function as a market regulator, an expert body performing advisory and regulatory functions and the establishment of a Competition Appellate Tribunal which would be a quasi-judicial adjudicatory body.

The material sections of the amendments made in 2007 and in 2009, repealing the MRTP Act, their scope and effect are incorporated in the text at the appropriate places in the text of the relevant chapters of the book. Throughout the book, the Competition Act, 2002, thus amended, will be referred to as the Competition Act, 2002, or the Act.

Antitrust Issues

What are the basic antitrust issues that any legislation should provide against? Whatever the system, the question, in essence, is one of dealing with conduct that impairs the process of competition. In a theoretical market, suppliers have the freedom to compete amongst themselves and the consumers have knowledge of the suppliers, the relative prices and quality, and decide to buy or not depending on their preferences and purchasing power. Market forces are stated to determine the price of a product or a service. However, the actual market is entirely different from this description.

Consumers everywhere, and this includes purchasers even in the most developed countries, have poor information of the necessary particulars of any product, including the current market price, the price range or the quality of the suppliers, and comparable products or services. Suppliers, who over a period of time, have acquired, on account of various factors, the power to manipulate the market, do everything in their power to prevent the development of a market that is free from interference. One reason for this is their intention of retaining a fixed percentage of profits, and this is possible only by either restraining or eliminating competition. Eliminating competition altogether is their objective. The means to achieve that objective are myriad and that is the reason why any legislative definition of an anti-competitive practice or conduct is general, inclusive, and also states that the practices prescribed as anti-competitive are not exhaustive.

Section 1 of the Sherman Act, the principal antitrust statute of the US, and perhaps, the earliest in the world, enacted in 1890, proscribes agreements in restraint of trade in the most general terms. The opening sentence of the section states that: 'Every contract, combination in the form of trust or otherwise, or conspiracy, in restraint of trade or commerce among the several States, or with foreign nations, is declared to be illegal.' The US Supreme Court in *Standard Oil Co. of New Jersey* v. *US*[2] declared: 'That in view of the many new forms of contracts and combinations which were being evolved from existing economic conditions, it was deemed essential by an all-embracing enumeration to make sure that no form of contract or combination by which an undue restraint of interstate or foreign commerce was brought about could save such restraint from condemnation.' The Court also added that the standard for determining whether there was a violation of the statute was the rule of reason. The concepts behind the 'rule of reason' and the 'per se' violation will be discussed later in this chapter.

Once again, the US Supreme Court explained in *Business Electronics Corp. v. Sharp Electronics Corp*[3] the scope of the term 'restraint of trade' in section 1 of the Sherman Act thus: 'The term "restraint of trade" in the Sherman Act, like the term at common law before the statute was adopted, refers not to a particular list of agreements, but to a particular economic consequence, which may be produced by quite different sorts of agreements in varying times and circumstances.'

Article 81 of the Treaty of Rome is the law of the European Union. Article 82 deals with abuse of a dominant position. Now, after the Treaty of Lisbon (1 December 2009), that is, the Treaty on the Functioning of the European Union (TFEU), Articles 81 and 82 of the EC Treaty are renumbered Articles 101 and 102 of the TFEU.

Article 81 is also very broad in the definition of the prohibition, though it refers to certain specific practices also as falling under the prohibition. Article 101 (Formerly Article 81 of TEC) is set out as follows:

1. The following shall be prohibited as incompatible with the common market: all agreements between undertakings, decisions by associations of undertakings and concerted practices which may affect trade between Member States and which have as their object or effect the prevention, restriction or distortion of competition within the common market, and in particular those which: (a) directly or indirectly fix purchase or selling prices or any other trading conditions; (b) limit or control production, markets, technical development, or investment; (c) share markets or sources of supply; (d) apply dissimilar conditions to equivalent transactions with other trading parties, thereby placing them at a competitive disadvantage; (e) make the conclusion of contracts subject to acceptance by the other parties of supplementary obligations which, by their nature or according to commercial usage, have no connection with the subject of such contracts.

2. Any agreements or decisions prohibited pursuant to this Article shall be automatically void.
3. The provisions of paragraph 1 may, however, be declared inapplicable in the case of: any agreement or category of agreements between undertakings, any decision or category of decisions by associations of undertakings, any concerted practice or category of concerted practices, which contributes to improving the production or distribution of goods or to promoting technical or economic progress, while allowing consumers a fair share of the resulting benefit, and which does not: (a) impose on the undertakings concerned restrictions which are not indispensable to the attainment of these objectives; (b) afford such undertakings the possibility of eliminating competition in respect of a substantial part of the products in question.

The provision regarding 'abuse of a dominant position', Article 102 (formerly Article 82) is as follows:

Article 102
(ex Article 82 TEC)
Any abuse by one or more undertakings of a dominant position within the internal market or in a substantial part of it shall be prohibited as incompatible with the internal market in so far as it may affect trade between Member States. Such abuse may, in particular, consist in: (a) directly or indirectly imposing unfair purchase or selling prices or other unfair trading conditions; (b) limiting production, markets or technical development to the prejudice of consumers; (c) applying dissimilar conditions to equivalent transactions with other trading parties, thereby placing them at a competitive disadvantage; (d) making the conclusion of contracts subject to acceptance by the other parties of supplementary obligations which, by their nature or according to commercial usage, have no connection with the subject of such contracts.

Coverage of the Act—The New Regulatory System

The antitrust issues that are specifically covered by the Act are: (*a*) anti-competitive agreements (section 3), (*b*) abuse of a dominant position (section 4), and (*c*) any combination, whether by way of an acquisition of an enterprise or merger of enterprises, above the prescribed threshold level of the assets or turnover of the enterprises involved in the combination (section 5). The substance of these sections is discussed in the following paragraphs.

Anti-competitive Agreements

Section 3(1) of the Act is very general and broad in scope. It prohibits and declares void any agreement between enterprises in respect of production, supply, distribution, storage, acquisition, or control of goods or provision of services, which causes, or is likely to cause an appreciable adverse effect on competition within India. There are no statutory illustrations of anti-competitive practices or conduct. Section 3(2) declares that any agreement entered into in contravention of the provisions contained in section 3(1) shall be void. Section 3(3) specifies certain anti-competitive agreements that may be entered into, or practices that may be carried on, by enterprises supplying identical or similar goods or services, or cartels. Under section 3(3), those agreements or practices carried on by that class of enterprises are presumed to have an appreciable adverse effect on competition. They are per se violations of the Act.

The usual anti-competitive agreements relate to: price-fixing, resale price maintenance, allocation among suppliers of the areas in which each will operate, reducing supply or output enabling the imposition of high prices, exclusive dealing agreements, and tie-in arrangements, all of which will have the intended effect of shutting out other sources of supply to the consumers. These are anti-competitive practices that may be engaged in by any enterprise. As should be obvious, the aim of all anti-competitive activity is to reduce competition that will increase the power of the anti-competitive enterprises to fix prices and conditions of supply.

Section 3(4) deals with what are termed vertical restraints. These are restrictions amongst enterprises at different stages or levels of the production chain in different markets. This would cover supply of goods as well as services. A typical example of this relationship is between a manufacturer and a retailer selling his goods. A manufacturer stipulating that a dealer shall not sell the goods purchased from him below the price indicated by the manufacturer is engaged in the anti-competitive practice of resale price maintenance. The vice consists in restricting the freedom of the dealer to sell at a price considered by him to be profitable. What is restricted is the ability of the dealer to compete. Vertical restraints are to be examined under the rule of reason. The appreciable adverse effect on competition has to be established in each case.

Section 3(5) provides certain exceptions from section 3. The first set of exceptions protect the right of an owner of any of the intellectual property rights under the enactments listed in the sub-section, to restrain any infringement of any of his rights, or to impose reasonable restrictions necessary for protecting any of those rights.[4] Also excepted under section 3(5) are terms of an agreement relating exclusively to the export of goods or supply of services abroad.[5] All these are considered in detail in the next chapter.

Abuse of a Dominant Position

Section 4[6] prohibits certain practices that are considered to be abuse of a dominant position by an enterprise. Some of them are: imposition of discriminatory prices or trading conditions or predatory prices, limiting supply of goods or services, denial of market access, using a dominant position in one relevant market to enter into, or protect, other relevant market. A dominant position in substance means the capacity of an enterprise to act independently of competitive forces prevailing in the market or to affect the relevant market in its favour. A dominant position is usually acquired by an enterprise over a period of time and factors such as state of technology, barriers to entry, scale of operations, etc., influence the achievement of a dominant position. The market share of an enterprise does not, as under the Monopolies and Restrictive Trade Practices (MRTP) Act, 1969, determine the dominant position of an enterprise, though it is one of the factors to be considered, along with other factors, including the market shares of its competitors. The basic position is that there is no violation of the Act by an enterprise by the mere fact of its enjoying a dominant position. It is only the abuse of that position by any one of the anti-competitive practices set out in section 4 that is prohibited. Section 4 is discussed in detail in Chapter 3 'Abuse of a Dominant Position'.

Combination/Acquisition

A 'combination' as defined under section 5[7] would result, subject to the other prescriptions of the section, such as the monetary thresholds of assets or turnover of the enterprises specified therein, on: (a) acquisition of control, shares, voting rights, or assets of one or more enterprises by one or more persons; (b) acquiring of control by a person over an enterprise when such person has already direct or indirect control over another enterprise engaged in production, distribution, or trading of a similar or identical or substitutable goods, or provision of a similar or identical or substitutable service; (c) any merger or amalgamation. Section 6[1] prohibits any combination that causes, or is likely to cause, an appreciable adverse effect on competition within the relevant market in India. It declares that such a combination would be void. Section 6[2][8] sets out the procedure for the regulation of combinations.

In a given case, a merger could be a certain way of eliminating a competitor. It should be noted that prior to the introduction of this Act, there was no law prohibiting anti-competitive mergers or acquisitions. This aspect is dealt with in detail in Chapter 4.

The Background Setting Leading to the Act

Before considering the other provisions of the Act, it may be useful to understand the economic milieu which led India to enact this Act which aims specifically at dealing with issues relating to the protection of the process of competition. A number of factors impelled this step, the major ones being the obligations cast on India by the World Trade Organization (WTO) Agreements, viz. the General Agreement on Trade and Services (GATS), Trade Related Aspects of Intellectual Property Rights (TRIPS), etc., and the entry of large multinational companies into India, consequent on India's measures liberalizing trade. Most significantly Indian industry began to realize that, without legislation specifically aimed at protecting the significantly, competitive process, they would be at a disadvantage in the changed business environment. The government also considered that the MRTP Act was enacted to contain the concentration of economic power and was not the right mechanism suited to deal with issues relating to the preservation and protection of competition, especially in the new business environment. The Central Government appointed in 1999 a high-level committee on competition policy and law ('the Committee'), to study the Indian economic scene and to make appropriate recommendations for a competition policy that would meet the needs of the country and provide the basis for legislation.

The Committee's assessment of the new business environment, the obligations cast on India under the GATS and TRIPS, two of the WTO Agreements, and the relationship of those obligations in relation to the Act are discussed in detail below.

The Committee's Assessment

The Committee had perforce to start with the matrix and composition of Indian industry that was the result of various economic and fiscal policies that were followed by the government over several decades. The foundation of India's economic policy was planned economic development in a mixed economy, where the public sector operated in large key sectors, such as steel, energy, power, transportation, telecommunications, and the private sector, owned mostly by large industrial houses, operated in the other areas. The manufacture of certain notified items was reserved for the small-scale sector. The principal criterion for eligibility for entry into this reserved sector was the level of investment in the plant and machinery in that business. It was largely the Central Government that directed the priorities and pace of industrial operations. The shifts in the policies of the Central Government over the years left the industry in a static condition, with little flexibility to compete in a normal market without the protection of the government. The Central Government was not entirely to blame, however, as a large unutilized capacity in the industrial sector was one of the reasons for this lack of maneuverability.

After making an extensive study of the government's policies and their effect on the industrial structure in India, and the inadequacy of the industry to compete effectively on account of various factors, the Committee came to the conclusion that vigorous steps were necessary for creating an environment in which competition may be preserved within a legal framework. The assessment of the Committee, which submitted its report in 2000, was as follows:

To summarize, the strategy of import substituting development along with the distorted price structure led to an allocation of resources towards heavy industry and the capital goods sector, which was not based on the principles of comparative advantage. The absence of domestic competition, along with the unconditional protection from imports provided to domestic industry together with the other aspects of the licensing regime (...) fostered a high cost industrial structure which was domestically inefficient in the utilization of resources and not competitive abroad. In addition to the static misallocation and inefficient utilization of resources, the system was also dynamically inefficient in so far as it was not likely to encourage technical change. On the other hand, a competitive market structure with 'right' prices would have promoted a dynamic, efficient, productive and competitive industrial sector. A competitive financial sector would have ensured better utilization of scarce financial resources and have had a positive impact on the productivity of the industrial sector.[9]

The Committee noted the steps already taken to increase competition and suggested the following:

Although significant steps have been taken to increase competition in various sectors of the economy, a number of important things need to be done that are essential for a competition policy. There is the need for a Competition Law Tribunal (Competition Commission of India) that will act as a watchdog for the introduction and maintenance of competition policy. It will promote the introduction of the required changes in the policy environment and once this is done, it will perform a pro-active advocacy function for competition. Competition Law should deal with anti-competitive practices, particularly cartelisation, price-fixing and other abuses of market power and should regulate mergers. It is important to ensure that such legislation does not itself become anti-competitive and this is a real danger. For this, it is necessary to ensure that the law is precise and discretion is kept at a minimum.[10]

The Committee emphasized the importance of the proper coordination of different policy measures of the government that could affect the effectiveness of a competition policy. It also identified specific areas in which micro-industrial governmental policies could support or adversely impinge on the application of competition policy. These included industrial policy; reservations for the small-scale industrial sector; privatization and regulatory reforms; trade policy, including tariffs, quotas, subsidies, anti-dumping action, domestic content regulations and export restraints (essentially WTO-related); state monopolies policy; labour policy; environment; healthcare and financial markets.[11] The Committee made recommendations relating to each field for the government to consider and take appropriate action.

The Committee's major recommendations were: (*a*) the MRTP Act should be repealed and an Act called the Indian Competition Act be enacted; that this Act would regulate anti-competitive agreements or practices, abuse of dominance and combinations, which would include mergers; (*b*) there should be a progressive reduction and ultimate elimination of reservation of products for the small-scale industries and the handloom sector; (*c*) the economic reforms of liberalization, deregulation, and privatization should be further progressed; government should divest its shares and assets in state monopolies and public enterprises and privatize them in all sectors other than those subserving defence and security needs; (*d*) the proposed legislation should cover all industries in the public and private sector and professional services.

Following the report submitted to the government, the Competition Act, 2002, was passed.

WTO Obligations

The obligations under the agreements of the WTO as stated earlier, made it necessary for the government to provide a legal means that would assure reciprocal rights to the other members of the WTO.

The WTO provides a common institutional framework for the conduct of trade relations among its members in matters related to the agreements and annexes which are part of the agreement establishing the WTO. The material agreements under the WTO are, the General Agreement on Tariffs and Trade, 1994 ('GATT 1994'), the 'GATS', and 'TRIPS'. They are all multilateral agreements entered into by governments, which are member states. India is a member of the WTO. GATT and GATS provide for the liberalization of the international movement of goods, services, and service providers. The agreement on TRIPS is in recognition of 'the need to promote effective and adequate protection of intellectual property rights, and to ensure that measures and procedures to enforce intellectual property rights do not themselves become barriers to legitimate trade'. These agreements also prescribe guidance for the member states as to their trade regulations and other laws as they may affect trade.

GATS

GATS establishes a multilateral framework of principles and rules for trade in services with a view to the expansion of such trade under conditions of transparency and progressive liberalization.

GATS applies to measures by members affecting trade in services. Trade in services means the supply of a service. The supply may be (*a*) from one's own territory into a territory of another member; (*b*) in one's own territory to a consumer visiting that country (for example, tourism); (*c*) the supply of a service in another territory through the commercial presence of a service supplier (for example, banking); (*d*) through the presence of natural persons representing a service supplier of one territory in another territory (for example, construction projects or consultancies). Services are defined as including any service in any sector except services supplied in the exercise of governmental authority.

Substance of the Articles of GATS

The *Articles of GATS* that are relevant for the purpose of the law relating to competition are the following:

Domestic Regulation[12]

Article VI requires that any member that has undertaken specific commitments in any sector relating to the supply of any service shall ensure that its measures, which mean governmental action, affecting trade in services,[13] are administered in a reasonable, objective, and impartial manner. The purpose is that enterprises of one country operating in another country do not have cause for complaining that they are discriminated against.

There should also be provided, subject to the constitutional provisions of that member, a mechanism for review, at the request of an affected supplier of a service, of administrative decisions affecting trade in services. Measures relating to qualification requirements and procedures, technical standards and licensing requirements are not to constitute unnecessary barriers to trade in services.

In sectors where specific commitments regarding professional services are undertaken, each member shall provide for adequate procedures to verify the competence of professionals of any other member. The member country, through harmonization, or agreement with the country concerned, or by itself, may determine the requisite criteria for certification of such service suppliers. The recommendation is that wherever appropriate, recognition should be based on multilaterally agreed criteria.[14]

This issue is of special concern now, when the entry of foreign enterprises into the legal and accounting professions has become a subject of debate. The subject of 'professional services' is discussed later in this chapter.

Monopolies and Exclusive Service Suppliers[15]

This Article requires member states to ensure that any monopoly supplier of a service in its territory, does not, in the supply of the monopoly service in the relevant market, act in conflict with the obligations of that member to give equal treatment to all services and service suppliers to all countries and does not also act against any specific commitments that may have been given by that member.

A 'monopoly supplier of a service' means any person, public or private, which in the relevant market of the territory of a member is authorized or established formally or in effect by that member as the sole supplier of that service.

The provisions of this Article shall also apply to cases of exclusive service suppliers, where a member, formally or in effect, (*a*) authorizes or establishes a small number of service suppliers; and (*b*) substantially prevents competition among those suppliers in its territory.

Business Practices[16]

This Article provides the means for members to deal with certain business practices of service suppliers, other than monopoly and exclusive suppliers of services, covered by Article VIII, which may restrain competition and thereby restrict trade in services. The issue is expected to be resolved through consultations among the members involved, with a view to eliminating such practices.

TRIPS

TRIPS aims 'to promote effective and adequate protection of intellectual property rights, and to ensure that measures and procedures to enforce intellectual property rights do not themselves become barriers to legitimate trade'. The principal objective of TRIPS is to obtain the establishment of legislation in member states that would prevent the abuse of intellectual property rights by right holders, or their resort to practices which unreasonably restrain trade or adversely affect the international transfer of technology.[17] It makes provisions relating to the following: copyright and related rights, trademarks, geographical indications, industrial designs, patents, layout-designs (topographies) of integrated circuits, protection of undisclosed information, and control of anti-competitive practices in contractual licences.

Article 40 of TRIPS providing for the control of anti-competitive practices in contractual licences is relevant. It permits members to specify in their legislation what would constitute an abuse of intellectual property rights having an adverse effect on competition in the relevant market. The members may also take appropriate measures to prevent or control such practices. The following practices are given as examples of such practices: exclusive grant-back conditions, conditions preventing challenges to validity and coercive package licensing.

WTO Agreements and the Act

The obligations following from the WTO Agreements provided the immediate need for a governmental policy requiring actions to be reasonable, objective, impartial, and non-discriminatory in relation to suppliers who enter the Indian market pursuant to the liberalization of any sector on the commitment given by India to provide for market access. Nevertheless, the country, with its domestic and overseas suppliers already based in India, needed a competition policy and law for the pre-WTO market itself. Only, the new suppliers, who have changed the composition of the market, its mix, and its capabilities have brought into focus the urgency for a law to regulate the overseas providers of goods and services operating in India also so that, while they are assured of a policy relating to competition that is fair to everyone, they submit to the law of the country intended for preserving the process of competition from manipulation.

Some of the clauses of these agreements also require that an overseas supplier of a product or a service entering the Indian market taking advantage of the liberalization process is not discriminated against. It may be noted that the provisions of these agreements do not directly confer on any individual supplier any substantive right to enforce any of these obligations. The agreements are between governments and it is only an affected member state that may complain of a failure by another member state to comply with any part of any of the agreements and seek redress.

The New Competition Law—Repealing the MRTP Act[18]

The Competition Act, 2002 ('the 2002 Act') repealed the Monopolies and Restrictive Trade Practices Act, 1969, ('MRTP Act'). Section 66 of the Competition Act provides for the repeal of the MRTP Act and for connected matters. The repeal is on the ground that the MRTP Act is not suited to deal with issues of competition that may be expected to arise in the new liberal business environment.

Section 66 has been amended twice, first in 2007 and then in 2009. As provided in the original Act of 2002, the MRTP Commission could not be dissolved on the coming into force of section 66, as the Competition Commission had not then been established, and cases pending before the MRTP Commission on its dissolution could not be transferred to the Competition Commission as directed by the original section 66. The 2007 amendment provided that the MRTP Commission was authorized to continue to exercise jurisdiction and power under the repealed Act for a period of two years from the date of the commencement of the 2007 Act and section 66 was not brought into force. Section 66 of the Act was brought in force on 1 September 2009. The 2009 amendment of section 66 provides, among other matters, for the transfer of pending cases and investigations on the commencement of the Competition Amendment Act, 2009, to the specified authorities under the Competition Act, 2002, as amended. The substance of section 66 as amended is discussed in Chapter 5 'Enforcement' under the heading 'Repeal of the MRTP Act'.

The Committee had in its report noted that the MRTP Act was inadequate, in comparison with the competition laws of many countries, for regulating anti-competitive practices.[19] The general definition of a restrictive trade practice under that Act was seen as not specifically covering the numerous categories of anti-competitive agreements, practices, etc.[20] The Committee considered the following as specific forms of anti-competitive conduct for which the MRTP Act had not made express provision: abuse of dominance, cartels, collusion and price fixing, bid rigging, boycotts and refusal to deal, and predatory pricing. Considering the need to bring mergers under the new Competition Act and its recommendation for transferring the sections in the MRTP Act dealing with unfair trade practices to the Consumer Protection Act, 1986 (CPA), the Committee recommended that enacting a new law on competition would be more expedient.[21]

Fair Criticism?

The question is whether, independent of the suitability of the MRTP Act to protect the process of competition and the need to have a separate and comprehensive competition law for India, it was even effective for the purposes for which it was enacted, from 1970 to the date of its repeal. A review may also show the lessons for administration of the Competition Act, 2002.

It should be noted that the MRTP Act was enacted in 1969 and for a purpose that was relevant at that time. That Act was also passed after Parliament had considered the report of the Monopolies Inquiry Commission that had identified concentration of economic power in the hands of a few large industrial houses. Various factors had contributed to this position, such as the high cost of entry into industry, the rigid control by the Central Government of issue of capital by companies, issue of industrial licences, etc. The primary goal of that Act, as pursued by the government at that time, was to regulate the further activities of those industries that by the definition of the MRTP Act under Chapter III were undertakings where economic power was concentrated.

Concentration was measured in terms of the prescribed value of the assets owned or controlled by any undertaking, singly or along with interconnected undertakings or as a dominant undertaking.

The objective that was sought to be achieved at that time through the MRTP Act was ensuring that large industrial houses, which were covered by the definition under section 20 of Chapter III of that Act, in terms of the value of the assets they controlled, did not deprive smaller enterprises of their share of the resources of the country and that large industrial houses fell in line with the country's planning priority. The main purpose of the MRTP Act was containment of concentration of economic power not issues relating to competition though prohibition of monopolistic and restrictive trade practices restraining competition was also within the scope of the Act.

However, the question still remains: Did the MRTP Act serve the purposes for which it was intended? This requires a look at the law and the machinery for enforcing that law as provided in that Act.

The Scheme of the MRTP Act

This section examines the material provisions of the MRTP Act, viz. (a) those relating to concentration of economic power, monopolistic trade practices, restrictive trade practices, agreements registrable as providing for the exercise of a restrictive trade practice, and unfair trade practices; (b) the authorities to enforce the provisions of the MRTP Act; and (c) the manner in which the MRTP Act has been implemented.

The Material Provisions of the Law

The preamble to the MRTP Act was: 'An Act to provide that the operation of the economic system does not result in the concentration of economic power to the common detriment, for the control of monopolies, for the prohibition of monopolistic and restrictive trade practices and for matters connected therewith or incidental thereto.'

Concentration of Economic Power

Chapter III dealing with measures to regulate and control concentration of economic power consisted of Part A, Part B, and Part C. Sections 20 to 26 were the basic provisions that constituted Part A. Section 20 declared the yardstick for measuring concentration, viz. the value of assets controlled by an undertaking or interconnected undertakings, which was revised upwards from time to time to reflect values resultant on inflation. Section 26 of the Act required undertakings to which Part A of Chapter III applied, to register with the government the fact of their falling under the purview of that Part, giving the prescribed information about the undertakings. This was intended to provide information to the government to enable it to contain further concentration. Under the Act as it originally stood, substantial expansion, establishment of a new undertaking by, and merger and takeover of, Chapter III undertakings required the prior approval of the Central Government under sections 21, 22, and 23 of the MRTP Act respectively. This was in addition to any other approvals under other enactments as necessary.

Part B originally contained section 27 only. That section dealt with the division of undertakings and the division of the trade of any undertaking on the direction of the Central Government, in circumstances specified therein. Action may be initiated under this section where the working of an undertaking is complained of as prejudicial to the public interest, or has led or is likely to lead to the adoption of any monopolistic or restrictive trade practice. An amendment of the Act in 1984 introduced: (a) section 27A empowering the Central Government to direct the severance of any interconnected undertakings on the grounds of public interest or any of the grounds stated in that section; and (b) section 27B providing for the manner in which an order under section 27 or section 27A was to be carried out.

Part C consisted of sections 28 to 30. Section 28 set out the matters that were to be considered by the Central Government in exercising its powers under Part A or Part B of Chapter III. Sections 29 and 30 dealt with related matters.

The amendments to the Act in 1991 omitted sections 20 to 26, the whole of Part A, and sections 28 to 30, the whole of Part C. The reasons for the amendments and their effect will be considered later in this chapter.

Monopolistic Trade Practices

Chapter IV provided for the investigation into a monopolistic trade practice, defined by section 2(i),[22] by the MRTP Commission and for the nature of the orders it could pass. Under section 31, the MRTP

Commission could, on its own information, or on the application of the Director-General of Investigation and Registration, or on a reference from the Central Government, make an inquiry into whether a monopolistic trade practice was being practised by any undertaking, or if such a practice was prevalent in respect of any goods or services. If the Commission found, after an inquiry, that the monopolistic trade practice was likely to operate against the public interest, it could report that finding to the Central Government. The Central Government may pass such orders as it thought fit to remedy or prevent any mischief which resulted, or could result from that monopolistic trade practice.

Section 32 declared that every monopolistic trade practice was to be deemed to be prejudicial to public interest, except where excepted as provided in sub-sections (a) and (b) of this section, thus introducing a per se rule in the case of monopolistic trade practices. The exceptions were: (*a*) the trade practice was expressly authorized by any enactment for the time being in force; and (*b*) the Central Government, on being satisfied that the trade practice is necessary, permits, by a written order, the owner of any undertaking to carry on the trade practice. Before issuing this permission, the Central Government was to be satisfied that the trade practice was necessary: (*a*) to meet the requirements of the defence of India or any part of India or for the security of the state; (*b*) to ensure the maintenance of supply of goods and services essential to the community; (*c*) to give effect to the terms of any agreement to which the Central Government was a party.

Restrictive Trade Practice

Section 2(o) of the Act defined what a restrictive trade practice was.[23]

Sections 37 to 40 of Chapter VI provided for the control of certain restrictive trade practices. The starting point was registration, under section 33, of an agreement relating to a restrictive trade practice. Section 37 dealt with investigation, by the Commission into any restrictive practice and the nature of the orders it could pass. The Commission could act independently and pass final orders itself relating to any restrictive trade practice. Section 38 declared the 'gateways' by which it could be shown that a restrictive trade practice was not prejudicial to public interest. If a restrictive trade practice that was being inquired into could not be justified under any gateway, under the section, the restrictive trade practice was to be deemed to be prejudicial to public interest.

Sections 39 to 41 regulated 'resale price maintenance'.

Registrable Agreements Relating to Restrictive Trade Practices

An amendment in 1984 to section 33, containing provisions requiring undertakings to register with the Director-General, certain categories of agreements relating to restrictive trade practices, effected a drastic change in the legal position relating to restrictive trade practices. Section 33(1) as amended states that every agreement falling under one or more of the categories mentioned in sub-sections (a) to (l) shall be deemed for the purposes of the Act to be an agreement relating to restrictive trade practices and subject to registration. They are cases of conditions stipulating exclusive dealing, fixing prices on which a resale is to be made, allocation of area or market for the disposal of goods, etc. The anti-competitive effect of the agreements falling under these categories is presumed. A trade practice charged as a restrictive practice but not falling under section 31(1), will have to be considered under the general definition of a restrictive trade practice under section 2(o). However, in considering a case under section 2(o), the effect on competition has to be established under the rule of reason.

The *TELCO* case,[24] decided in 1977, before the 1984 amendment, when section 33(1) merely required the registration of agreements relating to any of the practices set out in that sub-section, without this deeming provision, ruled that on the law as it stood then, the question whether a trade practice was a restrictive trade practice or not had to be decided only under section 2(o), under the rule of reason and that the registrability, at that time, did not determine the issue.

Unfair Trade Practices

Part B on 'unfair trade practices' and their regulation was introduced, by an amendment in 1984 through sections 36A to 36E. Unfair trade practices were those that were found to be prejudicial to the public interest or to the interest of any consumer or consumers generally. These provisions related mainly to issues of consumer protection directly such as false representations regarding the quality of the goods or services, misleading representation regarding the usefulness of any goods or services, etc.

Enforcement Authorities

The Central Government was the authority to deal with matters falling under Chapter III of the MRTP Act. The MRTP Commission could pass final orders in respect of restrictive trade practices and unfair trade practices, but only had an advisory role in the disposal of cases of monopolistic trade practices. In this regard it was the Central Government that could pass final orders. The Commission also had the powers, under section 12A to grant temporary injunctions and under section 12B compensation for any loss or damage suffered by the central or a state government, or any trader or class of traders or a consumer, as a result of any monopolistic or restrictive or unfair trade practice.

Implementation of the MRTP Act

For a number of reasons, the Act was not found to be effective, and it was seen only as an enactment on paper.

One of the major reasons for the failure of the MRTP Act to achieve its original purpose was the frequent shifts in the government's industrial policy and extension to Chapter III undertakings of some of the changes. Some examples are the permission to these undertakings to enter into what were called the 'core sector' under certain conditions, rationalizing their licensed capacity by endorsing the capacity of these undertakings on the principle of minimum economies of scale of operations, diversification within the overall licensed capacity, etc. These were intended to further industrial growth and promote further utilization of industrial capacity. It is well known that one of the clogs to the growth of Indian industry even now is a large unutilized capacity built over decades, with its undesirable consequences. Nothing was done to reduce the concentration declared by undertakings at the time of registration under the Act, when it came into force.

Chapter III conferred power on the Central Government to regulate the substantial expansion of, the establishment of a new undertaking by, and merger relating to, any undertaking falling under Chapter III. The Central Government acted on the premise that the imposition of an export obligation on applicant undertakings would halt further concentration, while no action was ever seriously taken to dilute the concentration that existed at the time the Act came into force, though section 27 empowered the Central Government to order the division of any undertaking or the trade of any undertaking, or the interconnection between undertakings under section 27A. The record of action under these sections is very unsatisfactory.

In this state of affairs, pursuant to its new industrial policy declared in 1991 liberalizing the rules relating to industrial activity, the government removed from Chapter III the most important regulatory provisions, viz. sections 20 to 26, calling it *restructuring* the MRTP Act. Thus, it put an end to all concern of control of the concentration of economic power to the common detriment. The reason given was that 'pre-entry restriction under the MRTP Act on the investment decision of the corporate sector has outlived its utility and has become a hindrance to the speedy implementation of industrial projects.' The thrust of the industrial policy was stated as having been shifted to controlling and regulating the monopolistic, restrictive, and unfair trade practices.

The key sections of an enactment were removed and the question is if it was for the right reason. The further question is whether such a truncated enactment could have been expected to be an appropriate, much less, an effective vehicle to regulate competition. Now, enterprises big or small will have to conform to the rules of competition established by the Competition Act, regardless of whether such compliance is a 'hindrance to the speedy implementation of industrial projects' or not.

The regulation of restrictive trade practices was also limited to such of those undertakings that chose to file the agreements that they considered as falling under section 33. A more vigorous and comprehensive investigation as permitted by that Act would have served the purposes of the Act more fully.

While the exemption from the MRTP Act granted to trade unions of employees and co-operative societies is legitimate, there can be no justification for that part of section 3 of that Act excluding the application of the Act, in respect of government companies, undertakings owned or controlled by the government and undertakings owned by corporations established under a central or state Act, unless the Central Government by notification otherwise directed. This built-in defect has limited the scope for controlling restrictive trade practices or monopolistic trade practices of the Act that could be, and were, practiced by public sector undertakings such as airways, and the telecommunications sector. On the other hand, section 54 of the 2002 Act[25] permits the Central Government to exempt from the application of that Act any class of enterprises on grounds of security of the state or public interest; a practice or agreement arising out of any obligation under any international agreement; any enterprise performing a sovereign function on behalf of the Central Government or a state government. Section 54 should include an exemption for trade unions of employees and co-operative societies.

There was also little justification for the provisions of section 4(2) of the MRTP Act to the effect that the MRTP Act would not apply in respect of matters for which specific provisions were made in the sectoral legislation relating to banks, the State Bank of India and insurance companies. It is needless to add that in the matter of unfair trade practices and monopolistic trade practices this was indefensible, as has been shown by the numerous cases under the Consumer Protection Act, 1986, against banks and insurance companies.

The general perception is about the apparent inaccessibility of the MRTP Commission in that its sittings were almost always in Delhi and there were no regional sittings of the Commission in sufficient number and frequency. The expenditure in time and money involved in conducting protracted proceedings before the MRTP Commission discouraged small companies and consumers from seeking its aid.

THE COMPETITION ACT—AN OVERVIEW

In comparison, one may study the structure of the Competition Act, 2002, as amended in 2007 and 2009, in relation to its stated objectives. This will cover the major provisions dealing with antitrust issues, viz. regulation of anti-competitive agreements, abuse of a dominant position and a combination or an acquisition falling under the Act.

The Law Relating to Competition

A summary of the key provisions, viz. sections 3, 4, 5, and 6 dealing with anti-competitive agreements, abuse of a dominant position, combination and regulation of combinations have been set out at the beginning of this chapter. Certain aspects of the major provisions of this Act are reviewed below.

Anti-competitive Agreements

Two comments may be made on the provisions of section 3 that is intended for 'prohibition of certain agreements'. The basic one is on the starting point for determining that an agreement is an anti-competitive agreement within the meaning of the Act. The other relates to the rules of treatment, in considering whether an agreement is a per se violation, or is an agreement the anti-competitive effect of which is to be decided under the rule of reason.

Section 19(1) sets out the procedure for initiation of the process of inquiry into an anti-competitive agreement. It is to the effect, after the 2007 amendment, that the Commission may inquire into any alleged contravention of the provisions contained in section 3(1) on its own motion, or on the receipt of information (pre-amendment provision was 'on receipt of a complaint'), in such manner and accompanied by such fee as may be determined by regulations, from any person, consumer or their association or trade association or on a reference made to it by the Central Government or a state government or a statutory authority.

The important question is how are persons who are not parties to such agreements expected to know the terms of business agreements and their implications for competition? Anti-competitive agreements that any antitrust authority would be pursuing are those that are entered into by commercial organizations, many of which would be large domestic and foreign companies and agreements relating to supply of a product or a service would be kept away from everyone not concerned with their implementation. How would anyone know that there is an 'alleged contravention' of the provisions of section 3(1) as made necessary by the sub-section before one may make a complaint? Considering the large number of suppliers, sub-suppliers, agents, distributors and retailers in various industries and different points, it would be difficult for any individual to know of the terms of an agreement and also evaluate their effects on competition.

A provision similar to section 33 of the MRTP Act requiring certain categories of agreements to be registered with the Director-General, which serves as a starting point for investigation, could be considered for the Competition Act. However, an amendment after the Competition Act has been brought into force should be expected to generate protest, most likely on the ground of its being interference with the freedom to carry on trade effectively. Section 33 of the MRTP Act originally required the registration of certain categories of agreements and after the amendment of that Act in 1984, section 33(1) was modified to the effect that the agreements listed therein would be deemed for the purposes of the Act to be an agreement relating to restrictive trade practices and be subject to registration. This registration would be a convenient starting point for any investigation.

The reasons for the shift in the treatment, of a tie-in arrangement, an exclusive supply agreement, an exclusive distribution agreement, refusal to deal, and resale price maintenance, to that under the rule of reason, under sections 3(4)(a) to (e) of the Competition Act from the per se rule under section 33(1) of the MRTP Act which treated them as per se restrictive trade practices and registrable are not clear. As is well known, exclusive supply arrangements contain the possibility of limiting competition. Resale price maintenance is objectionable, as stipulations on an independent seller of prices at which he may sell restrict his ability to compete. Therefore, it would be logical to treat them as per se violations and economic benefits to the consumer justifying these practices will have to be specifically established. Though courts have accepted that there can be no doctrinaire approach to any delineation and that the issue is determined by the state of the industry, its composition, the economic forces impinging on the industry's operations and the internal structure of competition in that industry at a given point of time; they have also held that where the effect of any anti-competitive practice is so patently restrictive of competition that it will not admit any exceptions, the trade practice will have to be governed by the per se rule. Cases not falling under this kind may have to be decided under the rule of reason.

The rule of reason has been lucidly explained in *Board of Trade of City of Chicago* v. *US*, 246 US 231 (1918).

Every agreement concerning trade, every regulation of trade, restrains. To bind, to restrain, is of their very essence. The true test of legality is whether the restraint imposed is such as merely regulates and perhaps thereby promotes competition or whether it is such as may suppress or even destroy competition. To determine that question the court must ordinarily consider the facts peculiar to the business to which the restraint is applied; its condition before and after the restraint was imposed; the nature of the restraint and its effect, actual or probable. The history of the restraint, the evil believed to exist, the reason for adopting the particular remedy, the purpose or end sought to be attained, are all relevant facts. This is not because a good intention will save an otherwise objectionable regulation or the reverse; but because knowledge of intent may help the court to interpret facts and to predict consequences.

Cartels

Section 3(3) provides that price-fixing, territory allocation for the supply of goods or services, restricting supply, bid rigging, etc., engaged in by any association of persons or enterprises and cartels, will be presumed to have an appreciable adverse effect on competition. Section 2(c) of the 2002 Act defines 'cartel' as follows: 'Section 2(c) "cartel" includes an association of producers, sellers, distributors, traders or service providers who, by agreement amongst themselves, limit, control or attempt to control the production, distribution, sale or price of, or, trade in goods or provision of services.' Unless there is an effective machinery for identifying and keeping track of the activities of cartels and which has the authority and resources in terms of special skills enabling it to collect credible *prima facie* evidence against them, this will be a pious declaration. This takes us to the means for enforcement established by the Competition Act, and we may now consider only the role of the Director-General who may carry out an investigation on the directions of the Commission. The role of the Director-General is defined by the new section 16, introduced by the 2007 amendment and his duty is stated by section 41(1) which is that he shall, when so directed by the Commission, assist the Commission in investigating into any contravention of the provisions of the Act or any rules or regulations made thereunder.

What should be noted is that investigating into the activities of a cartel requires knowledge and training relating to the way commercial transactions of this nature are conducted, and special expertise in tracking cartel activities, which are offences. The normal approach to ordinary investigations of explicit transactions is not suitable for this work, as this is pursuing those engaged in a criminal activity. It is also well known that cartels operate across continents and that it is not easy to locate a cartel's headquarters from where the directions are issued, which will not always be through formal correspondence. This necessitates an appropriate staffing of the investigating agency, providing them with necessary training and powers.[26]

The Office of Fair Trading (OFT), UK states that they use information from purchases of goods or services as evidence of a cartel operating in a business. They state that, in the normal course, the following are indicators of the operation of a cartel: 'how can you spot a cartel?' According to the OFT, there are a number of signs that may indicate that a cartel is operating. Some examples are: where suppliers raise prices by the same amount, and at around the same time; offer the same discounts or have identical discount structures; quote or charge identical or very similar prices; refuse to supply a customer because of their location, and use give-away terms or phrases, such as 'the industry has decided that margins should be increased', 'we have agreed not to supply in that area', and 'our competitors will not quote you a different price.'[27]

Section 188 of the Enterprise Act, 2002, UK, also prescribes that a cartel offence is committed by one who dishonestly agrees with one or more other persons to make or implement arrangements for price-fixing, limiting supplies or dividing the markets, etc., relating to at least two undertakings. Section 191 of this Act provides for the extradition of a person charged with the offence under section 188, a conspiracy or an attempt to commit that offence.

To encourage members of cartels to provide evidence of the cartel in which they are involved, the leniency programme of the OFT can give total or partial immunity from fines to companies who come forward with such information. Similarly, the European Commission has, by its 'Commission Notice on immunity from fines and reduction of fines in cartel cases',[28] which came into force on 8 December 2006, provided for such an immunity from fine on cartels on the conditions stated in that notice.

Under the proviso to section 27(b) of the Competition Act, the Commission may impose penalty on a member of a cartel for breach of section 3, but it may impose a lesser penalty as permitted by section 46[29] subject to the conditions set out therein but total immunity is not provided for. This may be considered as a practical measure.

Abuse of a Dominant Position

The definition of a predatory price under Explanation (b) to section 4 is unsatisfactory in that the level of the cost of production of goods, or the provision of services below which a price would become a predatory price should not have been left to be determined by regulations that may be made by the Commission, leaving the principle unknown and, therefore, uncertain. The principle, on which a relevant cost of production is determined and the factors considered, should be known to the industry and acceptable. Usually a price below the average variable costs is considered predatory.

Combinations

It is not clear as to the basis on which the threshold values of assets or turnover of the undertakings, as set out in section 5, that will be the subject of a combination has been arrived at. They appear to be very high and several enterprises below this level but with significant market power, which is the only material factor to be considered, will be out of the scope of the Act. The effect on competition in the market the business engaged in by these enterprises is crucial, and the size of their assets or turnover is not the key factor, for example, where the business is one of providing services. In approving mergers under the Companies Act, 1956, so far, the courts were not bound to examine, under the merger provisions of the Companies Act, the probable anti-competitive effect of a merger on the relevant market. Some mergers injurious to competitions, in so far as they may now be unscrambled, may have to be reviewed by the Competition Commission to examine whether the division of an enterprise enjoying a dominant position, permitted by section 28 may be necessary.[30]

Most of the enterprises that would be covered by section 5 are companies. However, the basic position of companies that may merge or enter into agreements of acquisition is not properly synchronized under the Competition Act, 2002 and the Companies Act. Companies falling under section 5 of the Competition Act will necessarily have to go through the procedure under section 391 of the Companies Act also, in addition to meeting the requirements of section 6 of the Competition Act, 2002. Companies effecting a combination below the threshold levels in section 5 will have to comply only with the provisions of the Companies Act. It should have been stated in the Competition Act itself that any company falling under section 5 shall first obtain the sanction of the high court under the relevant provisions of the Companies Act. Or, that the Companies Act should be amended to this effect. The position is not properly settled by section 21 of the Competition Act,[31] which requires a statutory authority before which the issue is raised that its decision may be contrary to the Competition Act, 2002, to make a reference to the Commission for its opinion before passing any order.

ENFORCEMENT

Authorities Enforcing the Competition Act, 2002

They are the Competition Commission established for the purposes of the Act, called the Competition Commission of India,[32] a Director-General appointed for the purpose of assisting the Competition Commission in conducting inquiry into contravention of any of the provisions of the Act and for performing such other functions as may be provided by the Act,[33] and the Competition Appellate Tribunal exercising appellate powers as specified in the Act.[34] Chapter 5, dealing with 'Enforcement', covers a detailed analysis of their powers and functions.

The Competition Commission

Composition of the Commission—Section 8

The composition of the Competition Commission and the mode of selection of the chairperson and the members of the Commission had been at the centre of the criticism of the Act. Section 8 of the Act as it stood before the 2007 amendments provided for the composition of the Competition Commission.

It was as follows:

> S 8. (1) The Commission shall consist of a Chairperson and not less than two and not more than ten other members to be appointed by the Central Government: Provided that the Central Government shall appoint the Chairperson and a Member during the first year of the establishment of the Commission. (2) The Chairperson and every other Member shall be a person of ability, integrity and standing and who has been, or is qualified to be, a judge of a high court or, has special knowledge of, and professional experience of not less than fifteen years in international trade, economics, business, commerce, law, finance, accountancy, management, industry, public affairs, administration or in any other matter which, in the opinion of the Central Government, may be useful to the Commission. (3) The Chairperson and other Members shall be whole-time Members.

Apart from the delay in filling up the positions in the Competition Commission, the government was, as the litigation showed, conceptually in error in its idea of the functions of the Commission and therefore in creating an appropriate structure suitable for the purpose. Following from that, its determination of the necessary qualifications was shown as not matching the functions. More than that, as far as the necessary experience for carrying out the functions of the Commission, the original section 8 did not contain the basic experience, viz. experience in dealing with issues relating to competition in the supply of goods and services. Experience in business, commerce, law, finance, etc., stated in the original section 8 were too general. There was no recognition of the need to lay emphasis on the requirement of skills and knowledge necessary to make an effective competition analysis of the acts of business organizations. The government did not take note of how other countries provided for the constitution of competition commissions. The appointment of a civil servant as the chairperson led to the pursuit of a judicial pronouncement, in *Brahm Dutt* v. *Union of India*, on the validity of the basis of the constitution of the Commission under the provisions of the Act before the amendment.

As submitted to the Supreme Court in this case, the Competition Commission, under the amended Act, would be a market regulator, an expert body performing advisory and regulatory functions. The new section 8 reflects this in the description of the composition of the Competition Commission.

The new section 8 is as follows:

Section 8—Composition of the Commission

S 8. (1) The Commission shall consist of a Chairperson and not less than two and not more than six other Members to be appointed by the Central Government. (2) The Chairperson and every other Member shall be a person of ability, integrity and standing and who has special knowledge of, and such professional experience of not less than fifteen years in, international trade, economics, business, commerce, law, finance, accountancy, management, industry, public affairs or competition matters, including competition law and policy, which in the opinion of the Central Government, may be useful to the Commission. (3) The Chairperson and other Members shall be whole-time Members.

It may be noted that the new section 8 is different in two important elements. The first relates to the composition. The qualification that for one to be a member of the Commission, he or she should be one who, has been, or is qualified to be, a judge of a high court has been omitted. The obvious reason is that it is intended that the Commission would be an expert body and act as a market regulator. The establishment of the Competition Appellate Tribunal acting as an adjudicatory body is another reason for so designing the composition of the Commission. The other material change in section 8 is that one of the conditions for eligibility for appointment as a member of the Commission, which includes the chairperson, is that the person to be considered for appointment should have special knowledge and professional experience in competition matters, including competition law and policy.

Selection of the Chairperson and Members

Section 9 of the pre-amendment Act was, in itself, unsatisfactory. The section simply stated that the chairperson and other members shall be selected in the manner as may be prescribed. Rule 3 of the Competition Commission of India (Selection of Chairperson and Other Members of the Commission) Rules, 2003, enacted pursuant to section 9 was attacked in *Brahm Dutt* v. *Union of India* on the ground that the right to appoint the judicial members of the Commission should rest with the Chief Justice of India or his nominee and that Rule 3 did not so provide.

Section 9 has been substituted by a new section which is as follows:

S 9. Selection Committee for Chairperson and Members of Commission. (1) The Chairperson and other Members of the Commission shall be appointed by the Central Government from a panel of names recommended by a Selection Committee consisting of—(a) the Chief Justice of India or his nominee… Chairperson; (b) the Secretary in the Ministry of Corporate Affairs…Member; (c) the Secretary in the Ministry of Law and Justice…Member; (d) two experts of repute who have special knowledge of, and professional experience in international trade, economics, business, commerce, law, finance, accountancy, management, industry, public affairs or competition matters including competition law and policy…Members. (2) The term of the Selection Committee and the manner of selection of panel of names shall be such as may be prescribed.

Recommendation of the Standing Committee Ignored

Having recognized that the members of the Competition Commission would be chosen for their expertise in commercial issues and their ability to make effective competition analyses, it was inappropriate to provide for machinery for selection as provided by section 9. In fact it goes against what the Standing Committee recommended.

The Committee observed:

In so far as the composition of the Selection Committee under Clause 5 is concerned, the Committee observe that the government proposes to include Chief Justice of India or his nominee as head of the Selection Committee selecting the Chairperson and Members of CCI, which they do not find to be tenable. In their justification advanced, the Ministry have taken the stand that this would enable the selection to be seen as more fair and transparent. The Committee do not agree with this view as bringing transparency and fairness in selection of suitable candidates is definitely possible otherwise too. They are of the opinion, that CCI is intended to be an expert body in the field of Competition, which apart from law, also involves expert knowledge in the domain of economics, commerce, business, finance, management, industry, international markets, companies, accounts, consumer welfare and so on.

Bearing in mind the significance of the role that would be played by the CCI and the economic and financial stakes involved, it is absolutely critical to have a broad-based Selection Committee of high stature and experience who are well aware of the trends in economics, commerce, trade and business etc. In this regard, the Committee note that Selection Committees for Chairpersons and Members of other statutory regulatory bodies like IRDA, SEBI, CERC etc. are also headed by experts, and not Chief Justice or his nominees. The Committee, therefore, feel that in the same manner, the Chairperson and members of the CCI can be selected by a broad-based Selection Committee that can better appreciate the candidate's knowledge in the requisite areas. Moreover, the Committee are of the opinion that the basic objection, raised in the Writ Petition, which suggested that CCI being a quasi-judicial body, requires to be headed by a retired judge of the Supreme Court or high court, has been adequately met by the very fact that the adjudicatory powers of the CCI have now been proposed through this Amendment Bill, to be conferred on a quasi-judicial body, i.e. CAT, which will be headed by a person, who is or has been, a judge of the Supreme Court or the Chief Justice of a high court. They, therefore, desire that the Ministry may review Clause 5 in this light and suitably amend it in a way so that the Selection Committee for Chairperson and Members of the Commission is broad-based and headed by an expert of proven track record in the chosen fields.

The government has not considered legislation of other countries that have initiated and are successfully implementing competition law over the years. It has not recognized, or perhaps is not willing to accept, that more than the mode of selection, the calibre of the members of the Commission is the key to its effective functioning and acceptability in the commercial world. In the European Union, it is the European Parliament that approves the appointment of the President of the European Commission and the commissioners. The position in the UK is that the Secretary of State appoints the members of the Competition Commission. The judiciary is not involved in the selection process, relating to the Competition Commission, in these jurisdictions.

Again, sub-section (2) of section 9 which states that the manner of selection of panel of names shall be such as may be prescribed is open to criticism as this is certainly not a matter to be left to be decided by the government under its rule making powers. Section 8(2) is sufficiently clear for any committee to match the experience of an individual considered for appointment to the Commission with the functions to be exercised by the Commission. This is certainly unnecessary as the constitution of Selection Committee constituted under section 9(1) is such that it should be left free to take into account the relevant criteria for eligibility for appointment.

Skill and Knowledge Requirements

The Competition Act is fairly recent legislation, and is vital to the economic growth of the country which is presently in a transitional stage. Therefore, for an effective, and therefore credible, enforcement machinery, more than ordinary care should be taken in ensuring a proper composition of the Commission. The first step towards this would be unlearning the practice of laying too much emphasis on the formal qualifications of the persons to be appointed to the Commission. Equally so, one should not fall into the temptation to overawe others with reference to their past experience that may or may not be relevant to their duties as members of the Commission. What is essential is the necessary analytical skills that will ensure the protection of the structure of a market so that competition is preserved, ultimately serving the interests of the consumers. Past service in howsoever a high position in an unrelated field is no *automatic* guarantee that a member would bring to bear the required knowledge and skills necessary to perform his *present* duties, under the Act, which should in no case be permitted to be considered as an exercise of some administrative powers. While experience with the methods of operations of business enterprises would help, a sufficient degree of flexibility and creativity is necessary for offering the appropriate remedies to be considered by the contending parties, who may be expected to take extreme and rigid positions, so that the needs of the market are subserved and the terms of anti-competitive arrangements are rendered of no effect. But then this requires knowledge of the business, including the prevailing practices in that business.

In addition to knowledge of the business and the practices of that business, knowledge of how enterprises abroad carry on such businesses and the usual anti-competitive practices that have been prohibited in those countries is equally necessary. The purpose of any competition analysis is to determine if and how a market has been distorted by the alleged anti-competitive activity. Information is easy to obtain in the case of established businesses but new services such as telecommunications and Internet services present problems of inaccessibility to information on practices, relevant data on costs, pricing principles, etc. The need to exercise resourcefulness in dealing with such situations is obvious.

The basics in the composition of a commission are well known.[35] In all jurisdictions, what is sought after in the composition of a commission is knowledge of the mechanics of trade and industry and the markets in which they operate. The issues that any commission will have to consider relate to anti-competitive conduct in myriad ways, which will include the abuse of a dominant position in the market and mergers and acquisitions eliminating or restricting competition in the business of the enterprises effecting the merger or acquisition. What is necessary is a knowledge of the markets, their structure, the sub-markets, the level of concentration, if any, the factors that affect their operations, the position of buyers and consumers, their preferences, what products are substitutable, the reasonableness or otherwise of prices charged as anti-competitive and related issues. Further, these are not to be considered in a vacuum but are to be decided with reference to the factors set out in section 19(3) relating to anti-competitive agreements, section 19(4) for examining the existence of a dominant position, and section 20(4) for assessing if the combination has, or is likely to have, an appreciable adverse effect on competition in the relevant market. Determination of issues such as market power, a dominant position, particularly in new services, is a highly demanding and challenging task, requiring a deep knowledge of the business and the willingness to take expert advice, if necessary. The net is to be cast wide in the selection of members and the chairman, so that the Commission is perceived as a body with the necessary knowledge and understanding of the issues with the consequent competence to resolve complex commercial issues to the satisfaction of the parties seeking redress.

In the determination of such issues, no fine rules of procedure or strict evidence, which hamstring all civil litigation, will be allowed any play. Section 36 of the Competition Act permits the Commission to regulate its own procedure. It states that the Commission shall be guided by the principles of natural justice, which only means that parties are to be heard before passing any order against them.

Section 17(1) of the Act allows the Commission to appoint a secretary and such officers and other employees, as it considers necessary for the efficient performance of its functions under the Act. It may also engage, in accordance with the procedure specified by regulations, such number of experts and professionals of integrity and outstanding ability, who have special knowledge of, and experience in, economics, law, business or such other disciplines related to competition, as it deems necessary to assist it in the discharge of its functions under this Act. The Commission may, like the UK Competition Commission, appoint staff with the requisite experience to assist it.

The UK Competition Commission has a staff of about 150, headed by the chief executive and accounting officer. The staff includes administrators; professionals (accountants, economists, business advisers, and lawyers); and support staff, such as information services, finance and human resources. About two-thirds are direct employees; the remainder are on temporary contract or on loan from government departments. The EC also has such staff support, and recently, a chief economist has been appointed.

In addition to knowledge of the business of the applicants before it, independence of the Commission would enable it to carry out its functions effectively for the purposes for which it is established. When it is clearly difficult to get the requisite number of members possessing the necessary knowledge and skills, the conditions of their service as members should be crafted with imagination, as otherwise it would only attract those who look upon the position as sinecures at the end of one employment. Section 12 of the Act, as amended, is not certainly the appropriate means of attracting persons to serve as members of the Commission. It states that the chairperson and the members shall not, for a period of two years from the date on which they cease to hold office, accept employment in, or, be connected with the management or administration of any enterprise that was a party to a proceeding under the Act. But this prohibition does not apply to employment under the government or a government company. The prohibition, if it is to remain, should apply to any employment after leaving the Commission.

Term of Office—Section 10

Section 10 as it originally stood simply provided that the chairperson and every other Member shall hold office as such for a term of five years from the date on which he entered upon his office and shall be eligible for reappointment. The 2007 amendment has introduced a proviso to section 10(1) to the effect that the upper age limit for a chairperson as well as a member shall be sixty-five years.

Restriction on Employment after Ceasing to Hold Office in the Commission

Section 12 prescribes the period for which the chairperson and other members of the Commission are not to accept any employment, in certain cases, after ceasing to hold office in the Commission. The prohibition is against their accepting any employment, for a specific period, commencing from the date on which they cease to hold office in the Commission, in, or connected with the management or administration of any enterprise which has been a party to a proceeding before the Commission under this Act.

Under the pre-amendment section 12, the prohibition was for a period of one year from the date of their ceasing to hold office in the Commission. The amendment has raised this period to two years from that date. Such a provision, regardless of the period which is the subject of the amendment, is difficult to justify. The presumable objective should be that the members should not be exposed to the influence, howsoever speculative or distant, of a possible employment, after their leaving the Commission, with any litigant before the Commission. Where the decisions are of the Commission acting as a collegium, every litigant knows that no one member may act out of personal interest in favouring any of the parties.

But there is no logic in the proviso to section 12 which excludes from this prohibition any member taking up any employment under the Central Government or a state government or local authority or in any statutory authority or any corporation established by or under any Central, State or Provincial Act or a government company as defined in section 617 of the Companies Act, 1956 (1 of 1956). Even if any justification may be found for the prohibition, it should apply to employment with any business, whether in the private sector or the public sector. On the other hand, towards a more effective method of taking personal interest out of the process of making a decision, the Commission may, under section 36, which enables it to regulate its own procedure, prescribe, on the lines of the Companies Act, 1956, that any member personally interested in the enterprise in proceedings before it shall declare that interest in writing and shall not participate in the proceedings relating to that enterprise.

In this context, the recommendations of the Standing Committee are to be noted. It said:

The Committee is broadly in agreement with the proposed amendment of Section 12, which proposes to prohibit the Chairperson and Members of the Commission to take employment in any enterprise that had been a party to a proceeding before the Commission, for two years after ceasing to hold office. However, they feel that the restriction of 2 years on re-employment should also be made applicable for the Director-General, who has a very significant position in conducting inquiries and other investigative functions of the Commission, if he is borne permanently on the cadre of Competition Commission. In this connection, the Committee understand that at present the Director-General is a Joint Secretary level officer on deputation to the Commission. In such a situation, the suggestion for 2-year restriction on his re-employment will not be applicable. Therefore, the Committee are of the view that while framing the rules, government should see that the Director-General is an officer who is an expert borne permanently on the cadre of Competition Commission and not a deputationist on whom such a restriction could be imposed. The Committee recommend that the government may examine the matter and carry out necessary changes in Clause 7 to that effect.

Competition Advocacy—Section 49

Section 49 deals with competition advocacy. There are three amendments to section 49. The section as it originally stood was as follows:

S 49. (1) In formulating a policy on competition (including review of laws related to competition), the Central Government may make a reference to the Commission for its opinion on a possible effect of such policy on competition and on receipt of such a reference, the Commission shall, within sixty days of making such reference, give its opinion to the Central Government, which may thereafter formulate the policy as it deems fit. (2) The opinion given by the Commission under sub-section (1) shall not be binding upon the Central Government in formulating such policy. (3) The Commission shall take suitable measures, as may be prescribed, for the promotion of competition advocacy, creating awareness and imparting training about competition issues.

There are three amendments to section 49. They are: (i) sub-section (1) has been substituted by a new section; (ii) in sub-section (2) 'or the state government, as the case may be' has been inserted; (iii) in sub-section (3) the words 'as may be prescribed' have been omitted. After the amendments, the new section 49 is as follows:

S 49. (1) The Central Government may, in formulating a policy on competition (including review of laws related to competition) or any other matter, and a State Government may, in formulating a policy on competition or on any other matter, as the case may be, make a reference to the Commission for its opinion on possible effect of such policy on competition and on the receipt of such a reference, the Commission shall, within sixty days of making such reference, give its opinion to the Central Government, or the State Government, as the case may be, which may thereafter take further action as it deems fit. (2) The opinion given by the Commission under sub-section (1) shall not be binding upon the Central Government or the State Government, as the case may be in formulating such policy. (3) The Commission shall take suitable measures for the promotion of competition advocacy, creating awareness and imparting training about competition issues.

COMPETITION ADVOCACY

Competition advocacy and the Commission's role in it are well explained by the High Level Committee on Competition Policy and Competition Law. It stated:

The mandate of the CCI needs to extend beyond merely enforcing the Competition Law. It needs to participate more broadly in the formulation of the country's economic policies, which may adversely affect competitive market structure, business conduct and economic performance. The CCI therefore, needs to assume the role of competition advocate, acting proactively to bring about governmental policies, that lower barriers to entry, promote de-regulation and trade liberalization, and promote competition in the market place. There is a direct relationship between competition advocacy and enforcement of Competition Law. The aim of competition advocacy is to foster conditions that will lead to more competitive market structure and business behaviour without the direct intervention of the Competition Law Authority, namely, the CCI.[36]

The new sub-section (1) does not appear to give full effect to this objective. It relates to what the government, whether the Central Government or a state government, will do on receipt of the opinion of the Commission on the reference made to the Commission. Whereas the previous sub-section ended by stating that the government 'may thereafter formulate the policy as it deems fit', the new sub-section (1) ends by stating that the government 'may take further action as it deems fit'. It is common ground that the opinion of the Commission is not binding on the government and also that the making of any policy is the exclusive right of the government. But having asked for an opinion, it should not be that the opinion lies in limbo without any response whatever. At least the Commission is entitled to know how it was dealt with and the reasons for that action.

As part of its Advocacy Series, addressed for the layman, the Competition Commission has brought out the following quick guides on abuse of dominance, bid rigging, cartels, combination, competition compliance for enterprises, and the Competition Act—an overview.[37] The Competition Commission has also decided a number of cases.

Draft National Competition Policy

The Ministry of Corporate Affairs had constituted a committee for framing of National Competition Policy and related matters. The draft report dated 28 July 2011, has been placed on the Commission's website inviting comments from the public. Some of the major recommendations are discussed below. It is best that this is read along with the report of the high-level committee on competition policy and law appointed by the Central Government in 1999, relating to competition policy and related matters, which have been discussed in the previous paragraphs of this chapter, particularly the following comments, especially its emphasis on the importance of the proper coordination of different policy measures of the government that could affect the effectiveness of a competition policy. It also identified specific areas in which micro-industrial governmental policies could support or adversely impinge on the application of competition policy. These included industrial policy; reservations for the small-scale industrial sector; privatization and regulatory reforms; trade policy, including tariffs, quotas, subsidies, anti-dumping action, domestic content regulations and export restraints (essentially WTO related); state monopolies policy; labour policy; environment; healthcare and financial markets.[38] The Committee made recommendations relating to each field for the government to consider and take appropriate action.

In the introductory part, the draft 2011 report states that 'this Policy is aimed at laying down an overarching policy framework for infusing competition principles in various policies, statutes and regulations and promoting a competitive market structure in the economy, thereby striving to achieve maximum economy efficiency in various spheres, and public welfare.' In its view competition policy means government measures, policies, statutes, and regulations including a competition law, aimed at promoting competitive market structure and behaviour of entities in an economy and that it is a proactive and positive effort to build a competition culture in an economy. Notable among its premises of what a national competition policy will seek to achieve is to 'strive for single national market as fragmented markets are impediments to competition.' This Committee appointed in 2011 has suggested in its draft report a list of parameters that would enable a study, for purposes of competition assessment of what government policies or institutions limit competition. The proposal in its final shape is yet to be progressed.

Power to Make Rules, Regulations—Sections 63, 64

Section 63 sets the matters on which the Central Government may make rules under the Act and the amendment of section 63 effects the changes necessary to provide for matters required for the purposes of the amended Act.

Power of the Commission to Make Regulations—Section 64

Section 64 deals with the power of the Commission to make regulations to carry out the purposes of the Act. After its establishment, the Competition Commission has issued a number of notifications and regulations dealing with General Regulations, 2009, Transactions of Business Regulations, 2009, and Procedure in Regard to the Transaction of Business Relating to Combinations, 2011.

Director-General

Section 16 relates to the appointment of a Director-General, and additional, joint, deputy or assistant directors general or such other advisers, consultants or officers. The amendments to this section were two. The amendment to sub-section (1) limited the role of the Director-General and the other was the introduction of the new sub-section (1A), providing for the appointment of additional directors general and others.

The amended section 16(1) is as follows: 's 16(1) The Central Government may, by notification, appoint a Director-General for the purposes of assisting the Commission in conducting inquiry into contravention of any of the provisions of this Act and for performing such other functions as are, or may be, provided by or under this Act.'

The noticeable difference in the new sub-section is that now the work of the Director-General will be limited only to assisting the Commission in (a) conducting inquiry into contravention of any of the provisions of the Act and (b) performing such other functions as are, or may be, provided by or under this Act. The responsibility for conducting cases before the Commission has been omitted. The reason is not known, though it could be said that it could be covered by the general functions to be discharged under the Act. Section 41(1) of the Act defining the duties of the Director-General only states that he 'shall, when so directed by the Commission, assist the Commission in investigating into any contravention of the provisions of this Act or any rules or regulations made thereunder.'

Section 16(1A) is as follows: 's 16(1A) The number of other additional, joint, deputy or assistant directors-general or such officers or other employees in the office of Director-General and the manner of appointment of such additional, joint, deputy or assistant directors-general or such officers or other employees shall be such as may be prescribed.'

Secretary to the Commission, Experts, and Other Professionals to Assist the Commission

Section 17 has been amended by substitution of a new section in the place of the original section 17, which provided only for the appointment, by the Commission, of a registrar and other employees as it may consider necessary for the efficient performance of its functions under this Act. The new section 17 provides for the appointment of a secretary, other officers and employees and experts and professionals. Sub-section (3) gives some specific criteria for selection. It is as follows: 's 17(3) The Commission may engage, in accordance with the procedure specified by regulations, such number of experts and professionals of integrity and outstanding ability, who have special knowledge of, and experience in, economics, law, business or such other disciplines related to competition, as it deems necessary to assist the Commission in the discharge of its functions under this Act.'

Competition Appellate Tribunal

Having made the Competition Commission a market regulator, it was necessary to establish a separate body to perform adjudicatory functions under the Competition Act, 2002, and the 2007 amendment introduced by a new chapter, Chapter VIIIA. Chapter VIIIA provides for the establishment of the Competition Appellate Tribunal, its functions, powers, composition, selection, and related matters, through sections 53A to 53U.[39] The Competition Appellate Tribunal will be a quasi-judicial body with adjudicatory powers. It shall hear appeals from any direction or decision or order of the Commission passed under certain specified sections of the Act and shall also adjudicate on claims for compensation that may arise from the findings of the Commission or the Appellate Tribunal in appeals against findings of the Commission, or under certain other sections of the Act. Any person aggrieved by any decision or order of the Appellate Tribunal may file an appeal to the Supreme Court within the prescribed period.

The Competition Appeal Tribunal, UK

The position in the UK relating to the constitution of the Competition Appellate Tribunal,[40] which is also a quasi-judicial body is governed by section 12(2)(a–c) of the Enterprise Act, 2002. The Tribunal shall consist of (a) a person appointed by the Lord Chancellor to preside over the Tribunal 'the President'; (b) members appointed by the Lord Chancellor to form a panel of chairmen; and (c) members appointed by the Secretary of State to form a panel of ordinary members. Paragraph 1 of Schedule 2 to the Enterprise Act, 2002, prescribes the qualifications for being appointed as president and chairman of a panel.

Paragraph 1(1) is as follows: A person is not eligible for appointment as president unless (a) he has a 10 year general qualification; (b) he is an advocate or solicitor in Scotland of at least 10 years' standing; or (c) he is a member of the Bar of Northern Ireland or solicitor of the Supreme

Court of Northern Ireland of at least 10 years' standing; and he appears to the Lord Chancellor to have appropriate experience and knowledge of competition law and practice.

Paragraph 1(2) states: 'A person is not eligible for appointment as a chairman unless (a) he has a 7-year general qualification; (b) he is an advocate or solicitor in Scotland of at least 7 years' standing; or (c) he is a member of the Bar of Northern Ireland or solicitor of the Supreme Court of Northern Ireland of at least 7 years' standing; and he appears to the Lord Chancellor to have appropriate experience and knowledge (either of competition law and practice or any other relevant law and practice)'. Cases are heard before a panel consisting of three members: either the president or a member of the panel of chairmen and two ordinary members. The members of the panel of chairmen are judges of the Chancery Division of the high court and other senior lawyers. The ordinary members have expertise in law and/or related fields.

Competition Appellate Tribunal—The 2002 Act

The substance of the important sections of the 2002 Act relating the Competition Appellate Tribunal may now be considered.

Establishment of Competition Appellate Tribunal—Section 53A

The amended Act has provided for the establishment of a quasi-judicial body, viz., the Competition Appellate Tribunal. The Appellate Tribunal shall consist of a chairperson and not more than two other Members to be appointed by the Central Government.[41] The chairperson of the Appellate Tribunal shall be a person, who is, or has been a judge of the Supreme Court or the Chief Justice of a high court. A member of the Appellate Tribunal shall be a person of ability, integrity and standing having special knowledge of, and professional experience of not less than twenty-five years in, competition matters including competition law and policy, international trade, economics, business, commerce, law, finance, accountancy, management, industry, public affairs, administration or in any other matter which in the opinion of the Central Government, may be useful to the Appellate Tribunal.[42] Section 53E provides for the process of selection of the chairperson and Members.[43] This structure is expected to meet the challenges made in Brahm Dutt.

Appeals to Competition Appellate Tribunal—Section 53B

This section provides for an appeal to the Competition Appellate Tribunal against orders made by the Commission under certain specific sections of the Act. They are as follows: [a] closure of the matter by the Commission on the ground that there is no *prima facie* case [section 26(2)]; [b] closure of the matter by the Commission agreeing with the report of the Director-General that there is no contravention [section 26(6)]; [c] orders of the Commission after inquiry into agreements or abuse of dominant position [section 27]; [d] an order directing the division of an enterprise enjoying dominant position [section 28]; [e] orders under section 31, relating to a proposed combination such as, approval of or prohibition of a proposed combination, suggesting modifications to the scheme of combination, accepting modifications suggested by the parties, prohibiting: acquisition referred to in clause (a) of section 5; or (b) the acquiring of control referred to in clause (b) of section 5; or (c) the merger or amalgamation referred to in clause [c] of section 5; [f] acts taking place outside India but having an effect on competition in India [section 32]; [g] an interim order passed under section 33; [h] rectification of order under section 38; [i] an order of reference to the income-tax authority for recovery of monetary penalty imposed on a party [section 39]; [j] levy of penalty for failure to comply with directions of Commission under sub-sections (2) and (4) of section 36 or the Director-General while exercising powers referred to in sub-section (2) of section 41 [section 43]; [k] power to impose penalty for non-furnishing of information on combinations [section 43A]; [l] penalty for making false statement or omission to furnish material information [section 44]; [m] penalty for offences in relation to furnishing of information [section 45]; [n] power to impose lesser penalty, in cartel cases [section 46].

The penalties for such breaches are discussed in Chapter 5 dealing with enforcement. The Commission is vested with power to impose lesser penalty in certain cases.[44]

An appeal may be made by the Central Government or the state government or a local authority or enterprise or any person, aggrieved by any direction, decision or order referred to above and also in respect of a claim for adjudication of compensation.

Restriction on Employment of Chairperson and Other Members of Appellate Tribunal in Certain Cases—53L

The chairperson and other members of the Appellate Tribunal are prohibited for a period of two years from the date on which they cease to hold office, from accepting any employment in, or connected with the management or administration of, any enterprise which has been a party to a proceeding before the Appellate Tribunal under this Act. However, this prohibition will not apply to their accepting any employment under the Central Government or a state government or local authority or in any statutory authority or any corporation established by or under any Central, State or Provincial Act or a government company as defined in section 617 of the Companies Act, 1956 (1 of 1956).[45]

It is not clear as to how the next employer being the government should make any difference.

Appeal to the Supreme Court—Section 53T

This section provides for an appeal to the Supreme Court by the Central Government or any state government or the Commission or any statutory authority or any local authority or any enterprise or any person aggrieved by any decision or order of the Appellate Tribunal. The appeal is to be made within sixty days from the date of communication of the decision or order of the Appellate Tribunal to the appellant. But the Supreme Court may extend this period if it is satisfied that the applicant was prevented by sufficient cause from filing the appeal within the said period. An appeal should be entertained only on a question of law.

Power to punish for contempt—Section 53U

This section empowers the Appellate Tribunal to punish, as high court, for contempt of itself in accordance with the Contempt of Courts Act, 1971.

The procedure and powers of the Competition Commission and the Appellate Tribunal set out in other sections of Chapter VIIIA dealing with the powers of the Appellate Tribunal are discussed in the chapter on Enforcement.

SOME ISSUES IN ENFORCEMENT

This section considers (a) the provisions prescribing the penalties under the Competition Act; (b) some specific areas containing potential for conflict in enforcing the regulatory powers under the Act; and (c) the composition of the Commission, the appointment of a Director General, the establishment of the Competition Appellate Tribunal and related matters.

India has some unique features including a mixed economy, where private sector participation has been allowed in some public sector undertakings. In addition, some of its markets have recently opened up, resulting in foreign direct investment in various permitted sectors. Eventually, it is envisaged that the old practice of state-protection to companies will vanish, giving way to a more open, independent way of working for each enterprise.

On the other hand, the US had a free economy from the start. In fact, their problems were reining in the anti-competitive conduct of big business. The EU is also largely a group of developed countries and their objective has been to bring about a single common market. The point is that those countries did not have to experience the kind of transition that is taking place in India, and readjust to the changed business environment and the introduction of a regulatory mechanism to protect competition in the market. It is in this changing situation that the Competition Act is to commence its operation. This requires that reorientation in outlook is necessary not only for the government but for business also.

The Act, patterned largely on the EU model, has to be worked to assess its appropriateness to the country's present scene.[46] A further opening up of markets in new sectors would invite more entrepreneurs who would demand an effective law relating to competition and one under which they are not discriminated against. More than the set of sections prescribing the substantive law, what is necessary to make the Act serve the intended purpose would be effective and consistent enforcement. The success of the EC antitrust law is largely due to the severe fines imposed on undertakings found to have breached the law.

Penalties under the Act

Chapter VI of the Act provides for the penalties for *the following*: contravention of any order of the Commission,[47] compensation in cases of contravention of orders of the Commission, that may be ordered by the Appellate Tribunal, a new section,[48] failure to comply with any directions of the Commission and the Director-General,[49] power to impose penalty for non-furnishing of information on combinations,[50] making a false statement or omission to furnish material information,[51] and for offences in relation to furnishing of information[52] and contravention by companies.[53] The penalties for such breaches are outlined in Chapter 5 dealing with enforcement.

Only after a considerable period of working of the Competition Act, and after the level of compliance with the Act has been ascertained, may one be in a position to conclude if these are deterrents sufficient enough to compel enterprises to plan business on the premise that it is more economical to comply with the law. The key problem in enforcement, particularly entailing criminal sanctions, is the extent of effective supervision of the activities of those engaged in commerce. In a large country such as India, and in a new area like regulation of competition, the magnitude of the task in terms of the resources needed such as manpower, their skills, training and motivation, and the need to create a vibrant and flexible enforcement machinery would be apparent. Those dealing with breaches such as these should also understand that they are to be resolved consistent with the objective of the preservation of the process of competition. A mechanical approach would certainly not serve the purposes of the Act.

Since all enterprises, whether in the private or public sector, except activities of the government relatable to its sovereign functions, are covered by the Act, a consistent and uniform enforcement of the Act against all these enterprises would lend it credibility and make it more acceptable to all enterprises, domestic and foreign.

Potential for Conflict

The business environment in India described earlier is likely to present some special problems in the regulation and early recognition of those areas that would aid in the effective implementation of the Act. One is the gradual elimination of state monopolies consequent on deregulation, requiring from those enterprises the flexibility to adapt to the new regime by reorienting their attitude to doing business in the new legal and commercial environment. Just as important it is for those businesses to cease to expect a special treatment, the enforcing authorities also should treat them simply as commercial enterprises falling under the Act.

The Committee, in Chapter III of its report, dealing with 'Prerequisites for a Competition Policy', emphasized the need 'to pursue an appropriate Competition Policy without being constrained by or conflicting with other public policy objectives.' As stated earlier in this chapter, the following are the areas, listed by the report, of microindustrial governmental policies that may support or adversely impinge on the application of competition policy: industrial policy, reservations for the small-scale industrial sector, privatization and regulatory reforms, trade policy, including tariffs, quotas, subsidies, anti-dumping action, domestic content regulations and export restraints (essentially WTO-related) state monopolies policy and labour policy.[54] The report has cautioned that building too many objectives into the competition policy such as protection of the small-scale sector, trade, investment and regional development policies, etc., would, where the thrust of any on these policies ignores the economic inefficiencies that may either result from any of those policies, or shields economic inefficiency, defeat the purposes of the legislation on competition. The acquiescence in the poor management of the public sector undertakings is an example of a policy that would help continue economic inefficiency. The continuance of a policy of reservation for the small-scale industry is an example of a policy that shields economic inefficiency. Here, consider the position relating to two areas: the small-scale industry and state monopolies.

Industrial Policy—Small-scale Industry

While it is generally understood that industrial licensing as a means of controlling or directing industrial activity in areas other than defence, atomic energy and the sovereign functions of the government, is no longer relevant and is certainly an interference with the growth of industrial activity, the lack of logic in reserving certain items exclusively for the small-scale industry is overlooked for reasons other than economic justification. The value of the assets of the business treated, as a small-scale industry for this purpose, is not an appropriate test either for exempting it from industrial licensing or following from that position, for restricting the entry of other enterprises into the reserved sector. For one thing, the ceiling on investment in plant and machinery to qualify for being treated as a small-scale industry is fixed by the government as an administrative decision and that ceiling has been frequently revised. On the other hand, any exemption, if based on the small-scale industry's *status*, for example, if it were a co-operative society, not operating for profit, would be logical. But the present division, as a policy of the government, does not aid free competition.

The Committee recommended that there should be no reservation for the small-scale sector of products which are on Open General Licence (OGL) for imports and that there should be a progressive reduction and ultimate elimination of reservation of products for the small-scale industrial and handloom sectors.[55] As the Committee has rightly pointed out, the inefficiencies[56] of the small-scale sector would infect the industries to which they supply their products, leading to the overall poor quality of products to consumers. The latest industrial policy of the Government of India states that as of now there are only twenty one industries in the small-scale sector and their number was reduced after continual review.[57]

State Monopolies

Now that the government is divesting its interest in state monopolies as part of the process of deregulation, those enterprises will also come under the purview of the Competition Act and any monopolistic, restrictive and unfair trade practices engaged in by them would be a breach of the Act. But as state monopolies present some special problems, in the regulation of competition we may consider some examples.

Monopolies Created by the State—the EU

One of the arguments raised in *CBEM*[58] was whether Article 82 dealing with the abuse of a dominant position would apply to an undertaking that had been granted certain exclusive rights to enjoy a monopoly. The case related to telemarketing and the complaint was that the telemarketing company was denied television time on the television station of the first defendant, if it were to use a telephone number other than that of the second defendant (an exclusive agent of the first defendant) for television advertising for telephone marketing operations, and this was alleged to be an abuse of a dominant position. The first defendant enjoyed a legal monopoly granted by the state in television service and at the relevant time there was no commercial advertising on national television stations in Belgium.

The question referred to the court was whether Article 82 could be held to be applicable in the case of a monopoly that did not result from any act of a party but was the result of some provision of law as a consequence of which there was no real competition. Citing its earlier decision in *Italy v. Commission*,[59] the court ruled that the fact that the absence of competition or its restriction on the relevant market is brought about or encouraged by provisions laid down by law in no way precluded the application of Article 82. The court cited *SACCHI*,[60] which had ruled that though an undertaking might be granted a monopoly, as an undertaking entrusted with the operation of services of general economic interest, Article 86(2) itself provided that such undertakings remained subject to the Treaty rules on competition and in particular those contained in Article 82, as long as it was not shown that the said prohibitions set out in the rules of competition of the Treaty were incompatible with the performance of their tasks.

Article 86 of the Treaty offers scope for such an argument as raised on behalf of the television company. Article 86(1) permits the state to grant special or exclusive rights to public undertakings and other undertakings.

Special or exclusive rights to operate a service of general economic interest are given by the state to any agency where, market forces alone do not provide a satisfactory service. The EU policy on the granting of such rights is stated thus: 'In certain circumstances, in particular where market forces alone do not result in a satisfactory provision of services, public authorities may entrust certain operators of services with obligations of general interest and where necessary grant them special or exclusive rights and/or devise a funding mechanism for their provision.'[61]

However, the special or exclusive right granted by the state under Article 86(1) is subject to the qualification, set out in Article 86(2), that even though undertakings may be granted such monopoly rights, they would still be subject to the rules of competition, unless the enforcement of the rules of competition obstructs the performance, in law or fact, of the particular tasks assigned to them. Article 86(2) is as follows:

> Undertakings entrusted with the operation of services of general economic interest or having the character of a revenue-producing monopoly shall be subject to the rules contained in this Treaty, in particular to the rules on competition, insofar as the application of such rules does not obstruct the performance, in law or in fact, of the particular tasks assigned to them. The development of trade must not be affected to such an extent as would be contrary to the interests of the Community.[62]

With the grant of monopoly rights, the undertaking should be able to perform its task and have the benefit of economically acceptable conditions. The enforcement of competition rules are not to come in the way of its performing its services in conditions of economic equilibrium, in the sense, that it should be possible to offset less profitable sectors against the profitable sectors.[63] Economically unacceptable conditions resulting from the removal of the exclusive rights, for example, by permitting competition in that sector, would amount to 'obstructing the performance'. But what is an economically unacceptable condition is a question of fact to be determined in each case.

It should be noted that with increasing liberalization, the number of services holding exclusive rights to operate a service of general economic interest would decline. The OFT document 'Services of general economic interest exclusion'—Draft competition law guideline for consultation, April 2004, states in paragraph 3.8:

> Over the last two decades privatization and liberalization in the United Kingdom has significantly reduced the number of services for which exclusive rights are held. In addition, the introduction of EC directives concerning common rules

for the internal market in electricity, natural gas and postal services and the development of measures to promote competition in electronic communications and rail services since the above Article 86(2) cases were considered will also render these precedents less relevant in the EU as more of the markets are opened up to competition and the number of exclusive rights over aspects of services are reduced.

The Indian government should note the possible problems that may arise from the grant of such rights.[64] One is being able to offer a justification satisfactory to the private operators who would complain against such protection to those obtaining exclusive rights and remaining out of the net of the Competition Act. Equally important is the care with which claims like 'unacceptable economic conditions' are evaluated. Then, the exercise of concurrent authority by two agencies in respect of one anti-competitive Act, which, for historical reasons, other countries have had to endure, should be avoided. For example, in the UK, both the Office of Fair Trading and the Regulators, in respect of regulated sectors, such as communications matters, gas, electricity, water and sewerage, railway and air traffic services (under section 54 and schedule 10 of the Competition Act, 1998), exercise concurrent jurisdiction in matters falling under the Competition Act, but they are required to consult each other.

The need for one authority only to decide on issues relating to the containment of anti-competitive activities cannot be overemphasized. While the Telecom Regulatory Authority of India Act, 1997, amended in 2000, specifically states, as explained later, that it shall not exercise any jurisdiction relating to issues in competition among the service providers in the telecommunications business, the Banking Laws (Amendment) Bill, 2011 states as follows: '2A. Notwithstanding anything to the contrary contained in section 2, nothing contained in the Competition Act, 2002 shall apply to any banking company, the State Bank of India, any subsidiary bank, any corresponding new bank or any regional rural bank or co-operative bank or multi-state co-operative bank in respect of the matters relating to amalgamation, merger, reconstruction, transfer, reconstitution or acquisition under this Act....' It refers to the Banking Regulation Act, 1949, and other enactments relating to certain classes of banks. Merger of banks could raise competition issues such as reduction in the area of operations, services rendered and so on. In the interest of consistency it is appropriate that the Competition Commission alone should determine such issues.

Areas Needing Further Consideration

Though the Act has elaborately provided for various forms of anti-competitive conduct, there are some special areas that are to be given closer attention and to be specifically provided for. For example, many of the enterprises in the sectors that are being deregulated, particularly services which are new and in the provision of which technology plays a large part, as in the case of provision of telecommunication services, will, in addition to domestic competition, have to face competition from foreign enterprises that have been allowed to invest to a substantial extent in Indian operations. In the same way, the supply in India of professional services from overseas enterprises in the financial, legal, and other areas present special problems and the rules of the professional bodies governing those professions are to be recast in such a way that they do not limit the ability of the members of these professions to compete as in an open market. It is to be noted that the means of enforcing the decisions of the Commission against overseas enterprises that do not operate in India are not yet in place. These issues are considered below.

Telecommunications

Liberalization measures have implications of national obligations towards service providers who invest in India pursuant to the commitments that may have been made for granting market access under any of the agreements under the WTO, as already noted. The nature of the industry, the structure of the markets, the technology employed by the service providers, the level of transparency among them relating to their business practices in providing the services and terms of supply are special features of each industry and this should be recognized by those in charge of enforcement of the law of competition in that industry.

The telecommunications business cannot be placed in the category of conventional trade. The telecommunications sector is a burgeoning field with several peculiar features such as the number and variety of telecommunication services and the technological changes affecting them, and the nature of the business itself. There has been an unprecedented growth in this sector and this is attributed to intense competition and aggressive pricing. In view of the nature and volume of business in the tele-communications sector, the Commission should be the only authority to determine issues that may arise under the Competition Act, viz. anti-competitive practices, abuse of a dominant position by those providing telecommunication services and combinations among those enterprises.

Competition Issues in Telecommunication Services

Issues like those raised in the *Alsatel*[65] case are of relevance here also. The clauses of the agreement that were the subject of complaint, for rental and maintenance of telephone equipment which *Alsatel* offered to its subscribers were: the contract was for an initial duration of 15 years, but was to be renewed for a further term of 15 years if, as a result of one or more modifications to the installation, the initial rental was increased by 25 per cent or more.

The issue came up before the European Court for a preliminary ruling on the interpretation of Article 82 relating to the position of *Alsatel* and the attention of the court was drawn to these contractual terms which could be abusive, but their validity was not necessary to be determined, as the finding was that *Alsatel* was not dominant in the domestic market in telephone installations. The court observed:

... the fact that the price of the supplements to the contract entailed by those modifications is not determined but is unilaterally fixed by the installer and the automatic renewal of the contract for a 15-year term if as a result of those modifications the rental is increased by more than 25 per cent may constitute unfair trading conditions prohibited as abusive practices by Article 86 of the Treaty if all the conditions for the application of that provision are met.

Issues such as unfair prices, abuse of dominance, lack of transparency, and denial of opportunity to negotiate terms of supply are of equal concern to the consumer using telecommunication services. Competition among the providers of telecommunication services of every description at all levels is to be protected. The need is urgent as the sector is opening up and operators already in the field should be expected to do everything in their power to continue to remain in their entrenched position, which would ultimately cause loss to the consumers. *Wanadoo Interactive*, charging predatory prices for Internet access services, referred to in the chapter on abuse of a dominant position, is one such example.

The common anti-competitive practice in the developing area of telecommunication services is for the operators already in the field to deny access to the new participants to their infrastructure, which is called 'unbundling the local loop'. In May 2003, the European Commission levied a fine of €12.6 million on finding that *Deutsche Telekom*, a dominant provider of broadband and narrowband retail access, with a market share of 95 per cent, was charging new entrants higher fees for wholesale access to the local loop than what its subscribers paid for fixed line subscriptions. This discouraged new companies from entering the market and reduced the choice of suppliers of telecommunication services as well as price competition for consumers.[66]

In the field of satellites, telecommunications operators could enter into agreements providing for pooling of their space segment capacity, the effect of which may be such as to limit their own ability to compete among themselves. They may also enter into agreement among themselves to limit their supplies in quality and/or quantity to third parties. Direct or indirect imposition of any kind of agreement by a telecommunication operator, for instance, by making the uplink subject to the conclusion of an agreement with a third party, would constitute an abuse of a dominant position.[67]

All such anti-competitive practices should be brought under the purview of one Act, viz. the Competition Act, 2002 and should be decided only by one authority, viz. the Competition Commission so that unintended conflicts of the exercise of jurisdiction are avoided.

The Telecom Regulatory Authority of India Act (TRAI), 1997

Section 2(k) of the TRAI defines 'telecommunication service', as:

'Telecommunication service' means service of any description (including electronic mail, voice mail, data services, audio text services, video text services, radio paging and cellular mobile telephone services) which is made available to users by means of any transmission or reception of signs, signals, writing, images and sounds or intelligence of any nature, by wire, radio, visual or other electro-magnetic means but shall not include broadcasting services.

The Functions of TRAI—Aligning with the Competition Commission

Section 11(1) of the Act sets out the functions of the TRAI. Clauses (h) and (i) of that sub-section only provide that TRAI shall facilitate competition and promote efficiency in the operation of telecommunication services so as to facilitate growth in such services and protect the interest of the consumers of telecommunication services. Under clause (n) it will also settle disputes between service providers. The types of disputes that may be settled by TRAI under section 14(2) between providers of telecommunications services or between any of the service providers and a group of consumers are limited to: (*a*) technical compatibility and interconnections between service providers; (*b*) revenue-sharing arrangements between different service providers; and (*c*) quality of telecommunication services and interest of consumers.

The proviso to section 14(2) expressly excludes from the jurisdiction of TRAI the authority to deal with any matter relating to: (a) any monopolistic trade practice, restrictive trade practice and unfair trade practice that would fall under the jurisdiction of the Monopolistic and Restrictive Trade Practices Commission (MRTPC); or (b) any complaint of a consumer under section 9 of the CPA before any of the consumer disputes redressal agencies. With the full enforcement of the Competition Act, the consequent repeal of the MRTP Act, and the transfer of the provisions relating to unfair trade practices from the MRTP Act to the CPA, the proviso to section 14(2) will have to be appropriately amended to state that the Commission would be the only body authorized to deal with any matter relating to any provider of any telecommunications service falling under the Competition Act, particularly sections 3, 4, 5, and 6.

In this context the directives issued by the European Economic Community (EEC) would be relevant. The EEC had established full competition in the telecommunications market. In 1992, it issued a directive establishing a common regulatory framework for electronic communications networks and services, called the 'Framework Directive', along with four related directives. By a directive in 2002,[68] the services in this sector were redefined as 'electronic communications services' and 'electronic communications networks' in the place of the previously used terms 'telecommunications services' and 'telecommunications networks', to take account of the convergence phenomenon by bringing together under one single definition all electronic communications services and/or networks which are concerned with the conveyance of signals by wire, radio, optical or other electromagnetic means (i.e., fixed, wireless, cable television, satellite networks).

The transmission and broadcasting of radio and television programmes were also to be recognized as an electronic communication service and networks used for such transmission and broadcasting were to be recognized as electronic communications networks. The new definition of electronic communications networks was also stated as covering fibre networks which enabled third parties, using their own switching or routing equipment, to convey signals.

Among other provisions of the directive, aimed at full competition in this sector, two are worth noting. Member states were advised to remove exclusive and special rights for the provision of all electronic communications networks and electronic communications services. More than all, the directive required that the providers of electronic communications services were not to be subjected to a licensing regime but only a general authorization regime was to govern them. The authorization was to be based on 'objective, non-discriminatory, proportionate and transparent criteria'. An aggrieved party would be entitled to challenge a decision preventing him from providing electronic communications services or networks before an independent body and, ultimately, before a court or a tribunal.

In the future enforcement of the Competition Act, in the regulation of the business of providing telecommunications services, the principles of these directives should be borne in mind.

The telecommunications services is only one of the several activities that are being deregulated and the enforcement of the Competition Act, relating to the activities that are being deregulated and the state monopolies that will gradually cease to exist require legislative attention to eliminate the dual regime covering these activities.

Professional Services

The law relating to competition should, in the present context of the expansion in the range of professional services and entry of foreigners into India for providing professional services, pursuant to the undertakings under the WTO Agreement, pay special attention to preserving competition among those providing professional services. The issue is to be examined in a dual perspective. One is the conduct or practices of those rendering professional services, in so far as competition among them may be adversely affected, and the other is the implementation of the rules of the regulatory bodies governing admission of the practitioners to the concerned profession. The rules of such regulatory bodies would be treated as decisions of an association of persons and could be prohibited if they restrict the freedom of the members of that profession to compete. The cases illustrating this position are discussed in the next chapter. Then, the requirements of GATS would have to be complied with.

The definition of a 'service' under section 2(u) of the Act would cover all professions such as accountancy, law, and medicine and read with the definition of an 'enterprise' under section 2(h), individuals practising any profession as an economic activity would be governed by the provisions of the Competition Act. The bodies regulating the practice of such professions, for example, the Bar Council, or the Medical Council, would be associations of persons under section 2(l)(v) or under section 2(x), as the case may be. The effect is that their regulations relating to admission, practice, charging remuneration for services rendered, etc., should be such as to conform to the Act. The regulations should not have the effect of restricting competition among those practising the profession. But section 3(1) as it stands does not include 'decisions of association of persons' but refers only to *agreements* between association of enterprises or association of persons. This means that rules of a professional association would not by definition fall under section 3(1). This is a lacuna and is to be rectified at the earliest as only then can the rules of professional associations be checked for their conformity to the Act.

Similarly, members of any profession may not engage in anti-competitive practices in the course of practising their profession. *Goldfarb v. Virginia State Bar*, discussed in the next chapter, was a case where the US Supreme Court rejected the contention that the practice of a learned profession was not engaging in 'trade or commerce'.

In the chapter on 'Competition Policy and Professional Services',[69] the Committee's report has dealt at length on the need to improve the competitive ability of the professions, particularly for working overseas, taking advantage of the opportunity afforded by GATS, by removing the anti-competitive rules for professions that limit the freedom of the practitioners to compete. While noting that professional bodies required the power to make regulations for prescribing the qualifications and for disciplining the conduct of the members, the Committee observed that 'regulations which disallow normal promotional activity, which deny the consumers the benefit of full unrestricted and informed profile about professional firms and deny the consumers of the choice of firms should have no place.' It added that regulations limiting the size of a professional firm should have no place, if Indian professional firms were to compete globally in the market.[70]

Multidisciplinary Partnerships

However, a wider debate would be necessary on the Committee's recommendation that 'Rules should provide for multidisciplinary partnerships (lawyers, accountants and other professionals) which would permit delivery of composite services, as desired by the clients.'[71] The law relating to the professions of lawyers, chartered accountants, cost accountants, and company secretaries, as it stands now does not permit multidisciplinary partnerships. Representatives of the respective professions themselves have recommended the desirability of amending the relevant Acts to permit multidisciplinary partnerships. The reason given for this proposal is that foreign firms offer single-window multidisciplinary services which give them a competitive advantage, as a client would prefer to have all its legal, financial, commercial, and tax issues dealt with by only one organization.

Leaving aside for a moment, as a question of fact, the number and size of corporate clients in India who want such services at one place, as well as the frequency at which needs of this kind may arise, the principle on which such partnerships are held as undesirable as leading to a conflict of duties must be understood. In this context, the decision in *Wouters* Case C-309/99, discussed in the next chapter, is most appropriate. In this case, the challenge was by the members of the Bar of the prohibition against their practising as members of the Bar in full partnership with accountants.

It was argued on behalf of the appellants who had failed in the lower courts that the Regulation restricted competition and cited the following as the benefits of a multidisciplinary partnership, between lawyers and accountants: that multidisciplinary partnerships of members of the Bar and accountants would make it possible to respond better to the needs of clients operating in an ever more complex and international economic environment; members of the Bar, having a reputation as experts in many fields, would be best placed to offer their clients a wide range of legal services and would, as partners in a multidisciplinary partnership, be especially attractive to other persons active in the market in legal services; that accountants would be attractive partners for members of the Bar in a professional partnership as they were experts in fields such as legislation on company accounts, the tax system, the organization and restructuring of undertakings, and management consultancy. It was also urged that 'there would be many clients interested in an integrated service, supplied by a single provider and covering the legal as well as financial, tax and accountancy aspects of a particular matter.'

In defence, the Luxembourg Government claimed that a prohibition of multidisciplinary partnerships such as that laid down in the 1993 Regulation had a positive effect on competition. It pointed out that, by forbidding members of the Bar to enter into partnership with accountants, the national rules, in issue in the main proceedings, made it possible to prevent the legal services offered by members of the Bar from being concentrated in the hands of a few large international firms and, consequently, to maintain a large number of operators in the market.

Upholding the Regulation of the Amsterdam Bar prohibiting a partnership between a lawyer and an accountant, as a rule to ensure the proper practice of the legal profession, the European Court of Justice declared that the Bar of the Netherlands was entrusted with the responsibility for adopting regulations designed to ensure the proper practice of the profession, so that the essential rules adopted for that purpose covered, in particular, the duty to act for clients in complete independence and in their sole interest, the duty, mentioned above, to avoid all risk of conflict of interest and the duty to observe strict professional secrecy.

The European Commission considers the *Wouters* judgement also as 'giving some guidance on examining purely "deontological" (professional ethics) rules. Any examination of such rules in competition terms will have to take account of the court's finding that deontological rules are not called into question in so far as they are *reasonably necessary to guarantee the proper exercise of the profession*, (emphasis supplied) and to this extent are not caught by Article 81(1). For rules which are not reasonably necessary to guarantee this objective, they must be assessed to see if they qualify for an exemption under Article 81(3). In this way *Wouters* will affect the Commission's approach to other types of restrictive rules and practices in this area, such as restrictions on advertising, soliciting clients and access to the profession.'[72]

The message of *Wouters* is that the issue of multidisciplinary partnerships cannot be determined in a vacuum, disregarding the structure of the professions, their present rules of practice, the mix of those engaged in the provision of those services, the areas of their expertise, and the level of concentration or otherwise in each profession. In any case, it would appear that there ought to be a more explicit demand from the users of such services for a 'single-window' service. Despite the merits of the multidisciplinary partnerships widely advanced, the general view is, in conformity with the principle of the *Wouters* case, viz. that where the independence of the practitioner, as in the case of a lawyer, in having to render advice is crucial to protecting the interests of the client, and there is a need to avoid a conflict of interest, in being a partner of an accountant and having to advise as a lawyer, a multidisciplinary partnership, between a lawyer and accountants would not secure this safeguard to a client.

Competition in Professional Services

As of now, the subject of competition in professions has not been given the serious attention it requires. There is a need to identify the structure of the markets in these liberal professions, which means the number and category of suppliers of services in terms of their areas of specialization, the terms on which they offer their services, the type of users of such services, the conditions subject to which the providers of services are permitted by their professional associations or councils to render services, and if any of those conditions or the terms of supply of any services restrict or eliminate competition. The government should go beyond merely including professions within the definition of a 'service' and cause the necessary legislative amendments to the statutes governing the professions to eliminate terms in the professional rules that restrict competition in professional services. However, an analysis of the actual position is required before such a step can be taken. The experience of the European Union is informative in this context.

'Report on Competition in Professional Services' (European Commission)[73]

The Report, dealing only with lawyers, notaries, accountants, architects, engineers, and pharmacists, mentions five main categories of potentially restrictive regulations in the EU professions: price fixing, recommended prices, advertising regulations, entry requirements and reserved rights, and regulations governing business structure and multidisciplinary practices.

It points out that: 'Such restrictions may eliminate or limit competition between service providers and thus reduce the incentives for professionals to work cost-efficiently, to lower prices, to increase quality or to offer innovative services. Price regulation, advertising restrictions and entry barriers may for example allow prices to remain above competitive levels. Business structure regulations may inhibit the development of innovative services and cost-effective business models.'[74]

The Report cites three reasons as to why some regulation of professional services may be necessary: asymmetry of information between customers and service providers; externalities; public goods.

Asymmetry of information consists in the difference between the technical knowledge possessed by the one rendering a professional service and the ability of the customer to evaluate the quality of the services offered. Sometimes, the provision of a service may have effects on third parties and the ground for some professional rules would be to provide against the danger that the providers and purchasers of these services fail to take proper account of these external effects. The poor construction of a building that may cause damage to a third party is an example of an externality. Services that provide goods of value to the society, for example, high quality urban improvements, where, without some regulation, the services may be inadequately supplied, also need to be governed by regulations.

The European Commission applies the 'proportionality' test in evaluating rules of professional bodies. This means that rules 'must be objectively necessary to attain a clearly articulated and legitimate public interest objective and they must be the mechanism least restrictive of competition to achieve that objective.'

The position is well summarized in the resolution of the European Parliament referred to in the report:

In its resolution on market regulation and competition rules for the liberal professions, the European Parliament concluded that from a general point of view rules are necessary in the specific context of each profession, in particular those relating to the organisation, qualifications, professional ethics, supervision, liability, impartiality and competence of the members of the profession or designed to prevent conflicts of interest and misleading advertising, provided that they give end-users the assurance that they are provided with the necessary guarantees in relation to integrity and experience, and do not constitute restrictions on competition.[75] In its follow-up Report on Competition in Professional Services, 2004, the Commission, after a review of action so far taken by the Member States, stated in conclusion as follows: 'The Commission recognises that it is the Member States' prerogative to determine to what extent they want to regulate the professions directly by State regulation, or to leave the matter to self-regulation by professional bodies. However, good governance would require that Member States oversee the impact of national self-regulation to guard against it becoming overly restrictive and detrimental to customers' interests.'[76]

Acts of Persons from Abroad Affecting Competition in India

Section 32 of the Act, which was amended in 2007, provides for the Commission to take action in such cases. That section states:

S 32. The Commission shall, notwithstanding that, — (a) an agreement referred to in section 3 has been entered into outside India; or (b) any party to such agreement is outside India; or (c) any enterprise abusing the dominant position is outside India; or (d) a combination has taken place outside India; or (e) any party to combination is outside India; or (f) any other matter or practice or action arising out of such agreement or dominant position or combination is outside India, have power to inquire [in accordance with the provisions contained in sections 19, 20, 26, 29, and 30 of the Act] into such agreement or abuse of dominant position or combination if such agreement or dominant position or combination has, or is likely to have, an appreciable adverse effect on competition in the relevant market in India [and pass such orders as it may deem fit in accordance with the provisions of this Act].

The amendments are the parts in the two brackets, viz., that the inquiry should be in accordance with the provisions contained in sections 19, 20, 26, 29, and 30 of the Act and the orders that may be passed are as deemed fit in accordance with the provisions of this Act.

A common problem in the enforcement of any antitrust legislation is countering the anti-competitive acts of those outside the country and not subject to the jurisdiction of local authorities, where the effects of those acts adversely affect competition within the country. Developed countries are equally keen to agree upon a workable mechanism that would give some legal basis for taking action to protect themselves from the fall-out within their countries of the effects of such activities. To be specific, they are concerned about cartels operating from outside their countries and affecting their commerce.

Section 32 of the Competition Act makes provision for the Competition Commission to deal with anti-competitive acts of persons who are not in India, but whose acts affect competition in India. In substance it means that the Commission may inquire into cases where: (*a*) an anti-competitive agreement falling under section 3 of the Act has been entered into outside India, or any party to such agreement is outside India; or (*b*) any party abusing the dominant position is outside India; or (*c*) a combination has taken place outside India or any party to a combination is outside India; or (*d*) any other practice arising out of such agreement or dominant position or combination is outside India, if such agreement or dominant position or combination has, or is likely to have, an appreciable adverse effect in the relevant market.

The principal defect in this section is that it does not state what the Commission is supposed to do at the end of the inquiry. It should have provided for the kind of orders that it would be competent to pass and also have provided the means of enforcing its orders under this section. Section 14 of the MRTP Act was much more explicit. It is as follows:

S 14. Orders where the party concerned does not carry on business in India—where any practice substantially falls within monopolistic, restrictive or unfair, trade practice, relating to the production, storage, supply, distribution or control of goods of any description or the provision of any services and any party to such practice does not carry on business in India, an order may be made under this Act with respect to that part of the practice which is carried on India.

After all, the final implementation of an anti-competitive act in India requires an Indian party and if that party is restrained from participating in giving effect in India to any anti-competitive act caused from abroad, the Act would have been enforced to some extent. But where the consequences of anti-competitive acts taking place outside India and affecting the process of competition in India are sufficiently serious by affecting a larger market, the issue is one to be resolved by bilateral agreements providing for reciprocity in collecting information, evidence and prosecution of the offender in his host country. But courts have always maintained their authority to exercise jurisdiction even where a person does not carry on business in the country where the effects of his unlawful acts result. In the well-known *Wood Pulp* case, discussed in Chapter 5, the European Court of Justice established what is usually called the 'effects doctrine'. It was a case where wood pulp producers, having their registered offices outside the EC, in different countries, but not carrying on business within the EC entered into price-fixing agreements among themselves covering supplies to be made to purchasers within the EC. Some applicants raised submissions regarding the Community's jurisdiction to apply its competition rules to them. Their contention was regulation of conduct restricting competition adopted outside the territory of the Community merely by reason of the economic repercussions, which that conduct, produced within the Community would be against public international law. The European Court of Justice rejected this contention and held that these suppliers were to be held as to be in competition for the supply of wood pulp in the common market and that the rules of the EC competition applied to their conduct also and upheld the fines levied on some of the applicants.

How bilateral agreements between countries are used to meet such problems is discussed in the last chapter on 'Enforcement' under the section 'cross-border issues and competition'.

Provision should also be made, at the time of reviewing the working of the Competition Act, for dealing with such issues arising out of Internet trading.

The Future

Though it is too soon at present, it should be borne in mind that the effectiveness of any legislation may be improved by a periodic review of its working. Section 49 of the Act itself has provided for a review of the laws related to competition. The Central Government may formulate a policy on competition and refer it to the Competition Commission seeking its opinion on the possible effect of the proposed policy on competition. The opinion of the Commission is not binding on the government and it may formulate its competition policy as it deems fit. A responsibility is also cast on the Commission to take suitable measures for the promotion of competition advocacy, creating awareness and imparting training about competition issues.

***

Endnotes

[1] [2005] 64 CLA 214 SC.
[2] 221 US 1 (1910).
[3] 485 US 717 (1988).
[4] Section 3(5)(i)(a) to (f).
[5] Section 3(5)(ii).
[6] In 2007, this section was amended to include: abuse of a dominant position by a group, the definition of a 'group' being the same as clause [b] of the Explanation to section 5. The amendment also extended the definition of denial of market access, to the effect that the denial could be '*in any manner*'.
[7] Amended in 2007. See Chapter 4, under 'Combination—The Legal Framework Acquisition/Merger', for text of section 5 as amended.
[8] Amended in 2007.
[9] Paragraph 2.5.9 of the Report.
[10] Paragraph 2.9.7.
[11] Paragraphs 3.3.0 and 3.3.1.
[12] Article VI.
[13] Article 1.1.
[14] Article VII.
[15] Article VIII.

[16] Article IX.
[17] Article 8(2).
[18] Section 66 of the Competition Act, 2002; for text of section 66 as amended in 2009, see Chapter 5 on Enforcement under 'Repeal of the MRTP Act'.
[19] Paragraph 7.1.3.
[20] The relevant section 2(o) of the MRTP Act defining a restrictive trade practice and the landmark decision of the Supreme Court of India in *Tata Engineering and Locomotive Co. Ltd* v. *Registrar of Restrictive Trade Agreements* (1977) 47 Comp Cas 520 are discussed in the next chapter.
[21] Paragraph 7.2.2.
[22] Section 2(i): 'monopolistic trade practice' means a trade practice which has, or is likely to have, the effect of—(i) maintaining the prices of goods or charges for the services at an unreasonable level by limiting, reducing or otherwise controlling the production, supply or distribution of goods or the supply of any services or in any other manner; (ii) unreasonably preventing or lessening competition in the production, supply or distribution of any goods or in the supply of any service; (iii) limiting technical development or capital investment to the common detriment or allowing the quality of any goods produced, supplied or distributed, or any services rendered, in India to deteriorate; (iv) increasing unreasonably—(a) the cost of production of any goods; or (b) charges for the provision, or maintenance, of any services; (v) increasing unreasonably, (a) the prices at which goods are, or may be, sold or resold, or the charges at which the services are, or may be, provided; or (b) the profits which are, or may be, derived by the production, supply or distribution (including the sale or purchase) of any goods or by the provision of any services; (vi) preventing or lessening competition in the production, supply or distribution of any goods or in the provision or maintenance of any services by the adoption of unfair methods or unfair or deceptive practices.
[23] Section 2(o): restrictive trade practice means a trade practice which has, or may have, the effect of preventing, distorting or restricting competition in any manner and in particular. (i) which tends to obstruct the flow of capital or resources into the stream of production, or (ii) which tends to bring about manipulation of prices, or conditions of delivery or to affect the flow of supplies in the market relating to goods or services in such a manner as to impose on the consumers unjustified costs or restrictions.
[24] Discussed in the next chapter.
[25] Section 54. The Central Government may, by notification, exempt from the application of this Act, or any provision thereof, and for such period as it may specify in such notification—(a) any class of enterprises if such exemption is necessary in the interest of security of the State or public interest; (b) any practice or agreement arising out of and in accordance with any obligation assumed by India under any treaty, agreement or convention with any other country or countries; (c) any enterprise which performs a sovereign function on behalf of the

Central Government or a state government: Provided that in case an enterprise is engaged in any activity including the activity relatable to the sovereign functions of the government, the Central Government may grant exemption only in respect of activity relatable to the sovereign functions.

[26] Some leading cases on cartels are discussed in the next chapter.

[27] OFT—'Cartels and the Competition Act, 1998—A Guide for Purchasers', 2005.

[28] OFT's Guidance as to the appropriate amount of a penalty—2004.

[29] Section 46 was amended in 2007. See Chapter 5 for text of the section and commentary.

[30] Previous to the amendment in 2007, the Central Government could exercise this power, on the recommendation of the Competition Commission, under section 27(f), which has been omitted as part of the amendment. The power is now, after the 2007 amendment, vested with the Competition Commission, under section 28.

[31] Section 21.

[32] Section 7.

[33] Section 16.

[34] Chapter VIIIA, introduced by the 2007 amendment, containing sections 53A to 53U, deals with their appointment, powers etc; the new sub-section 2[ba] defines the 'Appellate Tribunal' as 'Appellate Tribunal' means the Competition Appellate Tribunal established under sub-section (1) of Section 53A.

[35] The position in the UK is explained in Chapter 5.

[36] Paragraph 6.4.7 of the Report.

[37] These and the other publications of the Commission may be browsed at the Commission's website www.cci.gov.in.

[38] Paragraphs 3.3.0 and 3.3.1.

[39] The provisions of this Chapter VIIIA deal with:
section 53A Establishment of Appellate Tribunal
section 53B Appeal to Appellate Tribunal
section 53C Composition of Appellate Tribunal
section 53D Qualifications for Appointment of Chairperson and Members of Appellate Tribunal
section 53E Selection Committee
section 53F Term of Office of Chairperson and Members of Appellate Tribunal
section 53G Terms and Conditions of Service of Chairperson and Members of Appellate Tribunal
section 53H Vacancies
section 53I Resignation of Chairperson and Members of Appellate Tribunal
section 53J Member of Appellate Tribunal to act as Its Chairperson in Certain Cases
section 53K Removal and Suspension of Chairperson and Members of Appellate Tribunal

section 53L Restriction on Employment of Chairperson and Other Members of Appellate Tribunal in certain cases
section 53M Staff of Appellate Tribunal
section 53N Awarding Compensation
section 53O Procedures and Powers of Appellate Tribunal
section 53P Execution of Orders of Appellate Tribunal
section 53Q Contravention of Orders of Appellate Tribunal
section 53R Vacancy in Appellate Tribunal not to invalidate Acts or Proceedings
section 53S Right to Legal Representation
section 53T Appeal to Supreme Court
section 53U Power to Punish for Contempt

[40] 'Section 53A(1) The Central Government shall, by notification, establish an Appellate Tribunal to be known as Competition Appellate Tribunal—(a) to hear and dispose of appeals against any direction issued or decision made or order passed by the Commission under sub-sections (2) and (6) of section 26, section 27, section 28, section 31, section 32, section 33, section 38, section 39, section 43, section 43A, section 44, section 45 or section 46 of the Act; (b) to adjudicate on claim for compensation that may arise from the findings of the Commission or the orders of the Appellate Tribunal in an appeal against any finding of the Commission or under section 42A or under sub-section(2) of section 53Q of this Act, and pass orders for the recovery of compensation under section 53N of this Act.

(2) The headquarter of the Appellate Tribunal shall be at such place as the Central Government may, by notification, specify.'

[41] Section 53C.

[42] Section 53D.

[43] Section 53E provides that the appointment of the chairperson and the members of the Appellate Tribunal shall be from out of a panel of names recommended by a selection committee, consisting of the Chief Justice of India or his nominee, who will be the chairperson of the selection committee, and the Secretary in the Ministry of Corporate Affairs and the Secretary in the Ministry of Law and Justice as members of that committee.

[44] Section 46, amended in 2007.

[45] Section 53L.

[46] The dissenting note from one of the members of the Committee, Sudhir Mulji, was to the effect that there was little point in following the model of other countries for casting a law to suit Indian conditions, as their position was entirely different, as the developed countries enjoyed free competition and they were also not engaged in shifting of the focus from curbing monopolies to promoting competition. In his view, promoting freedom of the markets would be immediately desirable.

[47] Section 42, amended in 2007; sections 42 to 48 discussed in 'Enforcement'.

[48] Section 42A, introduced by the 2007 amendment.

[49] Section 43, amended in 2007.
[50] Section 43A introduced by the 2007 amendment.
[51] Section 44.
[52] Section 45, amended in 2007
[53] Section 48.
[54] Paragraph 3.3.0 of the Report of the Committee.
[55] Paragraph 3.5.2: 3.
[56] On the efficiency of the small industries as suppliers of ancillaries to organized producers, the Committee said: 'Efficiency of such suppliers is poor because of the lack of skills, low capital availability, poor quality of machinery, heavy labour orientation, poor cost control, low output and poor quality of outputs.' Paragraph 3.3.3.
[57] Industrial Policy statement (2011) of the Ministry of Commerce and Industry.
[58] Case 311/84 European Court Reports 1985 Page 03261.
[59] Case 41/83 ((1985) ECR 880).
[60] Case 155/73 ((1974) ECR 409).
[61] Communication from the Commission—Services of general interest in Europe (2001/C 17/04).
[62] Paragraph 4 of Schedule 3 of the Competition Act, 1998, UK, excludes services of general economic interest from the Prohibitions of Chapters I and II. It is as follows: 'Neither the Chapter I prohibition nor the Chapter II prohibition applies to an undertaking entrusted with the operation of services of general economic interest or having the character of a revenue-producing monopoly in so far as the prohibition would obstruct the performance, in law or in fact, of the particular tasks assigned to that undertaking.'
[63] *Paul Corbeau* Case C—320/91, (1993) ECR 2533.
[64] The European Commission's Communication on 'Services of general interest in Europe' (2001/C 17/04) sets out the considerations in creating a policy relating to the provision of general services by undertakings and the establishment of a mechanism to ensure the achievement of the basic objective of providing services of general interest to users of those services. It also explains the application of the rules of competition to such services.
[65] *Alsatel v. SA Novasam*—Case 247/86. European Court Reports 1988 Page 05987.
[66] Commission Press Release IP/03/717, 21 May 2003.
[67] Application of articles 81 and 82 in the field of satellites OJ C 233, 6 September 1991.
[68] Commission Directive 2002/77/EC of 16 September 2002 on competition in the markets for electronic communications networks and services.
[69] Chapter VIII.
[70] Paragraph 8.2.9.
[71] Paragraph 8.2.7.

[72] Paragraph 203 'European Union XXXIInd Report on Competition Policy 2002'.
[73] Communication from the Commission COM (2004) 83 Final, Brussels, 9 February 2004.
[74] Paragraph 221.
[75] Paragraph 29.
[76] COM(2005) 405 final, 5.9.2005.

2

Anti-competitive Agreements

One of the objects of the Act as stated in the Preamble is to prevent practices having adverse effect on competition. Competition among suppliers of goods and services will, in a market whose operation is unhindered, stabilize prices at a reasonable level. The principal objective of suppliers of goods and services who are in a position to manipulate the market is to maintain their profits at pre-determined levels. They seek to achieve this through various means. Agreements for price-fixing, limiting supply of goods or services, dividing the market, etc., are the usual modes of interfering with the process of competition and ultimately reducing or eliminating competition. Where competition is adversely affected to an appreciable extent, such agreements would be anti-competitive.

The law prohibiting agreements, practices, and decisions that are anti-competitive is contained in section 3 of the Act.[1] Section 3(1) is a general prohibition of an agreement in the supply of goods or services that causes or is likely to cause an appreciable adverse effect on competition within India. Section 3(2) declares such an agreement void. Section 3(3) deals with certain specific anti-competitive agreements, practices and decisions of those supplying identical or similar goods or services, acting in concert or such action by cartels. Section 3(4) deals with vertical restraints imposed through agreements among enterprises in different stages of production or supply. A simple example of such a relationship is one between a manufacturer and seller. Section 3(5) saves the rights of the proprietor of any of the intellectual property right listed therein to restrain the infringement of any of those rights regardless of section 3.[2]

Since the definition of an agreement is wide enough to include acts in concert and informal understanding, hereafter, the word 'agreement' is used to refer to them also. The agreement covered by the section is one that could be between enterprises, or associations of enterprises, or persons or associations of persons, or between any of these entities. The agreement should be in respect of production, supply, distribution, storage, acquisition or control of goods or provision of services. Where the agreement is one that will cause, or is likely to cause an appreciable adverse effect on competition within India, it is prohibited and declared void by section 3(1). What is requisite is the effect of the agreement on competition. Obviously, it would be an issue only when that effect prejudicially affects competition, in the sense that either existing competition in the relevant market is either reduced, or totally eliminated.

The factors that are to be taken into consideration in determining whether an agreement has an appreciable adverse effect on competition are set out in section 19(3) and will be discussed later in this chapter.

The Terms Used

Agreement

As their object is unlawful, anti-competitive agreements are not made through formal documents and are rarely reduced into writing. The term 'agreement' has been defined very widely.[3] It would bring within its ambit any arrangement or understanding or action in concert. It need not be a formal arrangement and it need not also be in writing. Even if the parties to the agreement do not intend their arrangement, understanding or action to be enforceable by legal proceedings, it would still be an agreement for the purposes of the Act.

In the case of the *Lombard Club*, referred to later in this chapter, the information that formed the basis for action against the cartel was contained in minutes of meetings, memoranda, records of telephone conversations, correspondence, etc.

An agreement requires that there should be two parties which should be independent of each other. It is to be noted that even what are called 'gentlemen's agreements' would fall under section 2(b) as an 'understanding' and if the effect of such an agreement were to cause or was likely to cause an appreciable adverse effect on competition within India, there would be a breach of section 3. The range of such understandings would be from innocuous information-sharing arrangements to express coordination of price or other terms of supply.

Cartel

Section 3(3) provides that in the case of suppliers of identical or similar goods or services, including cartels, certain agreements between those enterprises, practices carried on by them and decisions taken by them, will be presumed to have an appreciable adverse effect on competition.

A cartel[4] includes an association of producers, sellers, distributors, traders or service providers who, by agreement amongst themselves, limit, control or attempt to control the production, distribution, sale or price of, or, trade in goods or provision of services. The word 'includes' is intended to provide that a cartel may be an association or any other form of organization. A cartel is always with reference to a sector. There could be sugar cartels, tobacco cartels, cement cartels and so on.

Since most of such groups would have a unity of purpose it would be appropriate, for the rest of the discussion, to refer to them as a cartel. The members of a cartel fix prices at which a product or a service is to be supplied, or they may divide the market. The division of a market may be on the lines of types of the customers or territories to be dealt with by the agreed members of the group. Basically, the objectives of a cartel are anti-competitive as the effect of such practices would be the restriction of competition and consequent loss of benefits to the consumer that an unhindered market would have offered. Depending upon the size of the members of a cartel and the volume of business they control, the harm they could cause to the economy would be huge.

Parties to an Agreement

The classes of parties to an agreement could be enterprises, associations of enterprises, persons or associations of persons or any combination of these entities.

Enterprise

What is an enterprise for purposes of this Act is defined by section 2(h).[5]

The substance of the definition of an enterprise is that it can either be a 'person' or a department of the government (as qualified in the sub-section) carrying on an economic activity in the supply of goods or services. Supply of goods would cover production, storage, and distribution or control of goods and in the case of services, it would refer to the provision of services. Supply at any stage towards selling in the market would be covered.

Since the definition of 'enterprise' states that it means a person or department of the government, any other entity cannot, for purposes of the Act, be treated as an enterprise.

Person

The term 'person' has been defined very widely and it would cover every conceivable entity.[6] It would include an individual, a Hindu Undivided Family (HUF), a company, a firm, an association of persons, whether incorporated or not, in India or outside India, a body corporate incorporated under the laws of a country outside India, a registered cooperative society, a local authority and every artificial juridical person, not falling under any of the above categories.

Association of Persons—Professions

Some comments on an 'association of persons' would be necessary in the context of anti-competitive acts. In business parlance, trade associations are usually considered relevant as enterprises. In the present definition however, in an Act intended to protect competition among enterprises described above, it would include every form of association of persons, whether engaged in conventional 'trade' or in any other economic activity, which is the business of an 'enterprise'. It would also include professional associations such as the Medical Council, Bar Council, and other such professional organizations. But as the Act stands now, it is only an *agreement* that may be entered into by any of these enterprises that may be caught by section (3)(1).

The regulatory rules of a profession are decisions of an association of persons. They are also to be evaluated for their effect on competition among members governed by those regulations. Such rules regulating entry into and practice of a profession may exceed the limits of what is barely necessary to stipulate the qualifications for admission to the profession and conditions of practice. Where this happens, the ability of members to compete among themselves is restricted. For example, a rule of an association fixing a scale of fees, especially if it is unrelated to the complexities of the job, but dependent on the size of the firm or population in the area, would be an anti-competitive decision of the rule-making body of that profession, which is an enterprise, as an association of persons. This lacuna is to be plugged by the insertion of the words in the opening sentence of section 3(1), after '... shall enter into any agreement', the words 'or take any decision'. Then, the rules of any association would be a decision of an enterprise and if they are such as to restrict competition among members, section 3 would come into operation. Article 81 of the EC Treaty and section 2 of the Competition Act, 1998, UK, include agreements, decisions and concerted practices of undertakings.

In the same way, members of a profession may not engage in anti-competitive practices such as fixing fees or other terms of practice. The case of members of a profession may be brought under section 3(3)(b) or (c), as the case may be, as an association of persons engaged in the provision of similar or identical services enforcing an anti-competitive agreement, or a practice or a decision taken by that association.

As the question is of serious importance to those engaged in competitive and concentrated professions, and with emerging competition from abroad entering pursuant to GATS,[7] and who may not be subject to the rules of the profession amounting to a restriction on competition, the legal position should be made specific, ensuring that decisions of such professional associations do not go beyond what is necessary for their purpose and limit the ability of the members to compete. The position would still be unfair even when there is no consistency in the rules or standards of the various associations even within India.

The explanation to section 2(h) defining 'enterprise' clarifies that for the purposes of that clause 'activity' includes profession or occupation. This would also mean that members of any profession would have to conform to the provisions of the Competition Act. The decisions of courts illustrating how such rules of professional associations may limit the ability of members to compete among themselves are considered later in the chapter.

Companies Incorporated Outside India

The definition of a person would include any body corporate incorporated under the laws of a country outside India.

Section 32 of the Act empowers the Commission to inquire into anti-competitive acts taking place outside India, but having an effect on competition in India. The scope of the powers and the steps necessary to give full effect to the Act will be discussed in the chapter on 'Enforcement'.

Goods

The term 'goods'[8] would have the same meaning as in the Sale of Goods Act, 1930. It would also include products resulting from manufacture, processing or mining; debentures, stocks and shares after allotment; and imported goods that are supplied or controlled in India. Obviously, the law relating to competition will apply, in the case of goods, only to moveable goods. Immoveable property is outside the purview of the Act.

Government Companies

Government companies, within the meaning of section 617 of the Companies Act, 1956, where not less than 51 per cent of the paid-up share capital is held by the Central Government or any state government, or by both of them are also covered by this Act. So also, are corporations established by any central, state or provincial Act.

Government

The two kinds of enterprises recognized under the Act are: a person and any department of the government engaged in the supply of goods or services set out in section 2(h). But the definition excludes the following activities of the government from the purview of the Act: any activity of the government relatable to the sovereign functions of the government including all activities carried on by the departments of the central government dealing with atomic energy, currency, defence and space. Therefore, all economic activity other than these exceptions carried on by the government or government undertakings, public sector undertakings, by whatever name they are called, are covered by the Act.

Practice

Section 3(3) dealing with cartels and groups supplying identical or similar goods or services has enumerated as anti-competitive certain agreements between them, practices carried on by them and decisions taken by them and declared that they shall be presumed to have an appreciable adverse effect on competition. While the meanings of 'agreements' and 'decisions' are obvious, it would be necessary to state the meaning of the word 'practice' for the purpose of this Act. The meaning of the definition[9] would include any practice towards carrying on the trade or for the purpose of the trade by any person on enterprise. 'Trade' is explained below.

Price

Price, in relation to goods to be supplied or services rendered, includes any form of valuable consideration. That consideration may be paid directly or in some indirect mode, agreed to between the parties. It may, if parties agree, be a deferred payment. The consideration will be treated as price for the goods or services, if in effect it is related to the supply of goods or services, though ostensibly it may relate to any other matter.[10]

Service

'Service' means the service of any description which is made available to potential users and includes the provision of services in connection with business of any industrial or commercial matters such as banking, communication, education, finance, insurance, chit funds, real estate, transport, storage, material treatment, processing, supply of electrical or other energy, boarding, lodging, entertainment, amusement, construction, repairs, conveying of news or information and advertising.[11]

Trade

Trade means any trade, business, industry, profession or occupation in the supply of goods or services.[12]

SECTION 3—SUBSTANCE

The components of this section dealing with anti-competitive agreements are:

(a) prohibition generally of anti-competitive agreements in respect of the supply of goods or services that cause or are likely to cause an appreciable adverse effect on competition in India (sub-section (1));

(b) the declaration that such agreements in contravention of that sub-section are void (sub-section (2));

(c) any agreement, or a practice or a decision to which enterprises which are engaged in the supply of identical or similar trade of goods or provision of services, which would include cartels, are parties, which determines any of the following shall be *presumed* to have an appreciable adverse effect on competition:

1. the prices at which goods may be sold or services provided; price-fixing may be done directly or indirectly;
2. limiting or controlling any of the following: the production, supply of goods or services, or markets, or technical development or investment;

3. sharing the market or source of production or provisions of services. The partitioning of the market, i.e., deciding the customers who may be able to buy, or the decision who shall supply where, either goods or services, may be done by allocation of a geographical area of the market for supply, or by deciding on the type of goods or services that are to be offered or the number of customers in the market to be served. These are only illustrations of market-sharing agreements and it could be done in other similar ways also (sub-section 3).

(d) bid rigging or collusive bidding, whether done directly or indirectly;

the proviso to sub-section (3) exempts joint venture agreements if they increase efficiency in production, supply, or control of goods or provision of services.

(e) vertical restraints in trade, some of which are expressly set out in the Act but are not exhaustive, shall be a contravention of the prohibition, if an agreement stipulating to any such restraint causes or is likely to cause an appreciable adverse effect on competition in India; they are to be examined under the 'rule of reason' (sub-section 4);

(f) the entire section 3 will not apply to: any restriction that the owner of any intellectual property rights under any of the specified enactments set out in sub-section (5) may impose, in the exercise of his rights, to restrain infringement of any of his rights (5)(i), or to the right of any person to export goods from India under the conditions stated in sub-section (5)(ii).

Section 3(1) is a general prohibition of any agreement in respect of production, supply, distribution, storage, acquisition or control of goods or provision of services, which causes or is likely to cause an appreciable adverse effect on competition within India. Sub-sections (3) and (4) deal with certain kinds of anti-competitive agreements. The first, section 3(3), deals with certain decisions made by a group of persons or associations, including cartels. Section 3(4) indicates certain vertical restraints in trade, and they are not exhaustive.

Anti-competitive agreements that do not fall under sub-sections (3) and (4) and which are general will be covered by sub-section (1). As there has been no enumeration of anti-competitive practices set out in sub-section (1) showing the range and kinds of practices that would restrain or restrict competition, the question will have to be decided upon, each time, on the facts the particular case, and by the rule of reason, a principle that will be illustrated later, along with the per se rule.

COMPARATIVE LAW

Before analysing in detail the sub-sections of section 3, a summary of the comparative law on anti-competitive agreements of the European Economic Community (EEC), the UK, and the US may be made.

Competition Law of the EEC

Section 3(1) dealing with anti-competitive agreements and section 4 dealing with abuse of a dominant position, of the Competition Act, are based largely on the model of the law of the EEC relating to antitrust, viz. Articles 81 and 82 (now 101 and 102 respectively). Article 81 of the Treaty of Rome is the law regulating anti-competitive agreements in the EC. Article 82 deals with abuse of a dominant position. Though the decisions under those Articles are not binding on the authorities in India, they are useful guides in understanding the intent of the legislation. The fact that the primary goal of the Treaty of Rome is stated as to integrate the EC into a common market and not to protect competition, as such, as in the US, should not also make any difference in considering the logic of the EC decisions.

Article 81 of the EC Treaty (previously Article 85) prohibits agreements between undertakings that may affect trade between member states and which have as their object or effect the prevention, restriction or distortion of competition within the Common Market. Article 81 lists the following as prohibited as incompatible with the Common Market: (*a*) price-fixing agreements; (*b*) those that limit or control production, markets, technical development, or investment or share markets or sources of supply; (*c*) agreements that impose dissimilar conditions to equivalent transactions, placing trading parties at a disadvantage; and (*d*) agreements that place the other party to the contract under supplementary obligations commercially unrelated to the subject of the contract.

The list of prohibited agreements is illustrative and not exhaustive. A prohibited agreement is automatically void. Article 81(3) exempts certain categories of agreements from Article 81(1) subject to certain qualifications that remove the anti-competitive nature of the agreement. An agreement is exempted if it contributes to improving the production or distribution of goods, or to promoting technical or economic progress, while allowing consumers a fair share of the resulting benefit. This is subject to the proviso that the agreement also does not impose unrelated restrictions on the undertakings concerned and also does not enable the undertaking to eliminate competition in respect of a substantial part of the products in question.

The basic principle is that agreements falling under Article 81(1) are automatically void, unless they are specifically exempted under sub-section (3) of that Article. It should be noted that the qualifying conditions to be satisfied for claiming exemption under this sub-section are cumulative. The Commission's interpretation of the conditions for exception contained in Article 81(3) is exhaustively set out in its 'Guidelines on the application of Article 81(3) of the Treaty' (2004/C 101/08) of 27 April 2004. They are stated to be more detailed than earlier guidelines. Though they are not binding on courts and authorities in member states, they are intended to give guidance to them on the application of Article 81(1) and (3) of the Treaty.

The EEC has granted a number of 'block exemptions' to agreements in various sectors so that it is unnecessary for individuals to apply for exemption. They relate to agency agreements, exclusive distribution agreements, motor vehicle distribution agreements, agreements relating to research and development, specialization agreements, vertical agreements and concerted practices, certain categories of technology transfer agreements, etc. The new Commission Regulation (EC) No. 772/2004 of 27 April 2004, on the application of Article 81(3) of the Treaty to categories of technology transfer agreements replacing Regulation 240/96 relating to block exemption to certain categories of technology transfer agreements, will be discussed at the end of this chapter when dealing with section 3(5).

Modernizing Legislation—EEC

Council Regulation (EC) No. 1/2003 of 16 December 2002, on the implementation of the rules on competition laid down in Articles 81 and 82 of the Treaty, which is called the 'Modernization Regulation'[13] has redefined the manner of application of these Articles, effecting considerable decentralization of authority to national competition authorities in enforcing antitrust law.

The Competition Act, 1998, UK

The principal domestic law relating to competition in the UK is the Competition Act, 1998. The Enterprise Act, 2002, is complementary to their Competition Act. Section 2,[14] of the UK Competition Act, deals with anti-competitive agreements, decisions and concerted practices. Section 2(1), subject to section 3,[15] prohibits, unless they are exempt in accordance with the provisions of Part I, 'agreements between undertakings, decisions by associations of undertakings or concerted practices which—(a) may affect trade within the UK, and (b) have as their object or effect the prevention, restriction or distortion of competition within the UK'. They are broadly the same as set out in Article 81, as according to section 60 of the Competition Act, 1998, the domestic law in the UK relating to competition should be consistent with the treatment of corresponding questions arising in Community law in relation to competition within the Community. Any issue relating to the effect on competition with a Community Dimension will be dealt with in accordance with the European Community law, viz. Articles 81 and 82 of the EEC Treaty. The Act grants individual exemptions, under section 4, block exemptions under section 6, when the criteria under section 9[16] are met. A parallel exemption may be available where the agreement has been exempted under Article 81(3).

Competition Law of the US

Sections 1 and 2 of the Sherman Act,[17] 1890, and section 2 of the Clayton Act, 1914,[18] are the key antitrust provisions. Section 7 of the Clayton Act deals with the acquisition of stocks or assets of another. The substance of section 1 of the Sherman Act is that every contract or conspiracy, in restraint of trade or commerce among the several States, or with foreign nations, is declared to be illegal. Section 2 prescribes that monopolizing or conspiring with any other person or persons, to monopolize any part of the trade or commerce among the several States, or with foreign nations, is an offence. Section 2 of the Clayton Act prohibits as unlawful any price discrimination the effect of which discrimination may be substantially to lessen competition or tend to create a monopoly in any line of commerce.

It should be noted that much of the US law relating to antitrust is judge-made law, viz. the Supreme Court of the United States. It was that Court which, in several of its landmark decisions, gave flesh and blood to the broad provisions of law such as 'in restraint of trade', 'monopolizing a trade', 'line of commerce', which did not give any illustrative list, which the Court stated was well-advised, as it would enable the courts to deal with concepts such as the structure of a market, effect on competition in a particular market, interchangeability of products, etc., in relation to the market which is always subject to the dynamics of change.

SECTION 3—THE ELEMENTS

We may now consider in sequence the scope of section 3(1) of the Competition Act imposing a general prohibition on anti-competitive agreements, without specifying the purpose of any particular agreement; section 3(3) dealing with cartels, section 3(4) dealing with vertical restraints; and section 3(5) which saves the rights of owners of intellectual property rights from the operation of section 3.

Section 3(1)—Appreciable Adverse Effect on Competition within India

The basic requirement for section 3(1) to come into operation is that an agreement between enterprises relating to the supply of goods or services should cause or be likely to cause an appreciable adverse effect on competition within India. The key elements are: agreement, effect of the agreement on competition, that effect being adverse on competition, and that adverse effect being appreciable. The territory where the effect on competition is to be considered relevant for the purpose of the Act is India.

Each of these may be considered in some detail.

Agreement

There could be some overlap between the anti-competitive agreements that may fall under the general provision of section 3(1) and the specific anti-competitive agreements entered into among members of a cartel (section 3(3)) and vertical restraints (section 3(4)). Anti-competitive agreements are usually those that stipulate price-fixing, allocation of territory, exclusive dealings, etc. When agreements that are listed in section 3(3) are entered into between members of a cartel, that sub-section would apply. Section 3(4) would apply to vertical restraints. Section 3(1) would cover all anti-competitive agreements not expressly covered by these sub-sections.

Sometimes an agreement may be called by an apparently insignificant name and be in effect an anti-competitive agreement. Agreements for information exchange are one such and what is necessary is to examine the effect of that agreement on competition and not go by its name.

Agreements for exchange of information

Exchange of information will normally be among members of a trade association. The Office of Fair Trading (OFT) considers that the question of whether exchange of information will adversely affect competition will depend on the type of information, the market, and the manner of the exchange of information. Competition may be considered to be enhanced by the sharing of information, for example, on new technologies or market opportunities. This kind of exchange of information would have no adverse effect on competition, even if competitors exchanged the information.

In the view of the OFT, exchange of information may, however, be treated as likely to have an adverse effect on competition 'where it serves to reduce or remove uncertainties inherent in the process of competition. As a general principle, the OFT will consider that there is more likely to be an appreciable effect on competition the smaller the number of undertakings operating in the market, the more frequent the exchange and the more sensitive, detailed and confidential the nature of the information which is exchanged. There is also more likely to be an appreciable effect on competition where the exchange of information is limited to certain participating undertakings to the exclusion of their competitors and consumers.'[19]

Exchange of price information, non-price information

The following is the position of the OFT on exchange of price information and non-price information:[20]

The exchange of information on prices may lead to price coordination and, therefore, diminish competition that would otherwise be present between the undertakings. This will be the case whether the information exchanged relates directly to the prices charged or to the elements of a pricing policy, for example, discounts, costs, terms of trade and rates and dates of change.

The more recent or current the information exchanged, the more likely that exchange will have an appreciable effect on competition. Therefore, the circulation of purely historical information or the collation of price trends is unlikely to have an appreciable effect on competition, for example, where the exchange forms part of a scheme of inter-business comparison which is intended to spread best industrial practice. Exchange of information that is aggregated, and which cannot be disaggregated is also unlikely to have an appreciable effect on competition.

The exchange of information on matters other than price may have an appreciable effect on competition depending on the type of information exchanged and the structure of the market to which it relates. The exchange of aggregated statistical data, market research, and general industry studies, for example, are unlikely to have an appreciable effect on competition, since exchange of such information is unlikely to reduce individual undertakings' commercial and competitive independence.

In general, the exchange of information on output and sales should not affect competition provided that it is aggregated or, if it enables participants to identify individual undertakings' competitive behaviour, provided that it is sufficiently historic. In such circumstances, it is unlikely that an agreement to exchange such information would influence the participants' competitive market behaviour. There may, however, be an appreciable effect on competition if the information exchanged is current, or recent, or concerns future plans and if it can be ascribed to particular undertakings, whether because it is broken down in this way or because it can be disaggregated.

UK Agricultural Tractor Registration Exchange[21]

It was a case of information exchange that was held anti-competitive. The Agricultural Engineers Association Ltd (AEA), the UK trade association of manufacturers and importers of agricultural machinery, notified an information exchange agreement called the UK Agricultural Tractor Registration Exchange ('the Exchange'). That agreement concerned an exchange of information identifying the volume of retail sales and market shares of eight manufacturers and importers of agricultural tractors on the UK market with detailed breakdowns by product, territory, and time periods. The market position was that imports of tractors from Community countries into the UK accounted for over 50 per cent of the total UK market, and members of the Exchange together held some 87 to 88 per cent of the UK tractor market while the remaining 12 per cent of the market was shared by several small manufacturers who were not members.

The European Commission noted that the business of supply of agricultural tractors in the UK was highly concentrated and that 'the information exchange itself considerably increases the barriers to entry because it permits the established suppliers to recognize immediately any new penetration into the UK market or any increase in sales by non-members and then to react and defend their market positions. It is indeed the case that the market share of non-members has shown no substantial change over the entire period of the existence of the Exchange.'

In the view of the Commission, the nature of the information exchanged, that is, the exact quantities of the retail sales and the exact market shares which were trade secrets between genuine competitors in a highly concentrated market, clearly led to restrictions of competition for two reasons: (*a*) prevention of hidden competition in a highly concentrated market; and (*b*) increase of barriers to entry for non-members.

The Commission ruled that the Exchange restricted competition because it created a degree of market transparency between the suppliers in a highly concentrated market that was likely to destroy what hidden competition there remained between the suppliers in that market on account of the risk and ease of exposure of independent competitive action. It observed: 'In this highly concentrated market, "hidden competition" is essentially that element of uncertainty and secrecy between the main suppliers regarding market conditions without which none of them has the necessary scope of action to compete efficiently. Uncertainty and secrecy between suppliers is a vital element of competition in this kind of market. Indeed active competition in these market conditions becomes possible only if each competitor can keep its actions secret or even succeeds in misleading its rivals.' It also held that while small enterprises would certainly be handicapped if they chose to remain outside the Exchange, for lack of information, it was not advantageous for them to enter the Exchange and make available their level of activities known to others in the Exchange.

'Decisions' of Associations of Persons—Professional Rules
India

By virtue of the definition of 'activity' stated in the Explanation, the law relating to competition will apply to professions such as medical, legal, accountancy and such other professions. But section 3(1) as it stands now, does not extend to 'decisions' of the regulatory bodies covering these professions, which would be associations of persons. The rules of a professional regulatory body governing its members would be its decisions. Such of those decisions of a regulatory body as may affect the ability of its members to compete among them should be regulated by the Act.

The Competition Act, UK—professional services

Section 3(1) of that Act excluded matters provided for in Schedules 1–4 from the operation of the Chapter I prohibition, viz. anti-competitive agreements or decisions. Section 3(1)(d) dealt with professional rules set out in Schedule 4 to that Act. The principal provisions of Schedule 4 were, that Chapter I prohibition would not apply to an agreement to the extent to which the agreement (either on its own or when taken together with another agreement) (*a*) constituted a designated professional rule; (*b*) imposed obligations arising from designated professional rules; or (*c*) constituted an agreement to act in accordance with such rules.

Anybody regulating a professional service or the persons who provided, or wished to provide, that service could apply to the secretary of state for rules of that body to be designated. 'Designated' meant designated by the secretary of state under paragraph 2. 'Professional rules' were rules regulating a professional service or the persons providing, or wishing to provide, that service. 'Professional service' meant any of the services described in Part II of this Schedule.[22] 'Rules' includes regulations, codes of practice, and statements of principle. The effect is that in the case of these specific professions listed in Part II of Schedule 4, where the rules regulating the professional service of persons in those professions were notified to the secretary of state, the prohibition of Chapter I would not apply to those professional rules governing the members of that profession. However, it should be noted that any rule of the professional body going beyond what was necessary to regulate the profession, such as entry requirements, and code of practice and individual agreements between practitioners, such as one on fees to be charged, would have fallen under the prohibition if they were anti-competitive.

However, the Enterprise Act, 2002 UK, removed this exclusion of agreements relating to 'designated professional rules'.[23] The repeal was on the principle that professional services should be subject to competition law in the same way as other goods and services in the economy. Therefore, the Chapter I prohibition would apply also to decisions of associations regulating the professions as well as to individual agreements of those supplying professional services.

European Union

The application of EU competition law to the liberal professions is stated as follows in 'European Union XXXIInd Report on Competition policy 2002':[24]

Liberal professions are occupations requiring special training in the liberal arts or sciences, for example, lawyers, notaries, engineers, architects, doctors and accountants. The sector is usually characterized by a high level of regulation, either imposed by national governments or self-regulation by the professional bodies. This regulation can affect, *inter alia*, the numbers of entrants into the profession; the prices professionals may charge and the permitted charging arrangements (e.g., contingency fees); the organizational structure of professional services undertakings; the exclusive rights they enjoy; and their ability to advertise. Such regulation clearly has the potential to affect competition and when it is decided by associations of undertakings it may therefore come within the scope of Article 81(1) of the EC Treaty.

The Commission's policy with respect to the liberal professions is to fully apply the competition rules to this sector, whilst recognizing its specificities, such as the asymmetry of information between customer and service provider. The policy does not question the existence of professional bodies as such, but it requires, for example, that professional bodies must use their self-regulatory powers to benefit consumers, and not merely the interests of their own members. The overall goal is to improve the welfare of consumers of professional services.

The European Commission has been periodically assessing the position relating to competition in the professional services and the possible scope for reform or for modernizing specific professional rules of current legislation. The five main categories of potentially restrictive regulation found in the EU professions were: (i) price fixing, (ii) recommended prices, (iii) advertising regulations, (iv) entry requirements and reserved rights, and (v) regulations governing business structure and multi-disciplinary practices. The Commission considers that 'Professional services have an important role to play to improve the competitiveness of the European economy, as they are inputs for the economy and business, so their quality and competitiveness have important spillover effects. Professional services are also important because of their direct import for consumers.'

In its Annual Report of 2004, the Commission highlighted the need for national governments which had delegated the power to legislate on the regulation of professional duties emphasizing that it was their responsibility to ensure that the legislation did not contravene the Articles of the EC Treaty Regulation. It said: 'Where a State delegates its policy-making power to a professional association without sufficient safeguards, that is, without clearly indicating the public interest objectives to respect, without retaining the last word and without control of the implementation, the Member State can also be held liable for any resulting infringement.'

The rules of professional bodies relating to the regulation of professional services in India are its decisions and they are not 'agreements' and therefore at present they would not fall under section 3(3) of the Act. But they would be covered by Article 81.

The report continues as follows: 'As regards self-regulation by the professions Article 81(1) of the EC Treaty prohibits all agreements between undertakings, decisions by association of undertakings and concerted practices which may affect trade between Member States and which have as their object or effect the prevention, restriction or distortion of competition within the common market.'

Following this up, the European Commission emphasized the need for regulatory authorities in the Member States and professional bodies to review their existing rules taking into consideration whether those rules are necessary for the public interest, whether they are proportionate and whether they are justified.[25]

Two recent cases decided by the European Court of Justice may be considered.

Manuele Arduino—Case C-35/99

The criteria for determining fees and emoluments payable to members of the Bar, in Italy, in respect of civil and criminal proceedings and out-of-court work were to be set every two years by decision of the CNF (National Council of the Bar). Thereafter, it would have to be approved by the minister. The criteria referred to above were to be based on the monetary value of disputes, the level of the court and, in criminal matters, the duration of the proceedings. For each procedural step, or series of steps, maximum and minimum limits were to be set. Fees were settled by the court on the basis of these criteria having regard to the seriousness and number of the issues dealt with.

The question referred to the court for a preliminary ruling was: did the decision of the CNF, approved by Ministerial Decree No 585/94, fixing binding tariffs for the professional activity of members of the Bar, come within the scope of the prohibition in Article 85(1) (now Article 81(1)) of the EC Treaty?

The court ruled that Articles 5 (duty of the Members to act towards fulfillment of Treaty objectives) and 85 of the Treaty did not preclude a member state from adopting a law or regulation 'which approves, on the basis of a draft produced by a professional body of members of the Bar, a tariff fixing minimum and maximum fees for members of the profession, where that State measure forms part of a procedure such as that laid down in the Italian legislation'.

Wouters—Case C-309/99
Multidisciplinary Partnerships
The issue was the prohibition, by Supervisory Boards of Amsterdam and Rotterdam Bars, of members of the Bar from practising as members of the Bar in full partnership with accountants. The Regulation on Joint Professional Activity 1993, issued under the authority of the Law on the Bar, relating to the Netherlands, provided for: professional partnership, duty not to accept to any obligations which might jeopardize the free and independent exercise of their profession, etc. 'Professional partnership' was defined as 'any joint activity in which the participants practise their respective professions for their joint account and at their joint risk or by sharing control or final responsibility for that purpose'. The setting up or altering the constitution of a professional partnership required the affirmation of the Supervisory Board that the conditions on which that partnership was formed or its constitution altered, including the way in which it presented itself to other parties, satisfied the requirements imposed by, or under the Regulation.

The material part of the Regulation was Article 3 of this Regulation of 1993, which prohibited members of the Bar from entering into professional partnerships with one who was not practising law. It stated that: 'Members of the Bar shall not be authorized to enter into or maintain any professional partnership unless the primary purpose of each partner's respective profession is the practice of the law.'

The Regulation, however, permitted members of the Bar to enter into or maintain professional partnerships with members of another professional category accredited for that purpose by the General Council in accordance with Article 6. The principal conditions imposed by

Article 6 were: the members of that professional category were subject to disciplinary rules comparable to those imposed on members of the Bar; and entering into partnership with members of that other professional partnership was not contrary to Article 2 or 3, the basic provisions.

The recitals of the 1993 Regulation showed that members of the Bar were already authorized to enter into partnership with notaries, tax consultants and patent agents. Accountants were mentioned as an example of a professional category with which members of the Bar were not authorized to enter into partnership. The Regulation also provided for avoiding conflicts of interest, professional secrecy, and registration of documents in cases where members of the Bar entered into professional partnerships with such accredited members of another professional category.

The first point that the Court decided was that registered members of the Bar in the Netherlands carried on an economic activity and were, therefore, undertakings for the purposes of Articles 85, 86, and 90 of the Treaty. It added: 'The complexity and technical nature of the services they provide and the fact that the practice of their profession is regulated cannot alter that conclusion.'

The next issue before the Court was: whether, when it adopts a regulation such as the 1993 Regulation, a professional body is to be treated as an association of undertakings or, on the contrary, as a public authority. The Court ruled that the professional body was not acting as a public authority and only acted as the regulatory body of a profession, the practice of which constitutes an economic activity. It held that the 1993 Regulation was a decision of an association of undertakings within the meaning of Article 85(1) and that a professional organization with regulatory powers, such as the Bar of the Netherlands, cannot escape the application of Article 85 of the Treaty.

The key issue before the Court was if the 1993 Regulation, prohibiting multidisciplinary partnerships had the object of restricting competition. In the opinion of the Court, the 1993 Regulation, in so far as it prohibited absolutely any form of multidisciplinary partnership, whatever the respective sizes of the firms of lawyers and accountants concerned, restricted competition. But it ruled: 'The 1993 Regulation adopted by a body such as the Bar of the Netherlands does not infringe Article 85(1) of the Treaty, since that body could reasonably have considered that that regulation, despite the effects restrictive of competition that are inherent in it, is necessary for the proper practice of the legal profession, as organized in the Member State concerned.'

The Court reasoned: 'The Bar of the Netherlands was entitled to consider that members of the Bar might no longer be in a position to advise and represent their clients independently and in the observance of strict professional secrecy if they belonged to an organization which is also responsible for producing an account of the financial results of the transactions in respect of which their services were called upon and for certifying those accounts.' The Court ruled that the effects restrictive of competition for members of the Bar resulting from the 1993 Regulation did not go beyond what was necessary in order to ensure the proper practice of the legal profession. In other words, it was upheld as a rule of the profession regulating the practice of the profession of a lawyer, viz. ensuring the proper practice of the legal profession.

It is time for professional bodies in India to evolve a set of rules regarding their respective activities, which do not contain any condition that may be termed restrictive of competition.

United States of America

In the US, the position has been that the mere fact of one carrying on any profession, outside industrial activity, does not, without more, make available any exemption from the operation of the Sherman Act. *FTC* v. *Indiana Federation of Dentists*, and *Arizona* v. *Maricopa County Medical Society* discussed below related to the agreements covering medical services.

FTC v. Indiana Federation of Dentists[26]

A group of dentists formed the Indiana Federation of Dentists, in order to pursue their association's policy of resisting insurers' requests for X-rays for reference in considering settlement of claims relating to the dental patients. The insurers required the X-rays to enable them to contain the cost of treatment limiting payment of benefits to the cost of the 'least expensive yet adequate treatment' suitable to the needs of individual patients. Some dentists viewed such review of diagnostic and treatment decisions as a threat to their professional independence and economic well-being. They promulgated a 'work rule' forbidding its members to submit X-rays to dental insurers in conjunction with claim forms. The Federal Trade Commission (FTC) charged the association of an unfair method of competition in violation of section 5 of the FTC Act, pursuant to a conspiracy in restraint of trade that was unreasonable and hence unlawful under the standards for judging such restraints developed by the US Supreme Court in interpreting section 1 of the Sherman Act. The Supreme Court ruled that the rule of the Association forbidding the submission of X-rays to the insurers was in restraint of trade under section 1 of the Sherman Act. It declared:

The fact remains that the dentists' customers (that is, the patients and their insurers) sought a particular service: cooperation with the insurers' pretreatment review through the forwarding of X-rays in conjunction with claim forms. The Federation's collective activities resulted in the denial of the information the customers requested in the form that they requested it, and forced them to choose between acquiring that information in a more costly manner or forgoing it altogether. To this extent, at least, competition among dentists with respect to cooperation with the requests of insurers was restrained.

Goldfarb v. *Virginia State Bar*[27]—minimum fees

The petitioners, husband and wife, were unable to obtain the services of any lawyer, in Fairfax County, Virginia, to conduct an examination of title to the property they intended purchasing in Fairfax, for fees below the minimum fee prescribed by the Fairfax County Bar Association. They brought a class action against the State Bar and the County Bar alleging that the operation of the minimum-fee schedule, as applied to fees for legal services relating to residential real estate transactions, constituted price fixing in violation of section 1 of the Sherman Act. They sought both injunctive relief and damages.

Rejecting the contention that the learned professions were not 'trade or commerce' and so would be excluded from antitrust legislation, the Court ruled that Congress did not intend any sweeping exclusion. It stated: 'The language of section 1 of the Sherman Act, of course, contains no exception.' It held that title examination was a service, and the exchange of such a service for money was 'commerce' in the common usage of that term. Since financing of purchase of property in Fairfax could be from any part of the country outside that country, the Court concluded that interstate commerce had been sufficiently affected. It held that the petitioners had clearly proved that the fee schedule fixed fees and thus deprived purchasers or consumers of the advantages which they would derive from free competition. The Court also held that *Parker* v. *Brown* 317 US 341 (1943) did not apply to this case as the activity objected to could not be attributed to any act of the state acting in its sovereign capacity.

Evaluating Appreciable Adverse Effect on Competition within India[28]

To ascertain the effect on competition of an agreement stated as being anti-competitive, the first step is to determine the market where the competition is complained of as having been adversely affected. The market that has to be taken into consideration for this purpose is called the 'relevant market'. The relevant market is to be divided into the relevant product market and the relevant geographic market relating to the product or service supplied. Once the boundaries of the market are determined in this manner, the effect of the agreement said to be anti-competitive is to be considered, that is, whether it has reduced existing competition or eliminated competition in the supply of the product or service in the relevant market. If the effect were adverse and appreciable, meaning thereby in a substantial part of that market, the agreement would be one prohibited by section 3 and, therefore, void.

Two comments may be made on the use of the words in describing the harm to competition sought to be prevented. There is no uniformity in the Act. While this sub-section and sub-section (4) use the phrase 'appreciable adverse effect on competition in India', sub-section (3) simply refers to 'appreciable adverse effect on competition.' Section 6 dealing with regulation of combinations refers to 'an appreciable adverse effect on competition within the relevant market in India'. It is axiomatic that any examination of the effect on competition of any practice is always with reference to a market for a product or a service, the said market being further sub-divided into a product market and a geographical market. This principle should be adopted in examining, under the Act, all agreements or practices.

The European Commission's Notice of 9 December 1997, on the definition of the relevant market for the purposes of Community competition law states: 'Basically, the exercise of market definition consists in identifying the effective alternative sources of supply for the customers of the undertakings involved, both in terms of products/services and geographic location of suppliers.'[29]

Relevant market

Determining the relevant market[30]

Sub-sections (5) to (7) of section 19[31] state what factors are to be taken into consideration for the purpose of determining the 'relevant market' which will further be split into the 'relevant product market' and the 'relevant geographic market'. Then, what is to be ascertained is whether the extent of competition in the market for the goods or services, which may be the subject of the issue, that existed before the agreement has been reduced or eliminated as a result of the enforcement of the agreement.

The relevant geographic market

The definition under section 2(s) of a 'relevant geographic market' furnishes the basic test for determining a relevant geographic market. It should be a market comprising the area in which the conditions of competition for supply of goods or provision of services, or demand for goods or services are *distinctly homogenous* and can be distinguished from the conditions prevailing in the neighbouring areas. Homogeneity means uniformity of composition. The factors set out in section 19(6) such as local specification requirements, transport costs, and customer preferences are those that would, where they are different, negate homogeneity in conditions of competition. For example, if customer preferences for a particular quality or price of the product are different in a neighbouring area, the composition of the geographical market is different in the two places and what should be considered as the relevant geographic market in that case is only the area where the conditions of competition are homogenous. Uniformity of composition of the market is of the essence in a specific geographic market.

The relevant product market

The substance of the definition, under section 2(t) is that a 'relevant product market' means a market comprising all those products or services that are considered by the consumer as interchangeable or substitutable. This conceived interchangeability or substitutability should be by reason of the characteristics of the products or services, their prices and intended use. Interchangeability or substitutability on these grounds is what will determine the relevant product market. Section 19(7) also sets out these factors as necessary to be considered while determining the relevant product market.

Usually, a supplier would prefer to describe his product under as broad a classification as possible to dilute a possible anti-competitive effect. On the other hand, the government, in enforcing antitrust legislation may attempt to bring the product under as narrow a group as possible. Ultimately the issue will have to be decided by the competition authorities or the court, considering the market, the commercial practices, consumer application and other such matters.

Interchangeability of a product—the cellophane case

United States v. *Du Pont & Co.*[32] is the case usually referred to in connection with interchangeability of a product while determining a product market. The appellant in that case produced almost 75 per cent of the cellophane sold in the US. But cellophane constituted less than 20 per cent of all flexible packaging materials sold in that country. The US Supreme Court affirmed the judgement of the lower court, that the relevant market was the market for flexible packaging materials, as cellophane was interchangeable with numerous other materials, and was a part of the market for flexible packaging materials and competition from other materials in that market prevented the appellant from exercising any monopoly power in the supply of cellophane.

In examining the existence of cross-elasticity of demand between cellophane and other wrappings, the Court stated: 'This interchangeability is largely gauged by the purchase of competing products for similar uses considering the price, characteristics and adaptability of the competing commodities.'

Sub-markets

In *Brown Shoe Co. Inc.* v. *US*[33] the US Supreme Court pointed out that within the broad product market, well-defined sub-markets may exist which, in themselves, may constitute product markets for antitrust purposes. It stated that the boundaries of such a sub-market may be determined by examining such practical indicia as industry or public recognition of the sub-market as a separate economic entity, the product's peculiar characteristics and uses, unique production facilities, distinct customers, distinct prices, sensitivity to price changes, and specialized vendors. Though reaching out to identify sub-markets is not expressly provided under the Indian Act, 'consumer preference' under section 19(7)(c) would permit, where necessary, ascertaining a sub-market.

Effect on Competition

Having defined the relevant product and geographic market, which in plain terms means identifying the constituents of that market, viz. the suppliers, their products or services, their respective shares of the market, and the extent of the ability of individual suppliers to operate independently in competition in that market, the next important step will be to ascertain the effect of the agreement on the existing structure of that market. If the effect of the agreement, which as has been explained, will include any arrangement or understanding or action in concert, is such that it will significantly reduce the level of competition existing at the time the agreement is given effect to, the agreement may be stated to be one that has an adverse effect on competition. However, for the purposes of the Act, the agreement must fall under the description of one 'which causes or is likely to cause appreciable adverse effect on competition within India'. Where existing competition is totally eliminated, there is an appreciable adverse effect on competition and there is no need for further proof. But in cases where the erosion of competition is not so blatant and is subtle, leaving scope for argument on the effect on competition, a close examination of the issue is necessary. The question of when an agreement may be considered to be one which causes or is likely to cause *appreciable adverse effect on competition*, is a question of fact.

Section 3 has not directly defined what an anti-competitive agreement is, but has only provided that an agreement which causes or is likely to cause an appreciable effect on competition within India is prohibited and has declared that such an agreement is void. Therefore, it is necessary to ascertain in each case whether an agreement does have that effect. Section 19(3) specifies what factors are to be taken into consideration by the Commission in determining whether an agreement has an appreciable adverse effect on competition under section 3:

The Commission shall, while determining whether an agreement has an appreciable adverse effect on competition under section 3, have due regard to all or any of the following factors, namely—(a) creation of barriers to new entrants in the market; (b) driving existing competitors out of the market; (c) foreclosure of competition by hindering entry into the market; (d) accrual of benefits to consumers; (e) improvements in production or distribution of goods or provision of services; (f) promotion of technical, scientific and economic development by means of production or distribution of goods or provision of services.

In the first place, (a) to (c) are not the actual anti-competitive practices themselves, but the result of anti-competitive agreements or decisions. One will have to examine the agreements to ascertain if they would offend section 3(1). The usual anti-competitive practices are, fixing prices at which goods or services may be sold by others, market allocation, exclusive dealings and other such arrangements.

Rules for Determining Effect on Competition

Taking all the relevant factors into account, there should still be found a principle on which one can arrive at a conclusion on the effect of the anti-competitive conduct or practice on competition. It should be noted that the rules for determining the effect of any anti-competitive conduct or practice on the relevant market are: the rule of reason and the per se rule.

The Rule of Reason

Under the rule of reason, the effect on competition is found on the facts of the case, the market, and the existing competition, the actual or probable limiting of competition in the relevant market, etc. What determines the issue is, on the facts, the actual or probable restraint on competition. The rule of reason in examining the legality of restraints on trade was explained by the US Supreme Court in *Board of Trade of City of Chicago* v. *US*[34] as follows:

Every agreement concerning trade, every regulation of trade, restrains. To bind, to restrain, is of their very essence. The true test of legality is whether the restraint imposed is such as merely regulates and perhaps thereby promotes competition or whether it is such as may suppress or even destroy competition. To determine that question the court must ordinarily consider the facts peculiar to the business to which the restraint is applied; its condition before and after the restraint was imposed; the nature of the restraint and its effect, actual or probable. The history of the restraint, the evil believed to exist, the reason for adopting the particular remedy, the purpose or end sought to be attained, are all relevant facts. This is not because a good intention will save an otherwise objectionable regulation or the reverse; but because knowledge of intent may help the court to interpret facts and to predict consequences.'

The Per Se Rule

Under the per se rule, the acts or practices specified by the Act as deemed or presumed to have an appreciable adverse effect on competition are by themselves prohibited. It is unnecessary to consider, under the per se rule, if they limit or restrict competition. This is on the basis of established experience of their nature to produce anti-competitive effects. Therefore, it is no longer necessary to prove the anti-competitive nature of per se violations. Only, if any defence is permitted under the Act—the proviso to section 3(3) is an example, providing efficiency increases in a joint venture—may a justification for the conduct or practice charged be advanced.

The US Supreme Court explained, in *Northern Pac. R. Co.* v. *United States*, 356 US 1, the basis on which the per se rule was based thus:

However, there are certain agreements or practices which because of their pernicious effect on competition and lack of any redeeming virtue are conclusively presumed to be unreasonable and therefore illegal without elaborate inquiry as to the precise harm they have caused or the business excuse for their use. This principle of per se unreasonableness not only makes the type of restraints which are proscribed by the Sherman Act more certain to the benefit of everyone concerned, but it also avoids the necessity for an incredibly complicated and prolonged economic investigation into the entire history of the industry involved, as well as related industries, in an effort to determine at large whether a particular restraint has been unreasonable—an inquiry so often wholly fruitless when undertaken.

The Supreme Court cited the following cases where it had held price fixing (*United States* v. *Socony-Vacuum Oil Co.*, 310 US 150, 210); division of markets (*United States* v. *Addyston Pipe & Steel Co.*, 85 F. 271, aff'd); group boycotts (*Fashion Originators' Guild* v. *Federal Trade Comm'n*, 312 US 457); and tying arrangements (*International Salt Co.* v. *United States*, 332 US 392) as deemed to be unlawful in and of themselves.

The Two Rules under the Competition Act

The Competition Act has been ambivalent about the application of these rules. The breaches under section 3(3) by cartels or such groups, through anti-competitive agreements or practices that have the effects set out in section 3(3)(a) to (d) have been declared as those that shall be presumed to have an appreciable adverse effect on competition and it cannot be criticized. In the case of agreements set out in section 3(4)(a) to (e), viz. tie-in arrangement, exclusive supply agreement, exclusive distribution agreement, refusal to deal and resale price maintenance, they shall be in contravention of section 3(1), if they cause or are likely to cause an appreciable adverse effect on competition in India, meaning thereby that they will be examined under the rule of reason. The position regarding anti-competitive agreements that do not fall under section 3(3) or section 3(4), but fall under section 3(1) is not expressly stated and, therefore, it should be understood that such cases will have to be considered only under the rule of reason.

What needs to be criticized is the reversal of the position regarding the treatment of the agreements falling under section 3(4)(a) to

(e) with regard to tie-in arrangement, exclusive supply agreement, exclusive distribution agreement, refusal to deal and resale price maintenance. Under the MRTP Act, after the amendment in 1984, of section 33(1) of that Act, any agreement falling within one or more of the categories set out in section 33(1) (a) to (l) was 'deemed for the purposes of the Act, to be an agreement relating to restrictive trade practices ....' The practices that may be covered by section 33(1) (a) to (l), as a consequence, became per se restrictive trade practices. Those agreements stipulating the per se restrictive practices were required to be registered under that Act and were the starting point of investigation into restrictive practices. Even though these trade practices were per se restrictive trade practices, section 38 of the MRTP Act provided certain 'gateways' through which any of such practices could be shown as not prejudicial to the public interest.

Tie-in arrangements, exclusive supply agreements, exclusive distribution agreements, refusal to deal and resale price maintenance, covered by section 3(4)(a) to (e) of the Competition Act, 2002 are covered by section 33(1) of the MRPT Act,[35] under which they are per se restrictive trade practices. Further, section 39 of the MRTP Act is a specific provision declaring void the establishment of a minimum price to be charged on the resale of goods in India, thus regulating resale price maintenance. Some legal basis resting on commercial experience is necessary to change the treatment of these restrictive trade practices to one under the rule of reason from the per se rule. None seems to have appeared from 1969 till the enactment of the Competition Act, and the mere fact of repeal of the MRTP Act cannot be an occasion for changing the rule thus.

Rule of Reason—Section 3(1)

Cases falling under section 3(1) of the Competition Act are to be decided under the rule of reason. The principle of appreciable adverse effect on competition in India, the subject of section 3(1), is also contained in section 2(o) of the MRTP Act, which is as follows:

... restrictive trade practice means a trade practice which has, or may have, the effect of preventing, distorting or restricting competition in any manner and in particular. (i) which tends to obstruct the flow of capital or resources into the stream of production, or (ii) which tends to bring about manipulation of prices, or conditions of delivery or to affect the flow of supplies in the market relating to goods or services in such a manner as to impose on the consumers unjustified costs or restrictions; ...

Tata Engineering and Locomotive Co. Ltd v. *Registrar of Restrictive Trade Agreement*[36] is a landmark decision of the Supreme Court of India where, among other principles, the rule of reason was illustrated. It was a case under the MRTP Act and the decision rested on the interpretation of section 2(o) of that Act, defining a 'restrictive trade practice'.

The question before the Supreme Court of India, on appeal from the decision of the MRTP Commission ('the Commission'), was whether the agreement between Telco and its dealers allocating territories to its dealers within which only the dealers could sell bus and truck chassis referred to as the vehicles produced by the company, constituted a 'restrictive trade practice'.

The complaint before the Commission was that the clauses in the agreements, between Telco and its dealers for commercial vehicles, fixing an area in which only a Telco dealer may sell the vehicles purchased from Telco, prohibiting a dealer from selling commercial vehicles supplied by enterprises other than Telco, and fixing minimum prices for resale by a dealer of commercial vehicles purchased from Telco, were all restrictive trade practices. During the hearing before the Commission, Telco reported that it had discontinued the practice of resale price maintenance, thus putting an end to that complaint. Telco contended before the Commission that allocation of an area was considered necessary so that unequal and unfair distribution of these vehicles in various parts of the country could be avoided. The company defended exclusive dealership arrangements on the ground that there was no system of preferred buyers and that dealers were selected after a careful study of their experience so that they would be in a position to extend to the buyers of Telco vehicles high quality after-sales service, and the only way by which this could be secured was through exclusive dealership agreements, which was also common to that trade. Telco claimed that the issues were to be determined under section 2(o) of the MRTP Act and that none of the practices that were the subject of the complaint would cause any restraint on competition within the meaning of that section. Following from this, it also argued that the agreements containing these clauses were not registrable under section 33(1) of that Act. It should be noted that it was only in 1984, that section 33(1) was amended to declare certain categories of agreements as agreements deemed to be agreements relating to restrictive trade practices. The Commission ruled that the issues were to be decided under section 2(o), viz. whether any of the practices would fall under the definition of a restrictive trade practice, and if so whether it was open for Telco to avail of any of the gateways under section 38 showing that the practice was not prejudicial to the public interest.

The Commission held that exclusive dealership was a restrictive trade practice, but that Telco had the benefit of section 38(1)(h) which was a defence on the ground that the restriction did not directly or indirectly restrict or discourage competition to any material degree in any relevant trade or industry and was not likely to do so. The Commission noted that there were only four manufacturers, including Telco, of commercial trucks and bus chassis in India and that each major manufacturer had its own exclusive channels. Therefore Telco's exclusive dealership agreements did not directly or indirectly restrict or discourage competition to any material degree. The Commission held that allocation of territory was a restrictive trade practice as there was no material before it to show that it led to ensuring fair distribution of vehicles among different areas of the country and that no evidence was furnished by Telco about the economics of dealership or service points. It held further that no justification under section 38 providing the gateways was also shown.

Telco appealed to the Supreme Court of India. First, in explaining section 2(o), the Court stated: 'The instances set forth in the definition of restrictive trade practice emphasize the factors which go to establish a restrictive trade practice. Clauses (i) and (ii) in section 2(o) of the Act afford graver instances of restrictive trade practice.' On the application of section 2(o), the Court said: 'The definition of restrictive trade practice is an exhaustive and not an inclusive one. The decision whether trade practice is restrictive or not has to be arrived at by applying the rule of reason and not on the doctrine that any restriction as to area or price will per se be a restrictive trade practice.'

The Court explained that the following was required to be determined for deciding whether a restraint promoted competition or suppressed competition: 'To determine this question three matters are to be considered. First, what facts are peculiar to the business to which the restraint is applied. Second, what was the condition before and after the restraint is imposed. Third, what is the nature of the restraint and what is its actual and probable effect.' The Court also held that an agreement would be registrable under section 33(1), as it stood then, only if the trade practice fell under section 2(o) defining a restrictive practice, and that the agreements set out in section 33(1) were not statutory illustrations of section 2(o).

Considering the fact that the supply of commercial vehicles in India was far below demand, and keeping in view the great demand for Telco vehicles and the need to establish good quality after-sales service, of the kind assured by Telco throughout the country, the Court was satisfied that from the point of view of the consumer, there should be the widest and equitable geographical distribution of Telco vehicles, avoiding concentration of sales only in big cities. If the territorial restrictions were to be removed, it would be possible to divert sales to more profitable areas, depriving certain areas of supply of these vehicles.

Telco showed that there was a basis in allocating territories to dealers, which took note of; (*a*) population of commercial vehicles in the dealer's territory; (*b*) orders from customers pending with the dealer; (*c*) preference for Tata diesel vehicles as against other makes in the territory of the dealer; (*d*) past sales performance of the dealer; (*e*) effective after-sales service provided by the dealers; (*f*) special requirements of the territory during the erection of government projects such as steel plants, construction of dams, etc.; (*g*) emergency requirements of the territory on account of drought, flood relief, etc.; (*h*) government recommendations for meeting certain specific requirements; (*i*) dependence of the particular territory on road transport; and (*j*) requirements of state government and nationalized transport undertakings procured through dealers.

The Supreme Court held that when supply was shown as being far below demand and when the dealers were not in a position to sell below permissible prices, the charge of territorial restrictions restraining competition had no merit. The Court also stated that the territorial restriction ensured equitable distribution of the commercial vehicles in all parts of the country, where Telco had appointed dealers, and that if, without that restriction, Telco dealers were free to sell anywhere, the commercial vehicles would find their way to big cities and upcountry locations and small backward states would be deprived of the supply. It decided that the territorial restriction imposed by Telco did not fall under section 2(o).

As stated earlier, with the amendment of section 33(1) of the MRTP Act in 1984, after this judgement, allocation of an area for the disposal of goods sold became per se a restrictive trade practice, under section 33(1)(a) of that Act.

Some leading cases that decided when the adverse effect on competition was substantial are considered below. Section 19(3)(d) to (f) that offer gateways to what can be considered anti-competitive agreements are then discussed.

Causing Entry Barriers

In *Ford Motor Co. v. United States*,[37] Ford acquired the assets of Autolite, an independent manufacturer of spark plugs and other automotive parts and a supplier to Ford. Ford was a major customer in an oligopolistic industry. It was held that the acquisition was likely to substantially lessen competition in automotive spark plugs as the acquisition by a buyer of a substantial share of the total industry output 'foreclosed' access to independent spark plug manufacturers. The US Supreme Court held that Ford's position of a buyer of spark plugs as an original equipment manufacturer would 'maintain the virtually insurmountable barriers to entry to the aftermarket'.

Eliminating Competition

Standard Oil Co. of New Jersey v. US[38]

This was a case where competition was virtually eliminated. The charge was that the defendants were engaged in conspiring 'to restrain the trade and commerce in petroleum, commonly called "crude oil," in refined oil, and in the other products of petroleum, among the several states and territories of the US and the District of Columbia and with foreign nations, and to monopolize the said commerce.' The conspiracy was stated to be for the purpose of fixing the price of crude and refined oil and the products thereof, limiting its production, controlling its transportation and thereby, restraining trade and commerce among the several states, and monopolizing the said commerce.

The combination was the acquisition by Standard Oil Company of New Jersey of the majority of the stock of a large number of companies in the oil industry. The combination was charged with having obtained a complete mastery over the oil industry, controlling 90 per cent of the business of producing, shipping, refining, and selling petroleum and its products, and being in a position to fix the price of crude and refined petroleum, and to restrain and monopolize all interstate commerce in those products.

The combination abused its control, and the anti-competitive practices levelled against them were: rebates, preferences, and other discriminatory practices in favour of the combination by railroad companies; restraint and monopolization by control of pipelines, and unfair practices against competing pipelines; contracts with competitors in restraint of trade; unfair methods of competition, such as local price cutting at the points where necessary to suppress competition; espionage of the business of competitors, the operation of bogus independent companies, and payment of rebates on oil, with the like intent; the division of the US into districts, and limiting the operations of the various subsidiary corporations as to such districts so that competition in the sale of petroleum products between such corporations had been entirely eliminated and destroyed.

The US Supreme Court held that so far as the decree of the lower court held that the ownership of the stock of the New Jersey Corporation constituted a combination in violation of section 1, and an attempt to create a monopoly or to monopolize under section 2, both of the Sherman Act,[39] and commanded the dissolution of the combination, the decree was clearly appropriate.

In elucidating the necessity to adopt the rule of reason as a standard in determining whether a contract was in restraint of trade, the US Supreme Court stated:

The merely generic enumeration which the statute makes of the acts to which it refers, and the absence of any definition of restraint of trade as used in the statute, leaves room for but one conclusion, which is, that it was expressly designed not to unduly limit the application of the act by precise definition, but, while clearly fixing a standard, that is, by defining the ulterior boundaries which could not be transgressed with impunity, to leave it to be determined by the light of reason, guided by the principles of law and the duty to apply and enforce the public policy embodied in the statute, in every given case whether any particular act or contract was within the contemplation of the statute.

Agreement to Sell at Fixed Minimum Prices

Dr Miles Medical Co. v. *John D. Park & Sons Co.*[40]

The complainant, Dr Miles Medical Company, was a manufacturer of proprietary medicines prepared in accordance with secret formulae. The agreement between the complainant and the wholesale distributing agents, required, among other obligations, that the goods were to be sold at not less than the prices indicated therein. In the case of retailers, they were not to sell at less than the full retail price as printed on the packages. The wholesalers and retail agents were also prohibited from selling the proprietary medicines at any price to wholesale or retail dealers who were not accredited agents of the Dr Miles Medical Company.

The complaint against the defendant was that it obtained the goods of the complainant from its wholesale and retail agents by false and fraudulent representations and in violation of their contracts with the complainant. The allegation was that the defendant had procured the complainant's products for selling them at 'cut rates' and, in fact, sold them at less than the prices established by the complainant.

No material was placed before the Court showing from whom the vendor to the defendant had acquired the medicines. The Court considered it possible that the goods procured by the defendant may have been purchased by the defendant's vendors from other wholesale agents who were entitled to sell them to anyone.

The Court observed: 'It is, as we have seen, a system of interlocking restrictions by which the complainant seeks to control not merely the prices at which its agents may sell its products, but the prices for all sales by all dealers at wholesale or retail, whether purchasers or sub purchasers, and thus to fix the amount which the consumer shall pay, eliminating all competition.'

Holding the agreements as in restraint of trade, the US Supreme Court held that the agreements were designed to maintain prices after the complainant had parted with the title to the articles, and to prevent competition among those who traded in them. The Court declared: 'The complainant having sold its product at prices satisfactory to itself, the public is entitled to whatever advantage may be derived from competition in the subsequent traffic.'

Since the complainant's products were not patented and were not protected by any statutory grant, the Court rejected the contention that the restrictions objected to were legitimate in the case of products manufactured by a secret process.

OFT on Price Fixing

According to the OFT, price fixing may be done in many ways. It states:[41]

There are many ways in which prices can be fixed. Price fixing may involve fixing either the price itself or the components of a price, setting a minimum price below which prices are not to be reduced, establishing the amount or percentage by which prices are to be increased, or establishing a range outside which prices are not to move.

Price fixing may also take the form of an agreement to restrict price competition. This will include, for example, an agreement to adhere to published price lists or not to quote a price without consulting potential competitors, or not to charge less than any other price in the market. An agreement may restrict price competition even if it does not entirely eliminate it. Competition may, for example, remain in the ability to grant discounts or special deals on a published list price or ruling price.

An agreement may also have the object of fixing prices while only indirectly affecting the price to be charged. It may cover the discounts or allowances to be granted, transport charges, payments for additional services, credit terms or the terms of guarantees, for example. The agreement may relate to the charges or allowances quoted themselves, to the ranges within which they fall, or to the formulae by which ancillary terms are to be calculated.

Price fixing issues are not limited to agreements between competing undertakings. They can also arise between undertakings operating at different levels in the supply chain, where an agreement directly or indirectly (whether on its own or in combination with other factors under the control of the parties) has the object of restricting a buyer's ability to determine its resale price.

Termination of a Dealer's Appointment by a Manufacturer

Business Electronics v. Sharp Electronics[42]

Termination of the agreement with a price-cutting dealer on the representation of another dealer cannot be said, in the absence of some agreement between the remaining dealer and the manufacturer on prices to be maintained after the termination of the appointment of the dealer, to be per se illegal. Proof of its anti-competitive effects will have to be shown, which was not done in this case. A non-price restraint was held as not per se illegal under the Act.

Territory Restriction, Franchisee

Continental T.V. Inc. v. Gte Sylvania Inc.[43]

Where there is a vertical restriction on a franchisee that the products are to be sold only from the location franchised and not any other place and the manufacturer appoints another franchisee, within its rights reserved, at a location of about mile from the first franchisee's location, it cannot be termed a per se violation of the Sherman Act. The issue is to be decided under the rule of reason principle, on anti-competitive effects of the arrangement being shown.

Benefits that may Flow from an Agreement

Section 19(3)(d) to (f) deal with benefits that outweigh the possible adverse anti-competitive effect that an agreement may cause and which could be grounds for allowing the agreement to remain, either in the same form or in any altered form. They are:

(d) accrual of benefits to consumers;
(e) improvements in production or distribution of goods or provision of services;
(f) promotion of technical, scientific, and economic development by means of production or distribution of goods or provision of services.

Under section 27(d) the Commission has the power to direct that an agreement shall stand modified to the extent and in the manner as may be specified in the order by the Commission.

The factors to be considered under the above sub-sections are some of the criteria for granting individual or block exemption, as meeting the requirements of section 9 of the Competition Act 1998, UK,[44] to an agreement falling under the Chapter I prohibition. The agreement may also be eligible to a 'parallel' exemption, where it is exempted under any Regulation under the EEC law or specifically exempted by the European Commission. Pursuant to the EEC Modernization Regulation referred to above, the Competition Act 1998, UK, has been amended to the effect that an agreement that falls within the Chapter I prohibition but which satisfies the conditions set out in section 9(1) of that Act is not prohibited, no prior decision to that effect being required. The burden of proving that the conditions are satisfied rests on the undertaking(s) claiming the benefit of section 9(1) of the UK Act.

The OFT has explained as to when the criteria for exemption may be claimed to have been met. On improvements in production or distribution of goods it states: 'Examples of improvements in production or distribution include lower costs from longer production or delivery runs, or from changes in the methods of production or distribution; improvements in product quality; increase in range of products produced or services provided. In each case, the nature of the improvement claimed must be clearly identified and justified.' On promotion of technical progress, it states: 'Examples of the promotion of technical or economic progress include efficiency gains from economies of scale and specialization in research and development with the prospect of an enhanced flow or speed of innovation, and technical progress.'[45] On benefits to the consumer, the requirement is that they should flow from the improvements in production or distribution, such as a faster development of a new product or of new markets or better distribution systems.

The Indian Competition Act could also have provided for individual or block exemptions, as made available by the UK Act and the EEC legislation. Block exemptions save administrative costs and introduce certainty. The power of the central government, under section 54 to provide exemptions from the Act, does not deal with this subject.

SECTION 3(2)

An agreement in contravention of the provisions of section 3(1) is void.

The prescribed mode of enforcement of the provisions of the Act relating to agreements falling under section 3 will be outlined later in this chapter.

SECTION 3(3)—CARTELS AND SIMILAR GROUPS

Section 3(3) deals with enterprises that are engaged in the supply of identical or similar goods or services or constitute a cartel and which engage in certain anti-competitive agreements, practices or take certain decisions set out therein.

Section 3(3) of the Act states that (i) the agreements entered into between the entities of the class described therein, or (ii) any practice carried on by them, or (iii) any decision taken by them and (iv) containing the terms set out in clauses (a) to (d), shall be *presumed* to have an appreciable adverse effect on competition.

They are deemed to be per se in violation of section 3. It would be for the party claiming that it has no such effect to prove that claim.

What is a Cartel?

The Office of Fair Trading, UK explains the nature of a cartel and how cartels operate.[46]

In its simplest terms, a cartel is an agreement between businesses not to compete with each other. The agreement is usually verbal and often informal. Typically, cartel members may agree on: prices, output levels, discounts, credit terms, which customers they will supply, which areas they will supply, who should win a contract (bid rigging).

Cartels can occur in almost any industry and can involve goods or services at the manufacturing, distribution or retail level.

However, some sectors are more susceptible to cartels than others because of the structure or the way in which they operate. For example, where there are few competitors, the products have similar characteristics, leaving little scope for competition on quality or service, communication channels between competitors are already established, the industry is suffering from excess capacity or there is general recession.

The classes of parties to an agreement dealt with by section 3(3) are: enterprises, associations of enterprises; persons or associations of persons and they could act in any combination. For the purposes of this sub-section there is a supply-related qualification as to the nature of the relationship between these entities that alone would bring them within the purview of this sub-section. It is that they are to be an association of persons or enterprises or a cartel, and be 'engaged in identical or similar trade of goods or provision of services'. Where the association of persons or enterprises is publicly identified as a group with a unity of purpose they are named as a cartel.

The Act has specifically listed in section 3(3)(a) to (d) the anti-competitive agreements, practices or decisions of such an association or cartel that shall be presumed to have an appreciable adverse effect on competition. In substance, they are fixing prices, limiting supply of goods or services or technical development, sharing the market, and bid rigging or collusive bidding. The explanation to the sub-section has defined 'bid rigging' as any agreement that has the effect of eliminating or reducing the competition for bids or manipulating the process of bidding. The purpose of inviting bids is to obtain an offer on terms submitted by competitors acting independently and honestly. The aim of bid rigging is to defeat this objective. Collusion among competing bidders will eliminate competition in bidding and manipulated terms will cause prejudice to the enterprise inviting bids for a job.

On the harmful effects of cartels the European Union XXXIInd Report on Competition Policy—2002 says:

They diminish social welfare, create allocative inefficiency and transfer wealth from consumers to the participants in the cartel by modifying output and/or prices in comparison with market-driven levels. Cartels are harmful also over the long run. Engaging in cartels to avoid the rigours of competition can result in the creation of artificial, uneconomic and unstable industry structures, lower productivity gains or fewer technological improvements and sustained higher prices. Furthermore, the weakening of competition leads to a loss of competitiveness and threatens sustainable employment opportunities.[47]

Cartel Cases

United States v. *Trenton Potteries Co. et al.*[48] was one of the early cases that were decided by the US Supreme Court. The complaint, under the

Sherman Act, was that the respondents, controlling some 82 per cent of the business of manufacturing and distributing in the US vitreous pottery of the type described, combined to fix prices and to limit sales in interstate commerce to jobbers. One of the arguments on behalf of the respondents was that where the prices fixed were reasonable, the practice could not be deemed to be an unreasonable restraint of commerce. The Court emphasized that the reasonableness or otherwise of the restraint of commerce was a distinct, and the only issue, and the reasonableness of the stipulated prices, under an agreement that was shown as an unreasonable restraint of commerce did not affect the basic issue, viz. whether an agreement was in restraint of commerce. On price-fixing, the Court stated:

> The aim and result of every price-fixing agreement, if effective, is the elimination of one form of competition. The power to fix prices, whether reasonably exercised or not, involves power to control the market and to fix arbitrary and unreasonable prices. The reasonable price fixed today may through economic and business changes become the unreasonable price of tomorrow. Once established, it may be maintained unchanged because of the absence of competition secured by the agreement for a price reasonable when fixed. Agreements which create such potential power may well be held to be in themselves unreasonable or unlawful restraints, without the necessity of minute inquiry whether a particular price is reasonable or unreasonable as fixed and without placing on the government in enforcing the Sherman Law the burden of ascertaining from day to day whether it has become unreasonable through the mere variation of economic conditions.

The Lombard Club[49]

The European Commission imposed fines totalling € 124,26 million on eight Austrian banks (the 'Lombard Club'), for their participation in a wide-ranging price cartel. The cartel covered the entire Austrian territory with a view to fixing deposit, lending and other rates to the detriment of businesses and consumers in Austria. The cartel extended to all banking products and services and the members fixed interest rates for loans and savings for private/household and for commercial customers as well as the fees consumers had to pay for certain services. The cartel also extended to money transfers and export financing. The minutes of meetings, memoranda, records of telephone conversations, correspondence, etc., unearthed a network of cartel committees ('Lending Rates Committees', the 'Deposit Rates Committees', etc.) The objective of the cartel was to avoid competition in 'interest rates'. Whenever there was a change in the key lending rates by the Austrian Central Bank, the members of the cartel would decide on increase or reduction in their own rates that they considered necessary as a consequence.

Auction Houses

Christie's and Sotheby's, the well-known auction houses, were found to be involved in a collusive agreement fixing trading terms. The purpose of the cartel agreement was to reduce the fierce competition between the two leading auction houses that had developed during the 1980s and early 1990s. The most important aspect of the agreement consisted in an increase in the commission paid by sellers at auctions (the so-called vendor's commission). But the collusive agreement also concerned other trading conditions, such as advances paid to sellers, guarantees given for auction results and payment conditions. The Commission fined Sotheby's 20.4 million, that is, 6 per cent of its worldwide turnover. The amount included a 40 per cent reduction for its cooperation in the investigation. Christie's, on the other hand, escaped a fine because it was the first to provide crucial evidence, which enabled the Commission to prove the existence of the cartel.[50]

Plasterboard Cartel

The members of the cartel, in order to protect themselves against a fall in prices of their product, plasterboard, a manufactured construction material, worked out a plan to exchange information among themselves on their sales volumes so as to provide mutual reassurance that the price war had ended. Similarly, they repeatedly gave each other advance warning of price increases. The companies covered by the decision of the European Commission produced virtually all the plasterboard manufactured in the countries concerned. The objective of the cartel was their common desire to reduce competition to a level that suited their interests on the German, French, UK and Benelux markets as, in previous years, the price of plasterboard had fallen sharply as a result of fierce competition, which had directly benefited consumers.

The Commission found that 'the concerted action took the form of discussions on the fringes of trade association meetings, the sending to competitors of letters announcing price increases to customers and even the sending to the private addresses of the directors of the German subsidiaries, of the instructions given to sales forces.' Holding that such conduct constituted a very serious infringement of the competition rules laid down in Article 81 of the EC Treaty, it imposed fines on members of the cartel as follows: (€ million): Lafarge: 249.60, BPB: 138.60, Knauf: 85.80 and Gyproc Benelux: 4.32. The Commission declared that the amount of the fines reflected the size of the plasterboard market, which was worth more than 1.2 billion in 1997, the last full year of the infringement, and the length of the period during which the cartel operated—more than six-and-a-half years.

Arizona v. Maricopa County Medical Society[51]
In this case, a number of foundations were established by doctors to promote fee-for-service medicine and to provide the community with a competitive alternative to existing health insurance plans. The foundations, by agreement of their member doctors, established the maximum fees the doctors could claim in full payment for health services provided to policyholders of specified insurance plans. The State of Arizona alleged that they were engaged in an illegal price-fixing conspiracy in violation of section 1 of the Sherman Act.

The question before the US Supreme Court was whether section 1 of the Sherman Act was violated by agreements among competing physicians, setting, by majority vote, the maximum fees that they could claim in full payment for health services provided to policyholders of specified insurance plans. The US Supreme Court held that the fee agreements disclosed by the record in the case, among independent competing entrepreneurs, doctors, fitted squarely into the horizontal price-fixing mould and was a per se violation of the Sherman Act.

Quoting its own judgement in *United States v. Socony-Vacuum Oil Co.*, 310 US 150 (1940), the Court said:

Any combination which tampers with price structures is engaged in an unlawful activity. Even though the members of the price-fixing group were in no position to control the market, to the extent that they raised, lowered, or stabilized prices they would be directly interfering with the free play of market forces. The Act places all such schemes beyond the pale and protects that vital part of our economy against any degree of interference. Congress has not left with us the determination of whether or not particular price-fixing schemes are wise or unwise, healthy or destructive. It has not permitted the age-old cry of ruinous competition and competitive evils to be a defense to price-fixing conspiracies. It has no more allowed genuine or fancied competitive abuses as a legal justification for such schemes than it has the good intentions of the members of the combination. If such a shift is to be made, the Congress must do it. Certainly Congress has not left us with any such choice. Nor has the Act created or authorized the creation of any special exception in favor of the oil industry.

Whatever may be its peculiar problems and characteristics, the Sherman Act, so far as price-fixing agreements are concerned, establishes one uniform rule applicable to all industries alike.

Limiting production, technical development, etc.

Enterprises may combine to limit supply to the market at the level they consider profitable to them. They may also impose conditions on other parties that would have the effect of restricting the dissemination of technology into the market.

Sarabhai Chemicals P. Ltd and Another, in re[52] decided by the MRTP Commission, as a restrictive trade practice, is one such.

The Indian company, Sarabhai Chemicals P. Ltd and the overseas collaborator, E. Merck A.G., had entered into a technical know-how agreement which provided for the provision of know-how to the Indian party for the manufacture of fine chemicals, pharmaceutical chemicals, vitamins, insecticides, analytical reagents and other allied products in India. The period of the agreement was 20 years, but after 10 years, they terminated the agreement releasing each other from their obligations under that agreement, but entered into a fresh agreement that contained a clause that was as follows:

(9) E.M. (2nd respondent) agrees that from the date both parties signed this agreement up to the 28th October, 1978, E.M. shall not directly or indirectly either by itself or by its licensees or agents manufacture within the Union of India any of the LISTED ITEMS and shall not package, sell or distribute such products within the Union of India. E.M., however, shall be free to import into the Union of India any such products and shall be free to package to sell and to distribute such imported product within the Union of India whether by itself or a licensee or an agent.

The Commission held that there was a denial of access to the technical know-how for manufacturing the products in India and that the impugned clause did have an adverse effect on competition and that it was highly likely to have such an effect, in terms of section 2(o), in future also. It ruled: 'We have no hesitation, therefore, in finding that cl. 9 in this case, which prevents the further flow of know-how into India subsequent to the termination of the original agreement in 1969, for a period as long as ten years in respect of an extremely wide range, including some important items, thus enuring to the benefit of the 1st respondent and not at all to the general public, acts as a barrier to entry to other intending manufacturers in the relevant field, is and amounts clearly to a restrictive trade practice within the mischief of section 2(o) of the Act.'

Sharing the market

Timken Co. v. United States[53] is a clear example of a manufacturing cartel dividing the market.

Three Timken corporations—Timken Roller Bearing Co, an American company, the appellant in this case, British Timken Ltd, a British company and, Societe Anonyme Francaise Timken, a French company manufacturing antifriction bearings—had allocated trade territories among themselves, fixed prices on products of one sold in the territory of the others, cooperated to protect each other's markets and to eliminate outside competition, and participated in cartels to restrict imports to, and exports from, the US. The District Court concluded that the appellant (the American company) had violated the Sherman Act as charged and entered a comprehensive decree designed to bar future violations. The Supreme Court confirmed the order of the District Court, except relating to divestiture of the holding of stock in overseas companies by the American company.

The Supreme Court rejected many of the arguments on behalf of the appellant. It was claimed that the agreements impugned were part of a larger arrangement, viz. a joint venture between one Dewar who, along with the appellant company, held a significant percentage of the share capital of the British company and the entire share capital of the French company; a trademark licensing agreement permitting the British and French companies to use the appellant's *Timken* mark. It was also contended that the terms of the agreement were reasonable and therefore, could not be held to be in violation of the Sherman Act. The Supreme Court agreed with the finding of the District Court that the dominant purpose of the restrictive agreements into which the appellant, British Timken and French Timken entered was to avoid all competition either among themselves or with others and ruled that 'agreements between legally separate persons and companies to suppress competition among themselves cannot be justified by characterizing the project as a 'joint venture' and that common ownership or control of the contracting corporations would not liberate them from the impact of the antitrust laws.

On the question of the trademark licensing agreement as being necessary and not attracting the provisions of the antitrust Act, the

Supreme Court agreed with the District Court's finding that the purpose of that agreement was not mere protection of the name covered by the trademark, and held that 'the agreements in the present case went far beyond protection of the name "Timken" and provided for control of the manufacture and sale of antifriction bearings whether carrying the mark or not.' It ruled that a trademark cannot be legally used as a device for Sherman Act violation.

The Supreme Court also held that acceptance of the argument on behalf of the appellant that conditions of trade abroad, like tariffs and quota restrictions, required such arrangements through companies incorporated outside the country would 'make the Sherman Act a dead letter insofar as it prohibits contracts and conspiracies in restraint of foreign trade.'

Flat Glass Cartel—EU[54]

The European Commission imposed fines totalling €486,900,000 on the following leading manufacturers of flat glass, Asahi, Guardian, Pilkington, and Saint-Gobain for coordinating price increases and other commercial conditions for deliveries of flat glass in the EEA. The action was initiated on the Commission's own initiative and it collected the evidence through surprise inspection of the premises of the members of the cartel. Asahi, Guardian, Pilkington, and Saint-Gobain, with a combined share of at least 80 per cent of the flat glass market in the EEA, organized several rounds of price increases, fixed minimum prices and other commercial conditions in an endeavour to raise or otherwise stabilize prices. They also monitored the implementation of the price increase agreements. The evidence uncovered described in detail several meetings in restaurants and hotels in different European countries during which Asahi, Guardian, Pilkington, and Saint-Gobain discussed and agreed upon the level and timing of price increases (including which undertaking was to lead the price increase), target prices, minimum prices, and/or exchanged sensitive commercial information.

Air Cargo Carriers—Price Fixing Cartel[55]

The European Commission charged a fine of €799 million on the following known airlines: Air Canada, Air France-KLM, British Airways, Cathay Pacific, Cargolux, Japan Airlines, LAN Chile, Martinair, SAS, Singapore Airlines, and Qantas. The carriers coordinated their action on surcharges for fuel and security without discounts over a six-year period. Lufthansa (and its subsidiary Swiss) received full immunity from fines under the Commission's leniency programme, as it was the first to provide information about the cartel.

The contacts on prices between the airlines concerned initially started with a view to discussing fuel surcharges. The carriers contacted each other so as to ensure that worldwide airfreight carriers imposed a flat rate surcharge per kilo for all shipments. The cartel members extended their cooperation by introducing a security surcharge and refusing to pay a commission on surcharges to their clients (freight forwarders).

The aim of these contacts was to ensure that these surcharges were introduced by all the carriers involved and that increases (or decreases) of the surcharge levels were applied in full without exception. By refusing to pay a commission, the airlines ensured that surcharges did not become subject to competition through the granting of discounts to customers. Such practices violated EU competition rules.

Lift and Escalator Cartels Fined over €990 Million[56]

The companies allocated tenders and other contracts for the sale, installation, maintenance, and modernization of lifts and escalators with the aim of freezing market shares and fixing prices. Business secrets and confidential information on bidding patterns and prices between the cartel participants were also exchanged. Projects that were rigged included lifts and escalators for hospitals, railway stations, shopping centres, and commercial buildings.

The allocation of projects was similar in all four member states. The companies informed each other of calls for tender and coordinated their bids according to their pre-agreed cartel quotas. Fake bids, too high to be accepted, were lodged by the companies who were not supposed to win the tender, in order to give the impression of genuine competition. The companies kept and circulated amongst themselves updated project lists for Belgium, Germany, and Luxembourg. In Germany and The Netherlands, it was often agreed that the company that had a longstanding or good relationship with a particular customer should secure most of that customer's contracts; referred to by the companies as the 'existing customers remain' principle.

Bid Rigging

Rigging a bid occurs when by collusion among bidders, actual and potential, the members of that group keep the bid amount at a predetermined manipulated level. The substance of the explanation to section 3(3) is that 'bid rigging' occurs when there is an agreement, between enterprises or persons, engaged in the supply of identical or similar products or services, which has the effect of eliminating or reducing competition for bids, or adversely affects or manipulates the process of bidding. The essence is that independence in the bidding process is taken away and the bid offered is the result of collusion. This would lead to the enterprise inviting bids having to deal with contracts that do not represent real costs and suffer economic loss.

The US Department of Justice has issued *Price Fixing, Bid Rigging, and Market Allocation Schemes: An Anti-trust Primer.* On bid rigging, it states as follows:

Bid rigging

Essentially, competitors agree in advance who will submit the winning bid on a contract being let through the competitive bidding process. As with price fixing, it is not necessary that all bidders participate in the conspiracy. Bid rigging also takes many forms, but bid-rigging conspiracies usually fall into one or more of the following categories:

Bid Suppression: In bid suppression schemes, one or more competitors who otherwise would be expected to bid, or who have previously bid, agree to refrain from bidding or withdraw a previously submitted bid so that the designated winning competitor's bid will be accepted.

Complementary Bidding: Complementary bidding (also known as 'cover' or 'courtesy' bidding) occurs when some competitors agree to submit bids that are either too high to be accepted or contain special terms that will not be acceptable to the buyer. Such bids are not intended to secure the buyer's acceptance, but are merely designed to give the appearance of genuine competitive bidding. Complementary bidding schemes are the most frequently occurring forms of bid rigging, and they defraud purchasers by creating the appearance of competition to conceal secretly inflated prices.

Bid Rotation: In bid rotation schemes, all conspirators submit bids but take turns being the low bidder. The terms of the rotation may vary; for example, competitors may take turns on contracts according to the size of the contract, allocating equal amounts to each conspirator or allocating volumes that correspond to the size of each conspirator company. A strict bid rotation pattern defies the law of chance and suggests collusion is taking place.

Subcontracting: Subcontracting arrangements are often part of a bid-rigging scheme. Competitors who agree not to bid or to submit a losing bid frequently receive subcontracts or supply contracts in exchange from the successful low bidder. In some schemes, a low bidder will agree to withdraw its bid in favor of the next low bidder in exchange for a lucrative subcontract that divides the illegally obtained higher price between them.

Almost all forms of bid-rigging schemes have one thing in common: an agreement among some or all of the bidders which predetermines the winning bidder and limits or eliminates competition among the conspiring vendors.

The *Primer* adds: 'Some of the industry conditions favourable to collusion are: (i) there are few sellers; (ii) higher degree of standardization of a product, making it easy for competing firms to agree on a common price structure; (iii) repetitive purchasers enabling the vendors to know of other bidders.'

The Proviso to Section 3(3)

As stated earlier, section 3(3)(a–d) lists agreements, practices and decisions that may be effected by cartels or enterprises engaged in the supply of identical or the same goods or services that will be presumed to have an appreciable adverse effect on competition. However, the proviso exempts from section 3(3) any agreement entered into by way of joint ventures, if such agreement increases the efficiency in production, and supply of goods or services. Enterprises may, without interfering with the process of competition, agree upon improved methods of production or distribution leading to efficiency in costs. Such agreements would be outside section 3(3). The only two basic requirements are that such agreements should be part of a joint venture and they should be shown to increase efficiency in the supply of goods or services. The principle of this exemption is the same as Article 81(3) of the EC law on anti-competitive agreements and section 9 of the Competition Act, 1998, UK, discussed earlier in this chapter in section 'benefits that may flow from an agreement'.

Specialization Agreements

The European Commission by Regulation (EC) No. 2658/2000 of 29 November 2000 on the application of Article 81(3) of the Treaty to categories of specialization agreements has granted block exemption to certain classes of specialization agreements on the conditions stated therein. Certain joint venture operations are also covered by this Regulation and it would be useful to understand its substance.

A specialization agreement is an agreement between undertakings relating to the conditions under which they specialize in the production of goods and/or supply of services.

This Regulation, exempting certain specialization agreements from Article 81(1), will apply to unilateral specialization agreements between competitors, and all other agreements between undertakings relating to the conditions under which they specialize in the production of goods and/or services.

Specialization agreements covered by this Regulation fall into three categories: (a) a unilateral specialization agreement, where one undertaking agrees to cease production of certain products or to refrain from producing those products and to purchase them from a competing undertaking, and the competing undertaking agrees to produce and supply those products; (b) reciprocal specialization agreements, by which two or more parties on a reciprocal basis agree to cease or refrain from producing certain but different products and to purchase these products from other parties, who agree to supply them, and (c) joint production agreements, by virtue of which two or more parties agree to produce certain products jointly. This last class would arise in the case of joint ventures.

The exemption from Article 81(1) would also be available to provisions contained in specialization agreements, which do not constitute the primary object of such agreements, but are directly related to and necessary for their implementation, such as those concerning the assignment or use of intellectual property rights. The obvious reason for permitting conditions relating to the rights in the related intellectual property of any of the parties is that the transaction intended under the specialization agreement should not give any opportunity to the other party to infringe that right. However, as the legislative intent is that the owner of such right is only entitled to protect that right from infringement and no more, the following terms enumerated in Article 5(1) may not be included, as their object is the restriction of competition:

The exemption provided for in Article 1 shall not apply to agreements which, directly or indirectly, in isolation or in combination with other factors under the control of the parties, have as their object: (a) the fixing of prices when selling the products to third parties; (b) the limitation of output or sales; or (c) the allocation of markets or customers.

However, parties may, in their agreements provide for:

(*a*) an agreed amount of products in the context of unilateral or reciprocal specialization agreements, or the capacity and production volume of a production joint venture in the context of a joint production agreement; (*b*) the setting of sales targets and the fixing of prices that a production joint venture charges to its immediate customers in the case of joint distribution or the appointment of a non-competing third party distributor, appointed on an exclusive or non-exclusive basis.

These do not adversely affect competition.

The exemption would also be available to agreements under which the parties accept an exclusive purchase and/or exclusive supply obligation (i) in the context of a unilateral or reciprocal specialization agreement or a joint production agreement, or (ii) when the parties do not sell the products which are the object of the specialization agreement independently but provide for joint distribution, or agree to appoint a third party distributor on an exclusive or non-exclusive basis in the context of a joint production agreement provided that the third party is not a competing undertaking.

The Regulation rests on the basis that specialization agreements 'generally contribute to improving the production or distribution of goods, because the undertakings concerned can concentrate on the manufacture of certain products and thus operate more efficiently and supply the products more cheaply'. The same would be the position regarding the provision of services leading to the consumers receiving a fair share of the resulting benefit. Article 4 provides that for the exemption to apply, the combined market share of the participating undertakings should not exceed 20 per cent of the relevant market. Paragraph 3 of the Recitals to this Regulation states: 'Below a certain level of market power it can, for the application of Article 81(3), in general be presumed that the positive effects of specialization agreements will outweigh any negative effects on competition.' This qualification and the non-exemption of certain classes of agreements, set out in Article 5 of the Regulation, and the conditions of the Regulation are expected to 'ensure that the agreements to which the block exemption applies do not enable the participating undertakings to eliminate competition in respect of a substantial part of the products or services in question.'[57]

Dealing with Cartels—Penalty

The nature of the constitution and the operations of cartels are such that it would be very difficult for any investigating agency to be able to furnish the standard of proof possible in other types of cases of criminal activity. It should be understood that a cartel is a close and secretive group. Participating in a cartel, within the meaning of section 3(3), is an offence. The present proviso to section 27(b), after the 2007 amendment, provides the punishment for breach of section 3 by a cartel thus: Provided that in case any agreement referred to in section 3 has been entered into by a cartel, the Commission may impose upon each producer, seller, distributor, trader, or service provider included in that cartel, a penalty of up to three times its profit for each year of the continuance of such agreement or 10 per cent of its turnover for each year of the continuance of such agreement, whichever is higher.

Section 46 empowers the Commission to impose a lesser penalty, not total immunity, as under EC law discussed below, where an alleged violator belonging to a cartel makes full and true disclosures of the alleged violation, as required under section 46. Section 48 renders the company, the persons in charge of the conduct of the company and the directors privy to the violations of the Act, liable for punishment. Section 188 of the Enterprise Act 2002, UK, also prescribes that a cartel offence is committed by one who dishonestly agrees with one or more other persons to make or implement price-fixing and other agreements specified therein. Section 191 of this Act provides for the extradition of a person charged with the offence under section 188, a conspiracy or an attempt to commit that offence.

Immunity under the EC Law—Cartels

It is well known that one of the principal reasons for the effective enforcement of legislation prohibiting anti-competitive activities within the European Community is the stern approach of the European Commission as reflected in the very heavy fines it imposes on violators, whether they are individuals or overseas corporations operating within the Community. In calculating fines in cartel cases, the Commission takes account of the gravity of the infringement, its duration and any aggravating or mitigating circumstances. It also takes account of the market share held by the companies and their overall size, so as to ensure that the fine reflects each company's participation in the infringement and its capacity to harm other operators, particularly consumers, and so as to ensure that the fine acts as a deterrent.

But considering the nature of cartel activity the Commission has been adopting a policy of granting immunity to whistle-blower members of a cartel. Superceding its 1996 Notice relating to leniency in the matter of members of a cartel, the Commission issued a new notice, 'Notice on immunity from fines and reduction of fines in cartel cases' (2002/C 45/03), which came into force on 14 February 2002. Replacing this

Notice, the Commission has issued Commission Notice on Immunity from fines and reduction of fines in cartel cases (Text with EEA relevance) of 8 December 2006.

Immunity from Fine

The 2006 Notice sets out the framework for 'rewarding cooperation' in the Commission investigation by undertakings which are or have been party to secret cartels affecting the Community. It is considered to be in the Community interest to reward any member of a cartel who is prepared to cooperate with the Commission's investigation, regardless of the attitudes of the other members of the cartel. The immunity from any fine which would otherwise have been imposed will be granted when a member of a cartel seeking immunity is the first to submit information and evidence and which, in the Commission's view, will enable it to carry out a targeted inspection in connection with the alleged cartel or find an infringement of Article 81 EC (anti-competitive practices) in connection with the alleged cartel.

The information and evidence to be submitted by the applicant undertaking are: (a) a corporate statement containing the following information: a statement which includes, in so far as it is known to the applicant at the time of the submission, a detailed description of the alleged cartel arrangement, including, for instance, its aims, activities and functioning; the product or service concerned; the geographic scope; the duration of and the estimated market volumes affected by the alleged cartel; the specific dates, locations, content of and participants in alleged cartel contacts; and all relevant explanations in connection with the pieces of evidence provided in support of the application; the name and address of the legal entity submitting the immunity application as well as the names and addresses of all the other undertakings that participate(d) in the alleged cartel; the names, positions, office locations, and, where necessary, home addresses of all individuals who, to the applicant's knowledge, are or have been involved in the alleged cartel, including those individuals who have been involved on the applicant's behalf; information on which other competition authorities, inside or outside the EU, have been approached or are intended to be approached in relation to the alleged cartel; (b) other evidence relating to the alleged cartel in possession of the applicant or available to it at the time of the submission, including in particular any evidence contemporaneous to the infringement.

Immunity will not be granted if, at the time of the submission, the Commission had already sufficient evidence to adopt a decision to carry out an inspection in connection with the alleged cartel or had already carried out such an inspection.

Immunity will only be granted on the cumulative conditions that the Commission did not have, at the time of the submission, sufficient evidence to find an infringement of Article 81 EC in connection with the alleged cartel and that no undertaking had been granted conditional immunity from fines in connection with the alleged cartel. In addition, an undertaking must be the first to provide contemporaneous, incriminating evidence of the alleged cartel. The further requirements are that the undertaking should continuously cooperate with the Commission, it should have ended its involvement in the alleged cartel immediately following its application, except for what would, in the Commission's view, be reasonably necessary to preserve the integrity of the inspections.

An undertaking which took steps to coerce other undertakings to join the cartel or to remain in it is not eligible for immunity from fines, but however, it may still qualify for a reduction of fines if it fulfils the requisite requirements.

Reduction of Fine[58]

Undertakings disclosing their participation in an alleged cartel affecting the Community that do not meet the conditions for applying for immunity may be eligible to benefit from a reduction of any fine that would otherwise have been imposed. In order to qualify for seeking a reduction of fine, an undertaking must provide the Commission with evidence of the alleged infringement which represents significant added value with respect to the evidence already in the Commission's possession and must meet the prescribed conditions. The concept of 'added value' refers to the extent to which the evidence provided strengthens, by its very nature and/or its level of detail, the Commission's ability to prove the alleged cartel.

UK—Cartels, Leniency Programme

To encourage members of cartels to provide evidence of the cartel in which they are involved, the OFT's leniency programme offers, on conditions stipulated, total or partial immunity from fines to companies who come forward with such information.

Dealing with Cartels—the Purchasers

Some very practical suggestions are offered by the OFT, UK, through its booklet *Cartels—Detection and Remedies, a Guide for Purchasers*, on the means available to purchasers to protect themselves against a cartel, when they sense the operation of one. The main steps recommended to reduce the power of cartels are: encourage the largest possible number of bidders, for example, by minimizing bidder restrictions and qualifications, or by breaking the project into several smaller parts; if possible, obtain a disinterested cost estimate or prepare one in-house. This is desirable since the essential aim of bid-rigging is to secure a higher price than the competitive price; require bids to be broken down in as much detail as possible; a declaration of non-collusion should be included within contract documents and made a fundamental term of the contract. The declaration should cover collusion with associated or affiliated companies or subsidiaries, as well as unrelated competitors. As part of the tender return a list of all affiliates and subsidiaries should be required. It may also be required that main contractors should insist on sub-contractors operating a competitive tendering process and stipulate the intention of employing organization to inspect that process on demand.

SECTION 3(4)

Vertical Restraints

Another way in which competition in the supply of a product or a service may be reduced is through practices that control or remove the freedom of one of the parties in concluding an agreement in the way in which it would be enough to meet its actual needs that the transaction is intended to procure. Inevitably, the imposing of this unwanted burden will be by the economically stronger of the parties. Where the parties are in different stages or levels of the production chain, this practice is called a vertical restraint. Under section 3(4),[59] it would be anti-competitive only if the agreement providing for this practice causes or is likely to cause an appreciable adverse effect on competition in India. In other words, the restraint is to be evaluated under the rule of reason. The following are the vertical restraints specifically stated as to be considered anti-competitive if they fall under the prescription of the sub-section: (*a*) tie-in arrangement; (*b*) exclusive supply agreement; (*c*) exclusive distribution agreement; (*d*) refusal to deal; (*e*) resale price maintenance.

Anti-competitive Agreements 121

There could be other types of agreements falling under section 3(4) as those stated in the sub-section are not exhaustive.

The explanation to this sub-section gives an 'inclusive' definition of each of the vertical restraints, which means that there could be vertical restraints other than those stated in the sub-section.

A tie-in arrangement would arise only where the intending purchaser of a product or service is required by the supplier to purchase some other product or service, as *a condition of that purchase,* that is, there would be no supply of the first product or service if the buyer did not buy the second product or service also, offered by the supplier. Obviously, if the buyer is only persuaded of the advantage of buying the second product or service, tying does not take place.

An exclusive supply agreement includes one that restricts the purchaser from acquiring any goods or service from anyone other than the seller or any other person who may be nominated.

An exclusive distribution agreement includes an agreement that stipulates limiting, restricting or withholding output or supply of any goods, or allocating any area or market for the sale of any goods.

Such exclusive arrangements limit the sources of supply and, therefore, limit competition.

An agreement providing for refusal to deal includes any agreement that restricts by any method, the persons or classes of persons to whom goods may be sold or from whom the goods may be bought. Such agreements also limit the number of suppliers and are anti-competitive.

'Resale price maintenance', as is self-explanatory, means the imposition of a condition by a seller fixing the price at which his purchaser may resell the goods. But there would be no resale price maintenance, if having thus indicated the price at which the goods may be resold, the seller also indicates to his buyer that that buyer may sell at prices lower than the price indicated. Resale price maintenance is a negation of the right of the buyer to resell the goods at a price he considers appropriate, considering the market conditions, as on sale, the seller has transferred the property in the goods sold to the buyer. The Act prohibits it because it is a clog on the free play of market forces which alone shall determine the prices at which goods are sold.

Tie-in

A product or a service is to be treated as being the subject of a tie-in arrangement when its supply is offered on the condition that the buyer who ordered for some product or service, the basic product, must also purchase some other product or service. The product or service that is required by the buyer is called the tying product or service and the one that is forced on the buyer is called the tied product or service. The basic objection that would arise from the point of view of the buyer is that he is required, by business compulsion, to buy a product or service that he does not need and so is forced to incur unnecessary costs. But under the law protecting the competitive process this is objectionable on the ground that it reduces competition in the supply of the tied product.

International Salt Co. v. US[60]

The US Government brought a civil action to enjoin the International Salt Company from carrying out provisions of the leases of its patented machines to the effect that lessees would use therein only International's salt products. The restriction was alleged to violate section 1 of the Sherman Act, and sections 1 and 3 of the Clayton Act. International Salt was the country's largest producer of salt for industrial uses. International Salt also owned patents on two machines for the utilization of salt products. One, the 'Lixator,' was for dissolving rock salt into brine used in various industrial processes. The other, the 'Saltomat,' was usable for injecting salt, in tablet form, into canned products during the canning process. The principal distribution of each of these machines was under leases that, among other things, required the lessees to purchase from International Salt all unpatented salt and salt tablets consumed in the leased machines.

The US Supreme Court confirmed the decree of the lower court which held that the term in the lease deeds providing for discrimination was illegal. On the condition of tying in of the unpatented salt and salt tablets with the lease of the patented equipment, the Court observed:

The appellant's patents confer a limited monopoly of the invention they reward. From them appellant derives a right to restrain others from making, vending or using the patented machines. But the patents confer no right to restrain use of, or trade in, unpatented salt. By contracting to close this market for salt against competition, International has engaged in a restraint of trade for which its patents afford no immunity from the antitrust laws.

International Salt contended that its obligation to maintain and repair the equipment under lease caused it necessary to stipulate that the lessees were required to use to its own salt because 'its high quality assured satisfactory functioning and low maintenance cost.' The Court stated that while a lessor may impose on a lessee reasonable restrictions designed in good faith to minimize maintenance burdens and to assure satisfactory operation, there was no material to show that the machine was allergic to salt of equal quality produced by anyone except International. The effect of the tying clause was that other manufacturers who could produce salt equal to reasonable specifications for machine use were 'shut out of the market by a provision that limits it, not in terms of quality, but in terms of a particular vendor.' The Court ruled: 'Rules for use of leased machinery must not be disguised restraints of free competition, though they may set reasonable standards which all suppliers must meet.'

Tying-in—necessary market power
Jefferson Parish Hospital Dist. No. 2 v. Hyde[61]
In this case, the Jefferson Parish hospital had a contract with a firm of anesthesiologists, Roux & Associates, providing, for the firm to offer, anesthesiological services to the hospital on an exclusive basis. The relevant term was that the hospital shall restrict the use of its anesthesia department to Roux & Associates and that no other persons, parties or entities shall perform such services within the hospital for the term of the contract.

Due to this condition, the respondent's application for admission to the hospital's medical staff was rejected. He moved the action charging that the exclusive contract violated section 1 of the Sherman Act.

The Court of Appeals found the tying arrangement as a contract illegal per se. In the view of the Court of Appeals: (*i*) the tying arrangement consisted of users of the hospital's operating rooms (the tying product); (*ii*) the hospital's chosen anaesthesiological services (the tied product); (*iii*) the hospital possessed sufficient market power in the tying market to coerce purchasers of the tied product; (*iv*) since the purchase of the tied product constituted a 'not insubstantial amount of interstate commerce,' the tying arrangement was therefore illegal 'per se.'

The Supreme Court reversed this judgement on the grounds that the hospital did not have the requisite market power in relation to the tying product and no restraint on competition was established.

Reiterating the position of the nature of an invalid tying arrangement the Supreme Court stated:

...the essential characteristic of an invalid tying arrangement lies in the seller's exploitation of its control over the tying product to force the buyer into the purchase of a tied product that the buyer either did not want at all, or might have preferred to purchase elsewhere on different terms. When such 'forcing' is present, competition on the merits in the market for the tied item is restrained and the Sherman Act is violated.

The Supreme Court explained that a tying arrangement could be considered to be illegal per se only when it is shown that the seller has sufficient market power in relation to the tying product. The facts showed that the hospital did not have that requisite market power. Since there was also nothing in the record before it to show that the hospital forced such services on unwilling patients, the Court held that there was no basis for applying the per se rule against the arrangement.

Then, the arrangement had to be evaluated only by the rule of reason, viz. that it had unreasonably restrained competition. The Supreme Court held that there was no evidence of any restraint on competition. In fact, the Court noted that there was no evidence that the price, the quality, or the supply or demand for either the 'tying product' or the 'tied product' involved in this case had been adversely affected by the exclusive contract between Roux and the hospital, and that it was not shown that the market as a whole has been affected at all by the contract.

It should be noted that the first pre-requisite for consideration of the issue of tying is the existence of two separate markets for the tying and the tied product. Then, the effect on competition in the market for the tied product should be evaluated. Where the supplier has sufficient market power relating to the tying product, tying would be treated as per se illegal. Otherwise, it would be a matter to be determined under the rule of reason.

In *Eastman Kodak Co.* v. *ImageTech. Svcs*[62] the US Supreme Court, quoting its earlier decisions, again explained when appreciable economic power in the tying market may be considered to exist. The principles held to have been established were: market power is the power 'to force a purchaser to do something that he would not do in a competitive market.' It also held that the existence of such power ordinarily is inferred from the seller's possession of a predominant share of the market.

The Eastman Kodak Company manufactured and sold photocopiers and micrographic equipment. It also sold service and replacement parts for its equipment. The respondents, about 18 independent service organizations (ISOs), also serviced Kodak copying and micrographic equipment. Kodak subsequently adopted policies to limit the availability of parts to ISOs and made it more difficult for the ISOs to compete with Kodak in servicing Kodak equipment. That policy was limiting the selling of replacement parts for micrographic and copying machines only to buyers of Kodak equipment who used Kodak service or repaired their own machines.

The respondents brought the action under the Sherman Act.

On the question of tying, the US Supreme Court stated that it should be shown first, that service and parts were two distinct products, and, second, that Kodak had tied the sale of the two products. The Court found that there was sufficient evidence of a tie between service (the tied product) and parts, and that the record indicated that Kodak would sell parts to third parties only if they agreed not to buy the service from the ISOs.

The Court considered that the evidence showed that Kodak had the market power to raise prices and drive out competition in the aftermarket.

Exclusive Supply Agreements

Standard Oil Co. of California v. *United States*[63] was a case where Standard Oil, like its competitors, had entered into agreements with its retailers that they would buy all their requirements of gasoline and petroleum products only from Standard. The US Supreme Court held that this requirement under the agreement violated section 3 of the Clayton Act, as it restricted access for its retailers of other channels of procuring petrol and petroleum products and that therefore, competition had been foreclosed in a substantial share of the line of commerce.

Tampa Electric Co. v. *Nashville Co.*[64] Tampa Electric entered into a 20-year agreement with respondents for the supply of coal, as a boiler fuel for its electrical generating plants at Gannon. The material part of the agreement was as follows: 'total requirements of fuel ... for the operation of its first two units to be installed at the Gannon Station ... not less than 225,000 tons of coal per unit per year.'

The agreement provided that Tampa would also be entitled to give notice of further requirements of coal for additional units using coal it may build during the first 10 years of the term of the agreement. Two years after the agreement, after having spent approximately $7,500,000 towards performance of the contract for the supply of coal, the respondents advised Tampa that the contract was illegal under the antitrust laws, would therefore not be performed, and no coal would be delivered. Whereupon Tampa placed its order on another coal company.

The Supreme Court disagreed with the determination, by the lower courts, for the purpose of section 3 of the Clayton Act, of a smaller area, as the relevant competitive market while, on facts, the relevant competitive market area was much larger. Determination of the relevant competitive market was the prime factor in deciding whether the contract foreclosed competition in a substantial share of the line of commerce involved. The Court found that the proportionate volume of the total relevant coal product as to which the challenged contract pre-empted competition, less than 1 per cent was, conservatively speaking, quite insubstantial. It decided that there was no substantial foreclosing of competition in the relevant coal market.

The Court set out that in considering the effect of such an agreement on competition, the factors to be examined were the line of commerce, viz. the product, the area of effective competition, that is, the market affected, and whether a substantial share of the relevant market was affected by the agreement.

Its elucidation of 'substantiality' is instructive:

To determine substantiality in a given case, it is necessary to weigh the probable effect of the contract on the relevant area of effective competition, taking into account the relative strength of the parties, the proportionate volume of commerce involved in relation to the total volume of commerce in the relevant market area, and the probable immediate and future effects which pre-emption of that share of the market might have on effective competition therein.

Section 3 of the Clayton Act prohibits any provision in an agreement restraining a buyer from the use of or dealing in goods offered by any competitor. In this case there was no express clause in the agreement for the supply of coal prohibiting Tampa from acquiring coal from any competitor of the respondents. But since the agreement was for the supply of 'total requirements' for a period of 20 years, the lower courts came to the conclusion that 'the "total requirements" provision had the same practical effect, for it prevented Tampa Electric for a period of 20 years from buying coal from any other source for use at that station.' The US Supreme Court, for the purposes of this case, assumed, but did not decide, since the main question was not decided by the lower court and the case was remanded, that the contract was an exclusive-dealing arrangement within the compass of section 3 of the Clayton Act, and that the line of commerce was bituminous coal.

Exclusive Distribution Agreements

Timken Co. v. *United States* discussed earlier in this chapter is one case of allocation of a market for the sale of goods.

Refusal to deal

Business Electronics v. *Sharp Electronics* referred to earlier in this chapter was to the effect that the termination of an agreement with a price-cutting dealer on the representation of another dealer cannot be said, in the absence of some agreement between the remaining dealer and the manufacturer on prices to be maintained after the termination of the appointment of the dealer, to be per se illegal. The anti-competitive effects of such an action will have to be shown. The Court also explained the meaning of the term 'restraint of trade' as follows: 'The term "restraint of trade" in the statute, like the term at common law, refers not to a particular list of agreements, but to a particular economic consequence, which may be produced by quite different sorts of agreements in varying times and circumstances. The changing content of the term "restraint of trade" was well recognized at the time the Sherman Act was enacted.' The Court decided: 'In sum, economic analysis supports the view, and no precedent opposes it, that a vertical restraint is not illegal per se unless it includes some agreement on price or price levels.'

Where no issue of the effect on competition is involved, as for example, the dealer does not make due payments to the supplier regularly, the supplier may refuse to deal with that dealer on that ground.

Agreement Restricting Buying from Certain Classes of Sellers

United States v. *General Motors*[65]

General Motors found that some of its franchised dealers were selling new Chevrolets through 'discount houses' and 'referral services' at bargain prices. At the instance of non-participating dealers who lost sales, General Motors and three associations of Chevrolet dealers in and around Los Angeles, took steps, in concert, for the purpose of eliminating the sales of new Chevrolets through their 'discount houses' and 'referral services', by procuring, from all its franchised dealers, agreements not to deal with discounters. Also, a number of Chevrolet dealers were induced to repurchase cars they had sold through discounters.

General Motors relied upon the 'location clause' in the dealer selling agreement that prohibited a franchised dealer from moving to or establishing 'a new or different location, branch sales office, branch service station, or place of business ... without the prior written approval of Chevrolet.'

The action of General Motors and the dealers' associations was held to be a per se violation of the Sherman Act. The US Supreme Court ruled: 'There can be no doubt that the effect of the combination or conspiracy here was to restrain trade and commerce within the meaning of the Sherman Act. Elimination, by joint collaborative action, of discounters from access to the market is a per se violation of the Act.'

On the obtaining of the promises from the franchised dealers not to deal with the discounters the Supreme Court observed:

What resulted was a fabric interwoven by many strands of joint action to eliminate the discounters from participation in the market, to inhibit the free choice of franchised dealers to select their own methods of trade and to provide multilateral surveillance and enforcement.

Resale Price Maintenance

Between independent sources of supply, the seller and the reseller, there can be no restriction on the price at which the goods may be resold.

Dr Miles Medical Co. v. *John D. Park & Sons Co.* discussed earlier in this chapter in relation to fixing minimum prices at which the products could be sold is one example of resale price maintenance.

State Oil Co. v. *Khan No. 96–871*

The respondents in this case entered into an agreement with the State Oil Co. to lease and operate a gas station and convenience store owned by State Oil. Under the agreement, the respondents could charge any amount for gasoline sold to the station's customers, but if the price charged was higher than State Oil's suggested retail price, the excess was to be rebated to State Oil. The respondents could sell gasoline for less than State Oil's suggested retail price, but any such decrease would reduce their 3.25 cents-per-gallon margin. The respondents complained that the agreement restricted their freedom to charge appropriate prices.

The US Supreme Court held, overruling *Albrecht*,[66] that vertical maximum price fixing, like the majority of commercial arrangements subject to the antitrust laws, should be evaluated under the rule of reason. It stated: 'In our view, rule of reason analysis will effectively identify those situations in which vertical maximum price fixing amounts to anti-competitive conduct.'

The Treatment of Vertical Restraints

Under Section 3(4) of the Act, as noted, vertical restraints are to be evaluated under the rule of reason. The anti-competitive nature of the restraint is to be established.

Pro-competitive Benefits of Vertical Restraints

Sometimes, a vertical restraint, depending upon the structure of the market for a product, may be shown to be pro-competitive without any harm to the competitive process. The restraints may be necessary in some situations to ensure that the sales support to the retailers extended by the manufacturers may not be exploited by the free riders.

Commission Regulation (EC) No. 2790/1999 of 22 December 1999 on the Application of Article 81(3) of the Treaty to Categories of Vertical Agreements and Concerted Practices

The European Commission has granted a block exemption to certain vertical restraints, called 'vertical agreements', specified in this Regulation., subject to the conditions set out therein. Vertical agreements are agreements between undertakings at a different level of the production or distribution chain, and relating to the conditions under which the parties may purchase, sell or resell certain goods or services. The exemption will apply only if the agreement is one that falls within the scope of Article 81(1).

The premise on which this Regulation is based is stated in recital (6): 'Vertical agreements of the category defined in this Regulation can improve economic efficiency within a chain of production or distribution by facilitating better coordination between the participating undertakings; in particular, they can lead to a reduction in the transaction and distribution costs of the parties and to an optimization of their sales and investment levels.' It is further presumed that where the share of the supplier of the relevant market does not exceed 30 per cent, vertical agreements which do not contain certain types of severely anti-competitive restraints generally lead to an improvement in production or distribution and allow consumers a fair share of the resulting benefits. There will be no exemption for vertical agreements containing restrictions which are not indispensable to the attainment of the positive effects mentioned above and in particular, to vertical agreements containing certain types of severely anti-competitive restraints, such as minimum and fixed resale prices, as well as certain types of territorial protection.

In view of the overall positive experience with the application of that Regulation, which expired on 31 May 2010, and taking into account further experience acquired since its adoption, the Commission adopted a new block exemption regulation: Commission Regulation (EU) No. 330/2010 of 20 April 2010, entering into force on 1 June 2010.[67]

The benefit of the block exemption established by this Regulation should be limited to vertical agreements, containing vertical restraints, for which it can be assumed with sufficient certainty that they satisfy the conditions of Article 101(3) of the Treaty, which permits exemption to any agreement or category of agreements between undertakings, any decision or category of decisions by associations of undertakings, any concerted practice or category of concerted practices, which contributes to improving the production or distribution of goods or to promoting technical or economic progress, while allowing consumers a fair share of the resulting benefit, and which does not: (a) impose on the undertakings concerned restrictions which are not indispensable to the attainment of these objectives; (b) afford such undertakings the possibility of eliminating competition in respect of a substantial part of the products in question.

The exemption provided for in the Regulation shall apply to vertical agreements entered into between an association of undertakings and its members, or between such an association and its suppliers, only if all its members are retailers of goods and if no individual member of the association, together with its connected undertakings, has a total annual turnover exceeding € 50 million. Vertical agreements entered into by such associations shall be covered by this Regulation without prejudice to the application of Article 101 of the Treaty to horizontal agreements concluded between the members of the association or decisions adopted by the association. Also, the exemption provided by this Regulation shall be available only on condition that the market share held by the supplier does not exceed 30 per cent of the relevant market on which it sells the contract goods or services and the market share held by the buyer does not exceed 30 per cent of the relevant market on which it purchases the contract goods or services. However, vertical agreements containing certain types of severe restrictions of competition such as minimum and fixed resale prices, as well as certain types of territorial protection are excluded from the benefit of the block exemption irrespective of the market share of the undertakings concerned.

To prevent collusion on the relevant market, the exemption of non-compete obligations are limited to obligations which do not exceed a defined duration. For the same reasons, any direct or indirect obligation causing the members of a selective distribution system not to sell the brands of particular competing suppliers are also to be excluded from the benefit of this Regulation.

The Regulation is based on the premise that the market-share limitation, the non-exemption of certain vertical agreements and the conditions provided for in this Regulation may be expected to ensure that the agreements to which the block exemption applies do not enable the participating undertakings to eliminate competition in respect of a substantial part of the products in question.

In respect of the motor vehicle industry, the European Commission has issued a similar regulation, viz. Commission Regulation (EC) No. 1400/2002 of 31 July 2002, on the application of Article 81(3) of the Treaty to categories of vertical agreements and concerted practices in the motor vehicle sector.[68]

In course of time, based on experience in the working of the Act, specific exemptions such as these are to be considered. The central government's power to exempt under section 54 cannot be used for this purpose.

SECTION 3(5)—EXERCISE OF INTELLECTUAL PROPERTY RIGHTS AND COMPETITION

In the apparent exercise of intellectual property rights, the owners of these rights, frequently patentees and copyright holders, impose conditions on their licensees that go beyond the limits of the rights conferred on them by law and which conditions may reduce competition or actually eliminate competition in the relevant market.

Usually, patentees resort to resale price maintenance, in addition to imposing other restrictions on their licensees. *International Salt* has been referred to earlier, in connection with tying. Competitors may also cross-licence their patents and allocate territories among themselves and create entry barriers. The law is that a patentee may impose only such conditions on his licensees or buyers that are an exercise of his rights granted under a patent issued to him and beyond that, the patentee, or for that matter, the owner of any other intellectual property right, cannot, in the purported exercise of those rights, directly or indirectly interfere with the competitive process.

What is the position when the owner of an intellectual property right imposes a condition in an agreement for sale of goods or a licence of that right that would have anti-competitive effects? Clearly, there ought to be a balancing of the interests of such persons exercising certain exclusive rights conferred on them and the need to preserve the process of competition free from adverse influences. Section 3(5) limits the right of the holder of any of the rights under the enactments listed therein to only taking steps to restrain any infringement of any of those rights or to impose reasonable conditions as may be necessary for protecting such rights. The enactments are: (*a*) the Copyright Act, 1957; (*b*) the Patents Act, 1970; (*c*) the Trade Marks Act, 1999; (*d*) the Geographical Indications of Goods (Registration and Protection) Act, 1999; (*e*) the Designs Act, 2000; and (*f*) the Semi-conductor Integrated Circuits Layout-Design Act, 2000.

Section 3 will not also restrict the right of any person to export goods from India to the extent to which the agreement relates exclusively to the production, supply, distribution or control of goods or provision of services for such export.

Before considering the adequacy of section 3(5) as a tool to prevent anti-competitive practices of owners of intellectual property rights, we may study some cases where the exercise of rights in patents concerned issues relating to restraint on competition in the relevant market.

Patents

Condition in License Agreement Fixing Prices

United States v. *General Electric Co.*[69]

General Electric held three patents to cover completely the making of modern electric lights with tungsten filaments. It licensed the Westinghouse Company to make, use, and sell lamps under the patents owned by the former. It was charged that the license in effect provided that the Westinghouse Company would follow prices and terms of sale from time to time fixed by General Electric and observed by it, and that Westinghouse would, with regard to lamps manufactured by it under the license, adopt and maintain the same conditions of sale as observed by General Electric in the distribution of lamps manufactured by it.

The question before the Supreme Court was: 'Had the Electric Company as the owner of the patents, entirely controlling the manufacture, use and sale of the tungsten incandescent lamps, in its license to the Westinghouse Company, the right to impose the condition that its sales should be at prices fixed by the licensor and subject to change according to its discretion?'

The Court upheld the condition in the licenses. It ruled that such a term would be valid 'provided the conditions of sale are normally and reasonably adapted to secure pecuniary reward for the patentee's monopoly. One of the valuable elements of the exclusive right of a patentee is to acquire profit by the price at which the article is sold. The higher the price, the greater the profit unless it is prohibitory. When the patentee licenses another to make and vend and retains the right to continue to make and vend on his own account, the price at which his licensee will sell will necessarily affect the price at which he can sell his own patented goods.' But this decision has been distinguished by lower courts in different contexts, as for example, where the patentee does not manufacture the product, but only licenses another to work the patent.

Fixing Prices for Product Processed by a Licensee
United States v. *Univis Lens Co.*[70]
Univis Lens Co. was the owner of a number of patents and two trademarks relating to multifocal lenses. It incorporated Univis Corporation, acquired the majority stock in the corporation and transferred its interest in the patents and trademarks to the Corporation. The patents were for lens blanks. The legality of the condition imposed by the patentee, for lens blanks, fixing the sale price to be charged by the licensee on making the finished lenses, processed under the license, in accordance with its specifications, was the issue in the case.

The Lens Company was licensed to manufacture lens blanks, according to the specifications of one of the patents of the Corporation, and to sell them to designated licensees of the Corporation, and pay to the Corporation an agreed royalty.

There were three other classes of licensees-wholesalers, finishing retailers and prescription retailers.

The wholesalers were authorized by the terms of their licenses to purchase the blanks from the Lens Company, to finish them by grinding and polishing, and to sell them to prescription licensees only at prices fixed by the Corporation.

Under their licenses, the finishing retailers could purchase the blanks from the Lens Company, grind and polish them and adjust the lenses, in frames or supports, to the eyes of the consumers. They were also bound to sell the finished lenses to the customers at prices prescribed by the Corporation.

The prescription retailer was granted a 'franchise to prescribe and fit Univis lenses'. He did not do any processing on the glasses. The license required that he sell finished lenses only to consumers and only at prices prescribed by the Corporation.

The contention of the government, before the US Supreme Court was, that when the patents were only for the structure of the lens blanks, there could be no stipulation by the Corporation of the sale prices of finished lenses which the wholesalers and finishing retailers processed from the blanks. The district court had held that there could be no restriction on the price at which a prescription retailer may sell the lenses.

The Supreme Court ruled that a patentee could not, after the sale of the patented article, control the price at which it may be sold and that the price-fixing term, with the three classes of licensees was a violation of the Sherman Act.

It stated:

Whether the licensee sells the patented article in its completed form or sells it before completion for the purpose of enabling the buyer to finish and sell it, he has equally parted with the article, and made it the vehicle for transferring to the buyer ownership of the invention with respect to that article.

Cross-licensing of Patents Among Competitors

Hartford-Empire Co. v. *United States*[71] was a case where competitors cross-licensed amongst themselves their patents relating to the manufacture of glass-making machinery, and as a result of the monopoly acquired through these patents, others were excluded from a fair opportunity to freely engage in commerce in such machinery and in the manufacture and distribution of glass products. All the patents had, by cross-licensing agreements, merged into a pool that effectually controlled the industry. Ninety-four per cent of the glass containers manufactured in the country on feeders and formers were made on machinery licensed under the pooled patents. The Supreme Court confirmed that the corporate defendants had violated the Sherman Act.[72]

Pooling of Patents and Price-fixing

United States v. *New Wrinkle, Inc.*[73]
In this case, the US government filed a civil suit charging the defendants with successfully conspiring to fix uniform minimum prices and to eliminate competition in the wrinkle finish industry in the country by means of patent license agreements, in violation of section 1 of the

Sherman Act. On its dismissal by the District Court an appeal was made to the Supreme Court.

One of the defendants and another company, each claiming superiority of the patents held by it for manufacture of wrinkle finish enamels, varnishes and paints, entered into an agreement for forming a new company called New Wrinkle Inc., to which they assigned their patents, accepting shares in that new company in exchange for the assignments of their patents. Under the arrangement, New Wrinkle licensed patents to manufacturers of the products covered by the patents, fixing the minimum prices at which the licensees might sell. The license agreements empowered New Wrinkle to change the prices and other terms with due notice as provided in those agreements. New Wrinkle advised the licensees of the terms and conditions of sale and the 'agreed-upon prices' of the products covered by the licensed patents, which the licensees were assured was necessary 'in order to establish minimum prices throughout the industry.'

New Wrinkle did not manufacture the products covered by the patents, but was only a licensor of rights under patents. Its defence was that engaging exclusively in the activity of licensing of patents was not commerce and that therefore, section 1 of the Sherman Act did not apply to it, and that licensing of a patent was a matter governed by patent laws.

Rejecting this contention, the Supreme Court accepted the US government's charge that price control under the patent licenses was an essential part of the restraint of interstate trade in enamels, varnishes and paints, even though the isolated act of contracting for the licenses was wholly within a single state.

The Supreme Court, reversing the decision of the district court, ruled: 'An arrangement was made between patent holders to pool their patents and fix prices on the products for themselves and their licensees. The purpose and result plainly violate the Sherman Act.'

Fixing Prices—*del credere* agent

United States v. *Masonite Corporation*[74]

Masonite Corporation appointed its competitors as *del credere* agents and fixed the prices at which they could sell the products, for which it claimed patent protection. The agent was given only a license to sell. The agreement for price-fixing was charged as being in violation of the Sherman Act.

Masonite claimed, relying upon the General Electric case, that the arrangement would not fall under the Sherman Act, as it was only exercising its rights as a patentee. Rejecting that argument, the US Supreme Court said that once a product passed into the hands of a purchaser, it was outside patent protection and that the form in which the parties chose the governing transaction was not relevant. It held that the patentee, in this case, had exhausted its limited privilege when it disposed of the product to the del credere agent.

Adequacy of Section 3(5)

We now return to section 3(5) and its adequacy in meeting the abuse of intellectual property rights in a manner restraining competition in the relevant market in India.

The effect of section 3(5) is that the entire section 3 dealing with prohibition of anti-competitive agreements will not apply where the owner of any of the intellectual property rights under the enactments set out in section 3(5)(a) to (f) does anything in the exercise of his right to restrain the infringement of any of those rights, or imposes reasonable conditions as may be necessary for the protection of any of those rights.

There are two points to be considered in examining this exception and which are material to the prohibition of anti-competitive agreements. One is that such an owner of an intellectual property right, be it a patent or copyright, etc., may stipulate only conditions that are towards imposing a restraint on the *infringement* of his right conferred by the relevant Act. He may also impose 'reasonable' conditions that are necessary for the *protection of such rights*. This is in confirmation of the exclusive rights conferred by the respective enactments on the owner of the intellectual property right concerned. The other point is that an enactment such as the Competition Act should *expressly* prescribe that except to the availability of the right to take steps necessary to protect the monopoly granted under those enactments, agreements, decisions or concerted practices of owners of intellectual property rights that cause, or are likely to cause an appreciable adverse effect on competition in India in the relevant market, are prohibited. Agreements that fix prices or allocate territories may be treated as per se illegal. Others may be examined under the rule of reason. The control of anti-competitive practices cannot be left to be determined under other separate Acts.

Obligation under TRIPS

In this context India's obligation to comply with the requirements of Article 40 of TRIPS may be noted. That Article states the recognition of member states that certain licensing practices or conditions relating to intellectual property rights that restrain competition may have adverse effects on trade and may impede the transfer and dissemination of technology. It states further that members are free to bring in legislation specifying what licensing practices or conditions may in particular cases constitute an abuse of intellectual property rights having an adverse effect on competition in the relevant market. By way of examples of such licensing practices, the Article cites exclusive grant-back conditions, conditions preventing challenges to validity, and coercive package licensing.

The amended section 140 of the Patents Act, 1970, complying with TRIPS, prohibits terms, in a contract for the sale or lease of a product, or in a license to manufacture a patented article or work a patented process, such as tying-in, exclusive dealing, exclusive grant back, coercive package licensing. There are other practices such as division of territory, cross licensing of patents that would reduce competition and price fixing.

Section 83 of that Act states the 'General Principles Applicable to the Working of Patented Inventions'. The opening part of the section runs as follows:

Without prejudice to the other provisions contained in this Act, in exercising the powers conferred by this Chapter, regard shall be had to the following general considerations, namely: (a)–(g). Clauses (f) and (g) of this section are relevant. Clause (f): 'that the patent right is not abused by the patentee or person deriving title or interest on patent from the patentee, and the patentee or a person deriving title or interest on patent from the patentee does not resort to practices which unreasonably restrain trade or adversely affect the international transfer of technology;' (g) 'the patents are granted to make the benefit of the patented invention available at reasonably affordable prices to the public.'

Surely, what is a reasonably affordable price is not a matter that may be left to be determined by the patentee or his licensee. But the more important point is that the Competition Act should be the mechanism to deal with all anti-competitive practices by owners of all intellectual property rights.

Evaluating Technology Transfer Agreements Under Competition Law

US

In the US, the Department of Justice and the FTC have issued the 'Antitrust Guidelines for the Licensing of Intellectual Property' 1995, which states their antitrust enforcement policy with respect to the licensing of intellectual property protected by patent, copyright, and trade secret law, and of know-how. The guidelines are intended to assist those seeking to know the approach these two agencies would adopt in evaluating a practice for its anti-competitive nature. Admittedly, the matter will have to be ultimately decided by the courts.

EU

The European Commission has established a new regulation, Commission Regulation (EC) No. 772/2004 of 27 April 2004, replacing, with effect from 1 May 2004, its earlier regulation, Commission Regulation (EC) 240/96 of 31 January 1996, which granted block exemption to certain classes of technology transfer agreements, subject to the conditions of that Regulation.

The object of the revision is stated to be to 'move away from the approach of listing exempted clauses and to place greater emphasis on defining the categories of agreements which are exempted up to a certain level of market power and on specifying the restrictions or clauses which are not to be contained in such agreements.' This Regulation has widened the scope of the block exemption, while providing for separate treatment of technology transfer agreements between competing undertakings and those that do not compete with each other.

The premises on which this new Regulation is based are stated in the recitals:

Technology transfer agreements concern the licensing of technology. Such agreements will usually improve economic efficiency and be pro-competitive as they can reduce duplication of research and development, strengthen the incentive for the initial research and development, spur incremental innovation, facilitate diffusion and generate product market competition.

The likelihood that such efficiency-enhancing and pro-competitive effects will outweigh any anti-competitive effects due to restrictions contained in technology transfer agreements depends on the degree of market power of the undertakings concerned and, therefore, on the extent to which those undertakings face competition from undertakings owning substitute technologies or undertakings producing substitute products.

The market-share thresholds, the non-exemption of technology transfer agreements containing severely anticompetitive restraints and the excluded restrictions provided for in this Regulation will normally ensure that the agreements to which the block exemption applies do not enable the participating undertakings to eliminate competition in respect of a substantial part of the products in question.

Some of the key provisions of the new regulation are as follows:

Article 1(b) defines a 'technology transfer agreement'.[75]

Article 2 provides the exemption from Article 81(1) to technology transfer agreements entered into between two undertakings permitting the production of contract products. 'Contract products' means products produced with the licensed technology. The exemption is granted pursuant to Article 81(3) of the treaty and is subject to the conditions stipulated in the regulation.

In the first place, the agreement should fall under Article 81(1). Then, the exemption should apply for as long as the intellectual property right in the licensed technology has not expired, lapsed or been declared invalid or, in the case of know-how, for as long as the know-how remains secret, except in the event where the know-how becomes publicly known as a result of action by the licensee, in which case the exemption shall apply for the duration of the agreement.

Article 3 prescribes the market share threshold levels to meet the eligibility requirements for the exemption. In the case of an agreement between competing undertakings, the combined market share of the parties should not exceed 20 per cent on the affected relevant technology and product market. Where they are not competing undertakings, the market share of each of the parties should not exceed 30 per cent on the affected relevant technology and product market. The market share of a party on the relevant technology market(s) is defined in terms of the presence of the licensed technology on the relevant product market(s). A licensor's market share on the relevant technology market shall be the combined market share on the relevant product market of the contract products produced by the licensor and its licensees.

Article 4 provides that the exemption will not be available where the technology transfer agreement contains certain hard core restrictions such as a restriction of a party's ability to determine its prices when selling products to third parties and, subject to certain exceptions, limitation of output or allocation of markets or customers. It applies both in the case of competing undertakings and those not competing with each other.

Article 5 states what restrictions are excluded from the benefit of the exemption. They are: an obligation requiring a licensee to grant, to the licensor or his nominee, an exclusive licence to use or to assign its own severable improvements to or its own new applications of the licensed technology; a condition providing that the licensee shall not challenge the validity of intellectual property rights held by the licensor in the common market. But the agreement may provide for termination of the technology transfer agreement in the event that the licensee challenges the validity of one or more of the licensed intellectual property rights. Where the parties to an agreement are not competing undertakings, the exemption shall not apply to any condition limiting the licensee's ability to exploit its own technology, or limiting the ability of any of the parties to the agreement to carry out research and development, unless such latter restriction is indispensable to prevent the disclosure of the licensed know-how to third parties.

Article 6 provides that the benefit of the exemption may be withdrawn if it is found that the exempted agreement has effects that are incompatible with the conditions laid down in Article 81(3) of the Treaty. Some other situations when it may be withdrawn are: when access of third parties' technologies to the market is restricted; access of potential licensees to the market is restricted; without any objectively valid reason, the parties do not exploit the licensed technology.

According to Article 7, where parallel networks of similar technology transfer agreements cover more than 50 per cent of a relevant market, this Regulation shall not apply to technology transfer agreements containing specific restraints relating to that market.

Need to Review Section 3(5)

Obviously, supplementary legislation may have to be considered in India to make specific provision for the regulation of anti-competitive practices in licensing technology. The place to provide for this is at section 3(5). Having recognized the right of the owners of intellectual property rights to protect their rights granted to them by law, the section should go on with a rider to the effect that however, in the exercise of those rights, they would be subject to the relevant provisions of the

Competition Act. As the section stands, anti-competitive practices in licensing technology would fall under section 3(1), as sub-sections (3) and (4) deal with specific groups.

ENFORCEMENT PROVISIONS

An agreement prohibited under section 3(1) is void.

Section 19(1) of the Act provides that the Commission may either on its own motion or on receipt of any information, accompanied by such fee as may be determined by regulations, from any person, consumer or their association or trade association, or a reference made to it by the central government or a state government or a statutory authority, inquire into any alleged contravention of the provisions contained in sub-section (1) of section 3 or sub-section (1) of section 4. The factors that the Commission ought to take into consideration under section 19(3) and (5) to (7) have already been referred to.

Orders that may be Passed by the Competition Commission

Section 27, a common provision covering anti-competitive agreements and abuse of dominance, sets out the orders that may be passed by the Commission after an inquiry into an anti-competitive agreement covered by section 3 and abuse of a dominant position as set out in section 4.

It may be noted that the orders that the Commission may pass under this section are common to cases of breach of section 3 and section 4. Section 27 was amended in 2007 and after the amendment, the section is as follows:

S 27. Where after inquiry the Commission finds that any agreement referred to in section 3 or action of an enterprise in a dominant position, is in contravention of section 3 or section 4, as the case may be, it may pass all or any of the following orders, namely:

(a) direct any enterprise or association of enterprises or person or association of persons, as the case may be, involved in such agreement, or abuse of dominant position, to discontinue and not to re-enter such agreement or discontinue such abuse of dominant position, as the case may be;

(b) impose such penalty, as it may deem fit which shall be not more than ten per cent of the average of the turnover for the last three preceding financial years, upon each of such person or enterprises which are parties to such agreements or abuse:

Provided that in case any agreement referred to in section 3 has been entered into by a cartel, the Commission may impose upon each producer, seller, distributor, trader or service provider included in that cartel, a penalty of up to three times of its profit for each year of the continuance of such agreement or ten per cent of its turnover for each year of the continuance of such agreement, whichever is higher.

(d) direct that the agreements shall stand modified to the extent and in the manner as may be specified in the order by the Commission;

(e) direct the enterprises concerned to abide by such other orders as the Commission may pass and comply with the directions, including payment of costs, if any;

(g) pass such other order or issue such directions as it may deem fit.

Provided that while passing orders under this section, if the Commission comes to a finding, that an enterprise in contravention to section 3 or section 4 of the Act is a member of a group as defined in clause (b) of the Explanation to section 5 of the Act, and other members of such a group are also responsible for, or have contributed to, such a contravention, then it may pass orders, under this section, against such members of the group.

It should be noted that the amendment omitted sub-section (c), which provided for ordering payment of compensation, and sub-section (f), providing for a recommendation by the Competition Commission to the Central Government for the division of an enterprise enjoying a dominant position.[76]

Interim Orders—Section 33

The section was amended in 2007 and as the Commission would only be a market regulator, with no adjudicatory functions, it was considered inappropriate to refer to 'temporary injunctions'. For the same reason, section 34, which empowered the Commission to award compensation for loss or damage, was omitted by the 2007 amendment.

Where it is pleaded that an act in contravention of any of the following sections, 3(1), 4(1), or 6, has been committed and continues to be committed or is about to be committed, the Commission is empowered under section 33 to restrain a party from carrying on an act in violation of the relevant section, till the conclusion of the enquiry or until further orders. The Commission is not bound to give notice to that party.

Compensation for Loss or Damage

Antitrust Injury

Brunswick Corp. v. *Pueblo Bowl-O-Mat,*[77] *Inc.* established that to succeed in a claim, under section 4 of the Clayton Act, for treble damages, for injury to one's business or property by reason of anything forbidden in the antitrust laws, it should be shown that the injury was an 'antitrust injury', viz. an injury 'by reason of anything forbidden in the antitrust laws.'

The facts were: The operators of certain bowling centres brought the action against acquisition of competing bowling centres by one which was one of the two largest bowling equipment manufacturers and the operator of the largest bowling centre. The acquisition of those centres was consequent on their default in payments for bowling equipment purchased by them from the acquirer, the petitioner before the US Supreme Court. While the charge was that the acquisitions might substantially lessen competition or tend to create a monopoly in violation of section 7 of the Clayton Act, the ground on which treble damages, for violation of section 7 of the Clayton Act, were claimed, under section 4, was loss of profits.

The argument of the respondents, who were complaining, was that if the petitioner, instead of acquiring the competing bowling centres, who were in default, had allowed them to close down, their own profits would have increased. It was alleged that the scope for such increased profits was removed by the continuance of competition from the acquired bowling centres.

The US Supreme Court ruled that the loss of anticipated market shares following from the continuance of the acquired businesses was not injury for which treble damages could be awarded under section 4. To be an 'antitrust injury', under section 4, the injury should be to one's business or property 'By reason of anything forbidden in the antitrust laws.' It held that the injury should reflect the anti-competitive effect either of the violation or of anti-competitive acts made possible by the violation and that losses not related to the antitrust laws, such as loss from continued competition, would not be compensated.

Contravention of the Orders of the Commission—Section 42

Section 42 provides the penalty for contravention of the orders of the Commission and the amendment to section 42 in 2007 has altered the penalties.[78]

Contravention by Companies—Section 48

Section 48 of the Act provides for action against companies that contravene any rule or regulation or order or direction made under the Act. It is the standard clause that renders the company and the person in charge of and responsible to the company for the conduct of the business of the company, liable for punishment. It is open to the person charged to plead that the contravention was committed without his knowledge, or that he had exercised all due diligence to prevent the commission of the contravention. But where the contravention had taken place with the consent or connivance of, or is attributable to any neglect on the part of any director, manager, secretary or other officer of the company, he will be deemed to be guilty of the contravention and liable for punishment.

The penalties provided for contraventions are sufficiently high to discourage anti-competitive activities. The success of the enforcement of the antitrust legislation in the EEC is largely due to the heavy fines imposed on undertakings that violate its antitrust legislation. Section 36(3) of the Competition Act 1998, UK, provides that the Director may impose a penalty on an undertaking under sub-section (a) dealing with anti-competitive agreements; or (b) dealing with the abuse of a dominant position, only if he is satisfied that the infringement has been committed intentionally or negligently by the undertaking.

Enforcement against Those not Carrying on Business in India—Section 32

Obviously, enforcement may be only against parties carrying on business in India where they may be directed to discontinue the agreement or modify it so that the offending clauses in an agreement are removed. The same is the position where enforcement is through a penalty or compensation. But where one of the parties to an anti-competitive agreement does not carry on business in India, either directly or through a subsidiary or any other representative, the means of enforcing any order against that party directly, particularly if the other party challenges the jurisdiction of the enforcement agency in India, the Commission, are not clearly set out in the Act, even after the amendment in 2007. As stated in the previous chapter, section 32 is not satisfactory and provision should be made through bilateral agreements with other countries for the enforcement of such orders. The position is discussed also in Chapter 5 referring to the *Wood Pulp* case decided by the European Court of Justice in dealing with such challenges to its jurisdiction by overseas enterprises not having any office within the EEC.

Endnotes

[1] Section 3. Anti-competitive agreements.

1. No enterprise or association of enterprises or person or association of persons shall enter into any agreement in respect of production, supply, distribution, storage, acquisition or control of goods or provision of services, which causes or is likely to cause an appreciable adverse effect on competition within India.

2. Any agreement entered into in contravention of the provisions contained in sub-section (1) shall be void.

3. Any agreement entered into between enterprises or associations of enterprises or persons or associations of persons or between any person and enterprise or practice carried on, or decision taken by any association of enterprises or association of persons, including cartels, engaged in identical or similar trade of goods or provision of services, which—

(a) directly or indirectly determines purchase or sale prices;

(b) limits or controls production, supply, markets, technical development, investment or provision of services;

(c) shares the market or source of production or provision of services by way of allocation of geographical area of market, or type of goods or services, or number of customers in the market or any other similar way;

(d) directly or indirectly results in bid rigging or collusive bidding, shall be presumed to have an appreciable adverse effect on competition:

Provided that nothing contained in this sub-section shall apply to any agreement entered into by way of joint ventures if such agreement increases efficiency in production, supply, distribution, storage, acquisition or control of goods or provision of services.

Explanation—for the purposes of this sub-section, 'bid rigging' means any agreement, between enterprises or persons referred to in sub-section (3) engaged in identical or similar production or trading of goods or provision of services, which has the effect of eliminating or reducing competition for bids or adversely affecting or manipulating the process for bidding.

4. Any agreement amongst enterprises or persons at different stages or levels of the production chain in different markets, in respect of production, supply, distribution, storage, sale or price of, or trade in goods or provision of services, including—

(a) tie-in arrangement;

(b) exclusive supply agreement;

(c) exclusive distribution agreement;

(d) refusal to deal;

(e) resale price maintenance, shall be an agreement in contravention of sub-section (1) if such agreement causes or is likely to cause an appreciable adverse effect on competition in India.

Explanation—for the purposes of this sub-section—

(a) 'tie-in arrangement' includes any agreement requiring a purchaser of goods, as a condition of such purchase, to purchase some other goods;

(b) 'exclusive supply agreement' includes any agreement restricting in any manner the purchaser in the course of his trade from acquiring or otherwise dealing in any goods other than those of the seller or any other person;

(c) 'exclusive distribution agreement' includes any agreement to limit, restrict or withhold the output or supply of any goods or allocate any area or market for the disposal or sale of the goods;

(d) 'refusal to deal' includes any agreement which restricts, or is likely to restrict, by any method the persons or classes of persons to whom goods are sold or from whom goods are bought;

(e) 'resale price maintenance' includes any agreement to sell goods on condition that the prices to be charged on the resale by the purchaser shall be the prices stipulated by the seller unless it is clearly stated that prices lower than those prices may be charged.

5. Nothing contained in this section shall restrict—

(i) the right of any person to restrain any infringement of, or to impose reasonable conditions, as may be necessary for protecting any of his rights which have been or may be conferred upon him under—

(a) the Copyright Act, 1957 (14 of 1957);

(b) the Patents Act, 1970 (39 of 1970);

(c) the Trade and Merchandise Marks Act, 1958 (43 of 1958) or the Trade Marks Act, 1999 (47 of 1999);

(d) the Geographical Indications of Goods (Registration and Protection) Act, 1999 (48 of 1999);

(e) the Designs Act, 2000 (16 of 2000);

(f) the Semi-conductor Integrated Circuits Layout-Design Act, 2000 (37 of 2000);

(ii) the right of any person to export goods from India to the extent to which the agreement relates exclusively to the production, supply, distribution or control of goods or provision of services for such export.

[2] Section 3 was brought into force with effect from 20 May 2009, vide by SO 1241[E] dated 15-5-2009.

[3] Section 2(b) has defined an 'agreement' as follows: (b) 'agreement' includes any arrangement or understanding or action in concert—(i) whether or not, such arrangement, understanding or action is formal or in writing; or (ii) whether or not such arrangement, understanding or action is intended to be enforceable by legal proceedings;

[4] Section 2(c)—'cartel' includes an association of producers, sellers, distributors, traders or service providers who, by agreement amongst themselves, limit, control or attempt to control the production, distribution, sale or price of, or, trade in goods or provision of services.

⁵ Section 2(h): 'enterprise' means a person or a department of the Government, who or which is, or has been, engaged in any activity, relating to the production, storage, supply, distribution, acquisition or control of articles or goods, or the provision of services, of any kind, or in investment, or in the business of acquiring, holding, underwriting or dealing with shares, debentures or other securities of any other body corporate, either directly or through one or more of its units or divisions or subsidiaries, whether such unit or division or subsidiary is located at the same place where the enterprise is located or at a different place or at different places, but does not include any activity of the Government relatable to the sovereign functions of the Government including all activities carried on by the departments of the Central Government dealing with atomic energy, currency, defence and space.

⁶ Section 2(l) 'person' includes—

(i) an individual;

(ii) a Hindu undivided family;

(iii) a company;

(iv) a firm;

(v) an association of persons or a body of individuals, whether incorporated or not, in India or outside India;

(vi) any corporation established by or under any Central, State or Provincial Act or a Government company as defined in section 617 of the Companies Act, 1956 (1 of 1956);

(vii) any body corporate incorporated by or under the laws of a country outside India;

(viii) a co-operative society registered under any law relating to cooperative societies;

(ix) a local authority;

(x) every artificial juridical person, not falling within any of the preceding subclauses.

⁷ The report of the High Level Committee on Competition Policy has devoted an entire chapter to this subject (Chapter VIII).

⁸ Section 2.

(i) 'goods' means goods as defined in the Sale of Goods Act, 1930 (8 of 1930) and includes—

(a) products manufactured, processed or mined; 126 Competition Law in India

(b) debentures, stocks and shares after allotment;

(c) in relation to goods supplied, distributed or controlled in India, goods imported into India.

⁹ Section 2(m) 'practice' includes any practice relating to the carrying on of any trade by a person or an enterprise.

¹⁰ Section 2(o) 'price', in relation to the sale of any goods or to the performance of any services, includes every valuable consideration, whether direct or indirect,

or deferred, and includes any consideration which in effect relates to the sale of any goods or to the performance of any services although ostensibly relating to any other matter or thing.

[11] Section 2(u).

[12] Section 2(x).

[13] Article 1. Application of Articles 81 and 82 of the Treaty

1. Agreements, decisions and concerted practices caught by Article 81(1) of the Treaty which do not satisfy the conditions of Article 81(3) of the Treaty shall be prohibited, no prior decision to that effect being required.

2. Agreements, decisions and concerted practices caught by Article 81(1) of the Treaty which satisfy the conditions of Article 81(3) of the Treaty shall not be prohibited, no prior decision to that effect being required.

3. The abuse of a dominant position referred to in Article 82 of the Treaty shall be prohibited, no prior decision to that effect being required.

Article 2. Burden of proof

In any national or community proceedings for the application of Articles 81 and 82 of the Treaty, the burden of proving an infringement of Article 81(1) or of Article 82 of the Treaty shall rest on the party or the authority alleging the infringement. The undertaking or association of undertakings claiming the benefit of Article 81(3) of the Treaty shall bear the burden of proving that the conditions of that paragraph are fulfilled.

[14] Section 2.

1. Subject to section 3, agreements between undertakings, decisions by associations of undertakings or concerted practices which—(a) may affect trade within the UK, and (b) have as their object or effect the prevention, restriction or distortion of competition within the UK, are prohibited unless they are exempt in accordance with the provisions of this part.

2. Sub-section (1) applies, in particular, to agreements, decisions or practices which—

(a) directly or indirectly fix purchase or selling prices or any other trading conditions;

(b) limit or control production, markets, technical development or investment;

(c) share markets or sources of supply;

(d) apply dissimilar conditions to equivalent transactions with other trading parties, thereby placing them at a competitive disadvantage;

(e) make the conclusion of contracts subject to acceptance by the other parties of supplementary obligations which, by their nature or according to commercial usage, have no connection with the subject of such contracts.

3. Sub-section (1) applies only if the agreement, decision or practice is, or is intended to be, implemented in the UK.

4. Any agreement or decision which is prohibited by sub-section (1) is void.

5. A provision of this part which is expressed to apply to, or in relation to, an agreement is to be read as applying equally to, or in relation to, a decision by

an association of undertakings or a concerted practice (but with any necessary modifications).

6. Sub-section (5) does not apply where the context otherwise requires.

7. In this section 'the UK' means, in relation to an agreement which operates or is intended to operate only in a part of the UK, that part.

8. The prohibition imposed by sub-section (1) is referred to in this Act as 'the Chapter I prohibition'.

[15] Excluded agreements—Section 3.

1. The Chapter I prohibition does not apply in any of the cases in which it is excluded by or as a result of—

(a) Schedule 1 (mergers and concentrations);

(b) Schedule 2 (competition scrutiny under other enactments);

(c) Schedule 3 (planning obligations and other general exclusions); or

(d) Schedule 4 (professional rules). Schedule 4 was later deleted.

[16] Section 9. The criteria for individual and block exemptions. This section applies to any agreement which—

(a) contributes to

(i) improving production or distribution, or

(ii) promoting technical or economic progress, while allowing consumers a fair share of the resulting benefit; but

(b) does not

(i) impose on the undertakings concerned restrictions which are not indispensable to the attainment of those objectives; or

(ii) afford the undertakings concerned the possibility of eliminating competition in respect of a substantial part of the products in question.

[17] § 1 Sherman Act, 15 U.S.C. § 1.

Trusts, etc., in restraint of trade illegal; penalty.

Every contract, combination in the form of trust or otherwise, or conspiracy, in restraint of trade or commerce among the several States, or with foreign nations, is declared to be illegal. Every person who shall make any contract or engage in any combination or conspiracy hereby declared to be illegal shall be deemed guilty of a felony, and, on conviction thereof, shall be punished by fine not exceeding $10,000,000 if a corporation, or, if any other person, $350,000, or by imprisonment not exceeding three years, or by both said punishments, in the discretion of the court.

§ 2 Sherman Act, 15 U.S.C. § 2.

Monopolizing trade a felony; penalty.

129 Anti-competitive Agreements

Every person who shall monopolize, or attempt to monopolize, or combine or conspire with any other person or persons, to monopolize any part of the trade or commerce among the several States, or with foreign nations, shall be deemed guilty of a felony, and, on conviction thereof, shall be punished by fine not exceeding $10,000,000 if a corporation, or, if any other person, $350,000, or by imprisonment not exceeding three years, or by both said punishments, in the discretion of the court.

[18] § 2 Clayton Act, 15 U.S.C. §§ 13(2).
Discrimination in price, services, or facilities.
(a) Price; selection of customers.

It shall be unlawful for any person engaged in commerce, in the course of such commerce, either directly or indirectly, to discriminate in price between different purchasers of commodities of like grade and quality, where either or any of the purchases involved in such discrimination are in commerce, where such commodities are sold for use, consumption, or resale within the US or any Territory thereof or the District of Columbia or any insular possession or other place under the jurisdiction of the US, and where the effect of such discrimination may be substantially to lessen competition or tend to create a monopoly in any line of commerce, or to injure, destroy, or prevent competition with any person who either grants or knowingly receives the benefit of such discrimination, or with customers of either of them:

Provided, that nothing herein contained shall prevent differentials which make only due allowance for differences in the cost of manufacture, sale, or delivery resulting from the differing methods or quantities in which such commodities are to such purchasers sold or delivered: Provided, however, that the FTC may, after due investigation and hearing to all interested parties, fix and establish quantity limits, and revise the same as it finds necessary, as to particular commodities or classes of commodities, where it finds that available purchasers in greater quantities are so few as to render differentials on account thereof unjustly discriminatory or promotive of monopoly in any line of commerce; and the foregoing shall then not be construed to permit differentials based on differences in quantities greater than those so fixed and established: And provided further, that nothing herein contained shall prevent persons engaged in selling goods, wares, or merchandise in commerce from selecting their own customers in bona fide transactions and not in restraint of trade: And provided further, that nothing herein contained shall prevent price changes from time to time where in response to changing conditions affecting the market for or the marketability of the goods concerned, such as but not limited to actual or imminent deterioration of perishable goods, obsolescence of seasonal goods, distress sales under court process, or sales in good faith in discontinuance of business in the goods concerned.

(b) Burden of rebutting prima-facie case of discrimination.

Upon proof being made, at any hearing on a complaint under this section, that there has been discrimination in price or services or facilities furnished, the burden of rebutting the prima-facie case thus made by showing justification shall be upon the person charged with a violation of this section, and unless justification shall be affirmatively shown, the Commission is authorized to issue an order terminating the discrimination: Provided, however, that nothing herein contained shall prevent a seller rebutting the prima-facie case thus made by showing that his lower price or the furnishing of services or facilities to any purchaser or purchasers was made in good faith to meet an equally low price of a competitor, or the services or facilities furnished by a competitor.

(c) Payment or acceptance of commission, brokerage, or other compensation.

It shall be unlawful for any person engaged in commerce, in the course of such commerce, to pay or grant, or to receive or accept, anything of value as a commission, brokerage, or other compensation, or any allowance or discount in lieu thereof, except for services rendered in connection with the sale or purchase of goods, wares, or merchandise, either to the other party to such transaction or to an agent, representative, or other intermediary therein where such intermediary is acting in fact for or in behalf, or is subject to the direct or indirect control, of any party to such transaction other than the person by whom such compensation is so granted or paid.

(d) Payment for services or facilities for processing or sale.

It shall be unlawful for any person engaged in commerce to pay or contract for the payment of anything of value to or for the benefit of a customer of such person in the course of such commerce as compensation or in consideration for any services or facilities furnished by or through such customer in connection with the processing, handling, sale, or offering for sale of any products or commodities manufactured, sold, or offered for sale by such person, unless such payment or consideration is available on proportionally equal terms to all other customers competing in the distribution of such products or commodities.

(e) Furnishing services or facilities for processing, handling, etc.

It shall be unlawful for any person to discriminate in favor of one purchaser against another purchaser or purchasers of a commodity bought for resale, with or without processing, by contracting to furnish or furnishing, or by contributing to the furnishing of, any services or facilities connected with the processing, handling, sale, or offering for sale of such commodity so purchased upon terms not accorded to all purchasers on proportionally equal terms.

(f) Knowingly inducing or receiving discriminatory price.

It shall be unlawful for any person engaged in commerce, in the course of such commerce, knowingly to induce or receive discrimination in price which is prohibited by this section.

Discrimination in rebates, discounts, or advertising service charges; underselling in particular localities; penalties, 15 U.S.C. § 13a.

131 Anti-competitive Agreements

It shall be unlawful for any person engaged in commerce, in the course of such commerce, to be a party to, or assist in, any transaction of sale, or contract to sell, which discriminates to his knowledge against competitors of the purchaser, in that, any discount, rebate, allowance, or advertising service charge is granted to the purchaser over and above any discount, rebate, allowance, or advertising service charge available at the time of such transaction to said competitors in respect of a sale of goods of like grade, quality, and quantity; to sell, or contract to sell, goods in any part of the US at prices lower than those exacted by said person elsewhere in the US for the purpose of destroying competition, or eliminating a competitor in such part of the US; or, to sell, or contract to sell, goods at unreasonably low prices for the purpose of destroying competition or eliminating a competitor.

Any person violating any of the provisions of this section shall, upon conviction thereof, be fined not more than $5,000 or imprisoned not more than one year, or both.

[19] Paragraphs 3.18, 3.19, 'Draft competition law guideline on Article 81 and the Chapter I Prohibition' April 2004—OFT 401.

[20] Paragraphs 3.20–3.23 'Draft competition law guideline on Article 81 and the Chapter I Prohibition' April 2004—OFT 401.

[21] Official Journal L 068, 13/03/1992 p. 0019–0033.

[22] Schedule 4, PROFESSIONAL RULES (Schedule 4 repealed by the Enterprise Act 2002).

PROFESSIONAL SERVICES

Legal 8. The services of barristers, advocates or solicitors.

Medical 9. The provision of medical or surgical advice or attendance and the performance of surgical operations.

Dental 10. Any services falling within the practice of dentistry within the meaning of the Dentists Act 1984.

Ophthalmic 11. The testing of sight.

Veterinary 12. Any services which constitute veterinary surgery within the meaning of the Veterinary Surgeons Act 1966.

Nursing 13. The services of nurses.

Midwifery 14. The services of midwives.

Physiotherapy 15. The services of physiotherapists.

Chiropody 16. The services of chiropodists.

Architectural 17. The services of architects.

Accounting and auditing 18. The making or preparation of accounts or accounting records and the examination, verification and auditing of financial statements.

Insolvency 19. Insolvency services within the meaning of section 428 of the Insolvency Act 1986.

Patent agency 20. The services of registered patent agents (within the meaning of Part V of the Copyright, Designs and Patents Act 1988).

21. The services of persons carrying on for gain in the UK the business of acting as agents or other representatives for or obtaining European patents or for the purpose of conducting proceedings in relation to applications for or otherwise in connection with such patents before the European Patent Office or the comptroller and whose names appear on the European list (within the meaning of Part V of the Copyright, Designs and Patents Act, 1988).

Parliamentary agency 22. The services of parliamentary agents entered in the register in either House of Parliament as agents entitled to practise both in promoting and in opposing Bills.

Surveying 23. The services of surveyors of land, of quantity surveyors, of surveyors of buildings or other structures and of surveyors of ships.

Engineering and technology, etc. 24. The services of persons practising or employed as consultants in the field of

(a) civil engineering;

(b) mechanical, aeronautical, marine, electrical or electronic engineering;

(c) mining, quarrying, soil analysis or other forms of mineralogy or geology;

(d) agronomy, forestry, livestock rearing or ecology;

(e) metallurgy, chemistry, biochemistry or physics; or

(f) any other form of engineering or technology analogous to those mentioned in sub-paragraphs (a) to (e).

Educational 25. The provision of education or training.

Religious 26. The services of ministers of religion.

[23] 207 Repeal of Schedule 4 to the 1998 Act:

section 3(1)(d) of and Schedule 4 to the 1998 Act (which provide for the exclusion from the Chapter 1 prohibition in cases involving designated professional rules) shall cease to have effect.

[24] Paragraphs 197, 198.

[25] Follow-up to the Report on Competition in Professional Services, COM (2004) 83 of 9 February 2004.

[26] 476 US 447 (1986).

[27] 421 US 773 (1975).

[28] Section 2(r), (s) and (t) of the Act deal with the 'market'. Section 2(r): 'relevant market' means the market which may be determined by the Commission with reference to the relevant product market or the relevant geographic market or with reference to both the markets; section 2(s): 'relevant geographic market' means a market comprising the area in which the conditions of competition for supply of goods or provision of services or demand of goods or services are distinctly homogenous and can be distinguished from the conditions prevailing in the neighbouring areas; section 2(t) 'relevant product market' means a market comprising all those products or services which are regarded as interchangeable or substitutable by the consumer, by reason of characteristics of the products or services, their prices and intended use.

[29] Published in the Official Journal: OJ C 372 on 9/12/1997; also referred to in the chapter on 'combination'.

[30] The following cases are discussed in the chapter on 'Combination': vertical integration (*United States v. Columbia Steel Co*). product market (*Boeing/McDonnell Douglas*); product market, end-uses (*United States v. Continental Can Co*); product market and geographic market (*Brown Shoe Co. Inc. v. US*); telecommunication services—market (*British Telecom/MCI* (II)—Case No IV/M.856).

[31] Section 19(5) for determining whether a market constitutes a 'relevant market' for the purposes of this Act, the Commission shall have due regard to the 'relevant geographic market' and 'relevant product market'; [6]. The Commission shall, while determining the 'relevant geographic market', have due regard to all or any of the following factors, namely—(a) regulatory trade barriers; (b) local specification requirements; (c) national procurement policies; (d) adequate distribution facilities; (e) transport costs; (f) language; (g) consumer preferences; (h) need for secure or regular supplies or rapid after-sales services; [7]. The Commission shall, while determining the 'relevant product market', have due regard to all or any of the following factors, namely—(a) physical characteristics or end-use of goods; (b) price of goods or service; (c) consumer preferences; (d) exclusion of in-house production; (e) existence of specialized producers; (f) classification of industrial products.

[32] 351 US 377 (1956).

[33] 370 US 294 (1962).

[34] 246 US 231 (1918).

[35] Tie-in arrangement—section 33(1)(b); exclusive supply agreement and exclusive distribution agreement—section 33(1)(c); refusal to deal—section 33(1)(a); resale price maintenance—section 33(1)(f).

[36] (1977) 47 Comp Cas 520 Supreme Court.

[37] 405 U.S. 562 (1972). Discussed in detail in the chapter on 'Combination'.

[38] 221 US 1 (1910).

[39] 'Section 1. Every contract, combination in the form of trust or otherwise, or conspiracy, in restraint of trade or commerce among the several states or with foreign nations, is hereby declared to be illegal. Every person who shall make any such contract, or engage in any such combination or conspiracy, shall be deemed guilty of a misdemeanor, and, on conviction thereof, shall be punished by fine not exceeding $5,000, or by imprisonment not exceeding one year, or by both said punishments, in the discretion of the court.

Section 2. Every person who shall monopolize, or attempt to monopolize, or combine or conspire with any other person or persons to monopolize, any part of the trade or commerce among the several states, or with foreign nations, shall be deemed guilty of a misdemeanor, and, on conviction thereof, shall be punished by fine not exceeding $5,000, or by imprisonment not exceeding one year, or by both said punishments, in the discretion of the court.' (26 Stat. at L. 209, chap. 647, US Comp. Stat. 1901, p. 3200)

[40] 220 US 373 (1911).

[41] Paragraphs 3.5–3.8 'Draft competition law guideline on Article 81 and the Chapter I Prohibition', April 2004—OFT401.

[42] 485 US 717 (1988).

[43] 433 US 36 (1977).

[44] See endnote 16 for the criteria for individual and block exemptions.

[45] Paragraphs 4.11 and 4.12 of the Chapter I Prohibition, OFT 401.

[46] Competition Act, 1998 – Cartels—'Competition Law, 2005'.
[47] Paragraph 26.
[48] 273 US 392 (1927).
[49] EC Press Release.
[50] EC Press Release DN: IP/02/1585 Dated: 30/10/2002 'Commission rules against collusive behaviour of Christie's and Sotheby's'.
[51] 457 US 332 (1982).
[52] (1979) 49 Company Cases 145 MRTP Commission.
[53] 341 US 593 (1951).
[54] Press Release: IP/07/1781, Date: 28/11/2007.
[55] Press Release IP/10/1487, Brussels, 9 November 2010.
[56] IP/07/209 - Brussels, 21 February 2007.
[57] With certain elaborations of the principles of this Regulation of 2000 expiring in 2010, this was renewed by a new Regulation (EU) No 1218/2010 of 14 December 2010.
[58] Power to impose lesser penalty on a member of a cartel is discussed in the chapter on 'Enforcement' under 'Power to impose lesser penalty–section 46'.
[59] Text of the sub-section at endnote 1.
[60] 332 US 392 (1947).
[61] 466 US 2 (1984).
[62] 504 US 451 (1992).
[63] 337 US 293 (1949).
[64] 365 US 320 (1961).
[65] 384 US 127 (1966).
[66] In *Albrecht* v. *Herald Co.* 390 US 145 (1968) the Supreme Court had held that vertical maximum price fixing was a per se violation of the Sherman Act.
[67] The European Commission has issued a notice setting out the guidelines on vertical restraints, considering the assessment of the vertical restraints and the exemption and related matters. SEC (2010) 411 final, which may be browsed at the European Union's website: www.eur-lex.ec.eu.europa.en.
[68] This Regulation has been replaced by Commission Regulation (EU) No 461/2010 of 27 May 2010 on the application of Article 101(3) of the Treaty on the Functioning of the European Union to Categories of Vertical Agreements and Concerted Practices in the Motor Vehicle Sector.
[69] 272 US 476 (1926).
[70] 316 US 241 (1942).
[71] 323 US 386 (1945).
[72] See *US* v. *National Lead Co.*, 332 US 319 (1947) and *United States* v. *Singer Mfg. Co.*, 374 US 174 (1963) for further cases of cross-licensing of patents between competitors.
[73] 342 US 371 (1952).
[74] 316 US 265 (1942).

[75] 'Technology transfer agreement' means a patent licensing agreement, a knowhow licensing agreement, a software copyright licensing agreement or a mixed patent, know-how or software copyright licensing agreement, including any such agreement containing provisions which relate to the sale and purchase of products or which relate to the licensing of other intellectual property rights or the assignment of intellectual property rights, provided that those provisions do not constitute the primary object of the agreement and are directly related to the production of the contract products; assignments of patents, know-how, software copyright or a combination thereof where part of the risk associated with the exploitation of the technology remains with the assignor, in particular where the sum payable in consideration of the assignment is dependent on the turnover obtained by the assignee in respect of products produced with the assigned technology, the quantity of such products produced or the number of operations carried out employing the technology, shall also be deemed to be technology transfer agreements.

[76] Section 27 as amended is discussed in the chapter on 'Enforcement'.

[77] 429 US 477 (1977).

[78] Contravention of orders of Commission: Section 42(1) The Commission may cause an inquiry to be made into compliance of its orders or directions made in exercise of its powers under the Act. (2) If any person, without reasonable clause, fails to comply with the orders or directions of the Commission issued under sections 27, 28, 31, 32, 33, 42A and 43A of the Act, he shall be punishable with fine which may extend to rupees one lakh for each day during which such non-compliance occurs, subject to a maximum of rupees ten crore, as the Commission may determine. (3) If any person does not comply with the orders or directions issued, or fails to pay the fine imposed under sub-section (2), he shall, without prejudice to any proceeding under section 39, be punishable with imprisonment for a term which may extend to three years, or with fine which may extend to rupees twenty-five crore, or with both, as the Chief Metropolitan Magistrate, Delhi may deem fit: Provided that the Chief Metropolitan Magistrate, Delhi shall not take cognizance of any offence under this section save on a complaint filed by the Commission or any of its officers authorized by it.

3

Abuse of a Dominant Position

The abuse of a dominant position is another way of interfering with competition in the market place. In simple terms it refers to the *conduct* of an enterprise that enjoys a 'dominant position', as defined by the Act. In substance, 'dominant position' means the position of strength enjoyed by an enterprise that enables it to act independently of competitive forces prevailing in the relevant market. Such an enterprise will be in a position to disregard market forces and unilaterally impose trading conditions, fix prices, etc. The abuse may result in the restriction of competition, or the elimination of effective competition. Some of the various forms of abuse are: price-fixing, imposing discriminatory pricing, 'predatory' pricing, limiting supply of goods or services, denial of market access, etc.

The market share of an enterprise does not, as under the MRTP Act, determine the dominant position of an enterprise, though it is one of the factors to be considered, along with other factors, including the market shares of its competitors, in determining whether it enjoys a dominant position or not. The Act sets out the factors that are to be considered by the competition authorities in determining whether an enterprise enjoys a dominant position,[1] as well as the method for determining the relevant product and geographic market in which the dominant position is to be found.[2] Finally, the analysis should reveal if the result of the conduct indicted as abusive is the restriction or elimination of competition in the relevant market for the goods or services in question. The regulatory provisions of the Act would be set in motion if the abuse were a breach of section 4 of the Act.

SECTION 4—DOMINANT POSITION ABUSE

Section 4 deals with the abuse of a dominant position.[3] Section 4(1) prohibits abuse by an enterprise of its dominant position. Sub-section (2) defines when there is abuse of a dominant position within the meaning of section 4(1). It lists the anti-competitive practices of imposing unfair or discriminatory trading conditions or prices or predatory prices, limiting the supply of goods or services, or a market or technical or scientific development relating to goods or services, denial of market access, imposing on other contracting parties obligations not related to the basic contract with them, and using a dominant position in one market to gain entry into another market or to protect that other market.

Amendments to Section 4

Certain limited amendments were made to section 4 by the 2007 amendments. One of the amendments to section 4 was to provide for the abuse of dominance by a group also and not only by an enterprise as provided by sub-sections (1) and (2) as they stood before the amendment. Before the amendment, section 4(1) stood as follows: 'S 4(1) No enterprise shall abuse its dominant position'. The amendment to this sub-section has included a 'group' within the ambit of this restriction. The section now reads as: 'S 4(1) No enterprise or group shall abuse its dominant position'. Section 4(2) stating when there will be an abuse of a dominant position has been correspondingly amended to include abuse of dominance by a group. Section 4(2)(c) which stood, as an instance of abuse of a dominant position, 'indulges in practice or practices resulting in denial of market access' has been enlarged with the addition, at the end of that clause, of the words, 'in any manner'.

The other amendment to this section is the addition of a clause as Explanation (c) to section 4 explaining the meaning of the word 'group'. It is as follows: '"group" shall have the same meaning as assigned to it in clause (b) of the Explanation to section 5'. Clause (b) of the Explanation to section 5 defines a group as: '"group" means two or more enterprises which, directly or indirectly, are in a position to—(i) exercise twenty-six per cent or more of the voting rights in the other enterprise; or (ii) appoint more than fifty per cent of the members of the board of directors in the other enterprise; or (iii) control the management or affairs of the other enterprise'.

Abuse of a dominant position held collectively by enterprises otherwise independent is also abuse which would fall under this amendment.

A case of this kind *Compagnie Maritime Belge Transports SA and Others* v. *Commission of the European Communities* is discussed later in this chapter. *Europemballage Corporation and Continental Can Company*

Inc. v. Commission of the European Communities, another case discussed in this chapter is one where a subsidiary's conduct was attributed to the holding company.

Acts in Bonafide Competition Excepted

The Explanation to section 4(2)(a) exempts such unfair or discriminatory trading conditions or unfair or discriminatory prices, or predatory pricing referred to in section 4(2)(a)(i) and (ii), setting out those practices as an abuse of a dominant position, from being considered as an abuse of a dominant position, when they are adopted to meet competition. The basis for this contention is that when enterprises are engaged in bonafide competition and readjusting their trading strategies to meet the terms of offers of competitors in a market as it evolves, there is no 'abuse' by any of the enterprises. They are only responding to the market situation. For example, if prices fall in the market, for reasons not the action of an enterprise, a reduction in the price by that enterprise to match its prices to the new prices cannot be termed unfair pricing or predatory pricing.

Dominant Position—Definition

The dictionary meaning of the word 'dominant' is 'overriding', or 'influential'. 'Predatory' means exploitation for financial purposes. But they have specific meanings under the Act and the second explanation to section 4, defines 'dominant position' and 'predatory price'.

The elements that constitute a dominant position are: (i) a position of strength; (ii) that position being enjoyed in a relevant market in India (both product and geographical markets) (iii) and such a position that gives the enterprise the power to 'operate independently of competitive forces in the relevant market', meaning thereby that it can at will, disregard market forces and conditions and impose its own trading conditions, which will include the prices at which it is prepared to supply goods or services.

Conduct amounting to an abuse of a dominant position may also be such that it affects its competitors or consumers or the structure of the market in its favour. This results when abuse of a dominant position would impair the ability of the competitors to compete as they would and consumers would, as a consequence, have to accept higher prices or reduced quality. Where the freedom of those constituting a market is eroded in this manner, the structure of the market is deemed to have been altered in favour of the dominant enterprise abusing its position.

Predatory Price

The explanation defines predatory price as the sale of goods or provision of services, at a price which is below the cost, as may be determined by regulations, of production of goods or provision of services, with a view to reducing competition or eliminating the competitors. The purpose of selling at a predatory price is to offer low prices, lower than the variable costs, that is, below the average variable costs of production, so that competitors unable to sell at that price level will be eliminated. The usual practice is to raise the price to abnormal levels, towards what is termed 'recouping the loss', after such competition has been either reduced or eliminated in a market.

Usually, where the price is below average variable costs, predation is presumed, that is, the existence of an intention to damage competitors. The definition states that predatory price would be one that is below cost as may be determined by regulations. The Commission is empowered to make regulations to carry out the purposes of the Act. This now leaves open what costs will be considered as relevant for this purpose. Further, enterprises should be able to agree that the costs so fixed by regulations are reasonably relatable to the purpose of fixing that price.

Dominant Position—Elaboration

As stated earlier, 'dominant position' has a specific meaning under section 4 of this Act, and in the European Community Law, in Article 82, on which both the Indian Act and the Competition Act, 1998, UK, are based. It does not contain the commonly understood connotations of dominant position, as constituted by size or market share of an enterprise, though they are relevant in ascertaining dominant position. The substance of the definition is that a dominant enterprise is one that has the power to disregard market forces, that is, competitors, customers and others and to take unilateral decisions that would benefit it and also, in the process, cause harm to the process of free competition, injuring the consumers by saddling them with higher prices, limited supplies, etc.

The capacity to engage in the market in this manner is what is called 'market power', which is quite different from 'market share', though, the structure of a particular market, may aid an enterprise with a significant market share in acquiring market power. A dominant position is acquired over a period of time and the many factors which may further the acquiring of a dominant position by an enterprise are: technological superiority, access to certain intellectual property rights in the supply of the products, early entry, weak competition, the nature of the industry, government regulations, etc.

The OFT believes that an enterprise cannot be in a dominant position when it does not have substantial market power. It says:

Market power arises where an undertaking does not face sufficiently strong competitive pressure. Both suppliers and buyers can have market power. However, for clarity, market power will in this guideline refer to supplier market power. Where buyer market power is the issue, the term 'buyer power' is employed to differentiate such market power from supplier market power. Market power and buyer power are not absolute but are matters of degree; the degree of power will depend on the circumstances of each case.[4]

It explains the concept of market power thus:

Market power can be thought of as the ability profitably to sustain prices above competitive levels or to restrict output or quality below competitive levels. An undertaking with market power might also have the ability and incentive to harm the process of competition in other ways, for example by weakening existing competition, raising entry barriers or slowing innovation. However, although market power is not solely concerned with the ability of a supplier to raise prices, this guideline, for convenience, often refers to market power as the ability profitably to sustain prices above competitive levels.[5]

Abuse of a Dominant Position

The dominant position of an enterprise is a question of fact to be determined in each case, taking into consideration a number of relevant factors, such as the product and geographic market, its market share, the market shares of the competitors, any technological advantages held by that enterprise, the strength of its competitors, and barriers to entry. Section 19(4) of the Act sets out the factors that ought to be taken into consideration by the Commission while inquiring into the question whether an enterprise enjoys a dominant position, within the meaning of section 4. An enterprise may acquire a dominant position over a period of time by its own efficiency in running the enterprise and also by the way the market evolves. Acquiring a dominant position is not prohibited, only its abuse is prohibited.

Section 4 deals with abuse of a dominant position. As stated earlier, section 4(1) prohibits abuse of its dominant position by an enterprise. Section 4(2)(a)–(e) sets out what conduct would be an abuse of a dominant position under the Act. In summary, they are: imposing unfair or discriminatory trading conditions or prices or predatory prices, limiting supply of goods or services or a market or technical or scientific development relating to goods or services, denial of market access, imposing on other contracting parties obligations not related to the basic contract with them, and using a dominant position in one market to gain entry into another market or to protect that other market.

It should first be noted that the practices stated in sub-section (2), when engaged in by an enterprise that is shown to be as a dominant undertaking, are prohibited under sub-section (1). Those practices are not declared void as in section 3 dealing with anti-competitive agreements and in section 6 dealing with the regulation of combinations. Any practice set out in section 4 is treated as anti-competitive and is subject to regulation by the Commission under section 27 and where necessary, under section 28,[6] the Commission may *direct* the division of any enterprise enjoying a dominant position. They are just prohibited, as an abuse of its position by a dominant enterprise *or a group*. The section ought to have been extended to provide explicitly that such abuse of a dominant position would be prohibited when it causes, or is likely to cause, an appreciable adverse effect on competition in the relevant market within India. As may be seen from the language of legislation of other jurisdictions shown below, the adverse effect on trade or commerce resulting from the abuse must be shown as an anti-competitive effect.

COMPARATIVE LAW

The language used in section 4 in prohibiting anti-competitive acts as an abuse of a dominant position would limit this abuse to only those modes of abuse stated in section 4(2)(a) to (e). On the other hand, Article 82 of the EC Treaty and section 18 of the Competition Act 1998, UK, which is based on EC law, use language clearly indicating that the list of acts of abuse are only particular illustrations of abuse of a dominant position and are not exhaustive of all practices that may amount to the abuse of a dominant position.

Article 106 of the EC Treaty (ex Article 82):

Any abuse by one or more undertakings of a dominant position within the common market or in a substantial part of it shall be prohibited as incompatible with the common market insofar as it may affect trade between Member States.

Such abuse may, in particular, consist in:

(a) directly or indirectly imposing unfair purchase or selling prices or other unfair trading conditions;
(b) limiting production, markets or technical development to the prejudice of consumers;
(c) applying dissimilar conditions to equivalent transactions with other trading parties, thereby placing them at a competitive disadvantage;
(d) making the conclusion of contracts subject to acceptance by the other parties of supplementary obligations which, by their nature or according to commercial usage, have no connection with the subject of such contracts.

There are no specific exclusions from Article 82 but under community law, the following types of conduct are, in effect, excluded from the application of Article 82: conduct which would result in a concentration with a Community dimension and thereby be subject to the EC Merger Regulation, or conduct which is carried out by an undertaking entrusted with the operation of services of general economic interest or having the character of a revenue producing monopoly, insofar as the application of Article 82 would obstruct the performance, in law or fact, of the particular tasks assigned to the undertaking.[7]

As stated in the chapter on Anti-competitive Agreements the *Modernization Regulation on the Application of the Rules of Competition* has, among others, declared: 'The abuse of a dominant position referred to in Article 82 of the Treaty shall be prohibited, no prior decision to that effect being required'. It has also laid the burden of proof of an infringement of any of these Articles on the party alleging infringement.

The Competition Act, 1998, UK

S. 18—(1) Subject to section 19, any conduct on the part of one or more undertakings which amounts to the abuse of a dominant position in a market is prohibited if it may affect trade within the UK.

(2) Conduct may, in particular, constitute such an abuse if it consists in

(a) directly or indirectly imposing unfair purchase or selling prices or other unfair trading conditions;

(b) limiting production, markets or technical development to the prejudice of consumers;

(c) applying dissimilar conditions to equivalent transactions with other trading parties, thereby placing them at a competitive disadvantage;

(d) making the conclusion of contracts subject to acceptance by the other parties of supplementary obligations which, by their nature or according to commercial usage, have no connection with the subject of the contracts.

Section 19 deals with certain exclusions but no exemption is provided in the case of abuse of a dominant position.

The principle of the Modernization Regulation of EEC stated above would apply to the UK also.

Monopolizing or attempting to monopolize any part of the trade or commerce among the several states, or with foreign nations, which is an offence under section 2 of the Sherman Act, would correspond to abuse of a dominant position.

ASCERTAINING THE DOMINANT POSITION—STATUTORY GUIDES UNDER THE COMPETITION ACT, 2002

In the enforcement of section 4, the first step is to establish that an enterprise against which the complaint of abuse is made enjoys a dominant position within the meaning of the second explanation to section 4, which in substance means that that enterprise's behaviour in the market is not constrained by market forces. This has to be proved by facts. Section 19(4) lists the factors that the Commission shall consider in an inquiry as to whether an enterprise enjoys a dominant position or not. They are: the market share of the enterprise; its size and resources; its economic power, including commercial advantages over its competitors; the existence of any vertical integration of the enterprises; consumers' dependence on the enterprise; the way a monopoly or dominant position was acquired by the enterprise, whether through being a government company or a public sector undertaking or by reason of any statute; entry barriers; countervailing buying power; market structure and size of the market; social obligations and social costs; any contribution to economic development by the enterprise enjoying a dominant position having or likely to have an appreciable adverse effect on competition.

The Central Government may prescribe further factors that may be considered in making this examination.

As stated earlier, the market share of an enterprise by itself is not determinative of the issue of a dominant position. The size of the market, the number of enterprises, the share of each in the market and the way it is shared by the competing enterprises will only show the importance of the market share of an enterprise for ascertaining its dominant position. For example, if an enterprise has a market share of 65 per cent and the rest is distributed among four or five enterprises as 20 per cent, 10 per cent, and 5 per cent, clearly the first enterprise may be said to be enjoying a dominant position. It is only this kind of a distribution of the share of the market that would give that enterprise 'market power' which is necessary to engage in abusive conduct. The *Hoffmann-La Roche* case discussed later in this chapter explains this position.

Commercial advantages that would help in building up a dominant position are access to raw materials, exclusive use of locations, etc. Similarly, vertical integration of a manufacturer with the only supplier of raw materials would promote a dominant position. If there are barriers to entry, in the form of high costs of investment that a new entrant may not or would not be willing to incur immediately, or there are statutory regulations preventing new entry, it would help existing enterprises to reach a dominant position. An existing enterprise may itself create barriers to entry through exclusive distribution and retail arrangements with itself.

Dominant Position—Relevant Market

A dominant position is always with reference to a relevant market, both the relevant product and relevant geographic markets. The Commission will have to make inquiries if the enterprise is dominant in the relevant product and relevant geographic markets.

Section 2(r), (s), and (t) of the Act deal with the 'market':

Section 2(r): 'relevant market' means the market which may be determined by the Commission with reference to the relevant product market or the relevant geographic market or with reference to both the markets;

Section 2(s): 'relevant geographic market' means a market comprising the area in which the conditions of competition for supply of goods or provision of services or demand of goods or services are distinctly homogeneous and can be distinguished from the conditions prevailing in the neighbouring areas; and

Section 2(t) 'relevant product market' means a market comprising all those products or services which are regarded as interchangeable or substitutable by the consumer, by reason of characteristics of the products or services, their prices and intended use.

The purpose of ascertaining the market is to be able to examine whether an enterprise is dominant in a specific market, made up of the product, or the service, the competing suppliers and the buyers of the product or service, all operating in a particular geographic area. If an enterprise is found to be enjoying a dominant position in a specific market, comprising a geographic and a product market, the next step would be to investigate if the prohibited abuse of a dominant position has taken place.

Relevant Geographic Market

A geographic market is not merely the physical territory in which the competing enterprises operate but only that part of the territory where the 'conditions of competition for supply of goods or provision of services or demand of goods or services are distinctly homogeneous and can be distinguished from the conditions prevailing in the neighbouring areas'. The dictionary meaning of 'homogeneous' is: *formed of parts that all are of the same type.* This refers to uniformity of composition that can be distinguished from the conditions of competition such as terms of supply, or the mix of the services offered or demanded in the neighbouring areas. Only that part of the geographic territory where uniformity of composition is present should be considered the geographic market. Conversely, when conditions prevailing in the neighbouring areas are different, the markets are different. The objective is that the exact sphere of competition, both in terms of a physical market and a specific product or service is to be identified towards ascertaining a dominant position.

Relevant Product Market

All products or services considered interchangeable or substitutes by the consumer by reason of characteristics of the products or services, their prices and intended use, constitute the relevant product market. All those products or services compete among themselves, in the perception of the consumer and, therefore, all such interchangeable products and services form the product market in a given case. The issue of a dominant position is to be determined in relation to such group of products.

Factors to be Considered in Determining the Geographic and Product Market

Having provided that a dominant position should be established with reference to a relevant geographic market and a relevant product market, the Act requires that the relevant geographical market and the relevant product market are determined on a consideration of all or any of the factors set out in sub-sections (6) to (7) of section 19.[8]

Relevant Geographic Market

The Commission may consider all or any of the following factors set out in section 19(6) in determining the relevant geographic market: regulatory trade barriers, local specification requirements, national procurement policies, adequate distribution facilities, transport costs, language, consumer preferences, the need for secure or regular supplies, or rapid after-sales services.

It may be noted that all these factors excepting the last one will negate uniformity of composition and would help in narrowing down the geographic territory to the actual geographic market that is to be considered.

Relevant Product Market

The factors that may be considered in determining the relevant product market are as set out in section 19[7]: physical characteristics or end-use of goods, price of goods or service, consumer preferences, exclusion of in-house production, existence of specialized producers, and classification of industrial products.

The first three would aid in assessing the interchangeability of products or services. In-house production does not enter the market and is therefore to be excluded. Specialized producers are a group by themselves. The classification of industrial products may be only of limited use as classification is done for various purposes and may not be directly relevant for determining a product market as a commercial unit.

Abuse of a Dominant Position

After an enterprise is shown to be enjoying a dominant position within the meaning of the Act and on a consideration of the factors set out in section 19(4), the next step would be to prove that it has abused its dominant position. The acts of abuse of a dominant position are set out in section 4(2)(a to e). On proof of the abuse of a dominant position, the Commission may pass any of the orders in section 27. It may also direct, under section 28, a division of the enterprise enjoying a dominant position for the purpose of ensuring that the enterprise does not abuse its dominant position.

The Act regulates only acts of abuse of a dominant position. If an enterprise somehow acquired a dominant position and remains so without engaging in any of the acts set out in section 4(2) no action is required against that enterprise.

The usual abuses of a dominant position are imposing discriminatory prices or trading conditions, predatory pricing, limiting supplies, exclusive dealing, denial of market access and such other anti-competitive practices. However, section 4(2)(a to e) has listed certain specific abuses of a dominant position.[9]

In essence they are: (a) directly or indirectly imposing unfair or discriminatory: (i) trading conditions in the supply of goods or services; (ii) prices, viz. unfair or discriminatory prices in the supply of goods or services, including charging predatory prices; (b) limiting supply or restricting the supply of goods or services, or a market for goods or services, or limiting technical or scientific development relating to goods or services to the prejudice of consumers; (c) denial of market access, for example, refusal to deal; (d) making the conclusion of contracts subject to acceptance by other parties of supplementary obligations, which according to their nature or commercial usage have no connection with the subject of the contracts; and (e) using the existing dominant position as a lever to strengthen its position in the same market or to enter into another market.

Unfair prices are excessively high prices, above competitive level. Discriminatory prices may be levied by charging different prices for different customers for the same product. Prices would be considered to be discriminatory when the same price is charged to different customers, though the cost of supplying the product to them varies. Discriminatory prices create an unequal position among suppliers of the same product buying at different prices, as these prices are unrelated to the quantity or characteristics of the product and can prejudice the competitive process.

The definition of a 'predatory price' has already been considered. Predatory pricing as the decisions cited later will show that, for a price to be predatory, that price should not only be below costs but should show an intention to injure competitors in such a manner that they would not be able to sell for long against such a predatory price. Obviously, it would be a question of fact.

Reducing the quantity of supply is also considered to be an abuse, as it would lead to the increase in prices to the prejudice of consumers. Denial of market access would also have the same effect, as it would eliminate one source of supply. Imposing supplementary obligations unrelated to the main agreement for the supply of a particular product or a service, like tie-in, exclusive supply arrangements, when imposed as a condition for entering into the basic contract for the supply of a product or a service is an abuse, as it restricts the freedom of the other party to negotiate and to that extent, limits his ability to compete.

Precedents

Some well-known decisions that illustrate the concept of abuse of a dominant position may now be studied.

Assessing Dominant Position

Hoffmann-La Roche & Co. Ag, Basle v. *Commission of the European Communities in Brussels*[10]

The European Commission held that Roche, with a dominant position within the common market, on the markets for certain vitamins, abused that position by concluding with 22 purchasers of these vitamins, agreements which contained an obligation upon them, or the grant of fidelity rebates offering them an incentive, to buy all or most of their requirements of vitamins exclusively, or in preference from Roche.

One of the grounds on which Roche appealed to the European Court was that the Commission had incorrectly interpreted the concept of a dominant position and had wrongly applied that interpretation to its case, particularly relating to the assessment and relevance of the market shares and other factors. Roche also contended that the agreements with the purchasers did not constitute an abuse.

The Commission decided that Roche was enjoying a dominant position in respect of certain groups of vitamins on the basis of Roche's market shares, which were high, by themselves and more so compared to that of its competitors, and also on account of certain other factors, which gave Roche a 'marked ascendancy on the relevant markets', even if the share of the markets were not to be the determinative criterion. The Court affirmed the finding of the Commission of the dominant position of Roche, except regarding one group of vitamins.

On the principles on which a dominant position is to be determined, the Court stated that a number of factors would show the existence of a dominant position, a highly important factor among them being the existence of a very large market share. It added that substantial market share as evidence of the existence of a dominant position was not a constant factor but varied from market to market, depending on the structure of those markets. However, in the opinion of the Court, '...very large shares are in themselves, and save in exceptional circumstances, evidence of the existence of a dominant position.'

The Court elaborated the concept further, stating:

An undertaking which has a very large market share and holds it for some time, by means of the volume of production and the scale of the supply which it stands for—without those having much smaller market shares being able to meet rapidly the demand from those who would like to break away from the undertaking which has the largest market share—is by virtue of that share in a position of strength which makes it an unavoidable trading partner and which, already because of this secures for it, at the very least during relatively long periods, that freedom of action which is the special feature of a dominant position.

The Court listed the following as the relevant factors in determining the existence of a dominant position: the relationship between the market shares of the undertaking concerned and of its competitors, especially those of the next largest; the technological lead of an undertaking over its competitors; the existence of a highly developed sales network; and the absence of potential competition.

The Court explained the abuse of a dominant position thus:

The concept of abuse is an objective concept relating to the behaviour of an undertaking in a dominant position which is such as to influence the structure of a market where, as a result of the very presence of the undertaking in question, the degree of competition is weakened and which, through recourse to methods different from those which condition normal competition in products or services on the basis of the transactions of commercial operators, has the effect of hindering the maintenance of the degree of competition still existing in the market or the growth of that competition.

The Court also upheld the Commission's decision that the exclusive purchase contracts and the fidelity rebates offered to the purchasers amounted to abuse of this dominant position because they distorted competition between producers in so far as they deprived the customers of Roche of the opportunity of choosing their suppliers and also because the effect of the contract was to apply dissimilar conditions to equivalent transactions, viz. Roche would be charging two different prices for the same quantity of the same product, depending upon whether the buyer was prepared to forego purchasing from Roche's competitors.

Collective Dominance—Sharing the Market on a Geographical Basis

Compagnie Maritime Belge Transports SA and Others v. Commission of the European Communities[11]

This case established the principle that though enterprises could be independent legal entities, a dominant position could be collectively held by them if they presented themselves to a market as a collective entity.

The members of Associated Central West Africa Lines (CEWAL) and two other shipping conferences brought this action contesting before the Court the decision of the Commission and the Court of First Instance. The Commission had decided that all the shipping conferences had violated Article 81(1) and the members of CEWAL had abused their dominant position, infringing Article 82.

They were held to have infringed Article 81(1) of the EEC Treaty by entering into non-competition agreements with one another, imposing on themselves a restraint to the effect that each member would refrain from operating as an independent shipping company (outsider) in the area of activity of the others. Their intention was to share out the liner market between northern Europe and western Africa on a geographical basis.

The abuse of their collective dominant position by the members of CEWAL, with the intention of eliminating the principal independent competitor, was alleged to be by: (i) participating in the implementation of the cooperation agreement with Ogefrem; (ii) modifying its freight rates by departing from the tariff in force in order to offer rates the same as or less than those of the principal independent competitor for vessels sailing on the same date or neighbouring dates (practice known as fighting ships); (iii) establishing 100 per cent loyalty arrangements (including goods sold fob) which went beyond the terms of Article 5(2) of Regulation (EEC) No 4056/86 of 22 December 1986.[12]

The appellants denied a collective dominant position held by the members of CEWAL and claimed that the cooperation agreement with Ogefrem, 'fighting ships' and loyalty contracts did not amount to an abuse of a dominant position.

It was argued on behalf of the appellants that for the purpose of showing that a dominant position was shared by more than one undertaking, close economic links between them had to be established and the mere fact that they consulted each other in committees would not be adequate to establish that those undertakings shared a collective dominant position. Rejecting this argument, the Court ruled:

> It follows that the expression 'one or more undertakings in Article 86 of the Treaty' implies that a dominant position may be held by two or more economic entities legally independent of each other, provided that from an economic point of view they present themselves or act together on a particular market as a collective entity. That is how the expression 'collective dominant position', as used in the remainder of this judgement, should be understood.

The Court outlined that for the purpose of analysis under Article 82, of such cases, it should be ascertained whether the undertakings constitute a collective entity vis-à-vis their competitors, their trading partners and consumers for a particular market, and if that collective entity actually holds a dominant position and whether its conduct constitutes abuse.

The Court confirmed that the cooperation agreement with Ogefrem, 'fighting ships' and loyalty contracts amounted to abuse of a dominant position.

Subsidiary's Conduct Attributed to Holding Company

Europemballage Corporation and Continental Can Company Inc. v. Commission of the European Communities[13]

Continental was already enjoying a dominant position through the control of one company, in a substantial part of the common market for certain types of containers. The Commission held that there was an abuse of that dominant position by the acquisition by Continental, through its subsidiary, Europemballage, of approximately 80 per cent of the shares and convertible debentures of Thomassen and Drijver-Verbliva N.V (TDV). The Commission held that by the acquisition, through a merger, competition in the containers mentioned was practically eliminated in a substantial part of the common market and that Article 82 was infringed. But the Commission's decision was annulled on grounds of procedure.

One of the grounds of challenge of the Commission's decision was that Continental had its registered office outside the common market and that the European Community's competition law did not apply to it. The Court overruled it as it was Continental that caused Europemballage to make the takeover bid to the shareholders of TDV and also made available the necessary means for this purpose. The transaction was to be attributed to Continental first and then to Europemballage. As the acquisition influenced market conditions within the Community, the contention of lack of competence was dismissed. The Court declared that though the subsidiary had a separate legal personality, its conduct could be attributed to the parent company, particularly where the subsidiary company did not determine its market behaviour autonomously, 'but in essentials follows directives of the parent company'.

Abusive Conduct Outside the Dominated Market

Tetra Pak International SA v. *Commission of the European Communities*[14]

The Tetra Pak group specialized in equipment for the packaging of liquid or semi-liquid food products in cartons. Its activities covered both the aseptic and the non-aseptic packaging sectors. Its business was essentially in manufacturing cartons and carton-filling machines. Tetra Pak held 90–95 per cent of the market in the aseptic sector. In the non-aseptic sector, where the structure was oligopolistic, Tetra Pak held 50–55 per cent of the market in the European Community. The complainant, Elopak, held 27 per cent, followed by another company, PKL which had approximately 11 per cent of that market.

The contracts for the sale or lease of Tetra Pak equipment for manufacturing cartons contained several clauses found to be anti-competitive. The following were some of the main clauses, though not all clauses were enforced in all member states. The buyers of Tetra Pak equipment were prohibited from changing the configuration of the equipment bought and they were also not allowed to add any part or accessory to that equipment. Tetra Pak reserved to itself the exclusive rights to inspect the equipment, maintain and repair it, and to supply spare parts. The intellectual property right in relation to any improvement made to the product by the buyer was to be assigned to Tetra Pak.

As far as the manufacture of cartons was concerned, the purchaser was required to use only Tetra Pak cartons on the machines and to obtain the supplies of cartons from Tetra Pak or a supplier designated by Tetra Pak. The sale or transfer of the equipment by the purchaser from Tetra Pak required the consent of Tetra Pak and Tetra Pak retained the right to buy the equipment itself at a pre-arranged price. The purchaser from Tetra Pak was to ensure that his buyer assumed his obligations to Tetra Pak. Any breach of this condition entailed a penalty. The contracts for the lease of Tetra Pak equipment also contained similar conditions.

The complaint by Elopak Italia before the European Commission was that Tetra Pak imposed unfair conditions on the supply of machines for filling the cartons and that the sale of the cartons, and in certain cases, the sale of the equipment, were at predatory prices. The Commission found that through its contracts Tetra Pak had partitioned the markets, discriminated in the prices of cartons and equipment between buyers in different states, and had eliminated competition in certain states.

One of the arguments of Tetra Pak before the European Court of Justice, in its appeal against the decision of the Court of the First Instance, rejecting its application for annulment of the decision of the Commission was, that conduct in a market other than the dominated market, which is not intended to reinforce the position on the dominated market, would not be covered by Article 82. The Court of First Instance had held that the practices of Tetra Pak in the non-aseptic sector were caught by Article 82, without its being shown that Tetra Pak was dominant in that sector, on account of the 'close associative links between those markets and the aseptic markets'.

That Court stated:

It follows from all the above considerations that, in the circumstances of this case, Tetra Pak's practices on the non-aseptic markets are liable to be caught by Article 86 of the Treaty without its being necessary to establish the existence of a dominant position on those markets taken in isolation, since that undertaking's leading position on the non-aseptic markets, combined with the close associative links between those markets and the aseptic markets, gave Tetra Pak freedom of conduct compared with the other economic operators on the non-aseptic markets, such as to impose on it a special responsibility under Article 86 to maintain genuine undistorted competition on those markets.

The essence of Tetra Pak's objection was that the acts alleged to constitute an abuse should either take place within a market where the enterprise was dominant, or where the abuse was committed in a market where the enterprise was not dominant, the acts of abuse should lead to strengthening of the existing dominant position and that if neither were the case, Article 82 would not apply. Tetra Pak was dominant in the aseptic sector and the abuse related to the non-aseptic sector. The Court of First Instance did not agree with this argument as Tetra Pak's leading position in the non-aseptic markets and its links with the aseptic markets made the position different.

On appeal, the European Court clarified the legal position in such cases. Stating that Article 82 gave no explicit guidance as to the requirements relating to where on the product market the abuse took place, it observed: 'In the case of distinct, but associated, markets, as in the present case, application of Article 86 to conduct found on the associated, non-dominated, market and having effects on that associated market can only be justified by special circumstances.'

The special circumstances in this case justifying the application of Article 82 to Tetra Pak's conduct in the non-aseptic sector were:

Tetra Pak held 78 per cent of the overall market in packaging in both aseptic and non-aseptic cartons, seven times more than its closest competitor; its quasi-monopolistic 90 per cent share in the aseptic markets, made Tetra Pak a favoured supplier of non-aseptic systems. The fact that the various materials involved were used for packaging the same basic liquid products showed that Tetra Pak's customers in one sector were also potential customers in the other.

The European Court concluded:

Given its almost complete domination of the aseptic markets, Tetra Pak could also count on a favoured status on the non-aseptic markets. Thanks to its position on the former markets, it could concentrate its efforts on the latter by acting independently of the other economic operators. Accordingly, the Court of First Instance was right to accept the application of Article 86 of the Treaty in this case, given that the quasi-monopoly enjoyed by Tetra Pak on the aseptic markets and its leading position on the distinct, though closely associated, non-aseptic markets placed it in a situation comparable to that of holding a dominant position on the markets in question as a whole.

Section 4(2)(e) of the Competition Act, 2002, deals with the abuse of a dominant position in one market with the object of entering into another relevant market, or to protect that other market. *Tetra Pak* was a case where an enterprise in a dominant position in one market abused that position in a related market.

Unfair Trading Conditions

NV Nederlandsche Banden Industrie Michelin v. Commission of the European Communities[15]

This was an appeal against the decision of the European Commission, which had imposed a fine on Michelin NV for abuse of its dominant position. The business of Michelin NV was production of new tyres for vans and lorries. Michelin was alleged to have abused its dominant position, in the market in new replacement tyres for lorries, buses and similar vehicles. The abuse was tying tyre dealers in the Netherlands to itself through the granting of selective discounts on an individual basis conditional upon sales 'targets' and discount percentages, which were not clearly confirmed in writing, and by applying to them dissimilar conditions in respect of equivalent transactions; and granting an extra annual bonus in 1977 on purchases of tyres for lorries, buses and the like and on purchases of car tyres, which was conditional upon attainment of a 'target' in respect of car tyre purchases.

Michelin challenged the Commission's decision on a number of grounds but the main grounds were that the Commission was wrong in its definition of the relevant market and the share of Michelin in relation to its competitors and that, therefore, a finding of a dominant position on that view was not sustainable. It denied that it had a dominant position in the market in new replacement tyres for heavy vehicles in the Netherlands. Michelin also contended that the discounts did not amount to an abuse within the meaning of Article 86 (now Article 81).

The Court agreed with the finding of the Commission that the Netherlands was the geographic market. In the opinion of the Court the requisite criteria in examining the existence of a dominant position were Michelin's share of the relevant product market, its position in relation to its competitors, customers and consumers. The Court also agreed with the Commission's ascertaining, for the purpose of establishing Michelin's dominant position, Michelin's market share, with reference to replacement tyres for lorries, buses and similar vehicles, excluding the consideration of car and van tyres, at 57 per cent to 65 per cent, as compared to that of its main competitors at 4 to 8 per cent. The Court held that that market share was a valid indication of Michelin's preponderant strength in relation to its competitors.

The Court held, disagreeing with Michelin's argument, that what was offered was only a quantity discount, that the annual variable discount to which the dealers were tied was different as it was fixed for a long reference period of a year, and a dealer who knew that if he did not achieve the target fixed for him would lose the entire discount was under a compulsion to achieve the target fixed as he had no other choice of the sources of supply. Further, when competitors were not strong enough to offer economically matching terms, Michelin dealers were bound to Michelin by the discount system that was held to be an abuse of a dominant position.

Abuse by Holder of Exclusive Right Conferred by State

General Motors Continental NV v. Commission of the European Communities[16]

The charge was a violation of Article 82 by General Motors Continental NV. The infringement was charging an excessive amount as inspection charges, relating to five motor vehicles manufactured in another member state and imported into Belgium, towards checking, for conformity with the specifications contained in the approval certificate prescribed by the Belgian authorities that General Motors Continental NV had to carry out as the sole authorized agent of the manufacturer in Belgium. The Belgian authorities did not provide any measures to fix or limit the charge imposed for the service rendered. Dealing with the first issue of whether the activity involved in issue of certificates of conformity would constitute a dominant position, the Court held that the legal monopoly granted to the manufacturer or his agent put them in a dominant position as the service of inspection in Belgium for conformity to specifications could be availed of only on the terms stipulated unilaterally by them.

The Court observed that the holder of such an exclusive right could abuse it. 'Such an abuse might lie, *inter alia*, in the imposition of a price which is excessive in relation to the economic value of the service provided, and which has the effect of curbing parallel imports by neutralizing the possibly more favourable level of prices applying in other sales areas in the community, or by leading to unfair trade in the sense of article 86(2)(a).' But as it was shown to the Court that General Motors Continental NV had refunded to the parties the excess charges over the actual economic cost of the operation, after complaints from them and before the Commission commenced its investigation, the Court held that there was no 'abuse'.

Discriminatory Pricing

Federal Trade Commission v. Morton Salt Co.[17]

Morton Salt's quantity discounts on its premium quality Blue Label and on other table salts were enjoyed by certain wholesalers and retailers who competed with other wholesalers and retailers to whom these discounts were refused. Morton also granted special allowances to certain favoured customers who competed with other customers to whom they were denied.

Morton contended that its standard quantity discounts, available to all on equal terms, as contrasted, for example, to hidden or special rebates, allowances, prices or discounts, were not discriminatory, within the meaning of the Robinson-Patman Act. The US Supreme Court observed that though theoretically, the discounts were equally available to all, functionally they were not, as the qualifying limit for eligibility to avail of these discounts was beyond the reach of several purchasers.

The Court pointed out that section 2(a) of the Clayton Act, introduced by an amendment by the Robinson-Patman Act, was intended to prevent large buyers enjoying the benefit of quantity discounts except when 'a lower price could be justified by reason of a seller's diminished costs due to quantity manufacture, delivery or sale, or by reason of the seller's good faith effort to meet a competitor's equally low price.'

Section 2(a) of the Clayton Act is the basic provision prohibiting price discrimination against purchasers of commodities of like grade and quality. The first part states:

> It shall be unlawful for any person engaged in commerce, in the course of such commerce, either directly or indirectly, to discriminate in price between different purchasers of commodities of like grade and quality, where either or any of the purchases involved in such discrimination are in commerce, where such commodities are sold for use, consumption, or resale within the United States or any Territory thereof or the District of Columbia or any insular possession or other place under the jurisdiction of the United States, and where the effect of such discrimination may be substantially to lessen competition or tend to create a monopoly in any line of commerce, or to injure, destroy, or prevent competition with any person who either grants or knowingly receives the benefit of such discrimination, or with customers of either of them ....

The Robinson-Patman amendment introduced the following proviso to section 2(a):

That nothing herein contained shall prevent differentials which make only due allowance for differences in the cost of manufacture, sale, or delivery resulting from the differing methods or quantities in which such commodities are to such purchasers sold or delivered.

But the materials before the Supreme Court did not show any facts that would bring the discounts within the first proviso. The Court held that it was established that Morton's quantity discounts were discriminatory. It also ruled that no actual injury to competition needed to be proved. It declared: 'The statute requires no more than that the effect of the prohibited price discrimination "may be substantially to lessen competition...or to injure, destroy, or prevent competition."'

Selling at a Lower Price

The defence provided under section 2(b) of the Clayton Act permitting a supplier to show justification for such differentials came up for interpretation in *Standard Oil Co.* v. *Trade Comm'n*.[18]

The Federal Trade Commission had ordered Standard Oil Co. to cease and desist from selling gasoline to four comparatively large 'jobber' customers in Detroit at a lower price than it did to many comparatively smaller service station customers in the same area.

Standard Oil's contention was that the tank-car price was made to each 'jobber' in order to retain that 'jobber' as a customer and in good faith to meet a lawful and equally low price of a competitor. But the Commission held that this did not constitute a defence in the face of affirmative proof that the effect of the discrimination was to injure, destroy and prevent competition with the retail stations operated by the said named dealers and with stations operated by their retailer-customers.

Standard Oil's defence was based on the proviso to section 2(b).

(b) Upon proof being made, at any hearing on a complaint under this section, that there has been discrimination in price or services or facilities furnished, the burden of rebutting the prima-facie case thus made by showing justification shall be upon the person charged with a violation of this section, and unless justification shall be affirmatively shown, the Commission is authorized to issue an order terminating the discrimination: Provided, however, That nothing herein contained shall prevent a seller rebutting the prima-facie case thus made by showing that his lower price or the furnishing of services or facilities to any purchaser or purchasers was made in good faith to meet an equally low price of a competitor, or the services or facilities furnished by a competitor.

The US Supreme Court did not agree with the view of the Commission and held that section 2(b) permitted a seller 'to retain a customer by realistically meeting in good faith the price offered to that customer, without necessarily changing the seller's price to its other customers.'

It may be noted that the principle of the above defence provided in section 2(b) is contained in the explanation to section 4(2)(a) of the Indian Competition Act.

Predatory Pricing

As discussed earlier in the chapter, charging a predatory price is one form of abuse of a dominant position. The explanation (b) to section 4 defines it as follows:

... 'predatory price' means the sale of goods or provision of services, at a price which is below the cost, as may be determined by regulations, of production of the goods or provision of services, with a view to reduce competition or eliminate the competitors.

The Commission has issued regulations stipulating what costs will be considered for this purpose.[19] However, to show that a predatory price is used as an abuse of a dominant position, it will have to be established that the predatory price was charged with a view to reducing competition or eliminating competitors.

Small competitors would not be able to sustain themselves for long in a market where predatory prices are charged by enterprises in a dominant position. After the elimination of effective competition, the enterprises would revert to their original or even higher prices, the burden of which will fall on consumers.

Utah Pie Co. v. Continental Baking and Others 386 US 685 (1967)[20]

Utah Pie charged the respondents with conspiracy under sections 1 and 2 of the Sherman Act and section 2(a) of the Clayton Act as amended by the Robinson-Patman Act.

Utah Pie, a small company with 18 employees, based in Salt Lake City, was in the business of selling frozen dessert pies in Utah and surrounding states. Its price was the lowest. The respondents were big companies.

Pet Milk, one of the respondents, was suffering losses. It then reduced its prices in the Salt Lake City Area and there was evidence that it wanted to injure Utah Pie. The Supreme Court found that the evidence showed that the price discrimination attributable to Pet milk rendered lessening of competition possible.

Continental Baking, another respondent, selling frozen apple pies at substantially higher prices elsewhere, started selling in the Salt Lake City at a price which was less than its direct cost plus an allocation for overheads. Utah Pie, in response, reduced its price on all its apple pies. In the view of the Court, the lower court was in error in coming to the conclusion that the prices reduced by Continental had no effect on Utah Pie, as Utah Pie's sales volume continued to climb, as that court had failed to take note of the fact that Continental's below cost price caused Utah Pie to reduce its price. The potential impact of Continental's price reduction absent any responsive price cut by Utah had not been considered and Continental could have been held to violate section 2(a).

Carnation Co.'s new pricing policy to regain business in the Salt Lake City market was selling at a price admittedly well below its costs, and well below the other prices prevailing in the market. Following this, two other major sellers in the market reduced their prices. The Court held that Carnation's conduct could have been found by a jury as with a possibility to injure competition.

Explaining the principle on which section 2(a) of the Clayton Act, as amended by the Robinson-Patman Act was based, the US Supreme Court said:

Section 2(a) does not forbid price competition which will probably injure or lessen competition by eliminating competitors, discouraging entry into the market or enhancing the market shares of the dominant sellers. But Congress has established some ground rules for the game. Sellers may not sell like goods to different purchasers at different prices if the result may be to injure competition in either the sellers' or the buyers' market unless such discriminations are justified as permitted by the Act.

The Court stated that along with cases of predatory price discriminations 'employed with the hope of immediate destruction of a particular competitor', one had to consider cases of price discrimination that eroded competition. Holding that the effect of such price discriminations by the respondents may be substantially to lessen competition or to injure competition, the Court ruled that the statutory test was one that necessarily looked forward on the basis of proven conduct in the past.

Conspiracy to Sell at Predatory Prices

Matsushita Elec. Industrial Co. and others v. *Zenith Radio Corp. and Others*[21]

The action was initiated, under sections 1 and 2 of the Sherman Act, 2(a) of the Robinson-Patman Act, and 73 of the Wilson Tariff Act, by certain American companies manufacturing and selling television sets, against a group of Japanese companies or Japanese-controlled American companies. The charge was that the Japanese companies had entered into an illegal conspiracy to drive American firms from the American consumer electronic products market by engaging in a scheme to fix and maintain artificially high prices for television sets sold by petitioners in Japan and, at the same time, to fix and maintain low prices for the sets exported to and sold in the US.

The Japanese companies denied any conspiracy, which they described as economically irrational and practically infeasible, and submitted that they had no motive to engage in the alleged predatory pricing conspiracy.

As there was no unambiguous evidence of conspiracy placed before the Court, it considered it necessary to examine the nature of the alleged conspiracy and the practical obstacles to its implementation.

The Court explained the concept thus:

A predatory pricing conspiracy is by nature speculative. Any agreement to price below the competitive level requires the conspirators to forgo profits that free competition would offer them. The forgone profits may be considered an investment in the future. For the investment to be rational, the conspirators must have a reasonable expectation of recovering, in the form of later monopoly profits, more than the losses suffered.

In the Court's opinion, while these were the limitations to a single firm in engaging in predatory pricing, the conspiracy alleged against twenty-one Japanese companies, to charge below-market prices, to stifle competition, for a number of years, was considered difficult to execute.

The Court reasoned:

The conspirators must allocate the losses to be sustained during the conspiracy's operation, and must also allocate any gains to be realized from its success. Precisely because success is speculative and depends on a willingness to endure losses for an indefinite period, each conspirator has a strong incentive to cheat, letting its partners suffer the losses necessary to destroy the competition while sharing in any gains if the conspiracy succeeds. The necessary allocation is therefore difficult to accomplish. Yet if conspirators cheat to any substantial extent, the conspiracy must fail, because its success depends on depressing the market price for all buyers of CEPs. If there are too few goods at the artificially low price to satisfy demand, the would-be victims of the conspiracy can continue to sell at the 'real' market price, and the conspirators suffer losses to little purpose.

The Court also held that predatory pricing conspiracies were generally unlikely to occur where the prospects of attaining monopoly power, necessary for recouping losses caused by below-cost prices, seemed slight, as in this case. Two American companies held the largest share of the American retail market in colour television sets.

The Court held that evidence of a conspiracy was not satisfactory and that the Court of Appeals had failed to consider the absence of a plausible motive for the Japanese companies to engage in predatory pricing.

Volume Rebates

Brooke Group Ltd v. Brown & Williamson Tobacco Corp.[22] established what one should prove in claiming loss on account of a predatory pricing system and what factors are to be considered in determining the issue.

Liggett charged that the volume rebates offered by Brown & Williamson to wholesalers amounted to price discrimination that had a reasonable possibility of injuring competition in violation of section 2(a) of the Clayton Act, as amended by the Robinson-Patman Act. The complaint was that the system of rebates was part of a predatory pricing scheme under which Brown & Williamson set prices for generic cigarettes below average variable costs, forcing Liggett to raise its list prices on its generics, restraining the growth of the economy segment. This helped preserve Brown & William's supracompetitive profits on branded cigarettes. The district court concluded that there was no evidence of coordination among the firms contending for shares of the economy segment.

The court of appeals agreed with the lower court that there was no injury to competition. It observed: 'to rely on the characteristics of an oligopoly to assure recoupment of losses from a predatory pricing scheme after one oligopolist has made a competitive move is ... economically irrational.'

Stating that the essence of a claim, whether under section 2 of the Sherman Act, or section 2(a) of the Clayton Act as amended by the Robinson-Patman Act, was the same, the US Supreme Court clarified it thus: 'a business rival has priced its products in an unfair manner with an object to eliminate or retard competition, and thereby gain and exercise control over prices in the relevant market.'

It said that the first requirement for a claimant seeking to establish competitive injury resulting from a rival's low prices was to prove that the prices complained of were below an appropriate measure of its rival's costs. The second requirement was 'a demonstration that the competitor had a reasonable prospect, or, under 2 of the Sherman Act, a dangerous probability, of recouping its investment in below-cost prices.'

The Court added:

Recoupment is the ultimate object of an unlawful predatory pricing scheme; it is the means by which a predator profits from predation. Without it, predatory pricing produces lower aggregate prices in the market, and consumer welfare is enhanced. Although unsuccessful predatory pricing may encourage some inefficient substitution toward the product being sold at less than its cost, unsuccessful predation is in general a boon to consumers.

That below-cost pricing may impose painful losses on its target is of no moment to the antitrust laws if competition is not injured: it is axiomatic that the antitrust laws were passed for 'the protection of competition, not competitors'.

As to when recoupment of losses caused by predatory prices may be expected, the Court said:

For recoupment to occur, below-cost pricing must be capable, as a threshold matter, of producing the intended effects on the firm's rivals, whether driving them from the market or, as was alleged to be the goal here, causing them to raise their prices to supracompetitive levels within a disciplined oligopoly. This requires an understanding of the extent and duration of the alleged predation, the relative financial strength of the predator and its intended victim, and their respective incentives and will.

Quoting its own judgement in *Matsushita,* the Court stated: '[i]n order to recoup their losses, (predators) must obtain enough market power to set higher than competitive prices, and then must sustain those prices long enough to earn in excess profits what they earlier gave up in below-cost prices.'

It added that determining whether recoupment of predatory losses was likely required an estimate of the cost of the alleged predation and a close analysis of both the schemes alleged by the plaintiff and the structure and conditions of the market.

The Court decided that there was no evidence to support the likelihood of an oligopolistic price coordination and sustained supracompetitive pricing in the generic segment of the national cigarette market. In the absence of these, there was no reasonable prospect of Brown & Williamson recouping its predatory losses and no injury to competition could be caused.

EC Position

In contrast, the analysis of the elements of predatory pricing is different in the European Community and the prospect of recoupment of losses is not always necessary to be shown. *Akzo* and *Tetra Pak* established that prices below average variable costs must always be considered abusive and prices below average total costs but above average variable costs are only to be considered abusive if an intention to eliminate competition can be shown.

Akzo Chemie BV v. *Commission of the European Communities*[23]

The abuse complained of against Akzo was that it pursued a conduct intended to damage the business of Engineering and Chemical Supplies (Epsom and Gloucester) Ltd (ECS), a competitor, and/or to secure its withdrawal from the EEC organic peroxides market. The Commission had decided that Akzo had abused its dominant position.

The following acts were held by the Commission to be abuse by Akzo of its dominant position: (i) Akzo had made direct threats to ECS at meetings with the aim of securing ECS's withdrawal from the market for organic peroxides for the 'plastics' application; (ii) from about December 1980 onwards, Akzo had systematically offered and supplied flour additives to Provincial Merchants, Allied Mills, and ECS's customers in the 'large independent' sector at unreasonably low prices designed to damage ECS's business viability, compelling ECS either to abandon the customer to Akzo, or to match a loss-making price in order to retain the customer; (iii) it had made quotations selectively to customers of ECS for flour additives while maintaining substantially (up to 60 per cent) higher prices to comparable buyers who were already their own regular customers; (iv) it had offered potassium bromate and a vitamin mix (the latter a product which it did not normally supply) at a bait price in a package with benzoyl peroxide to ECS's customers in order to attract their business for the full range of flour additives to the exclusion of ECS; (v) it had maintained, as part of the plan to damage ECS, the prices for flour additives in the UK at an artificially low level over a prolonged period, a situation which it could survive because of its superior financial resources in comparison with ECS; and (vi) it had pursued an exclusionary commercial policy in respect of the major customers RHM and Spillers by obtaining from those customers precise details of offers made by other suppliers of flour additives (including ECS) and then offering a price just below the lowest alternative offer in order to obtain the business, coupled (in the case of Spillers) with a requirement that the customers should agree to obtain their entire supply of flour additives from Akzo.

Akzo challenged the Commission's decisions on the grounds that the Commission's determination of organic peroxides as the relevant market was wrong; that the said market was not a single market; that the existence of the dominant position alleged was based on incorrect facts; and that it was wrongly considered that Akzo's behaviour was abusive.

ECS operated solely in the flour additives sector till 1979 and in the course of that year it decided to extend its activities to the plastics sector. Akzo's main business was in the plastics sector and its interest in the business of flour additives was small. Akzo sold at low prices flour additives, not to strengthen its position in the flour additives market but to prevent ECS from extending its activities to the plastic sector. It was in a position to set off losses that it incurred in the flour additives sector against profits from its activity in the plastics sector. The Court confirmed the Commission's determination of organic peroxides as the relevant market. In that market, Akzo's market share was 50 per cent, and as Akzo was shown as regarding itself as the world leader in the peroxides market, and also admitting that it had the most highly developed marketing organization, both commercially and technically, and wider knowledge than that of its competitors with regard to safety and toxicology, the Court also agreed that Akzo was in a dominant position in the organic peroxides market.

The Commission had held that Akzo had abusively exploited its dominant position by endeavouring to eliminate ECS from the organic peroxides market mainly by massive and prolonged price-cutting in the flour additives sector.

On the question of the abuse by price cutting, the Commission had held that Article 82 did not make costs the decisive criterion for determining whether price reductions by a dominant undertaking were abusive. It stated: 'There can be an anti-competitive object in price-cutting whether or not the aggressor sets its prices above or below its own costs, whatever the manner in which those costs are understood.'

Akzo challenged the reasoning of the Commission and contended before the Court that costs as a criterion ought to have been considered and with reference to a specific market situation. Rejecting that argument, the Court held:

Prices below average variable costs (that is to say, those which vary depending on the quantities produced) by means of which a dominant undertaking seeks to eliminate a competitor must be regarded as abusive. A dominant undertaking has no interest in applying such prices except that of eliminating competitors so as to enable it subsequently to raise its prices by taking advantage of its monopolistic position, since each sale generates a loss, namely the total amount of the fixed costs (that is to say, those which remain constant regardless of the quantities produced) and, at least, part of the variable costs relating to the unit produced. Moreover, prices below average total costs, that is to say, fixed costs plus variable costs, but above average variable costs, must be regarded as abusive if they are determined as part of a plan for eliminating a competitor. Such prices can drive from the market undertakings which are perhaps as efficient as the dominant undertaking but which, because of their smaller financial resources, are incapable of withstanding the competition waged against them.

The Court agreed that Akzo had abused its dominant position in the organic peroxides market to prevent a seller in the flour additives business from extending its activities further to the organic peroxides market.

Tetra Pak International SA v. Commission of the European Communities[24]
Tetra Pak was found charging predatory prices in the non-aseptic sector, a market in which it was not dominant. It was argued on behalf of Tetra Pak before the European Court that there was no reasonable prospect of recouping the losses caused by predatory prices, and that on that ground, a charge of predatory pricing could not be sustained.

Citing *Akzo*, the European Court ruled that there were two different methods of analysis for determining whether an undertaking had practised predatory pricing:

First, prices below average variable costs must always be considered abusive. In such a case, there is no conceivable economic purpose other than the elimination of a competitor, since each item produced and sold entails a loss for the undertaking. Secondly, prices below average total costs but above average variable costs are only to be considered abusive if an intention to eliminate can be shown.

Since the evidence showed that Tetra Pak had sold both at prices below average variable costs and between average variable costs and average total costs and had not challenged the decision of the Court of the

First Instance that, in the latter case, Tetra Pak intended to eliminate a competitor, the Court held: 'It would not be appropriate, in the circumstances of the present case, to require in addition proof that Tetra Pak had a realistic chance of recouping its losses. It must be possible to penalize predatory pricing whenever there is a risk that competitors will be eliminated.' It stated that the Court of the First Instance had found that there was such a risk in this case and that the aim of maintaining undistorted competition, ruled out waiting until such a strategy led to the actual elimination of competitors.

Predatory Pricing—Internet Access Services

Wanadoo Interactive[25]

The European Commission found that, up to October 2002, the retail prices charged by Wanadoo Interactive, a subsidiary of France Télécom, were below cost and had abused its dominant position by predatory pricing in ADSL-based Internet access services for the general public. This practice restricted market entry and development potential for competitors, to the detriment of consumers, on a market essential for the development of the information society. In view of the gravity of the abuse and the length of the period over which it was committed, the Commission imposed a fine of 1035 million Euros.

Legitimate Competition

The explanation to section 4(2) exempts any practice that may fall under that sub-section as long as it is a practice 'adopted to meet competition'. This means that discriminatory prices, including predatory price, unfair trading conditions, etc., that are necessary to be adopted as a commercial necessity will not be considered to be 'abuse of dominance' when they are 'adopted to meet competition'.

Actually, this explanation is a defence that may be urged by one charged with having abused a dominant position under section 4(2)(a). It should be noted that it is not available in the case of allegations of practices set out in section 4(2)(b) to (e).

The principle of this defence is set out in section 2(b) of the Clayton Act, referred to in *Standard Oil Co.* v. *Trade Comm'n*:

... That nothing herein contained shall prevent a seller rebutting the prima-facie case thus made by showing that his lower price or the furnishing of services or facilities to any purchaser or purchasers was made in good faith to meet an equally low price of a competitor, or the services or facilities furnished by a competitor.

The US Supreme Court pointed out that as a matter of business survival it may be essential for a seller to meet a 'temptingly lower price' offered by one of his competitors rather than lose the customer, particularly if the customer was a major buyer, when the loss would entail a much higher unit cost and higher sales price for other customers. The Court stated:

> There is nothing to show a congressional purpose, in such a situation, to compel the seller to choose only between ruinously cutting its prices to all its customers to match the price offered to one, or refusing to meet the competition and then ruinously raising its prices to its remaining customers to cover increased unit costs. There is, on the other hand, plain language and established practice which permits a seller, through 2(b), to retain a customer by realistically meeting in good faith the price offered to that customer, without necessarily changing the seller's price to its other customers.

Restriction of Territory of Sale, Persons, etc.[26]

White Motor Co. v. United States[27]

White Motor Co., a manufacturer of trucks (they also sold parts) imposed on its distributors and dealers, conditions restricting them to sell only within specified geographical territories. As to persons to whom they may sell, the condition was that they were not to sell such trucks except to individuals, firms, or corporations having a place of business and/or purchasing headquarters in the said territory. The distributor was also prohibited from selling trucks to any federal or state government, or any department or political subdivision thereof, unless specifically permitted by the company. Those practices were charged as violations of sections 1 and 3 of the Sherman Act.

The company argued before the district court that in competing with large enterprises, the only feasible method, in that business, was the distributor or dealer system and for that system to be effective against existing competition, it was necessary that the distributor or dealer should make vigorous and intensive efforts in a restricted territory. The object of the territory restriction was to protect him from other distributors or dealers of the company. It was stated that distributors and dealers were to concentrate on trying to take sales away from competing truck manufacturers rather than from each other.

The customer clause was defended on the ground that it was necessary protection in its competition with other truck manufacturers for sales to certain classes as 'National Accounts', 'Fleet Accounts' and federal and state governments and departments and political subdivisions thereof.

The district court granted summary judgement for the government. On appeal to the US Supreme Court it reversed that judgement ruling that the legality of the territorial and customer limitations of White Motor Co. should be determined only after a trial. The US Supreme Court said: 'This is the first case involving a territorial restriction in a vertical arrangement; and this Court knows too little of the actual impact of that restriction and the one respecting customers to reach a conclusion on the bare bones of the documentary evidence before us'.

Sarabhai Chemicals P. Ltd and Another, in re,[28] discussed in the chapter on Anti-competitive Agreements was a case involving contractual terms limiting production, technical development, etc.

Entry Barriers

United Brands Company and United Brands Continentaal BV v. Commission of the European Communities[29]

The abuse charged in this case was that the appellants, dealing in bananas, required their distributors/ripeners in certain areas of the Economic Union to refrain from reselling their bananas while still green. They charged, in respect of Chiquita bananas, dissimilar prices for equivalent transactions; imposed unfair prices on the sale of Chiquita bananas in certain areas and on certain customers, excluding a particular group from such pricing; refusing to supply Chiquita bananas to a customer in Denmark.

In the appeal against the order of the Commission, the appellants contended that (a) the Commission's analysis of the relevant market, the product market and the geographic market was wrong; and (b) they were not in a dominant position in the relevant market. It also contended that the clause relating to the conditions of sale of green bananas was justified by the need to safeguard the quality of the product sold to the consumer; that the refusal to supply to a dealer was justified; and that they had not charged unfair or discriminatory prices.

In determining the product market, the question was whether bananas were an integral part of the fresh fruit market, consisting of apples, oranges, grapes, peaches, strawberries, etc., or if the relevant market was only bananas—branded and unlabelled.

The Court held that the banana market was a market sufficiently distinct from the other fresh fruit markets. It came to this conclusion, on the material showing, that those having a constant need for bananas were not 'enticed' by the arrival of a fresh fruit into the market. In other words, there was no interchangeability, from the buyer's position, between bananas and fresh fruit.

The Court found that the appellants were vertically integrated to a high degree and that their share of the relevant market was always more than 40 per cent and nearly 45 per cent.

The Court held that considering the standing of the appellants' products in the market and the significant barriers to entry, they had a dominant position in the relevant market.

On the barriers to entry the Court observed:

The particular barriers to competitors entering the market are the exceptionally large capital investments required for the creation and running of banana plantations, the need to increase sources of supply in order to avoid the effects of fruit diseases and bad weather (hurricanes, floods), the introduction of an essential system of logistics which the distribution of a very perishable product makes necessary, economies of scale from which newcomers to the market cannot derive any immediate benefit and the actual cost of entry made up inter alia of all the general expenses incurred in penetrating the market such as the setting up of an adequate commercial network, the mounting of very large-scale advertising campaigns, all those financial risks, the costs of which are irrecoverable if the attempt fails.

The argument of the appellants in defence of the clause prohibiting the sale of the bananas while they were still green was that the bananas were to be left with experienced ripeners, who had the equipment and the technical knowledge who would release the bananas to the market when their quality was 'at its peak'.

But the Court ruled that that clause forbidding the sale of green bananas infringed Article 82 of the Treaty, as those who were not willing to accept the condition would be denied supply of the product, and consequently competition was restricted.

Refusal to Supply

United Brands also decided the question of refusal to supply goods on the ground that the dealer had participated in an advertising campaign for Dole bananas, a product of one of the competitors of *United Brands*. The Court held:

Such a course of conduct amounts therefore to a serious interference with the independence of small and medium sized firms in their commercial relations with the undertaking in a dominant position and this independence implies the right to give preference to competitors' goods.

In this case the adoption of such a course of conduct is designed to have a serious adverse effect on competition on the relevant banana market by only allowing firms dependant upon the dominant undertaking to stay in business.

Discontinuing Sale of Raw Material

Istituto Chemioterapico Italiano S.p.A. et Commercial Solvents Corporation v. Commission of the European Communities[30]

The case arose out of the expression of the inability of Istituto to continue to supply aminobutanol to a company called 'Zoja', a raw material for the manufacture of ethambutol, which it had been supplying for some years. Istituto was a reseller of aminobutanol and nitropropane produced by the Commercial Solvents Corporation (CSC) in the US. In 1970, CSC decided that it would no longer supply to the EEC these products and informed Istituto that it would no longer supply them, and that only quantities committed for resale would be supplied. The CSC controlled Istituto. It held 51 per cent of the voting stock in Istituto and had 50 per cent representation on the executive committee and on the board of directors of Istituto. After the change of the policy, CSC supplied Istituto exclusively with dextro-aminobutanol for processing into bulk ethambutol. The Commission found that CSC and Istituto had violated Article 82.

The Court found that CSC's dominant position on the world market in the production and sale of the raw material in question was established. Some of the arguments raised by CSC before the Court were: that the change of policy relating to the supply of the raw material was on its recognizing the advantages of making finished products; the Commission was wrong in determining that ethambutol, a derivative from the raw material aminobutanol was the relevant market, as ethambutol did not have a separate market but was only a part of a larger market in anti-tuberculosis drugs, and for that reason a separate market in the raw material for the manufacture of this product could not be established; CSC and Istituto were two separate legal entities and one could not be held responsible for the acts of another; that it was registered in the United States as a company and did not commit any act in the EEC and that Istituto was not dominant in the manufacture of the product.

The Court rejected all these arguments.

The documents showed that CSC's policy was really actuated by its intention to 'facilitate its own access to the markets for the derivatives from the raw material'.

The Court held that an abuse of a dominant position in the market in raw materials may have effects restricting competition in the market in which the derivatives of the raw material were sold and these effects must be taken into account in considering the effects of an infringement, even if the market for the derivative did not constitute a self-contained market. It ruled that an undertaking which had a dominant position in the market in raw materials and which, with the object of reserving such raw material for manufacturing its own derivatives, refused to supply a customer, which was itself a manufacturer of these derivatives, and therefore, risked eliminating all competition on the part of this customer, abused its dominant position within the meaning of Article 82. In as much as Istituto was a subsidiary of CSC and acted in unison with CSC in dealing with Zoja, the Court held that the two companies acted as a single economic unit.

Refusal to Licence Copyright Material

Radio Telefis Eireann (RTE) and Independent Television Publications Ltd (ITP) v. Commission of the European Communities[31]

This case dealt with the question whether prevention by television companies of third parties from reproducing television programmes contained in the television guides published by the television companies on the ground of copyright privilege amounted to abuse of a dominant position.

Radio Telefis Eireann and ITV were television stations. At that time there was no comprehensive weekly television guide covering Ireland or Northern Ireland. Each published a television guide covering exclusively its own programmes and claimed, under Irish and United Kingdom legislation, copyright protection for the weekly programme listings in order to prevent their reproduction by third parties. RTE itself published its own weekly television guide, while ITV did so through ITP, a company established for that purpose. ITP, RTE, and BBC used to provide programme listings to daily and periodical newspapers, on request, free of charge, but subject to certain conditions, as a licence. When Magill TV Guide Ltd attempted to publish a weekly television guide, it was restrained through an injunction by RTE, ITP, and BBC. On a complaint by Magill that refusal by the appellants and BBC to grant licences for the publication of their respective weekly listings was an abuse of a dominant position, the Commission determined that there was a breach of Article 82.

The Commission ordered the three organizations to put an end to that breach, in particular, 'by supplying...third parties on request and on a non-discriminatory basis with their individual advance weekly programme listings and by permitting reproduction of those listings by such parties'. It also ordered that, if the three organizations chose to grant reproduction licences, any royalties requested should be reasonable.

The Court of First Instance also found that there was abuse of dominance. It held:

ITP enjoyed, as a consequence of its copyright in ITV and Channel 4 programme listings, which had been transferred to it by the television companies broadcasting on those channels, the exclusive right to reproduce and market those listings. It was thus able, at the material time, to secure a monopoly over the publication of its weekly listings in the TV Times, a magazine specializing in the programmes of ITV and Channel 4.

It held that ITP held a dominant position both in the market represented by its weekly listings and in the market for the magazines in which they were published in Ireland and Northern Ireland, and was in a position 'to hinder the emergence of any effective competition in the market for information on its weekly programmes'. With regard to RTE also, it reached the same conclusion. On the question of abuse of dominance, the Court of First Instance held that while the exercise of the exclusive right to reproduce a protected work, subject of copyright, was not in itself an abuse, the position was different when, in a specific case, it was apparent that that right was being exercised in such ways and circumstances as in fact to pursue an aim manifestly contrary to the objectives of Article 82. In the view of that Court, the appellants were using their copyright in the programme listings produced as part of the activity of broadcasting in order to secure a monopoly in the derivative market of weekly television guides in Ireland and Northern Ireland as, by reserving the exclusive right to publish their weekly television programme listings, they were preventing the emergence in the market of a new product, namely a general television magazine likely to compete with their own magazines.

On appeal to the European Court of Justice, one of the challenges to the decision was on the ground that the interpretation of the Court of First

Instance overlooked the exclusive right granted to a copyright owner to reproduce the subject of the right. It was also argued that dominance could not be determined on mere ownership of a copyright, without reference to any analysis whatever of economic power in the marketplace. The Court held that though mere ownership of an intellectual property right cannot constitute dominance, RTE, ITP, and the BBC held a monopoly over the information necessary to compile programme listings, such as the basic information as to the channel, day, time, and title of programmes which are produced through programming by television stations and that constituted dominance. Confirming that abuse of a dominant position had been established, the Court stated: 'The appellants' refusal to provide basic information by relying on national copyright provisions thus prevented the appearance of a new product, a comprehensive weekly guide to television programmes, which the appellants did not offer and for which there was a potential consumer demand.'

THE PROCESS OF DEALING WITH ABUSE OF A DOMINANT POSITION

Section 19(1) of the Competition Act, 2002 provides that the Competition Commission may either on its own motion or on the receipt of information, accompanied by such fee as may be determined by regulations, from any person, consumer or their association or trade association or a reference made to it by the central government or a state government or a statutory authority, inquire into any alleged contravention of the provisions contained in sub-section (1) of section 3 or sub-section (1) of section 4. The powers of the Commission while inquiring into a case of abuse of a dominant position and the factors that are to be taken into consideration, as set out in section 19(4) to (7) have been referred to earlier.

Orders that the Commission may Pass

In the case of abuse of a dominant position the orders that the Commission may pass are set out in sections 27 and 28. Section 27, a common provision covering anti-competitive agreements and abuse of dominance, sets out the orders that the Commission may pass on finding that an enterprise has contravened section 3 or section 4. *Sections 27 and 28 were amended in 2007.*

Section 27[32]

We may consider the amended section 27 and in respect of abuse of a dominant position. The Commission may: (i) direct any enterprise or association of enterprises or person or association of persons, as the case may be, involved in such abuse of dominant position, to discontinue such abuse of dominant position, as the case may be; (ii) impose such penalty, as it may deem fit which shall be not more than ten per cent of the average of the turnover for the last three preceding financial years, upon each of such person or enterprises which are parties to such or abuse; (iii) direct the enterprises concerned to abide by such other orders as the Commission may pass and comply with the directions, including payment of costs, if any; (iv) pass such other order or issue such directions as it may deem fit; and (v) if the Commission finds any member of a group is responsible for, or has contributed to, such a contravention, then it may pass orders, under this section, against such members of the group.

The significant amendments to section 27 are that the penalty that may be ordered has been increased and the provision which empowered the Commission to award compensation has been omitted.

Discontinuance of Abuse/Penalties

Restraint of acts constituting an abuse of a dominant position is one method of eliminating interference with the normal competitive process but is not always truly effective. Monetary penalties are more effective. Much of the success of the European Community's enforcement of its antitrust legislation is due to the heavy fines imposed on errant undertakings. What the Act has prescribed, viz. 10 per cent of the average turnover for the last three preceding years on each of the parties is a sufficiently deterrent penalty.

Compensation

Since the Commission is only a market regulator and has no adjudicatory powers, the power to award compensation under section 34 to any person, for loss or damage suffered by him as a result of any contravention of the provisions of Chapter II by any enterprise, was omitted by the 2007 amendment. Therefore, the clause in section 27 empowering the Commission to award compensation under section 34 of the Act has, as a consequence, been omitted by the 2007 amendment.

Division of the Enterprise

Under section 28 as it originally stood, the Commission could only recommend to the Central Government that a dominant enterprise may be ordered to be divided. The 2007 amendment to section 28 authorizes the Commission itself to direct division of an enterprise enjoying dominant position to ensure that it does not abuse its dominant position.

Interim Orders—Section 33[33]

Under section 33 as it originally stood, the Commission was empowered to issue a temporary injunction where it found that an enterprise was contravening any of sections 3, 4 (abuse of dominant position), or 6, till the conclusion of the inquiry. Since issue of an injunction is only appropriate in the case of courts, section 33 has been amended to the effect that in such a case, the Commission may, by order, temporarily restrain any party from carrying on such act until the conclusion of such inquiry or until further order, without giving notice to such party, where it deems it necessary.

Endnotes

[1] Section 19(4): The Commission shall, while inquiring whether an enterprise enjoys a dominant position or not under section 4, have due regard to all or any of the following factors, namely—(a) market share of the enterprise; (b) size and resources of the enterprise; (c) size and importance of the competitors; (d) economic power of the enterprise including commercial advantages over competitors; (e) vertical integration of the enterprises or sale or service network of such enterprises; (f) dependence of consumers on the enterprise; (g) monopoly or dominant position whether acquired as a result of any statute or by virtue of being a government company or a public sector undertaking or otherwise; (h) entry barriers including barriers such as regulatory barriers, financial risk, high capital cost of entry, marketing entry barriers, technical entry barriers, economies of scale, high cost of substitutable goods or service for consumers; (i) countervailing buying power; (j) market structure and size of market; (k) social obligations and social costs; (l) relative advantage, by way of the contribution to the economic development, by the enterprise enjoying a dominant position having or likely to have an appreciable adverse effect on competition; (m) any other factor which the Commission may consider relevant for the inquiry.

[2] Section 19(4)–(7).

[3] Section 4. (1) No enterprise or group shall abuse its dominant position.

(2) There shall be an abuse of dominant position 4 [under sub-section (1)], if an enterprise or a group—

(a) directly or indirectly, imposes unfair or discriminatory—
(i) condition in purchase or sale of goods or service; or
(ii) price in purchase or sale (including predatory price) of goods or service.

Explanation: For the purposes of this clause, the unfair or discriminatory condition in purchase or sale of goods or service referred to in sub-clause (i) and unfair or discriminatory price in purchase or sale of goods (including predatory price) or service referred to in sub-clause (ii) shall not include such discriminatory condition or price which may be adopted to meet the competition; or

(b) limits or restricts—
(i) production of goods or provision of services or market therefore; or
(ii) technical or scientific development relating to goods or services to the prejudice of consumers; or

(c) indulges in practice or practices resulting in denial of market access in any manner; or

(d) makes conclusion of contracts subject to acceptance by other parties of supplementary obligations which, by their nature or according to commercial usage, have no connection with the subject of such contracts; or

(e) uses its dominant position in one relevant market to enter into, or protect, other relevant market.

Explanation: For the purposes of this section, the expression—

(a) "dominant position" means a position of strength, enjoyed by an enterprise, in the relevant market, in India, which enables it to—
(i) operate independently of competitive forces prevailing in the relevant market; or
(ii) affect its competitors or consumers or the relevant market in its favour.

(b) "predatory price" means the sale of goods or provision of services, at a price which is below the cost, as may be determined by regulations, of production of the goods or provision of services, with a view to reduce competition or eliminate the competitors.

(c) "group" shall have the same meaning as assigned to it in clause (b) of the Explanation to section 5.

[4] Paragraph 4.12 'Article 82 and the Chapter II prohibition—Draft competition law guideline for consultation' OFT402, April 2004.

[5] Paragraph 4.13 'Article 82 and the Chapter II prohibition—Draft competition law guideline for consultation' OFT402, April 2004.

[6] The amended sections 27 and 28 are discussed in the chapter on Enforcement.

[7] Paragraph 2.7 'Article 82 and the Chapter II prohibition—Draft competition law guideline for consultation' OFT402, April 2004.

[8] For comparison reference may be made to the *Commission Notice on the definition of the relevant market for the purposes of community competition law*. (Published in the Official Journal: OJC 372 on 9/12/1997); also referred to in the chapter on Combination.

[9] See note 3.

[10] Case 85/76.

[11] In joined cases C-395/96 P and C-396/96 P, Judgement of the European Court (Fifth Chamber) 16 March 2000.

[12] A Regulation laying down detailed rules for the application of Articles 81 and 82 of the Treaty to maritime transport.

[13] Case 6–72, Judgement of the Court of 21 February 1973; this case, covering a merger, was brought under Article 86 (now Article 82), in 1973, before the Regulation 4064/89 the exclusive instrument for regulating concentrations entered into force on 21 September 1990.

[14] Case C-333/94 P, Judgement of the Court (Fifth Chamber) of 14 November 1996.

[15] Judgement of the Court of 9 November 1983 Case 322/81.

[16] Case 26–75, Judgement of the Court of 13 November 1975.

[17] 334 US 37 (1948).

[18] 340 US 231 (1951).

[19] The Competition Commission of India has issued the (Determination of Cost of Production) Regulations, 2007 (No. 6 of 2009) dated 20 August 2009.

[20] 386 US 685 (1967).

[21] 475 US 574 (1986).

[22] 509 US 209 (1993).

[23] Case C-62/86 Judgement of the Court (Fifth Chamber) of 3 July 1991.

[24] Case C-333/94 P Judgement of the Court (Fifth Chamber) of 14 November 1996.

[25] Extract from European Commission Press release: IP/03/1025, Brussels, 16 July 2003.

[26] *Standard Oil Co. of New Jersey* v. *US* 221 US 1 (1910) and *Timken Co.* v. *United States* 341 US 593 (1959) cases of division of territory, and *Standard Oil Co. of California* v. *United States* 337 US 293 (1949) and *Tampa Electric Co.* v. *Nashville Co.* 365 US 320 (1961) relating to exclusive agreements have been dealt with in the chapter on 'Anti-competitive Agreements'.

[27] 372 US 253 (1963).

[28] (1979) 49 Company Cases 145 MRTP Commission.

[29] Case 27/76, Judgement of the Court of 14 February 1978.

[30] Joined cases 6 and 7/73 R.

[31] Joined cases C-241/91 P and C-242/91 P, Judgement of the Court of 6 April 1995.

[32] Section 27. Where after inquiry the Commission finds that any agreement referred to in section 3 or action of an enterprise in a dominant position, is in contravention of section 3 or section 4, as the case may be, it may pass all or any of the following orders, namely:

(a) direct any enterprise or association of enterprises or person or association of persons, as the case may be, involved in such agreement, or abuse of dominant position, to discontinue and not to re-enter such agreement or discontinue such abuse of dominant position, as the case may be; (b) impose such penalty, as it may deem fit which shall be not more than ten per cent of the average of the turnover for the last three preceding financial years, upon each of such person or enterprises which are parties to such agreements or abuse: [Provided that in case any agreement referred to in section 3 has been entered into by a cartel, the Commission may impose upon each producer, seller, distributor, trader or service provider included in that cartel, a penalty of up to three times of its profit for each year of the continuance of such agreement or ten per cent of its turnover for each year of the continuance of such agreement, whichever is higher.] (d) direct that the agreements shall stand modified to the extent and in the manner as may be specified in the order by the Commission; (e) direct the enterprises concerned to abide by such other orders as the Commission may pass and comply with the directions, including payment of costs, if any; and (g) pass such other 45[order or issue such directions] as it may deem fit. [Provided that while passing orders under this section, if the Commission comes to a finding, that an enterprise in contravention to section 3 or section 4 of the Act is a member of a group as defined in clause (b) of the Explanation to section 5 of the Act, and other members of such a group are also responsible for, or have contributed to, such a contravention, then it may pass orders, under this section, against such members of the group.]

[33] Section 33. Where during an inquiry, the Commission is satisfied that an act in contravention of sub-section (1) of section 3 or sub-section (1) of section 4 or section 6 has been committed and continues to be committed or that such act is about to be committed, the Commission may, by order, temporarily restrain any party from carrying on such act until the conclusion of such inquiry or until further orders, without giving notice to such party, where it deems it necessary.

4

Combination

For the purposes of evaluating the effect or possible effect of a transaction between enterprises on competition, or to be more specific, the ability of an enterprise to compete, it is necessary to ascertain the degree of autonomy it has. In a merger, the legal effect of which is that the merging company will lose its corporate status as a company and will be owned by the company with which it has merged, the merging company's autonomy is lost in its entirety to the merged company. Where the control of an enterprise is acquired through other modes, such as purchase of securities, assets, or contract, the loss of autonomy of the other company need not be total or as perceptible. Yet, the acquiring company would be in a position to decide what the other company should do, even though that enterprise continues to be a separate legal entity. Through an appropriate mode and level of acquisition, it is possible to restrict or eliminate competition. The objective of any competition law is to ensure that persons or enterprises obtaining this autonomy through merger or acquisition do not impair the structure of competition. The Act uses a composite expression—combination—to cover these modes, viz. merger, acquisition of shares, assets, acquiring control of an enterprise. The term 'amalgamation' is used in the Companies Act, 1956, but the words 'merger' and 'amalgamation' are interchangeable, and in this book, the word 'merger' will be used.

The provisions of the Companies Act, 1956, relating to mergers do not provide for specific examination of the effect on competition of such arrangements.

The MRTP Act

Section 23 of the MRTP Act, 1969, under Chapter III dealing with 'Concentration of Economic Power' provided for regulating mergers by undertakings falling under Chapter III of that Act, or mergers that would lead to the creation of a Chapter III undertaking. What was necessary to be examined, by the central government in considering a proposal for merger under that section was, whether the merger would lead to a concentration of economic power. That section also provided for the regulating takeover of an undertaking by an undertaking to which Chapter III applied. Chapter IIIA contained sections 30A to 30G, regarding the acquisition of and transfer of shares above the prescribed threshold levels by individuals, bodies corporate that formed a group, or were under the same management. The central government's previous approval was necessary for the acquisition or transfer of shares by the entities covered by this chapter. The entire Chapter III and all the parts thereof were omitted in 1991, with the result that mergers and acquisitions of shares became subject only to the applicable provisions of the Companies Act, 1956.

ACQUISITION OF SHARES

The Companies Act, 1956

In the same year, by an amendment to the Companies Act, 1956, sections 108A to 108H dealing with restriction on acquisition, transfer of shares, as set out in sections 108A to 108C, were introduced. The Central Government's approval was necessary for the acquisition of shares that would lead to an increase in the shareholding beyond the prescribed percentage and for the transfer of shares by bodies corporate holding a specified percentage of shares. By virtue of section 108G, the relevant sections would apply when either of the parties to the acquisition or transfer of shares was a dominant undertaking, within the meaning of the MRTP Act.[1] It is needless to add that none of these provisions deal with the effect on competition of acquisition or transfer of shares.

The Securities and Exchange Board of India (SEBI)

The SEBI (Substantial Acquisition of Shares and Takeovers) Regulations, 1997, as amended up to 3 January 2005, do not require any examination of a proposal for acquisition or takeover covered by those regulations for the effect of the proposal on competition in the business of the enterprises involved in the transaction. The objective of that legislation is only to ensure that the acquisition of shares or voting rights in or control of a target company is done in an open manner, equitable to the shareholders and the public investors. Regulations 10, 11, and 12, the key provisions, impose an obligation on those who may acquire shares, voting rights, control of a target company, in the manner and to the extent set out therein, to make a public announcement to acquire shares in accordance with the Regulations. Any violation of these requirements would invite penalties. The Supreme Court of India has interpreted the scope and ambit of Regulations 10, 11, and 12 in *Swedish Match and Another* v. *Securities Exchange Board of India and Another*,[2] where Wimco Ltd was a target company.

By virtue of Regulation 3(1)(j) of the SEBI (Substantial Acquisition of Shares And Takeovers) Regulations, 1997, as amended up to 3 January 2005, Regulations 10, 11, and 12 relating to the acquisition of 15 per cent or more of the voting rights of any company, consolidation of holdings and acquisition of control over a company respectively, will not apply to the acquisition of shares pursuant to a scheme framed under Section 18 of the Sick Industrial Companies (Special Provisions) Act, 1985, or of an arrangement or reconstruction including amalgamation or merger or demerger under any law or regulation, Indian or foreign.

Regulation 3(1)(k) provides that the SEBI Regulations above would also not apply to the acquisition of shares in companies whose shares are not listed on any stock exchange. However, this exemption will not be available if by virtue of acquisition or change of control of any unlisted company, whether in India or abroad, the acquirer acquires shares or voting rights or control over a listed company.

MERGERS—THE COMPANIES ACT, 1956

The legislative provisions governing mergers of companies are contained in sections 390 to 396A of the Companies Act, 1956. Sections 23 and 24 of the MRTP Act, 1969 dealing with mergers and takeovers of companies governed by that Act were omitted by an amendment of that Act in 1991. The Competition Act, 2002, has repealed the MRTP Act in its entirety.

Section 5(c) of the Competition Act describes the mode in which a combination may be brought about through a merger or an amalgamation, the implications of which shall be considered later. Section 5 while defining the three modes in which a combination may result, refers to 'enterprise', a wider term that would include entities such as companies and other entities also. Under the Companies Act, 1956 a scheme of merger, or amalgamation as it is referred to in the Act, is an 'arrangement' between a company and, usually, its members (there could also be an arrangement between a company and its creditors) by which the assets and liabilities of one company (the transferor) are transferred to the other company (the transferee) and if the scheme is approved by the prescribed majority of the members of both companies, the court may sanction the scheme of merger. Then, the transferor company, the assets and liabilities of which are transferred, by virtue of the order of the court, to the transferee company, will be dissolved, without being wound up, thereby losing its corporate status and becoming a unit of the transferee company.

Why a Merger?

A merger is sought to be effected for a variety of reasons: it is an inexpensive way of entering into a new activity or a new market; it gives the opportunity to use the spare capacity in the acquiring company with the assets of the other company; where the companies are under the control of the same group, a merger may be seen as a means of effecting economies in making a company just a unit of another company. A merger may also help rationalization of operations or advance synergies in management; and provide a means for tax saving in that the losses of the transferor company may be set off against the profits of the remaining company. Another advantage of a merger would be saving in stamp duty on the sale of large assets by one company to another. However, many state governments are in the process of amending their law relating to stamp duty by levying stamp charges on even mergers approved by courts, treating them as agreements under which property is transferred.[3]

The Companies Act uses the expression 'arrangement' which would include a merger. That Act does not prescribe what mergers would be approved and what would not be approved. The 'arrangement' could be of any kind: a reverse merger, where a financially strong company merges with a financially weak or actually a sick company; a holding company may merge with its subsidiary; a demerger, which occurs when a unit of a company is hived off to another company, which may be in existence or formed for this purpose; the merging companies need not have the same or identical business activities. The merger may have tax avoidance as its objective but not tax evasion.

The Courts' Approach

So far, the courts in approving mergers, under section 394 of the Companies Act, have emphasized their role only as supervisory and have consistently resisted attempts of litigants to invite the courts to consider the commercial merits of such schemes. Except where unfairness is pleaded and proved, the courts, in considering mergers, have confined themselves to examining their conformity to statutory requirements relating to the process of obtaining the approval of the members of the company, and the court, for the scheme. Before passing an order of dissolution of the transferor company, the court should have before it a report from the official liquidator, based on his scrutiny of the books and papers of the company, that the affairs of that company have not been conducted in a manner prejudicial to the interests of its members or to public interest. The Companies Act as it stands does not deal with issues of the effect on competition of the merger. A merger of two or more companies, whether they are covered by the Competition Act or not, will still have to be approved by the high court, as required under the Companies Act. The evaluation of the effect of a proposed merger on competition is an additional process that companies falling under the definition of section 5 of the Competition Act will have to go through.

Even sections 23 and 24 of the MRTP Act, now omitted, only required that what was necessary to be examined was that the proposed scheme of merger or takeover was not likely to lead to the concentration of economic power to the common detriment, or was not likely to be prejudicial to the public interest in any other manner. The power to approve a merger under section 23 of the MRTP Act rested with the central government. Under that Act also, the effect of a merger or takeover on competition did not have to be examined in approving the proposal.

Nor have the courts been willing to expand the scope for their interference with either the principle of a scheme submitted by the company or any of the components of a scheme by extending the content of the term 'public interest' in the second proviso to section 394(1) beyond the intended meaning of the words as applied to the facts of a case. That proviso is as follows: 'Provided that no order for the dissolution of any transferor company under clause (iv) shall be made by the (Tribunal) unless the Official Liquidator has, on scrutiny of the books and papers of the company, makes a report to the (Tribunal) that the affairs of the company have not been conducted in a manner prejudicial to the interests of its members or public interest.' In the first place, it is only the affairs of the transferor company that may be examined as to whether they have been in any way conducted against public interest. Again, the term public interest is not defined. In any case, issues of restraint on competition in a merger were never to be considered under section 394 and, still less whether 'public interest' referred to above, could be urged as a ground for a court to review the merits of a scheme, on the ground of its restraining competition. The question was raised before the Supreme Court of India in *Hindustan Lever Employees Union* v. *Hindustan Lever Ltd and Others*.[4]

The facts of this case were that the scheme provided that Tata Oil Mills Co. Ltd (TOMCO) would merge with Hindustan Lever Ltd (HLL), which was a subsidiary of Unilever, a multinational company based in London. The merger was approved by a substantial majority of the members of both companies, the creditors, financial institutions and others. The high court sanctioned the scheme, overruling the objections of some shareholders of TOMCO, the employees unions of the two companies and two consumer protection organizations. The appeals against the order sanctioning the scheme were also dismissed. Then the objections were taken through an appeal to the Supreme Court of India.

There were a number of objections to the scheme. They related to the exchange ratio of the shares, the price at which the shares were offered to Unilever, and on a preferential basis to ensure that the level of Unilever's holding in HLL remained the same after the merger, the position of the employees of TOMCO, and such matters but which are not relevant for the present study of this case. A specific objection was that, after the merger, TOMCO, one of the two major competing companies, HLL being the other, would cease to be an independent company and that it would eliminate competition in the market for soap and detergent, resulting in a virtual monopoly in favour of HLL, which could lead to the deterioration of quality and an increase in the prices of these products, and that on that ground the scheme would work against public interest.

The Supreme Court of India stated that considerations of public interest were very material in a case such as the one before it, where a merger of two companies, one of which was a subsidiary of a foreign company, had to be approved by the court. It observed: 'It is not the interest of the shareholders or the employees only but the interest of the society which may have to be examined. And a scheme valid and good may yet be bad if it is against public interest.' In the opinion of the Supreme Court, the said violations of public interest had 'to be examined in the prevailing atmosphere which opted for liberalization of the government's policies to promote economic growth of the country.' The Court pointed out that after the amendments to the MRTP Act, by which, sections 20 to 26 (which included the power of the central government, under section 23, to approve mergers of undertakings falling under Chapter III of that Act were omitted, and the amendments to the Foreign Exchange Regulation Act, 1973, increasing the level up to which non-residents could hold shares in any Indian company, it could not be said that the scheme of merger was against any legislative provision or policy of the government. The Court stated further that if after the merger, the merged company, viz. HLL, was shown as engaging in any activity falling under the definition of a monopolistic trade practice or a restrictive trade practice, the issue could be taken up before the MRTP Commission and, if necessary, a division of that undertaking could also be applied for under the MRTP Act.

TOMCO's losses were estimated to be around Rs 160 million. The Supreme Court noted that there was a sharp decline in the business of TOMCO and it was possible that it would become a sick company unless something was done to improve its performance. Considering TOMCO's position, the Supreme Court stated that it was in public interest that 'TOMCO with its 60,000 shareholders and also a very large work force does not deteriorate into a sick company.' It held that it was proper to sanction the merger.

In the absence of specific provisions in the Companies Act, to deal with mergers that are anti-competitive, not every case, without any special facts as relating to TOMCO, may pass through the test of 'public interest', which is not specific and for that reason too wide to be of use in application to actual cases of mergers.

THE NEED FOR CONTROL OF MERGERS AND ACQUISITIONS

So far, in India there was no need for a merger policy, particularly one with a view to protect competition. However, in the wake of liberalization measures compelling businesses to reorganize their enterprises to survive and compete in the new environment, it was considered necessary to make provisions for merger control towards avoiding its anti-competitive effects and provide for an appropriate competition policy for the country.

The opening up of the economy to foreign investment and the reduction of government control over investment decisions has changed the scene in which businesses are to operate, particularly with large multinational companies operating in India. The Report of the High Level Committee on Competition Policy and Law ('the Report') states the reason for a domestic competition law thus: 'One reason for having domestic competition law is that it should be a precursor to the international competition law, which is sought to be placed on the agenda of the WTO. Competition law must emerge out of a national competition policy, which must be evolved to serve the basic goals of economic reforms by building a competitive market economy.'[5]

One such reorganization is merger. But the basic tenet of the new regime would be to ensure that arrangements in the nature of merger, or acquisitions of assets and management control, do not adversely affect existing competition in the business of the supply of goods or services offered by the undertakings effecting the reorganization. Merger control is one aspect of the law relating to the protection of competition.

Mergers fall under three broad categories: vertical, conglomerate, and horizontal mergers. A vertical merger is one between enterprises in different stages of production or supplies, viz. a manufacturer and a supplier of a component or raw material. A conglomerate merger is between enterprises in unrelated businesses. A horizontal merger, usually the primary concern of anti-competition law, is of competing enterprises. Each type of merger would have to be assessed for its anti-competitive effects, in relation to the market for the products or services supplied by the enterprises involved in the merger and there can be no general assumption that any of these types of merger would not, by its nature, be anti-competitive.

COMBINATION—THE LEGAL FRAMEWORK

Acquisition/Merger

Section 5 of the Competition Act sets out when a 'combination' is to be taken as to have resulted. The term 'combination' is wider and will include transactions in addition to merger. The basic principle of this section is that a combination would result, subject to the other prescriptions of the section, such as the monetary thresholds of assets or turnover of the enterprises specified therein, on: (a) acquisition of control, shares, voting rights or assets of one or more enterprises by one or more persons; (b) acquiring of control by a person over an enterprise when such person has already direct or indirect control over another enterprise engaged in production, distribution or trading of a similar or identical or substitutable goods, or provision of a similar or identical or substitutable service; (c) any merger or amalgamation.

Section 5 was amended as part of the 2007 amendments. Section 5 states when a combination by acquisition or merger is to be considered as falling under that section and it is with reference to monetary limits of assets or turnover of the enterprises or persons concerned in the combination. The amendments to this section are by way of substitution of certain sub-sections, only including to the existing sub-sections, an additional condition relating to the value of the assets or turnover, either in India or abroad, of the parties to the combination. The original sub-sections providing for the various modes of combination, in such cases, stated the monetary limits only in US dollars. The amendments in each of these sub-sections provide that the values of these assets or turnover shall include at least a stated amount of rupees in India. The purpose that would be served by this amendment is that at least a minimum effect on competition in India shall have to be shown for the Act to apply.

The sub-sections thus amended are: section 5(a)(i)(B), section 5(a)(ii)(B), section 5(b)(i)(B), section 5(b)(ii)(B), section 5(c)(i)(B), and section 5(c)(ii)(B).

The whole of section 5 dealing with combination as amended is as follows:

S 5. The acquisition of one or more enterprises by one or more persons or merger or amalgamation of enterprises shall be a combination of such enterprises and persons or enterprises, if—(a) any acquisition where—(i) the parties to the acquisition, being the acquirer and the enterprise, whose control, shares, voting rights or assets have been acquired or are being acquired jointly have,—(A) either, in India, the assets of the value of more than rupees one thousand crores or turnover more than rupees three thousand crores; or (B) in India or outside India, in aggregate, the assets of the value of more than five hundred million US dollars, including at least rupees five hundred crores in India, or turnover more than fifteen hundred million US dollars, including at least rupees fifteen hundred crores in India; or (ii) the group, to which the enterprise whose control, shares, assets or voting rights have been acquired or are being acquired, would belong after the acquisition, jointly have or would jointly have,—(A) either in India, the assets of the value of more than rupees four thousand crores or turnover more than rupees twelve thousand crores; or (B) in India or outside India, in aggregate, the assets of the value of more than two billion US dollars, including at least rupees five hundred crores in India, or turnover more than six billion US dollars, including at least rupees fifteen hundred crores in India; or

(b) acquiring of control by a person over an enterprise when such person has already direct or indirect control over another enterprise engaged in production, distribution or trading of a similar or identical or substitutable goods or provision of a similar or identical or substitutable service, if—(i) the enterprise over which control has been acquired along with the enterprise over which the acquirer already has direct or indirect control jointly have,—(A) either in India, the assets of the value of more than rupees one thousand crores or turnover more than rupees three thousand crores; or (B) in India or outside India, in aggregate, the assets of the value of more than five hundred million US dollars, including at least rupees five hundred crores in India, or turnover more than fifteen hundred million US dollars, including at least rupees fifteen hundred crores in India; or (ii) the group, to which enterprise whose control has been acquired, or is being acquired, would belong after the acquisition, jointly have or would jointly have,—(A) either in India, the assets of the value of more than rupees four thousand crores or turnover more than rupees twelve thousand crores; or (B) in India or outside India, in aggregate, the assets of the value of more than two billion US dollars, including at least rupees five hundred crores in India, or turnover more than six billion US dollars, including at least rupees fifteen hundred crore in India; or

(c) any merger or amalgamation in which,—(i) the enterprise remaining after merger or the enterprise created as a result of the amalgamation, as the case may be, have,—(A) either in India, the assets of the value of more than rupees one thousand crores or turnover more than rupees three thousand crores; or (B) in India or outside India, in aggregate, the assets of the value of more than five hundred million US dollars, including at least rupees five hundred crores in India, or turnover more than fifteen hundred million US dollars, including at least rupees fifteen hundred crores in India; or (ii) the group, to which the enterprise remaining after the merger or the enterprise created as a result of the amalgamation, would belong after the merger or the amalgamation, as the case may be, have or would have,—(A) either in India, the assets of the value of more than rupees four-thousand crores or turnover more than rupees twelve thousand crores; or (B) in India or outside India, in aggregate, the assets of the value of more than two billion US dollars, including at least rupees five hundred crores in India, or turnover more than more than six billion US dollars, including at least rupees fifteen hundred crores in India;

Explanation—For the purposes of this section,—(a) 'control' includes controlling the affairs or management by—(i) one or more enterprises, either jointly or singly, over another enterprise or group; (ii) one or more groups, either jointly or singly, over another group or enterprise; (b) 'group' means two or more enterprises which, directly or indirectly, are in a position to—(i) exercise twenty-six per cent or more of the voting rights in the other enterprise; or (ii) appoint more than fifty per cent of the members of the board of directors in the other enterprise; or (iii) control the management or affairs of the other enterprise; (c) the value of assets shall be determined by taking the book value of the assets as shown, in the audited books of account of the enterprise, in the financial year immediately preceding the financial year in which the date of proposed merger falls, as reduced by any depreciation, and the value of assets shall include the brand value, value of goodwill, or value of copyright, patent, permitted use, collective mark, registered proprietor, registered trade mark, registered user, homonymous geographical indication, geographical indications, design or layout-design or similar other commercial rights, if any, referred to in sub-section (5) of section 3.

Section 6, as amended in 2007, deals with the procedure for regulation of combinations. It is as follows:

S 6. (1) No person or enterprise shall enter into a combination which causes or is likely to cause an appreciable adverse effect on competition within the relevant market in India and such a combination shall be void.

(2) Subject to the provisions contained in sub-section (1), any person or enterprise, who or which proposes to enter into a combination, [shall] give notice to the Commission, in the form as may be specified, and the fee which may be determined, by regulations, disclosing the details of the proposed combination, within [thirty days] of—(a) approval of the proposal relating to merger or amalgamation, referred to in clause (c) of section 5, by the board of directors of the enterprises concerned with such merger or amalgamation, as the case may be;

(b) execution of any agreement or other document for acquisition referred to in clause (a) of section 5 or acquiring of control referred to in clause (b) of that section.

[(2A) No combination shall come into effect until two hundred and ten days have passed from the day on which the notice has been given to the Commission under sub-section (2) or the Commission has passed orders under section 31, whichever is earlier.]

(3) The Commission shall, after receipt of notice under sub-section (2), deal with such notice in accordance with the provisions contained in sections 29, 30 and 31.

(4) The provisions of this section shall not apply to share subscription or financing facility or any acquisition, by a public financial institution, foreign

institutional investor, bank or venture capital fund, pursuant to any covenant of a loan agreement or investment agreement.

(5) The public financial institution, foreign institutional investor, bank or venture capital fund, referred to in sub-section (4), shall, within seven days from the date of the acquisition, file, in the form as may be specified by regulations, with the Commission the details of the acquisition including the details of control, the circumstances for exercise of such control and the consequences of default arising out of such loan agreement or investment agreement, as the case may be.

Explanation—For the purposes of this section, the expression—(a) "foreign institutional investor" has the same meaning as assigned to it in clause (a) of the Explanation to section 115 AD of the Income Tax Act, 1961(43 of 1961); (b) "venture capital fund" has the same meaning as assigned to it in clause (b) of the Explanation to clause (23 FB) of section 10 of the Income-tax Act, 1961(43 of 1961).

The amendments to section 6 are amendments to section 6(2) and the introduction of a new sub-section (2A). The two amendments to section 6(2) relate to the obligation of a person or an enterprise entering into a combination, to give notice of the proposed combination to the Competition Commission and the period at the end of which the combination of which notice has been given to the Commission will take effect. Sub-section (2) of section 6, originally gave the option for a person or enterprise proposing to enter into a combination to give notice to Competition Commission of the proposed combination and the time within which that notice was to be given was within seven days of—(a) approval of the proposal relating to merger or amalgamation, referred to in clause (c) of section 5, by the board of directors of the enterprises concerned with such merger or amalgamation, as the case may be; (b) execution of any agreement or other document for acquisition referred to in clause (a) of section 5 or acquiring of control referred to in clause (b) of that section.

The two amendments to section 6(2) are: (a) the option given to the person or enterprise proposing to enter into a combination has been taken away and a duty is cast on those entities to give notice to the Commission of the proposed combination and (b) the time within which it should be given is changed to thirty days instead of the previous period of seven days.

It should be noted that even before the original 2002 Act had been enacted, the High Level Committee on Competition Policy had recommended that in the case of mergers above a certain threshold level prior notification was necessary as according to it, a 'complete absence of a pre-notification requirement could lead to more post-merger unscrambling with high social costs.' That Committee had also noted that the pre-merger notification required by the Hart-Scott-Rodino Act of 1976 of the United States was to give the agencies 'an effective mechanism to enjoin illegal mergers *before* they occur.' This was ignored and the prior notification was made optional. The Standing Committee raised this issue with the ministry, during the discussions on the provisions of the Competition (Amendment) Bill, 2006.

The ministry represented that under the existing provision, with the threshold limits having been prescribed, the enterprises could assess if their proposals were or not likely to be violative of the law and decide if, a notification to the Commission was necessary or not and that prior notification was not made mandatory as prior approval of all cases could lead to delays and unjustified interventions. In the view of the government, according to the proviso to section 20(1), no reopening of any combination may be taken up for enquiry by the Commission after expiry of one year from the date on which that combination had taken effect, suggesting that no change was necessary. But the Committee did not agree that it should be voluntary as that would lead to the position that 'the Commission may miss out on certain important developments, which can ultimately hamper its functioning as a regulatory body.' The Standing Committee recommended that section 6(2) may be amended suitably to provide for mandatory pre-notification of combinations/mergers covered by the Act.

Another amendment to section 6(2) made in 2007 is of the period within which the notice will have to be given of a proposed combination. It has been raised to thirty days from the period of seven days.

The other amendment to section 6 is the introduction of sub-section 2A to that section. Section 6(2A) is as follows: 'No combination shall come into effect until two hundred and ten days have passed from the day on which the notice has been given to the Commission under sub-section (2) or the Commission has passed orders under section 31, whichever is earlier.'

This states negatively that a combination shall not take effect till the end of either of the periods stated above. The amendment to sub-section (11) of section 31, consistent with section 6(2A), has replaced the words 'ninety working days from the date of publication referred to in sub-section (2) of section 29', with the following: 'two hundred and ten days from the date of notice given to the Commission under sub-section (2) of section 6.'

The amended sub-section (11) of section 31 reads as follows: (11) 'If the Commission does not, on the expiry of a period of [two hundred and ten days from the date of notice given to the Commission under sub-section (2) of section 6], pass an order or issue direction in accordance with the provisions of sub-section (1) or sub-section (2) or sub-section (7), the combination shall be deemed to have been approved by the Commission.'[6]

Regulations Setting Out the Procedure Applicable to Combinations

The Competition Commission has, by its Notification no. 3 dated 11 May 2011 issued in detail 'The Competition Commission of India (Procedure in regard to the transaction of business relating to combinations) Regulations, 2011.'[7] They deal with categories of transactions not likely to have appreciable adverse effect on competition in India, form of notice for the proposed combination, obligation to file the notice, procedure for filing notice etc.

Section 6 deals with the procedure for regulation of combinations. For section 6 to apply, the combination, within the meaning of section 5, should be one that causes or is likely to cause an appreciable adverse effect on competition within the relevant market in India. Such a combination would be void.[8] Section 20(4) sets out the factors that the Commission shall have due regard to, in determining whether a combination would have such an adverse effect on competition.[9] Section 31 specifies what orders may be passed by the Commission on certain combinations.[10]

COMPARATIVE LAW

At this stage it may be appropriate to take note of the principles on which the law on acquisitions and mergers is based in other countries and have been in force for quite a long time.

The Clayton Act—USA

Section 7 of the Clayton Act applicable to such transactions is most instructive.[11] It lays emphasis on the effect of the acquisition of stock or assets on competition in 'any line of commerce'. The mere value of the assets or turnover of the enterprises effecting the combination has naturally been ignored as a criterion for determining the effect of the acquisition of stock or assets on competition. The operative portion of the section relevant for the present purpose is:

No person engaged in commerce or in any activity affecting commerce shall acquire, directly or indirectly, the whole or any part of the stock or other share capital and no person subject to the jurisdiction of the Federal Trade Commission shall acquire the whole or any part of the assets of another person engaged also in commerce or in any activity affecting commerce, where in any line of commerce or in any activity affecting commerce in any section of the country, the effect of such acquisition may be substantially to lessen competition, or to tend to create a monopoly.

No person shall acquire, directly or indirectly, the whole or any part of the stock or other share capital and no person subject to the jurisdiction of the Federal Trade Commission shall acquire the whole or any part of the assets of one or more persons engaged in commerce or in any activity affecting commerce, where in any line of commerce or in any activity affecting commerce in any section of the country, the effect of such acquisition, of such stocks or assets, or of the use of such stock by the voting or granting of proxies or otherwise, may be substantially to lessen competition, or to tend to create a monopoly.

The EC Merger Regulation

Council Regulation (EC) No 139/2004 of 20 January 2004 discusses the control of concentrations between undertakings (the EC Merger Regulation).[12] This Regulation will apply to a concentration with a community dimension.[13]

Article 1(2) and (3) define when a concentration with a community dimension arises. A concentration with a community dimension is determined by the geographical area of activity of the undertakings concerned, worldwide and in member states, and by the quantitative thresholds of turnover,[14] prescribed by Article 1(2) and (3). A concentration that would significantly impede effective competition, in the common market or in a substantial part of it, in particular as a result of the creation or strengthening of a dominant position, shall be declared incompatible with the common market.[15] A concentration that would not significantly impede effective competition in the common market or in a substantial part of it, in particular as a result of the creation or strengthening of a dominant position, shall be declared compatible with the common market.[16]

The national law of the member state will govern concentrations that do not have a community dimension, but that will have to be consistent with community law.

Concentration—Definition

A concentration may arise either through a merger or through the acquisition of 'control' over another undertaking or part of an undertaking. Such control may be acquired through the purchase of securities or assets or by contract or by any other means.

A 'concentration' shall be deemed to arise where a change of control on a lasting basis results from: (*a*) the merger of two or more previously independent undertakings or parts of undertakings; or (*b*) the acquisition, by one or more persons already controlling at least one undertaking; or by one or more undertakings, whether by purchase of securities or assets, by contract or by any other means, of direct or indirect control of the whole or parts of one or more other undertakings.[17]

A concentration shall not be deemed to arise when credit institutions, financial institutions or insurance companies, as part of their normal business hold securities for a short time with a view to sell them and do not exercise any voting rights in respect of those securities.

The Regulation makes no discrimination between the public and private sector in the control of concentrations. But in the case of a public sector undertaking, calculation of the turnover of an undertaking concerned in a concentration will take account of undertakings making up an economic unit with an independent power of decision, irrespective of the way in which their capital is held or of the rules of administrative supervision applicable to them.[18]

While a change of control on a lasting basis is obvious in the case of a merger of undertakings, it may not always be evident in the case of acquisition of control, particularly indirect control, and will require close examination of the fact of change of control on a lasting basis and also its effect on competition.

The creation of a joint venture performing on a lasting basis all the functions of an autonomous economic entity shall constitute a concentration within the meaning of Article 3(1)(b).[19] The objective of the Regulation is to cover all operations bringing about a 'lasting change in the control' of the undertakings concerned and consequently, the structure of the market. 'Concentration' has been defined with this purpose in view and therefore this Regulation will cover all joint ventures performing on a lasting basis all the functions of an autonomous economic entity.[20]

The Enterprise Act, 2002—UK

The Competition Act, 1998, and the Enterprise Act, 2002, constitute the domestic law in the UK relating to antitrust regulation. The Competition Act deals with agreements preventing, restricting or distorting competition (Chapter I), abuse of a dominant position (Chapter II), and monopolies (Chapter V, Part III). Chapter IV, sections 45 to 40 deals with the Competition Commission and Appeals.

The Enterprise Act deals with mergers and related matters. Part 3 of this Act deals with mergers. Part 4 deals with market investigations. Part 5 deals with the Commission. All antitrust issues with a Community Dimension will be dealt with under the EC Regulations, as UK is a member of the EEC.

Mergers

It is the duty of the OFT to report to the Commission, if it believes that a relevant merger situation is being created which has resulted, or may be expected to result, in a substantial lessening of competition within any market or markets in the UK for goods or services.[21] Such a reference need not be made on grounds of *de minimis*, that is, where adverse effect is negligible, benefits to customers, which is to be determined in accordance with section 30, or when the OFT is considering whether to accept undertakings from the enterprises, and on certain other grounds.

The creation of a relevant merger situation is defined by section 23 of the Enterprise Act, UK. A relevant merger situation may arise when: (*a*) two or more enterprises have ceased to be distinct enterprises at the prescribed time; and the value of the turnover in the UK of the enterprise being taken over exceeds 70 million pounds; or (*b*) two or more enterprises have ceased to be distinct enterprises at the prescribed time and in relation to the supply of goods of any description, at least one-quarter of all the goods of that description which are supplied in the UK, or in a substantial part of the UK: (i) are supplied by one and the same person or are supplied to one and the same person; or (ii) are supplied by the persons by whom the enterprises concerned are carried on, or are supplied to those persons. The same test would be applied to the supply of services.

For the purpose of determining the proportion of one-quarter, the following criteria will be applied: value cost, price, quantity, capacity, number of workers employed or any other combination of criteria as may be considered appropriate.

The Companies Act, 1956, in force in India does not use the term 'merger', but uses an equivalent term 'amalgamation'. The concept of an amalgamation of a company under the Indian Act requires that the amalgamating or, merging company, after the transfer of its assets and liabilities, through the order of the court, to the amalgamated or merged company, is dissolved without winding up. This is true merger in the normal sense. But under the Enterprise Act UK, a relevant merger situation is created, when two or more enterprises have ceased to be distinct enterprises under the conditions set out in section 23. This means that the corporate status of the merging company need not change.

Ceasing to be Distinct Enterprises

Section 26 of the Enterprise Act, UK, states that two enterprises cease to be distinct enterprises when they are brought under common ownership or common control. This is so regardless of whether or not the business to which either of them formerly belonged continues to be carried on under the same or different ownership or control.

Common ownership is easily understood as when the enterprise is a body corporate and those acting in association with one another hold all the shares.

'Common control' as defined by section 26 is discussed later in this chapter under 'Control'.

REGULATION OF COMBINATIONS—SECTION 6

We return now to the components of the operative part of section 6 of the Indian Competition Act, providing for the regulation of combinations. According to sub-section (1), a combination that causes or is likely to cause an appreciable adverse effect on competition within the relevant market in India is void.

The question of prejudice to the process of competition cannot be considered in the abstract. The starting point for the examination of the effect on competition, whether adverse or otherwise, is the determination of the market, which is where competition among the suppliers of goods or services to that particular market operates. Again, the market is not an isolated fact. It is related to specific goods or services and to a territory within which the suppliers of goods or services are engaged in the competitive process. The Act has defined a relevant market, a relevant geographic market, and a relevant product market[22] and indicated the factors that are to be considered by the Commission in determining whether a combination would have the effect of, or is likely to have an appreciable adverse effect on competition in the relevant market.[23]

The European Commission's notice of 9 December 1997, on the definition of the relevant market for the purposes of community competition law prefaces the subject as follows:

The objective of defining a market in both its product and geographic dimension is to identify those actual competitors of the undertakings involved that are capable of constraining their behaviour and of preventing them from behaving independently of an effective competitive pressure. It is from this perspective, that the market definition makes it possible, inter alia, to calculate market shares that would convey meaningful information regarding market power for the purposes of assessing dominance or for the purposes of applying Article 85. Stating that firms are subject to three main sources of competitive constraints, viz. demand substitutability, supply substitutability and potential competition, it continues: 'Basically, the exercise of market definition consists in identifying the effective alternative sources of supply for the customers of the undertakings involved, both in terms of products/services and geographic location of suppliers.'

DEFINITIONS UNDER THE COMPETITION ACT, 2002

Before proceeding to consider the effect of the sections relating to regulation of combinations, it would be appropriate to comprehend the meaning of certain crucial terms used in the Act.

Combination

What is a combination? The Act only states the conditions when a combination between persons and enterprises is caused but has not defined the term. Section 5 refers to acquisition of enterprises, by one or more persons or a merger or amalgamation, in the manner set out therein, which would be a combination. Under section 2(l) the term 'person' would include an individual, a company and certain other entities.[24] A combination is a relationship between two or more persons or enterprises through any agreement or understanding and for the purpose of sharing the properties or interest in any enterprise. Where the effect of this combination would adversely affect competition, the combination would have to be regulated as appropriate to the market affected.

Northern Securities Co. v. US[25] was a combination of individuals. It was an early case of a combination affirmed by the US Supreme Court to be one in restraint of interstate and international commerce, and violative of the Sherman Act.

The facts of the case were as follows.

The Great Northern Railway Company and the Northern Pacific Railway Company were competitors, engaged in the business of carrying freight and passengers. They owned, controlled, and operated separate lines of railroad. Certain stockholders of the Great Northern Railway Company and the Northern Pacific Railway Company, holding a controlling interest in the respective companies, entered into a combination for forming a holding company, Northern Securities Company, to which the controlling interest in their two companies was agreed to be transferred and that holding company was to issue shares in its capital to those stockholders of the two companies, on an agreed basis, in exchange for the shares in each company, conveying the controlling interest in those companies to Northern Securities. The intended purpose was to enable Northern Securities to act as owner of the two companies and to take such steps as it considered necessary to enhance the value of the stocks of those companies.

After the incorporation of Northern Securities, the defendants-stockholders of the Great Northern Railway Company and Northern Pacific Railway Company transferred to Northern Securities, shares required to convey the controlling interest in their companies in exchange for the agreed number of shares in Northern Securities.

The objection to this arrangement was that it eliminated competition between those two railway companies and that through the mechanism of a holding company, controlling two competitors, a monopoly of the interstate and foreign commerce formerly carried on by the two systems as independent competitors was established. It was also complained that the formation of Northern Securities was not done in good faith and was done solely to incorporate the pooling of the stocks of the said companies and carry into effect the above combination.

It was also charged that the consequence of the scheme being carried out would be, that the holding company, would thereafter, guard the interests of both sets of stockholders as a unit, and manage, or cause to be managed, both lines of railroad as if they were held in one ownership.

The circuit court below had determined that the defendants had entered into a combination or conspiracy in restraint of trade or commerce among the several states and that the investment by Northern Securities in the railway companies was in pursuance of such combination. That Court decreed that the Northern Securities Company be enjoined from:

(a) acquiring, or attempting to acquire further stock of either of the aforesaid railway companies; (b) from voting at any meeting of any of the two railway companies on the strength of its existing shareholding in those companies; (c) from exercising or attempting to exercise any control or influence whatsoever over the acts of said railway companies, by virtue of its holding such stock therein.

The railway companies were in turn enjoined from permitting Northern Securities from voting at any of their general meetings on the election of any directors or officers of any of them.

The US Supreme Court, confirming the decision of the lower court, ruled that the combination was in restraint of interstate commerce and fell within the prohibition of the statute. It said:

Necessarily, also, the constituent companies ceased, under such a combination, to be in active competition for trade and commerce along their respective lines, and have become, practically, one powerful consolidated corporation, by the name of a holding corporation, the principal, if not the sole, object for the formation of which was to carry out the purpose of the original combination, under which competition between the constituent companies would cease. The control of two competitors had passed on to a single entity, the holding company.

No scheme or device could more certainly come within the words of the act—'combination in the form of a trust or otherwise ... in restraint of commerce among the several states or with foreign nations,' or could more effectively and certainly suppress free competition between the constituent companies. This combination is, within the meaning of the act, a 'trust;' but if not, it is a combination in restraint of interstate and international commerce; and that is enough to bring it under the condemnation of the Act.

The mere existence of such a combination, and the power acquired by the holding company as its trustee, constitute a menace to, and a restraint upon, that freedom of commerce which Congress intended to recognize and protect, and which the public is entitled to have protected.

It was argued on behalf of Northern Securities that it had only exercised the ordinary right of any company to make an investment in the shares of another company and that it was not forbidden by its charter. The Court treated this as a fallacious argument not comporting with the actual transaction, the purpose of which was suppressing competition between the two railway companies, by the combination, consisting of the principal stockholders of those companies, acting through Northern Securities in restraint of inter-state trade and commerce. It observed: 'There was no actual investment, in any substantial sense, by the Northern Securities Company in the stock of the two constituent companies.' The investment was only in form.

Rejecting the objection on behalf of the railway companies that, as entities incorporated under a state law, the application of the antitrust legislation enacted by Congress would be an unauthorized interference by the national government with the internal commerce of the states creating those corporations, the Court held that Congress had the power under the Constitution to regulate restraints on interstate and international commerce.

To the objection that the application of such a law would adversely affect business, the Court replied: 'It is the history of monopolies in this country and in England that predictions of ruin are habitually made by them when it is attempted, by legislation, to restrain their operations and to protect the public against their exactions.'

The majority judgement determined that the acquisition of the stock of the two competing railway companies by Northern Securities was a plain violation of section 1 of the antitrust Act.

The dissenting judges held that while Congress had the power to regulate interstate and international commerce, it had no authority, as regulating such commerce, to regulate the ownership of stock in competing railway companies, as in their opinion, ownership of stock in companies was not 'commerce'.

This case was decided in 1904 and the Clayton Act was passed in 1914. Section 7 of that Act has provided for a specific mechanism for regulating anti-competitive investments. In India before the introduction of the Competition Act such acquisitions or mergers were not required to be examined for their effect on competition in the relevant business.

Acquisition

Section 2(a) defines what an acquisition is. It states:

2: In this Act, unless the context otherwise requires—
  (*a*) 'acquisition' means, directly or indirectly, acquiring or agreeing to acquire—
    (*i*) shares, voting rights or assets of any enterprise; or
    (*ii*) control over management or control over assets of any enterprise; ...

The acquisition of shares, voting rights, or assets of an enterprise, or control over the management or assets of an enterprise, has implications for the maintenance of the system of competition. Where the extent of acquisition of shares or voting rights in an enterprise is such that it gives control over the management of the other enterprise, there is potential for erosion of the power of the latter to compete. If the assets are disposed of after the acquisition and the business carried on with those assets is discontinued, one source of competition would have been eliminated. The acquisition may be direct or indirect or may just form the subject of an agreement to acquire. As noted earlier, the result of an approved merger is that the merging company's autonomy, along with its assets and liabilities, would devolve on the merged company.

A reading of section 5 will show that the section will apply to any acquisition or merger when, as a result of the acquisition or merger, the value of assets or turnover of the enterprises involved in the acquisition or merger crosses the threshold levels specified in that section. Then, a person who proposes to enter into such a combination is required under section 6(2), as amended, to give notice to the Commission of the proposed combination. The Commission may also act on its own knowledge or information, as permitted by section 20(1), and inquire into whether any of the modes of a combination as defined by section 5 has caused, or is likely to cause an appreciable adverse effect on competition in India. But the proviso to this sub-section does not permit the Commission to initiate any inquiry under this sub-section after the expiry of one year from the date on which such combination has taken effect.

The Act has prescribed a two-stage test for evaluating the effect of combinations: (*a*) the specified threshold level, under section 5, of the value of the combined assets or turnover of the enterprises that constitute the combination; and (*b*) whether, under section 6(1), such a combination causes or is likely to cause an appreciable adverse effect on competition within the relevant market in India.

The acquisition of assets or control over the assets of an enterprise would certainly make available to the acquirer the power to determine the activities of the former. However, for the purpose of determining the effect on competition 'in the relevant market', the materiality of the value of all combined assets of the enterprises involved in the acquisition, regardless of their use in the supply of the product constituting the market is doubtful. The threshold levels of assets and turnover stipulated in section 5 also seem to be very high, much higher than what the Report recommended,[26] presumably set with the purpose of covering large multinational companies also. This means that many anti-competitive acquisitions and mergers below that level would not be covered by the Act, even if they are able to engage in anti-competitive acquisition or merger by reason of their market power, technological superiority or other such factors. A mere probable anti-competitive effect of an acquisition or a merger, without the preliminary requirement of the value of assets or turnover, would have furthered a fuller achievement of the objects of the Act.

The Act has liberally borrowed the concepts of the EC antitrust legislation and prescription of turnover as a criterion for evaluating combinations is one example. The current EC law relating to mergers[27] has prescribed, among others, quantitative thresholds of turnover, as a criterion for determining whether a concentration is compatible with the common market or not. Aggregate turnover of the undertakings alone is to be considered as a factor and the value of the assets of the undertakings concerned has not been considered relevant for the purpose of determining the effect of the concentration on competition.

In India too, market share is a material indicator, and it is one of the factors that the Commission should consider in determining whether it would, under the Act, have the effect of or is likely to have an adverse effect on competition in the relevant market.[28] It is difficult to agree with the High Level Committee's general observation: 'The Committee is of the view that the threshold limit may be fixed on the basis of assets rather than market share, as the latter may not be an appropriate barometer to determine affectation adversely of competition.'[29]

According to the Competition Act, the provision of section 2(a)(i) and (ii) are the only means of acquisition contemplated in India.

Assets

The term has not been defined by the Act. By virtue of section 2(z), it can be given the meaning assigned to it under the Companies Act, 1956.

However, here too it has not been directly defined and one may have to take guidance from Schedule VI of that Act. However, Explanation (c) to section 5 gives some indication of the meaning of this term and deals with determining the value of assets as follows:

... the value of assets shall be determined by taking the book value of the assets as shown, in the audited books of account of the enterprise, in the financial year immediately preceding the financial year in which the date of proposed merger falls, as reduced by any depreciation, and the value of assets shall include the brand value, value of goodwill, or value of copyright, patent, permitted use, collective mark, registered proprietor, registered trade mark, registered user, homonymous geographical indication, geographical indications, design or layout-design or similar other commercial rights, if any, referred to in sub-section (5) of section 3.

Since the above-mentioned values are required to be included in the value of assets, the position appears to be that the value of the assets as shown in the books of account and of those assets, not shown in the books of account, but which fall within the group above shall be taken as the value of assets of the enterprise.

Control

The explanation to section 5(a) and (b) states when control of an enterprise can be said to have been acquired. The Explanation, (a), states that 'control' includes controlling the affairs or management by (*i*) one or more enterprises, either jointly or singly, over another enterprise or group; (*ii*) one or more groups, either jointly or singly, over another group or enterprise. Explanation (b) defines a 'group' as follows—when two or more enterprises are, directly or indirectly, in a position to exercise 26 per cent or more of the voting rights in the other enterprise, or appoint more than 50 per cent of the members of the board of directors of the other enterprise, or control the management or affairs of the other enterprise, they are to be treated as a group.

Under this definition, the control of an enterprise operates when the *affairs or management* of one enterprise or group of enterprises are controlled by any enterprise or enterprises forming a group. The only test expressly stated as required for the purpose of examining if there is control of one enterprise by another is the presence of the actual control of the affairs or management of one enterprise by another. In the first place, what is meant by controlling the 'affairs' of an enterprise is not clear, though the meaning of controlling the management of an enterprise is less unclear. The above definition of 'control' is an inclusive definition and may apply to other modes of controlling an enterprise, in addition to controlling the affairs or management of an enterprise. Actually, the definition of 'control', through the explanation to the section, is vague and does not specifically enumerate or indicate the elements constituting control of another enterprise.

An enterprise may be said to control another enterprise when the former controls the latter's power to make major policy decisions relating to the second enterprise, under whatever arrangement, through the authority conferred by the latter's articles of association, a management agreement, or through holding the controlling shares. A simple example is the power of a holding company over its subsidiary. An enterprise may control a group and a group may control another group.

Regulation 2(1)(c) of the SEBI Regulations, 1997, defines 'control' as: '"control" shall include the right to appoint majority of the directors or to control the management or policy decisions exercisable by a person or persons acting individually or in concert, directly or indirectly, including by virtue of their shareholding or management rights or shareholders agreements or voting agreements or in any other manner.'

In this context, it would also be useful to refer to the definition of 'control' in the EC Regulation No. 139/2004 of 20 January 2004. Article 3(1)(a) and (b) of this Regulation set out when a concentration shall be deemed to arise.[30] It is deemed to arise when there is a change of control on a lasting basis resulting from: (*a*) the merger of two or more previously independent undertakings or parts of undertakings; or (*b*) the acquisition of direct or indirect control of the whole or parts of one or more other undertakings, by one or more persons already controlling at least one undertaking, or by one or more undertakings, whether by purchase of securities or assets, by contract or by any other means.

The substance of Article 3(2) defining what *constitutes* control is: control shall be constituted by rights, contracts or any other means which, either separately or in combination, enable an undertaking to exercise decisive influence on another undertaking in particular by: (*a*) ownership or the right to use all or part of the assets of an undertaking; (*b*) rights or contracts which confer decisive influence on the composition, voting or decisions of the organs of an undertaking. This includes the power to nominate directors, voting rights and any special rights.[31]

A very early decision of the European Coal and Steel Community (ECSC) High Authority on 'control' is much more specific:[32]

Article 1 of this decision states that the rights stated therein shall constitute the elements of control of an undertaking enabling the undertaking with any of those rights to determine how that other undertaking, controlled by it, shall operate as regards production, prices, investments, supplies, sales and appropriation of profits.

The following are the rights that constitute the elements of control: ownership or the right to use all or part of the assets of an undertaking; rights or contracts which confer power to influence the composition, voting or decisions of the organs of an undertaking; rights or contracts which enable any person, by himself or in association with others, to manage the business of an undertaking; contracts made with an undertaking concerning the computation or appropriation of its profits; contracts made with an undertaking concerning the whole or an important part of its supplies or outlets, where the duration of these contracts or the quantities to which they relate exceed what is usual in commercial contracts dealing with those matters.

Exceptions are those rights held by one on behalf of another that are revocable and rights of banks or financial institutions which, upon formation of an undertaking or increase of its capital, acquire shares in that undertaking with a view to selling them on the market but do not exercise voting rights in respect of those shares.

Deutsche Telekom/BetaResearch discussed later in this chapter under 'Merger' was a case where by acquiring shares and through a restructuring agreement the acquirers obtained joint control of another company.

Section 23 of the Enterprise Act, 2002, UK, provides that a relevant merger situation would be created if two or more enterprises ceased to be distinct enterprises at a time or in circumstances falling within section 24 and on the conditions stated in section 23. Section 26(1) states that any two enterprises cease to be distinct enterprises if they are brought under common ownership or common control (whether or not the business to which either of them formerly belonged continues to be carried on under the same or different ownership or control).

The following is the position under the Enterprise Act, UK, regarding control of an enterprise:[33]

> (a) enterprises will be treated as being under common control if they are: interconnected bodies corporate; enterprises carried on by two or more bodies corporate of which one and the same person or group of persons has control; an enterprise carried on by a body corporate and an enterprise carried on

by a person or group of persons having control of that body corporate;

(b) a person who is, or a group of persons who are, able directly or indirectly, to control or materially influence the policy of a body corporate, or the policy of any person in carrying on an enterprise but without having a controlling interest in that body corporate or in that enterprise may be treated as having control of it;

(c) in the context of bringing two or more enterprises under common control, a person or group of persons may be treated as bringing an enterprise under his or their control, when (i) a person or group of persons already able to control or to materially influence the policy of the person carrying on the enterprise, that person or group of persons acquires a controlling interest in the enterprise; also when such persons acquire a controlling interest in a body corporate; (ii) a person or group of persons being already able to materially influence the policy of the person carrying on the enterprise, that person or group of persons becomes able to control that policy.

Under the UK's Enterprise Act, a merger situation may arise at any of the three stages: acquiring the ability to influence the policy, controlling the policy and, finally acquiring a controlling interest in the other enterprise or body corporate and each stage would be a merger situation. Only after the acquisition of the controlling interest in the other will there be no inquiry relating to the issue of control.

In the case of acquisition of control in respect of enterprises covered by section 5(a) of the Competition Act, 2002, it is only the value of the assets or turnover of the parties to the acquisition, as applicable, which has to be checked against the threshold limits set out in the sub-section. But in the case of acquisition of control of enterprises covered by section 5(b), that is, where control is acquired of an enterprise, by one who already has control—direct or indirect—of an enterprise producing similar, identical or substitutable products or service as the enterprise acquired, it is only the value of the assets or turnover, as applicable, of these enterprises that has to be considered, and not the value of the assets or turnover of other enterprises that may be controlled or owned by the acquirer, but not supplying the goods or services as set out in section 5(b).

Enterprise

This term has been defined by section 2(h).[34] It means a person or a department of the government. A person as defined under the Act could be just a natural person or other legally recognizable entity, such as a company, a firm, a body corporate or a department of the government. Thus, a person or a department of the government engaged in the production, supply, distribution of articles or goods or the provision of services of any kind or in the business of investment or dealing in shares, debentures, etc., is an enterprise. The activity engaged in should be an economic commercial activity. Where the activity is carried on by the government, the Act will apply to all such activities except those relatable to the sovereign functions of the government and the activities of the departments of the central government dealing with atomic energy, currency, defence and space.

Group

The definition of 'group' in clause (b) of the explanation to section 5 is self-explanatory:

'group' means two or more enterprises which, directly or indirectly, are in a position to—
 (i) exercise twenty-six per cent or more of the voting rights in the other enterprise; or (ii) appoint more than fifty per cent, of the members of the board of directors in the other enterprise; or
 (iii) control the management or affairs of the other enterprise; ...

Merger or Amalgamation

Section 5(c) of the Act provides the threshold limits of the value of the assets or turnover of the enterprise remaining after the merger, or created as a result of the amalgamation or the value of the assets or turnover of the group to which such an enterprise would belong after the merger or amalgamation.

Turnover

Section 2(y) defines 'turnover' thus: '"turnover" includes value of sale of goods or services'.

Section 28 of the Enterprise Act, 2002, UK, sets out first that the turnover for the purposes of merger control would be the turnover of the remaining enterprises after deducting the turnover of the enterprises that have ceased to be distinct enterprises. It also provides that the Secretary of State may determine: (*a*) the amounts which are, or which are not, to be treated as comprising an enterprise's turnover; (*b*) the date or dates by reference to which an enterprise's turnover is to be determined; and (*c*) the connection with the UK by virtue of which an enterprise's turnover is turnover in the UK. A similar provision should have found a place in the Indian Competition Act. As it stands now, the requirement may be met by a Rule under the Act.

CONTROL OF ANTI-COMPETITIVE COMBINATIONS

Sub-section (2) of section 6 requires that a prior notice has to be given to the Commission by a party proposing to enter into a combination disclosing details of the combination within the time limits set out therein. As stated earlier, sub-section (2A) has been added to section 6 by the 2007 amendments. It is as follows: 'S 6(2A) No combination shall come into effect until two hundred and ten days have passed from the day on which the notice has been given to the Commission under sub-section(2) or the Commission has passed orders under section 31, whichever is earlier.' Sub-section (3) states that such a notice shall be dealt with in accordance with sections 29, 30 and 31 of the Act. They set out the procedure for investigation of a combination, and the orders which the Commission may pass on certain combinations. Sub-section (4) exempts subscription of shares, etc., and acquisition by financial institutions. Sub-section (5) is about the procedure to be followed by financial institutions on acquisitions.

APPRECIABLE ADVERSE EFFECT ON COMPETITION

After the monetary threshold limits have been crossed by a combination, under section 5(a) or (b) or (c), the next test to be applied is to see whether that combination is one which causes or is likely to cause an appreciable adverse effect on competition within the relevant market in India. It is for the party claiming so to establish that the assailed combination does not cause 'an appreciable adverse effect on competition within the relevant market in India'.

The concept of appreciable adverse effect on competition within India in the relevant market was discussed in the chapter on anti-competitive agreements. However, the essentials may be restated, for the purpose of illustrating the evaluation of a combination for its effect on competition under the provisions of the Act relating to combinations. Section 6(1) declares as void a combination that causes or is likely to cause an appreciable adverse effect on competition within the relevant market in India.

The first step in examining whether a combination has any adverse effect on competition within the relevant market in India is to define the relevant market. The relevant market would be the geographic market and the market for the product or service. Section 2(r)(s) and (t) define 'relevant market', 'relevant product market' and 'relevant geographical market' respectively. In essence, homogeneity is the test in identifying a geographic market and interchangeability is the test in defining a market for a product or service. Defining a market means identifying the structure of the market for the relevant product or service, viz. the suppliers and their shares of the market and the conditions of supply. By virtue of section 19(5) the Commission shall have due regard to both the 'relevant geographic market' and the 'relevant product market'. Section 19(6) and (7) set out the factors to be considered while determining these two kinds of markets respectively.[35]

Evaluating a Combination

The issue of whether a combination is likely to cause or has actually caused an appreciable adverse effect on competition within the relevant market in India is a question of fact to be determined in each case. This would depend upon a number of factors, the principal ones being the structure of the market, viz. the suppliers, their shares of the market, their relative strengths, the actual conditions of competition in the relevant market and such matters. They would indicate whether at all the proposed combination would affect competition in the relevant market and if it would, whether it would be an adverse effect. Section 20(4) sets out the factors that are to be considered by the Commission in determining whether a combination would have the effect of, or is likely to have an appreciable adverse effect on competition in the relevant market. Also, any benefits that arise from the combination which outweigh the adverse impact of the combination are to be considered.

The factors set out in section 20(4) are:

1. Barriers to entry.

   Barriers to entry to the relevant market are a significant factor to be considered. The barriers to entry for new entrants, who could be expected to offer a countervailing force mitigating the anti-competitive effect of a combination, may have been created by the high initial cost of investment in the business, the requisite technology not being freely available, government restrictions on entry or new capacity, etc. This would inevitably place an enterprise possessing the advantages of early entry and access to the necessary technology at an advantageous position and with an opportunity to enjoy limited competition.

2. Market share, in the relevant market, of the persons or enterprise in a combination, individually and as a combination.

   As stated earlier, market share by itself is not conclusive, but considered in the light of other facts, it is a definite indicator of the potential for adversely affecting competition. For example, where the market share of an enterprise is 70 per cent and that of its next competitor is 10 per cent, and others share the remaining market, a combination of the first enterprise with any other enterprise supplying the same product or service would have an appreciable adverse effect on competition. The same would be the position where the market share of 70 per cent is shared by a group of enterprises effecting a combination.

3. The likelihood of the combination resulting in the removal of a 'vigorous and effective competitor or competitors' in the market.

   Acquiring control over an effective competitor or causing the merger of such a competitor with an enterprise with a very large market share is a certain way of eliminating competition to a significant extent, as a competing source of supply to the market would have been brought under the control of the acquiring enterprise or the merged enterprise.

4. The level of combination in the market.

   This would refer to the distribution of control over the market at the time of the examination of the proposed combination. If the position were that the market was a highly concentrated

one, a combination effected by those controlling the market should be expected to eliminate whatever competition existed before the implementation of the proposal.
5. Extent of competition likely to sustain in a market.

This is the core issue—the position after the combination is effected. If the effect of the combination could be shown to be with the possibility to substantially reduce competition in the relevant market, if not totally eliminate it, the combination would be one that should be prohibited.
6. Availability of substitutes or through imports.

As is obvious, the availability of substitute products or services would, to the extent they are available at any time, neutralize the anti-competitive effects of a combination affecting those products or services. Similarly, if the products are available through imports and help maintain the process of competition from being distorted, the impact of the combination on the market could be less serious.
7. Degree of countervailing power in the market.

Any scope for buyers to obtain substitutes as well for the suppliers to consider supplying substitute products or close substitutes would act as a constraint to a combination that may be considered to adversely affect competition in the relevant market.
8. Potential to increase prices or profit margins.

The section stipulates that a factor to be considered is the 'likelihood that the combination would result in the parties to the combination being able to significantly and sustainably increase prices or profit margins'. What should be implicit is that it is only an increase in price or profit margins that can be shown to be excessively high, on the facts of each case, that may be considered as with a potential to harm competition.
9. Nature and extent of vertical integration in the market.

A vertical integration of enterprises, where enterprises are in different stages of the supply of a product or service, for example, a manufacturer and a supplier, a combination has the possibility of reducing or eliminating competition, depending on the relevant market. Therefore, the present level of vertical integration in the relevant market is of importance in evaluating a combination.

10. Possibility of a failing business.

This refers to an enterprise that is no longer active and is not really a competitor, much less an effective one. The proponents of a combination use the presence of such enterprises to show that there is no competition to be affected by the combination. Whether an enterprise suggested to be failing in its business intends to cease its operations and exit from the business and there will be no assets to carry on its business or it is impossible to restore that company financially are questions of fact to be determined in each case and the assertion of one of the parties would not conclude the issue.

11. Benefits that may outweigh adverse impact of the combination, etc.

The Commission is also required to consider the following: whether the benefits of the combination outweigh the adverse impact of the combination, if any; relative advantage, by way of the contribution to the economic development, by any combination having or likely to have an appreciable adverse effect on competition; the nature and extent of innovation. If the proponents of a combination are able to substantiate significant specific benefits that the combination would bring, such as efficiencies or economies leading to any advantage to the consumer, like lower prices, and that they would outweigh the adverse effect of the combination, if any, on competition, the combination would not be anti-competitive.

The OFT, UK, lists the following efficiency claims that are possible to be claimed: cost savings (fixed or variable), more intensive use of existing capacity, economies of scale or scope, or demand-side efficiencies such as increased network size or product quality; pro-competitive changes in the merged entity's incentives, for example, by capturing complementarities like R&D activity, which in turn might increase incentives to invest in product development in innovation markets. The OFT would require to be satisfied that such claims are demonstrable, arise out of the merger, and that the benefits are likely to be passed on to customers.[36]

It is to be noted that what is required of the Commission is only that it takes due regard of any or all of the above-mentioned factors set out under section 20(4). The Act does not declare that any of these factors by itself will cause an appreciable adverse effect on competition. The sub-section, in effect, means that each case will have to be decided on the facts of that case, keeping in view these factors.

GUIDELINES FOR EVALUATING EFFECTS OF A MERGER ON COMPETITION

US

The Act has set out certain factors under section 20(4) as relevant, in examining the effects of a combination, which will include both an acquisition and a merger. The US has issued administrative guidelines showing how the enforcing authorities may consider a proposal, for example, *The Horizontal Merger Guidelines 1992* as amended on April 8, 1997. It states: 'The unifying theme of the Guidelines is that mergers should not be permitted to create or enhance market power or to facilitate its exercise. Market power to a seller is the ability profitably to maintain prices above competitive levels for a significant period of time.' The Department of Justice has also provided specific guidance on non-horizontal mergers in Section 4 of its 1984 Merger Guidelines.

UK

OFT's 'Mergers—Substantive Assessment Guidance'[37] begins by stating that it is published pursuant to section 106(1) of the Enterprise Act 2002 (the Act) to provide guidance to companies and their advisers on the criteria applied by the OFT when considering whether to refer a merger to the Commission for further investigation.

However, the matter when contested, will ultimately have to be decided by the courts.

The key points which the Guidance makes are: that a proper examination of the competitive effects of a merger rests on a sound understanding of the competitive constraints under which the merged firm will operate and that the core concept of the substantial lessening of competition test is a comparison of prospects for competition with and without the merger.

The European Commission's notice on the appraisal of horizontal mergers under the Council Regulation on the control of concentrations between undertakings[38] offers guidance as to how the Commission makes the appraisal of concentrations where the undertakings concerned are active sellers on the same relevant market or potential competitors on that market, which concentrations are termed 'horizontal mergers' in the Notice.

At paragraph 11 of the Notice, it states:

There are three main ways in which horizontal mergers may significantly impede effective competition as a result of the creation or the strengthening of a dominant position: (a) A merger may create or strengthen a paramount market position. A firm in such a position will often be able to increase prices without being constrained by actions of its customers and its actual or potential competitors. (b) A merger may diminish the degree of competition in an oligopolistic market by eliminating important competitive constraints on one or more sellers, who consequently would be able to increase their prices. (c) A merger may change the nature of competition in an oligopolistic market so sellers, who previously were not co-ordinating their behaviour, now are able to co-ordinate and therefore raise prices. A merger may also make co-ordinating easier for sellers who were co-ordinating prior to the merger.

The European Commission will, on a consideration of the various factors, enumerated in the Notice, determine the merged entity's economic power and ascertain 'whether the merging firms will face sufficient residual competition to make it unprofitable to increase prices or decrease output.' The Commission would also consider the competitive constraints that the merging firms exert on each other pre-merger and examine whether the elimination of these constraints will lead the merged firm to significantly raise prices.

THE 2002 ACT

Acquisitions and mergers set out in section 5(a)—acquisition of control, shares, voting rights or assets; (b) acquisition of control where enterprises supply identical or substitutable goods or provide similar services; and (c) merger or amalgamation are to be regulated, if warranted, under section 6.

We will now discuss how certain combinations have been considered in other jurisdictions while considering the effect on competition.

Acquisition

Control

The question that was decided in *Anglo American Corporation/Lonrho*,[39] was that sole control may also be acquired in the case of a 'qualified minority'.

The operation consisted of the acquisition by Anglo American Corporation (AAC) and its related companies, of a total of 27.47 per cent of Lonrho's shares. Among the several arguments urged by the AAC before the Commission, one was that this holding was insufficient to place the AAC, and its related companies, in a position to exert decisive influence over Lonrho. The Commission referred to its notice on the notion of a concentration (OJ C 385, 31. 12. 1994, p. 5) which set out the factors for determining whether sole control exists in the case of a 'qualified minority' shareholder and held that the AAC had acquired the possibility to exercise decisive influence, and therefore control, over Lonrho. The notice stated that control would arise, for example, where the minority shareholder had the ability to achieve a majority in a shareholders' meeting, given that the remaining shares were widely dispersed among a number of shareholders. The Commission has applied this policy in a number of decisions.

Causing Another Company to Become a Subsidiary

Boeing/McDonnell Douglas[40]

Under the proposal, Boeing Company, US, (Boeing) was to acquire control of the whole of McDonnell Douglas Corporation (MDC), another company incorporated in the US, whereby MDC would become a subsidiary of Boeing, attracting Article 3(1)(b) of the EC Merger Regulation then in force (4064/89): 'A concentration shall be deemed to arise where: one or more persons already controlling at least one undertaking, or one or more undertakings acquire, whether by purchase of securities or assets, by contract or by any other means, direct or indirect control of the whole or parts of one or more other undertakings.'

Boeing's principal areas of business were: commercial aircraft, and defence and space. MDC's business was in four principal areas: military aircraft, missiles, space and electronic systems, commercial aircraft, and financial services.

Besides satisfying the requirement relating to 'community dimension' for the purpose of treating the proposal as falling under the Merger Regulation, the facts showed that the proposal had an important economic impact on the large commercial jet aircraft market within the European Economic Area (EEA).

The Commission determined that the proposed acquisition of McDonnel by Boeing would affect the market for large commercial jet aircraft. In the Commission's opinion, the geographic market for large commercial jet aircraft to be taken into account was a world market.

In the view of the Commission, the overall market for large commercial jet aircraft contained two separate relevant markets, the market for narrow-body aircraft and the market for wide-body aircraft. It was also of the view that the structure of those segments was similar and that therefore, the competition problems raised by the proposal were the same for both markets.

The three competitors in the worldwide market for large commercial jet aircraft, at the time of the hearing were Boeing, Airbus, and MDC. Boeing was the world's leading company in large commercial jet aircraft, sales of which represented about 70 per cent of its revenues. Airbus Industrie was the world's second largest producer of large commercial jet aircraft. MDC was the world's third largest manufacturer of large commercial jet aircraft, as well as the world's leading producer of military aircraft and the second leading defence firm in the world.

The Commission observed that Boeing's own '1997 Current Market Outlook', forecast that over the next 10 years, the total market potential was 7,330 aircraft, or the equivalent of US $490 billion (in 1996 US dollar terms) and that most of that demand would correspond to three main regional areas: Asia-Pacific (1,750 aircraft), North America (2,460 aircraft), and Europe (2,070 aircraft). The position was that European customers would account for more than 28 per cent of the cumulated demand and buy aircraft of the value of US $137 billion.

As for market shares, the Commission found that the combined market share of Boeing and MDC from 1989 was more or less stable at around 70 per cent and the very high market shares of Boeing indicated a strong position in the overall market for large commercial aircraft, as well as in the two markets proposed in the notification, viz. wide body and narrow body aircraft and was 'an illustration of dominance, as defined by the Court of Justice of the European Communities in its judgement in Case 322/81 *Michelin* v. *Commission*'. The Commission held further that the market structure within the EEA showed more or less the same pattern as the world market.

The market for second-hand large commercial jet aircraft was noted as forming a distinct market and different from the market for new large commercial jet aircraft, in which (latter) market Boeing and MDC were active. The Commission did not consider the second-hand market for large commercial jet aircraft in deciding the effect of the proposal on the market.

Boeing had a large customer base, giving it an advantage. It had also entered into certain long-term exclusive arrangements for the supply of large commercial jet aircraft to American Airlines, Delta Airlines, and Continental Airlines, three of the biggest airlines in the world. The purchasers found it advantageous to enter into these exclusive supply agreements of aircraft from Boeing because of certain options given to them. American Airlines obtained price-protect 'purchase rights' for a specified number of additional jets it might order during the more than 20-year exclusivity period. These rights, granted in consideration of the commitment to buy only from Boeing, entitled the buyer to decide when to place the order on Boeing, the period being shorter than the normal delivery period. Boeing had also, under such agreements, offered American Airlines a retroactive price reduction on aircraft purchased in previous campaigns.

In the view of the Commission, though these arrangements would obtain economic benefits for the purchasers, they were 'likely to be more than offset by the rigidity incurred by being locked into a single supplier for so long a period, during which it might prove to be the case that competitors' prices become lower, their technology and related services superior.'

The Commission also noted that the exclusive deals should be expected to have important foreclosure effects on the worldwide market for large commercial jet aircraft over the next 20 years.

The Commission held that acquisition of McDonnel's competitive potential in large commercial aircraft business, eliminating one competitor, McDonnel, leaving Boeing with only one competitor, Airbus, the combination of Boeing's and MDC's know-how and patent portfolios would strengthen Boeing's dominant position in the field of supply of large commercial aircraft.

Another situation that was considered as strengthening the dominant position of Boeing was the opportunity the proposed concentration gave to Boeing to gain control over the operations of Douglas Aircraft Company (DAC). The DAC was under the control of MDC, and was operating the commercial aircraft business of MDC, but DAC's business declined and at the time of the hearing it was no longer a real force in the market on a stand-alone basis. The competition concern was that it gave Boeing the power to supply or not DAC's products and consequently increased its own share of the market.

The Commission held that Boeing, at the time of the proposed concentration, already enjoyed a dominant position in the overall market for large commercial aircraft as well as for narrow-body and wide-body aircraft. It reached this conclusion in view of the various characteristics of the current structure of the markets for large commercial jet aircraft, in particular, the existing market shares of Boeing, the size of its fleet in service, the conclusion of long-term exclusive supply deals with major customers, and the lack of potential new entrants.

The Commission held that the proposed concentration would lead to a strengthening of Boeing's dominant position in large commercial aircraft through the large increase in Boeing's overall resources and in Boeing's defence and space business, which had a significant spillover effect on Boeing's position in large commercial aircraft. It held that the proposed concentration would lead to the strengthening of that dominant position through which effective competition would be significantly impeded in the Common Market.

However, the Commission held that the undertakings given by Boeing adequately addressed the competition problems identified in the case and that the full implementation of those undertakings would remove the concerns about a strengthening of Boeing's dominant position in the market for large commercial aircraft.

In sum, the major undertakings were that: Boeing would keep the separate legal status of DAC for 10 years, and would not do anything to leverage the product support for the DAC fleet with respect to the purchase of new aircraft; Boeing would discontinue its existing exclusive supply deals and not enter into fresh exclusive agreements until 1 August 2007, except for those campaigns in which another manufacturer had offered to enter into an exclusive agreement; Boeing agreed to license any commercial aircraft manufacturer, on a non-exclusive, reasonable royalty-bearing basis, any 'government-funded patent', which could be used in the manufacture or sale of commercial jet aircraft.

However, Boeing was free to select its suppliers, enforce its contracts with respect to price, quality scheduling and delivery and to protect its proprietary information.

The Commission's final conclusion was that subject to full compliance with the commitments made by Boeing, the proposed concentration would not create or strengthen a dominant position as a result of which effective competition would be significantly impeded in the common market or in a substantial part of it.

This case also concerned the issue of application of the competition laws of the US and the treatment of such issues under the bilateral

Concentrated Industry

United States v. *Alcoa*[41]

In this case, the acquisition by the Aluminum Company of America (Alcoa) of the stock and assets of the Rome Cable Corporation (Rome) was charged as a violation of section 7 of the Clayton Act.

The acquisition of Rome was sought to be defended on the ground that the share of Rome in aluminum conductor market was only 1.3 per cent, and that there would actually be no increase in concentration. The US Supreme Court did not agree with that plea as the situation in the aluminum industry appeared to be oligopolistic and in that kind of market the presence of 'small but significant competitors' would thwart the emergence of parallel policies of mutual advantage. The percentage of Rome's share in the aluminum conductor market, viz. 1.3 per cent was not determinative of the issue as Rome was fourth among independents in the aluminum conductor market and the records showed that Rome was an effective competitor. In fact, Alcoa, after the merger, appointed Rome the distributor of its entire conductor line. The Court held: 'Preservation of Rome, rather than its absorption by one of the giants, will keep it "as an important competitive factor".'

Vertical Integration

Vertical integration would arise when the acquisition or merger is between enterprises in different stages of production or supply, for example, the manufacturer of a complete product and supplier of a part or other component to make that finished product. It is possible that such acquisitions or mergers may raise issues concerning the effect on competition in the supply of the products covered by such arrangements. Section 20(4)(j) of the Indian Competition Act provides that the Commission, while inquiring into a combination under section 5, shall have due regard, among other factors, to the nature and extent of vertical integration in the market.

United States v. *Columbia Steel Co.*[42]

This was a suit, under section 4 of the Sherman Act to restrain the United States Steel Corporation and its subsidiaries from purchasing the assets of Consolidated Steel Corporation, the largest independent steel fabricator on the West Coast of the US, whose acquisition was charged as in violation of sections 1 and 2 of the Sherman Act.

Columbia, a subsidiary of United States Steel, entered into an agreement for buying the physical assets of Consolidated and its four subsidiaries. United States Steel Corporation and its subsidiaries were engaged in the business of producing rolled steel products and in structural fabrication. At the time of these proceedings, they were the largest producer of rolled steel products in the US, producing about a third of all rolled steel products in the country.

While Consolidated decided to sell its assets, as it considered, that from a business point of view, withdrawing from the fabrication business with its cyclical fluctuations, by selling its assets at a favourable price would be advantageous, United States Steel considered that the acquisition of Consolidated would assure it a market for the plates and shapes produced at its factory at Geneva, Utah. This vertical integration, closing the opportunity to other suppliers of rolled steel products to Consolidated, who were so far supplying to Consolidated was alleged by the government as constituting an illegal restraint of interstate commerce and violating the Sherman Act.

The complaint of the government was: (*a*) that the acquisition of Consolidated would exclude present suppliers from meeting the requirements of Consolidated for making rolled steel products as Consolidated would, after the acquisition, would only buy those requirements from United States Steel; (*b*) competition existing between United States Steel and Consolidated in the sale of structural fabricated products and pipes would be eliminated; and (*c*) it was also an attempt by United States Steel to monopolize the trade in fabricated steel products in the markets of Consolidated through a series of acquisitions.

The defence on behalf of Consolidated was that the extent of competition that may have been said to be affected was insignificant and that the restraint was a reasonable restraint and there was no attempt to monopolize that trade.

The US Supreme Court on appeal against a dismissal of the suit by the lower court, held that the government had failed to prove that the acquisition of Consolidated would unreasonably lessen competition as well as to prove that the acquisition amounted to an attempt to monopolize trade.

Regarding the charge of the government that the acquisition would exclude all present suppliers of rolled steel products to Consolidated as that company would only buy, after the acquisition, from United States Steel, the Court ruled that the effect of such an acquisition on the other suppliers of rolled steel products in their freedom to market their products was the question to be determined. It said: 'Exclusive dealings for rolled steel between Consolidated and United States Steel, brought about by vertical integration or otherwise, are not illegal, at any rate until the effect of such control is to unreasonably restrict the opportunities of competitors to market their product.'

Further, as the demand of Consolidated for rolled steel products was about 3 per cent of the demand in what was described as the Consolidated market, the Court held that the acquisition could not be said to restrain the freedom of other suppliers of rolled steel products to market their products.

It would be instructive to read what the Court said in relation to the approach to be taken by a court in considering the legality of a vertical integration under antitrust law:

It seems clear to us that vertical integration, as such without more, cannot be held violative of the Sherman Act. It is an indefinite term without explicit meaning. Even in the iron industry where could a line be drawn at the end of mining the ore, the production of the pig-iron or steel ingots, when the rolling mill operation is completed, fabrication on order or at some stage of manufacture into standard merchandise? No answer would be possible and therefore the extent of permissible integration must be governed, as other factors in Sherman Act violations, by the other circumstances of individual cases. Technological advances may easily require a basic industry plant to expand its processes into semi-finished or finished goods so as to produce desired articles in greater volume and with less expense. It is not for courts to determine the course of the Nation's economic development. Economists may recommend, the legislative and executive branches may chart legal courses by which the competitive forces of business can seek to reduce costs and increase production so that a higher standard of living may be available to all. The evils and dangers of monopoly and attempts to monopolize that grow out of size and efforts to eliminate others from markets, large or small, have caused Congress and the Executive to regulate commerce and trade in many respects. But no direction has appeared of a public policy that forbids, per se, an expansion of facilities of an existing company to meet the needs of new markets of a community, whether that community is nation-wide or county-wide. On the other hand, the courts have been given by Congress wide powers in monopoly regulation. The very broadness of terms such as restraint of trade, substantial competition and purpose to monopolize have placed upon courts the responsibility to apply the Sherman Act so as to avoid the evils at which Congress aimed. The basic industries, with few exceptions, do not approach in America a cartelized form. If businesses are to be forbidden from entering into different stages of production that order must come from Congress, not the courts.

The Court referred to its own earlier decision in *United States* v. *Paramount Pictures*, 334 US 131, wherein it had outlined the factors significant in determining the legality of a vertical integration. They were: the nature of the market to be served and the effect of the vertical integration on that market. The Court held that by these tests, the acquisition of Consolidated did not lead to any unreasonable restrictions on the opportunities of the competitor producers of rolled steel products.

However, *Ford Motor Co.* v. *United States*, discussed below, was a case where vertical integration had drastically changed the structure of the market in the spark plug industry.

On the question of the elimination of competition between United States Steel and Consolidated in the supply of structural steel products, after the acquisition, the Court held that there was no evidence before it that the competition between the two companies, before the acquisition, was substantial, so that there could be any consideration of an unreasonable restraint on competition.

Acquisition of Assets

Ford Motor Co. v. *United States*[43]

This was an action under section 7 of the Celler-Kefauver Antimerger Act, against Ford acquiring the assets of Electric Autolite Co., viz. its domestic spark plug plant, the distribution organization and Autolite's trade name. Autolite was an independent manufacturer of spark plugs and other automotive parts and a supplier to Ford. Ford's intention in making this acquisition was to participate in the replacement market, called the 'aftermarket'. It was quicker for Ford to do this in this manner rather than establish its own facilities for the manufacture of the spark plugs, which as noted by the Court would not have been illegal. Ford did not prefer it, as the project would take a longer time and was considered by Ford as more costly than the acquisition.

The district court held that the acquisition of Autolite by Ford was a violation of section 7 since its effect was likely to substantially lessen competition in automotive spark plugs. The Court's reasoning was that Ford's pre-acquisition position as a major customer in an oligopolistic industry was a moderating influence on the independent companies, which would cease after the acquisition, and that the acquisition by a buyer of a substantial share of the total industry output 'foreclosed' access to independent spark plug manufacturers. It ordered the divestiture of the Autolite plant and the trade name of Autolite.

The US Supreme Court, affirming this decree, held that Ford's position of a buyer of spark plugs as an original equipment manufacturer would 'maintain the virtually insurmountable barriers to entry to the aftermarket.' The divestiture of Autolite ordered by the District Court was confirmed, as with Ford as a purchaser of spark plugs, it was to be expected the divestiture would restore the competition that existed among other spark plug producers to sell to Ford. The divestiture was also a means to eliminate the anti-competitive consequences in the aftermarket flowing from the second largest automobile manufacturer's entry through acquisition into the spark plug manufacturing industry, the structure of which the acquisition had changed drastically. The Court considered that the relief granted would also enable Autolite to reestablish itself in the Original Equipment (OE) and replacement markets and remain a viable competitor.

Acquiring Machinery for Standardization

US v. *United Shoe Machinery Co. of New Jersey*[44]

Northern Securities is to be contrasted with United Shoe, a company that manufactured shoe-making machinery, which apparently was a similar case. United Shoe was formed for the purpose of acquiring and consolidating, into United Shoe, seven companies, engaged in a similar business. The consolidation lay in the transfer of the businesses of these companies, along with the patents they held, to United Shoe. The Supreme Court held that it was not an anti-competitive combination prohibited by the Act, as the facts were that those companies, were not in competition, at the time of their union with United Shoe, with each other in the products they were making, and that the purpose of organization, as shown to the Court was 'the consolidating of all the machines in one modern factory and the standardizing of them.' The unexceptional reasons for the acquisitions of those companies were: some companies had equipment needed by United Shoe, as accessories or to meet specific operations. Certain companies were acquired so that frustrating litigation around infringement of patents owned by them could be avoided. Also, the acquisitions were not made at one point of time but were spread over a number of years and the Court held the effect of those was to be judged separately and not in accumulation.

Shares in a Competing Company

International Shoe Co. v. Federal Trade Commission[45]

International Shoe acquired substantially all the stock of W.H. McElwain Company said to be in competition with it. This acquisition was charged as a violation of section 7 of the Clayton Act, leading to lessening of competition between them and a restraint on commerce.

The defence was that there was no substantial competition between the two companies, that the acquired company was nearly insolvent and that liquidation and sale were the options before that company and that, therefore, there was no prospect of any competition.

The Court determined that, though the companies were in the business of selling dress shoes, they were not in the same market. The products of the two were different in appearance and workmanship and appealed to the tastes of entirely different classes of consumers. Further, International Shoe's trade was through dealers in small communities, whereas, the acquired company's trade was through wholesalers and large retailers. The observations of the US Supreme Court in the matter of deciding upon the existence or otherwise of competition in a given case states the fundamental position: 'The existence of competition is a fact disclosed by observation rather than by the processes of logic; and when these officers, skilled in the business which they have carried on, assert that there was no real competition in respect of the particular product, their testimony is to be weighed like that in respect of other matters of fact.' There was no evidence to the contrary.

The Court held that the acquisition of stock of McElwain by International Shoe did not lessen competition. The evidence was that the bulk of the trade of each company was in different sections of the country. The main product of each company was sold to a different class of dealers and entered distinctly separate markets. Therefore the Court held 'that the purchase of its capital stock by a competitor (there being no other prospective purchaser), not with a purpose to lessen competition, but to facilitate the accumulated business of the purchaser and with the effect of mitigating seriously injurious consequences otherwise probable, is not in contemplation of law prejudicial to the public and does not substantially lessen competition or restrain commerce within the intent of the Clayton Act.'

However, in the view of the dissenting judges, when the evidence in that case showed that the competing products of the two companies were not only offered through different systems of distribution to the same retailers but were offered and sold by them to the ultimate consumers in their communities, it could be inferred that the arrangement as it existed before the acquisition would increase the competition. They also considered the financial position of McElwain as that of a company in a passing phase of the depression in the shoe business, and agreed with the FTC's representation that a receivership or reorganization of McElwain would enable it to continue its business and compete with International Shoe. They did not agree that McElwain was beyond revival and had only to be sold in some way.

JOINT VENTURES

The formation or operation of a joint venture could lead to anti-competitive effects. This depends on the intention of the parties regarding the use of the joint venture as a vehicle for their purposes and whether they limit their own right to compete. The Competition Act has not expressly provided for the regulation of joint ventures as constituting a combination, but they would be brought under section 5, if any acquisition or merger is covered by the conditions of the section. Section 3 of the Act dealing with anti-competitive agreements sets out in sub-section (3) certain agreements which are presumed to have an appreciable adverse effect on competition and the proviso to that sub-section exempts, from that sub-section (3), any joint venture agreement 'if such agreement increases efficiency in production, supply, distribution, storage, acquisition or control of goods or provision of services.'

As stated earlier, according to Article 3(4) of Council Regulation (EC) No. 139/2004 of 20 January 2004 on the control of concentrations between undertakings (the EC Merger Regulation), the creation of a joint venture performing on a lasting basis all the functions of an autonomous economic entity shall constitute a concentration within the meaning of paragraph 1(b) of Article 3.

In the US, the question is decided under the Clayton Act or the Sherman Act as the case may be.

Agreement Among Joint Venture Partners

Restraint on Competition Outside the Country through Combination and a Joint Venture

Timken Co. v. United States[46]

Three Timken corporations, Timken Roller Bearing Co., an American company, British Timken Ltd, a British company and, Societe Anonyme Francaise Timken, a French company, manufacturing antifriction bearings had allocated trade territories among themselves, fixed prices on products of one sold in the territory of the others, cooperated to protect each other's markets and to eliminate outside competition, and participated in cartels to restrict imports to, and exports from, the US. The District Court concluded that the appellant (the American Company) had violated the Sherman Act as charged and entered a comprehensive decree designed to bar future violations. The US Supreme Court confirmed the order of the District Court, except relating to divestiture of the holding of stock in overseas companies by the American Company.

The Supreme Court rejected many of the arguments on behalf of the appellant. It was claimed that the agreements impugned were part of a larger arrangement, viz. a joint venture between one Dewar who, along with the appellant company, held a significant percentage of the share capital of the British company as well as the entire share capital of the French company, and the appellant; that a trademark licensing agreement permitted the British and French companies to use the appellant's Timken mark, and that the terms of the agreement were reasonable and therefore could not be held to be in violation of the Sherman Act. The Supreme Court agreed with the finding of the district court that the dominant purpose of the restrictive agreements into which appellant, British Timken and French Timken entered was to avoid all competition either among themselves or with others and ruled that 'agreements between legally separate persons and companies to suppress competition among themselves cannot be justified by characterizing the project as a "joint venture"' and that common ownership or control of the contracting corporations would not liberate them from the impact of the antitrust laws.

Dealing with the contention that conditions of international trade demanded that for successful conduct of business abroad, the Sherman Act be made not applicable, the Court said:

The argument in this regard seems to be that tariffs, quota restrictions and the like are now such that the export and import of antifriction bearings can no longer be expected as a practical matter; that appellant cannot successfully sell its American-made goods abroad; and that the only way it can profit from business in England, France and other countries is through the ownership of stock in companies organized and manufacturing there. This position ignores the fact that the provisions in the Sherman Act against restraints of foreign trade are based on the assumption, and reflect the policy, that export and import trade in commodities is both possible and desirable.

Those provisions of the Act are wholly inconsistent with appellant's argument that American business must be left free to participate in international cartels, that free foreign commerce in goods must be sacrificed in order to foster export of American dollars for investment in foreign factories which sell abroad. Acceptance of appellant's view would make the Sherman Act a dead letter insofar as it prohibits contracts and conspiracies in restraint of foreign trade. If such a drastic change is to be made in the statute, Congress is the one to do it.

Potential Competition—Section 7 of the Clayton Act

United States v. *Penn-Olin Co.*[47]

Penn-Olin Co. was a joint venture company, formed by two companies not in competition with each other at the time of the formation of the joint venture, but the question that had to examined in that case was if the joint venture blocked any potential competition from any one of the two companies.

Pennsalt Chemicals Corporation and Olin Mathieson Company formed a new company, Penn-Olin Chemical Company, for the manufacture and sale of sodium chlorate, a product which Pennsalt was engaged in manufacturing and for which Olin was a selling agent. Olin did not produce that product at the time of the complaint. Pennsalt and Olin owned 50 per cent each of the stock of the joint venture company.

One of the contentions of the promoters of the joint venture was that section 7 of the Clayton Act would not apply to a newly formed company such as Penn-Olin, as the requirement was that the acquired company was to be 'engaged' in commerce.

Section 7 of the Clayton Act, 38 Stat. 731, as amended, 15 U.S.C. 18, provides in part:

> No corporation engaged in commerce shall acquire, directly or indirectly, the whole or any part of the stock or other share capital and no corporation subject to the jurisdiction of the Federal Trade Commission shall acquire the whole or any

part of the assets of another corporation engaged also in commerce, where in any line of commerce in any section of the country, the effect of such acquisition may be substantially to lessen competition, or to tend to create a monopoly.

The US Supreme Court held that the joint venture in that case would be subject to the regulation of section 7 of the Clayton Act, as the joint venture was 'organized specifically to engage in commerce'. More than that, according to the record, the joint venture company was actually engaged in commerce at the time of the suit and the Supreme Court held that the economic effects of an acquisition were to be measured at that point rather than at the time of the acquisition.

On the criteria to be applied in considering the applicability of section 7 to such cases of promotion of joint ventures, the Supreme Court stated that what had to be considered was the elimination of potential competition by the joint venture. It said: 'Just as a merger eliminates actual competition, this joint venture may well foreclose any prospect of competition between Olin and Pennsalt in the relevant sodium chlorate market.'

Since the Court found that the District Court had not considered, in determining the effect of the joint venture on the competition between the two promoters, the reasonable probability, if there was no joint venture, of either one of them building a plant in the relevant market area for engaging in the business for which the joint venture was created, while the other would have remained a significant potential competitor, it remanded the case to the District Court for that purpose.

The US Supreme Court listed the following criteria for the District Court to take into consideration in assessing the probability of a substantial lessening of competition: the number and power of the competitors in the relevant market; the background of their growth; the power of the joint venturers; the relationship of their lines of commerce; the competition existing between them and the power of each in dealing with the competitors of the other; the setting in which the joint venture was created; the reasons and necessities for its existence; the joint venture's line of commerce and the relationship thereof to that of its parents; the adaptability of its line of commerce to non-competitive practices; the potential power of the joint venture in the relevant market; an appraisal of what the competition in the relevant market would have been if one of the joint venturers had entered it alone instead of through Penn-Olin; the effect, in the event of this occurrence, of the other joint venturer's potential competition; and such other factors as might indicate potential risk to competition in the relevant market.

The Court observed in conclusion: 'In weighing these factors the court should remember that the mandate of the Congress is in terms of the probability of a lessening of substantial competition, not in terms of tangible present restraint.' The Court ruled that section 7, as amended, relating to acquisition of stock was intended to arrest incipient threats to competition which the Sherman Act did not ordinarily reach and that in those cases actual restraints need not be proved.

The 'Antitrust Guidelines for Collaborations Among Competitors' issued by the FTC and the US Department of Justice in April 2000 are intended to explain how the Agencies analyse certain antitrust issues raised by collaborations among competitors. 'A "competitor collaboration" comprises a set of one or more agreements, other than merger agreements, between or among competitors to engage in economic activity, and the economic activity resulting therefrom. "Competitors" encompasses both actual and potential competitors.' The Agencies conform to the principles laid down by the courts on what agreements are per se illegal, viz. territory allocation, price fixing, etc., and what are to be determined by the rule of reason as to the effect on competition and procompetitive benefits.

MERGER

Joint Control—Shareholding and Restructuring Agreement

Deutsche Telekom/BetaResearch[48]

In this case, the intended concentration, to be effected through the purchase of shares, lay in the proposal whereby Deutsche Telekom AG (Telekom) and BetaTechnik AG (BetaTechnik) would acquire joint control, within the meaning of Article 3(1) of the Merger Regulation, of BetaResearch. Telekom, as a public telecommunications operator in Germany, was active, either directly or through subsidiaries, in all areas of telecommunications services, and the owner and operator of nearly all the German cable-television networks at level 3.

BetaTechnik, a company, part of the Kirch group, (Kirch), was engaged mainly in film post production work, such as dubbing. Kirch was the leading German supplier of feature films and television programming and also active in commercial television.

BetaResearch, a wholly-owned Kirch subsidiary, was the holder of exclusive, open-ended licences—granted for Germany, Austria and the

German-speaking part of Switzerland—for Beta encryption technology for the encryption of programmes on the basis of the d-box decoder. The access technology was licensed to BetaResearch by DigCo B V in which Kirch had a 50 per cent stake. BetaResearch as one developoing encryption and operating software for the d-box technology intended to licence this technology to pay-TV operators, providers of technical services for digital television and decoder manufacturers.

The agreement on the restructuring of BetaResearch among BetaResearch Telecom, Kirch and another company, provided for the intended joint control of BetaResearch. The relevant clause stated that certain important business decisions listed were to be taken by the proprietors. The proceedings before the European Commission arose out of a condition in that restructuring agreement relating to the licensing of Beta access technology. Under the agreement, Telecom agreed to use exclusively Beta access technology on the basis of the d-box decoder. The right to be given to Telekom to use the Beta access technology in respect of cable networks was to be exclusive. This exclusive right to be given to Telekom was held to be one that would create a concentration that was incompatible with the common market.

The EC identified technical services for pay-TV and cable networks as the product markets. Germany was considered the geographical markets for both products.

At that time, Telekom, one of the acquirers, had the preponderant share of the cable network market and was the only provider of technical services for digital signal transmission over cable networks. The Commission held that the exclusive licence shut other cable operators from access to the Beta access technology, depriving them of the ability to compete with Telekom. As the Commission considered that the undertakings given by the parties, initial and expanded, were inadequate to solve the 'existing competition problems', viz. strengthening of the dominant position of Telekom in both the markets, it declared the concentration as incompatible with the Common Market under Article 8(3) of the Merger Regulation then in force.

Merger Eliminating a Competitor

Brown Shoe Co. Inc. v. *US*[49]

This was an action to restrain the merger of Kinney Company Inc., a manufacturer of men's, women's, and children's shoes (the twelfth largest shoe manufacturer in the US) and a retailer, with Brown Shoe Company Inc., the third largest seller of shoes by dollar volume in the US and a leading manufacturer of men's, women's, and children's shoes, and a retailer with over 1,230 retail outlets.

Through acquisitions already made, Brown was the fourth largest shoe manufacturer in the US, producing about 4 per cent of the country's total footwear production.

Since the requirements of Kinney were agreed to be supplied by Brown (about 7.9 per cent of all Kinney's needs), it was contended that the proposed merger may substantially lessen competition or tend to create a monopoly in the production of shoes in the national market by eliminating actual or potential competition and also foreclosing the competition that was previously offered by Kinney in the retail market. The district court ordered divestiture by Brown of Kinney.

The Supreme Court noted that the legislative history of the Act showed that 'section 7 applied not only to mergers between actual competitors, but also to vertical and conglomerate mergers whose effect may tend to lessen competition in any line of commerce in any section of the country.' The Court also held that after the amendment of this section 7, it would be inappropriate to apply the standards relevant under the Sherman Act for judging the legality of business combinations.

Section 7 of the Clayton Act as amended, states that:

> no corporation engaged in commerce shall acquire, directly or indirectly, the whole or any part of the stock or other share capital of another corporation engaged also in commerce, where in any line of commerce in any section of the country, the effect of such acquisition may be substantially to lessen competition, or to tend to create a monopoly.

The US Supreme Court added that to determine the effect on competition, the area of effective competition would need to be ascertained and this, it ruled, had to be determined by reference to a product market (the 'line of commerce') and a geographic market (the 'section of the country'). In this case, the competing products of the merging companies had to be identified.

The Court indicated that while the outer boundaries of a product market would be determined by 'the reasonable interchangeability of use or the cross-elasticity of demand between the product itself and substitutes for it', there could be well-defined sub-markets which by themselves may constitute product markets for antitrust purposes. 'The boundaries of such a sub-market may be determined by examining such practical indicia as industry or public recognition of the sub-market as a separate economic entity, the product's peculiar characteristics and uses, unique production facilities, distinct customers, distinct prices, sensitivity to price changes, and specialized vendors.'

In this case, the product lines recognized by the public were men's, women's, and children's shoes, each directed toward a distinct class of customers. The whole country was the geographic market. In a vertical integration, foreclosing the market available, till the merger, to other suppliers, the crucial question to be decided was the size of the market. In the view of the Court, in determining the applicability of the section, the nature and purpose of the arrangement was the most important factor.

Considering the position of the two companies and their market shares, and the trend in the shoe industry of increasing vertical mergers, the Court held that the merger may tend to lessen competition substantially in the retail sale of men's, women's, and children's shoes in the majority of the cities in which the two companies sold directly or through controlled outlets.

Product Market, End-uses

United States v. Continental Can Co.[50]

Continental Can Company, the country's second largest producer of metal containers, acquired the assets, business and goodwill of Hazel-Atlas Glass Company, the third largest producer of glass containers in the country, by issue of shares in Continental for assets acquired. The Government of the United States brought an antitrust action, under section 7 of the Clayton Act, seeking divestiture of the assets of the acquired undertaking.

The US Supreme Court, reversing the decision of the District Court, held that the position that products for which containers were used were different and with distinctive characteristics would not automatically remove the competition between the suppliers of cans from the reach of section 7 of the Act. The relevant product market was determined as the combined glass and metal container industries and all the end-uses for which they competed.

The Court ruled that inter-industry competition, between metal and glass containers for the same end-uses, food, soft drinks, medicine, cosmetic, household, chemical industries, etc., had to be taken into consideration in determining the product market. It said: 'If an area of effective competition cuts across industry lines, the relevant line of commerce must do likewise.'

The Court stated as the proper way of examining a merger in determining anti-competitive effects of a merger: 'The merger must be viewed functionally in the context of the particular market involved, its structure, history and probable future.'

Continental's share among end-uses for which glass and metal competed was 21.9 per cent. Hazel-Atlas ranked sixth in the relevant line of commerce, its share of the product market being 3.1 per cent. The merger removed Hazel-Atlas as an independent factor in the glass industry and in the line of commerce which included both metal cans and glass containers. Its potential competition with Continental was held as foreclosed.

The Supreme Court held that the merger violated section 7, as it would have a probable anti-competitive effect within the relevant line of commerce.

Telecommunication Services

British Telecom/MCI (II)[51]

The principal activity of British Telecommunications plc (BT) was the supply of telecommunications services and equipment. MCI Communications Corporation (MCI) was a diversified communications company offering a portfolio of integrated services, including long distance, wireless, local, paging, messaging, Internet, information services, outsourcing and advanced global communications in the US. The scheme was to merge MCI into a subsidiary of BT incorporated in the US, to rename that subsidiary as MCI Communications Corporation, and then to change name of BT to Concert plc, which would be incorporated in London. Business and consumer services were to continue to be sold in the UK and the US, under the BT and MCI brand names respectively, and through separate operations.

Among the various segments of the markets for telecommunication services offered by the companies, viz. domestic public switched voice services, enhanced value-added services, private leased lines, and international telecommunications, the Commission found that the relevant product markets, in that case, were only the market for international voice telephony services and audio-conferencing, and that the merger could be considered to have an impact on competition in those two markets. In the opinion of the EC, in considering international voice telephony services, cable and satellite were not substitutable for the provision of international voice telephony services at the required standards. In this case, the service was through cables and the control of BT over cable capacity in the relevant route was significant.

The Commission held that the relevant geographic market for international voice telephony services had to be defined with reference to call traffic routes between any country pair, on the UK–US route in this case, since different international routes could not be considered as viable demand substitutes. The Commission also noted that the possibility of hubbing, that is, re-routing US–UK traffic through third countries, did not appear to be a viable commercial possibility at that time, since under the system of accounting rates existing then and proportionate return it would be more expensive than using direct routes.

The geographical market for audio conference was held as national as 'customers do not generally purchase the service globally or internationally, even if an audio conference includes participants from different countries.'

The revenues of BT showed its dominant position in the market for the provision of international voice telephony service in the UK–US route.

The Commission ruled that the control of the cable capacity in the relevant route by the companies was likely to place the merged entity in a position to restrict new entrants. The substantial market share of BT and an associate company in the business of providing audio conferencing facilities was held as with the potential to restrict new entrants. The possible anti-competitive effects of the proposed merger were neutralized by the undertakings given by the parties.

Internet Access Services

WorldCom/MCI[52]

WorldCom, Inc. (WorldCom) and MCI Communications Corporation (MCI) were US-based telecommunication companies. The proposal was to merge MCI into TC Investments Corp., a Delaware corporation and a direct wholly-owned subsidiary of WorldCom.

In considering internet access services as a product, the EC held that though the provision of specific end-user to end-user data transmission facilities using other data protocols might well enable customers to reach a limited number of other customers using the same protocol, it would not provide the permanent, unfettered access to the community of Internet users which is the main purpose of buying the service and that, therefore, other forms of data transmission service would not be significantly substitutable.

In determining, for purposes of market definition, whether Internet Service Providers (ISPs) all compete against one another to provide the same Internet connectivity services, or whether there are any distinct and narrower markets within the sector, the Commission stated that the inter-relationships of the ISPs' networks was crucial. It stated that the offering of one network may be considered a substitute for that of another network only when both offered equivalent service standards but not when the service standards were widely differentiated. The content and price of the product on offer from any given ISP will depend on factors, such as the size of the ISP's network, and the precise nature of the relationships it has with other networks.

In the Commission's analysis, the industry was 'structured with a hierarchy of ISPs with progressively larger and geographically more wide-ranging networks providing transit for smaller and more localized ISPs unable to deliver traffic on their own account.'

The Commission found that the relevant product market on which the merging parties were active was the market for the provision of top level or 'universal' Internet connectivity, meaning that they were those 'capable of delivering complete Internet connectivity entirely on their own account' and that the said market was 'effectively one global market'.

The Commission recognized the practical difficulty in determining as conclusive an acceptable unit of measurement of the share of the market for providing Internet access services. This was compounded by the absence of industry consensus on such units.[53] But in this case, it ascertained the market shares of the two enterprises on revenue earned and traffic flow and found that the combined entity would hold over 50 per cent of the market. It held that the merger would produce anti-competitive effects such as entry barriers, the two companies raising their costs and decreasing the quality of their service offerings. The Commission concluded that the concentration, if not altered, would lead to the creation of a dominant position in the market for the provision of top level or universal Internet connectivity.

The Commission accepted the undertakings given by parties, the principal one being the provision for divesting the entire Internet business of MCI to a new company and approved the merger.

REGULATION OF COMBINATIONS UNDER THE COMPETITION ACT

The Process

Having set out, earlier in this chapter, the principles governing the regulation of combination, we may now refer to the provisions relating to the process by which this regulation is sought to be enforced. Section 20(1) and (2) states how the process of inquiry into a combination is initiated by the Commission.[54] Sub-section (1) is to the effect that the Commission may commence the process on its own knowledge or information. But where there is a notice under section 6(2) of a combination, the Commission shall make the inquiry on receipt of the notice. Section 6(2) referred to above requires a person or an enterprise proposing to enter into a combination to give notice to the Commission disclosing the details of the proposed combination.[55] After the 2007 amendment to section 6(2), the notice is mandatory and no longer at the option of the party. This notice should be given within thirty days of (a) approval of a merger by the board of directors of the enterprises concerned; or (b) execution of any document or agreement for acquisition covered by section 5(a) or section 5(b). The Commission shall deal with such a notice in accordance with the provisions of sections 29, 30, and 31.

Section 29 deals with combinations that come to the notice of the Commission and section 30 deals with cases where it has received a notice under section 6(2) of a proposed combination. In both cases, the Commission ought to inquire into whether the combination has, or is likely to cause an appreciable adverse effect on competition within the relevant market in India. While acting under section 29, the Commission should issue a notice to the parties of its intention to proceed with an investigation into the combination. A material amendment of 2007 of section 29 is the option given to the Commission to call for a report from the Director-General. If the Commission is prima facie of the opinion that the combination has, or is likely to have, an appreciable adverse effect on competition, it should also direct the parties to the said combination to publish details of the combination for bringing the combination to the knowledge or information of the public and persons affected, or likely to be affected by such combination. After receipt of all information from the parties and the objectors, if any, and the report of the Director-General, if any, the Commission should deal with the case as provided under section 31.

Section 31—Orders of the Commission on Certain Combinations[56]

Under section 31, the Commission shall approve a combination where it is of the opinion that any combination does not, or is not likely to, have an appreciable adverse effect on competition. This will apply to a combination in respect of which a notice under section 6(2) has been given to the Commission.

Where the Commission is of the opinion that the combination has, or is likely to have, an appreciable adverse effect on competition, it should direct that the combination shall not take effect. The Commission may propose appropriate modifications to the combination if it is of the opinion that the combination has, or is likely to have, an appreciable adverse effect on competition but such adverse effect can be eliminated by suitable modification to such combination. The parties may either accept the modification or submit an amendment to the modification. If the Commission accepts the amendment it may approve the combination. But if the Commission does not accept the amendment and the parties do not accept the modification within the prescribed time, the combination should be deemed to have an appreciable adverse effect on competition and be dealt with in accordance with the provisions of the Act.

Where the Commission has directed that a combination shall not take effect, or that the combination is deemed to have an appreciable adverse effect on competition under sub-section (9), the Commission may order that: (*a*) the acquisition referred to in sub-section (a) of section 5; or (*b*) the acquiring of control referred to in sub-section (b) of section 5; or (*c*) the merger or amalgamation referred to in sub-section (c) of section 5, shall not be given effect to. This would be in addition to any penalty that may be imposed or any prosecution which may be initiated under the Act.[57] The Commission may also, in appropriate cases, frame a scheme to implement its order under section 31(10).

Section 31(11), amended in 2007, is as follows: 'If the Commission does not, on the expiry of a period of two hundred and ten days from the date of notice given to the Commission under sub-section (2) of section 6 pass an order or issue direction in accordance with the provisions of sub-section (1) or sub-section (2) or sub-section (7), the combination shall be deemed to have been approved by the Commission.'[58]

Sub-section (13) declares that where the Commission has ordered a combination to be void, the acquisition or acquiring of control or merger or amalgamation referred to in section 5, shall be dealt with by the authorities under any other law for the time being in force as if such acquisition or acquiring of control or merger or amalgamation had not taken place, and the parties to the combination shall be dealt with accordingly. Nothing contained in this chapter shall affect any proceeding initiated or which may be initiated under any other law for the time being in force.[59]

Reliefs

Interim Orders—Section 33

The Commission had powers, under section 33, to grant a temporary injunction restraining any party from carrying on an act in contravention of section 3(1) (entering into anti-competitive agreements), or section 4(1) (abusing a dominant position) or section 6,[60] or importing any goods in contravention of the above-mentioned sections, until the conclusion of an inquiry or until further orders, without giving notice to the opposite party, where it deems it necessary.

The 2007 amendment removed the Commission's power to grant a temporary injunction, which was more appropriate to courts and not to a market regulator, and also omitted the position relating to import of goods. Now under the amended section 33, the Commission may only issue interim orders.[61]

Awarding Compensation

Under section 34 of the Competition Act 2002, the Commission was empowered to order compensation to any person or persons to be paid by any enterprise for any loss or damage shown to have been suffered, by such persons, as a result of any contravention of the provisions of sections 3 to 6 committed by such enterprise. It should be noted that the loss or damage for which compensation may be claimed should arise out of the breach of these sections. Since this power now vests with the Competition Appellate Tribunal, under section 53A(1)(b), section 34 has been omitted by the 2007 amendment. The compensation claimable was called 'antitrust injury' which claimants seeking damages under sections 4 (actual injury) and 7 (threatened injury) of the Clayton Act should prove.

Antitrust Injury

Cargill, Inc. v. Monfort of Colorado, Inc.[62] was a case where an alleged price-cost squeeze, pursuant to an apprehended post-merger price competition was held as not an antitrust injury to which section 16 of the Clayton Act was intended to apply.

The relevant part of section 16 of the Clayton Act provides: that '[a]ny person, firm, corporation, or association shall be entitled to sue for and have injunctive relief ... against threatened loss or damage by a violation of the antitrust laws ....' The Court held that the threat of loss of profits due to possible price competition following a merger does not constitute a threat of antitrust injury. Antitrust injury means injury caused by practices prohibited by the statute. Showing of loss or damage due merely to increased competition would not constitute such injury.

The Court cited its earlier decision in *Brunswick Corp. v. Pueblo Bowl-O-Mat Inc.*,[63] which was a case relating to a claim for treble damages under section 4 of the Clayton Act, for actual loss, and not threatened loss as in Cargill, where it had rejected the contention that the acquisition of competing bowling centres that had defaulted in payments for bowling equipment that they had purchased from the petitioner might substantially lessen competition or tend to create a monopoly in violation of section 7 of the Clayton Act. The loss that was claimed was the profits the petitioners would have earned if the acquired companies had been allowed to be closed, instead of being acquired. The Court ruled that the loss was not an antitrust injury.

Multijurisdiction Mergers

Multijurisdiction mergers present special problems and enforcement authorities of any domestic law relating to competition should recognize them. It would enable cooperation from parties to such mergers who may not have a place of business in India and are subject to a different jurisdiction. The primary concern of such parties is the delay and consequent costs in effecting such mergers. More than that they wish to have consistency in the broad concept of antitrust issues such as product market, dominant position, threshold levels, etc. While they know that determination of such issues is always subject to the domestic law in force in the enforcing country and that there cannot be uniformity in law, at least in the foreseeable future, like anyone doing business, they would prefer to have less uncertainty and more acceptable consensus.

US Study

Chapters 2 and 3 of the Final Report to the Attorney General and Assistant Attorney General for Antitrust, 2000, of the International Competition Policy Advisory Committee of the Department of Justice ('the ICPA Committee'), US, deal with multijurisdiction mergers. Chapter 2 deals with 'Multijurisdiction Mergers: Facilitating Substantive Convergence and Minimizing Conflict'. Chapter 3 deals with 'Rationalizing the Merger Review Process Through Targeted Reform'.

Minimizing conflict

Chapter 2 of the Report begins with the statement that issues raised by the proliferation of merger control laws are at the cutting edge of economic globalization. The challenges identified by the Report are the differences in the competition laws and regulations of various countries, reflecting divergent policy goals and the extraterritorial reach of many merger control laws.

Some of the major problems that companies implementing multijurisdiction merger schemes face are highlighted thus:

> For the merging parties, these challenges may include heightened uncertainty regarding the ultimate legality of the proposed transaction; the necessity for interacting and negotiating with multiple reviewing authorities; the possibility of inconsistent and perhaps conflicting rulings; and the potential for overly burdensome remedies. These challenges increase transaction costs for merging parties and, in the worst-case scenario, may result in the abandonment of procompetitive transactions.

Further problems that are to be anticipated, the Report adds, are the likelihood of decisions of an enforcement authority in one country imposing remedies with 'extra-territorial effects', or of a remedy that may make the enforcement by another authority difficult. It draws attention to the divergence in outcome where the transaction of a merger is subject to multiple agencies in countries with their own domestic law relating to competition. The report considered that a solution that may aid in meeting such problems could be 'facilitating where possible, substantive harmonization and convergence of substantive standards and approaches to merger review'.

The report draws attention to two circumstances in which multi-jurisdiction review of mergers may precipitate international friction. One is, ignoring 'externalities', meaning thereby that competitive benefits or harm in foreign markets is not taken into account by a reviewing authority. Also, a conflict may arise on account of contradictory decisions as to the effect on competition of such a merger. The other source of potential conflict is the imposition of remedies with extraterritorial effects.

The Committee considered the following steps as likely to minimize conflicts and to promote a degree of convergence among nations: facilitating greater transparency, developing disciplines for the review of transactions with significant transnational or spillover effects, enhancing cross-border cooperation among antitrust enforcement agencies, through the development of a framework for cooperation and the exchange of confidential business information, and developing work-sharing arrangements.

The Committee did not consider it as practicable, suggestions for a uniform code on international mergers or an international dispute settlement mechanism relating to those mergers.

Transaction costs

Chapter 3 of the report emphasizes the need 'to focus on those unnecessary and unduly burdensome costs imposed by merger control regimes that have little or no relationship to antitrust enforcement goals'. The costs referred to are the transaction costs imposed by the notification and review procedures implemented by various jurisdictions. They are: direct costs of filing fees, fees to counsel, indirect costs of executive time, and the lost opportunity costs resulting from the long time taken in deciding on the proposal for merger.

The Committee noted however, that for the present, such costs are best taken by the companies as normal cost of doing business.

The Committee believes that one way of improving the environment for such multijurisdiction mergers would be that individual countries enforcing an antitrust legislation focus only on 'those transactions that raise competitive concerns within their territory and refrain from unduly burdening transactions, particularly those that lack anti-competitive potential'.

India, with its new competition law to be tested through experience, should take note also of a number of other observations of this Committee.

Prior Notification

The ICPA Committee recommended that prior notification to the merger reviewing authorities of an intended merger should be required as it saves time and money. Unscrambling a consummated merger is costly. Also, after a merger has been effected it would be difficult to restore the pre-merger competitive market structure. The Committee noted that the pre-merger notification required by Hart-Scott-Rodino Act of 1976 (HSR Act or HSR) was to give the agencies 'an effective mechanism to enjoin illegal mergers before they occur'.

The Committee's report cites two cases where the FTC was able to show that the proposed mergers were anti-competitive and the blocking of the mergers led to savings to consumers. One was where it obtained a preliminary injunction to prevent two office supply superstores from merging in 1997 and the savings to consumers was estimated to be approximately $250 million annually. The agency also estimates that it had saved consumers another $300 million annually by blocking two nearly simultaneously proposed mergers in the drug wholesaling industry in 1998.

The rationale behind the requirement of prior notification is best stated in the Committee's own words:

Reliance on premerger notification systems to provide advance notice of proposed transactions is based in large part on the recognition that competition authorities have neither the time nor the resources to monitor all business transactions in an attempt to identify those that pose a threat to competition. Nor do they have the ability to detect those 'midnight mergers' that are consummated without public notice. Moreover, it is not practical to place the burden of notification on concerned competitors and consumers. Reliance on these entities to provide advance notice may prove imperfect either because these entities may not know about transactions before their consummation or because the transaction costs incurred by these entities in notifying the competition authorities may outweigh any benefits obtained by having the proposed transactions reviewed.

Threshold levels

In the view of the IPAC Committee, one of the factors that led to high transaction costs was low notification thresholds. It recommended several *best practices* that jurisdictions may consider and, where necessary, refine them so that the 'merger review net is cast appropriately'. It suggested the following that would lead to reduction in unnecessary transaction costs, without significantly reducing the public benefit from advance notification:

1. In establishing its premerger notification thresholds, each jurisdiction should seek to screen out mergers that are unlikely to generate appreciable anticompetitive effects within the reviewing jurisdiction.
   - This screening can be achieved, first, by implementing threshold tests that require an *appreciable nexus to the jurisdiction*, such as transaction-related sales or target assets in the jurisdiction.
   - Second, jurisdictions should set notification thresholds *only as broadly as necessary* to ensure the reporting of potentially problematic transactions. If an indexing mechanism is not employed, the Advisory Committee recommends that jurisdictions review their notification thresholds periodically (at least every four years) to determine whether they should be adjusted.
2. Additional steps that can be taken at this stage to reduce costs for international mergers include establishing objectively based notification thresholds and ensuring their transparency.
3. To better ensure that potentially anti-competitive transactions do not escape scrutiny under merger review systems, the Advisory Committee recommends that competition authorities be given the authority to pursue potentially anticompetitive transactions even if those transactions do not satisfy notification thresholds. Although the federal antitrust agencies in the United States already possess this authority, many existing merger regimes authorize regulators to review transactions only when notification requirements are satisfied.
4. Any efforts to revise notification thresholds also must consider filing fees, which currently constitute a significant source of revenue for numerous competition authorities, including the federal antitrust agencies in the United States. Ideally, no competition agency should be dependent on filing fees for its budget or staff salaries. To ensure that these competition authorities will be able to pursue their enforcement missions vigorously, it is imperative to provide agencies with alternative sources of funding to offset the loss of any funds that may result from revising notification thresholds or 'delinking' filing fees from agency budgets.

India should at the earliest review its notification threshold levels.

Bilateral Agreements

Till such time as convergence of substantive standards is within reach, the working alternative is a bilateral agreement, whether in the field of mergers or other anti-competitive conduct across countries. The EU and the US have entered into the necessary bilateral agreements. The following is a summary of an understanding between the two countries on best practices on cooperation in merger investigations.

US-EU Merger Working Group—Best Practices on Cooperation in Merger Investigations

Pursuant to an agreement on 23 September 1991, between the Government of the United States of America and the Commission of the European Communities regarding the application of their competition laws,[64] the EU and the US, through their respective Merger Working Groups entered into an understanding on 'Best Practices on Cooperation in Merger Investigations'. This document sets out the best practices, 'United States federal antitrust agencies and the Commission of the European Union will seek to apply, to the extent consistent with their respective laws and enforcement responsibilities, when they simultaneously review the same merger transaction'.

The substance of the agreement

The objective is to reach, as far as possible, consistent, or at least non-conflicting outcomes as divergent decisions on the same transaction would undermine public confidence in the merger review process. The major terms of this agreement cover the timing of the investigations by the US and EU antitrust investigating agencies, collection and evaluation of evidence, such as sharing publicly available information and, consistent with their confidentiality obligations, discussing their respective analyses at various stages of an investigation, including tentative market definitions, assessment of competitive effects, efficiencies, theories of competitive harm, economic theories, and the empirical evidence needed to test those theories.

The agencies will also advise the parties to consider coordinating the timing and substance of remedy proposals being made to the EU and US agencies, to avoid the risk of inconsistent results or difficulties in implementation.

Review of the Provisions of the Act

The position regarding companies that plan to merge, but do not meet the criterion of the value of assets or turnover and also which do not raise issues affecting competition should have been expressly stated to be governed only by the Companies Act, 1956. Also, the position regarding companies that do not meet that criteria, but raise competition issues should have been specifically laid down. Section 21(1) of the competition Act only provides that in a case where a statutory authority proposes to take a decision or has taken a decision, a party contends that that decision taken or proposed to be taken would be contrary to any of the provisions of this Act, that statutory authority may make a reference in respect of that issue to the Commission. But instead of providing for such specific issues of practical concern, the amendments of 2007 have only dealt with the question of overlapping of authority of the Competition Commission and a statutory authority.

The 2007 amendment has introduced a proviso to this sub-section that the statutory authority may also make, suomoto, a reference to the Commission and also provided that on receipt of the reference, the Commission shall give its opinion, within sixty days of receipt of such reference, to such statutory authority. Then the statutory authority shall consider the opinion of the Commission and thereafter, give its findings recording reasons therefore on the issues referred to in the said opinion.

If it is shown to the Commission that any decision it may take impinges on the powers of any statutory authority, the Commission may make a reference of the issue, on the representation of a party or suomoto, to the statutory authority. Then, the statutory authority shall give its opinion, within sixty days of receipt of such reference, to the Commission which shall consider the opinion of the statutory authority, and thereafter give its findings recording reasons therefore on the issues referred to in the said opinion.[65]

Countries that have had antitrust and merger control regulations for significant periods periodically review and revise legislation. In the UK, the regulation of mergers, from 2002, is under the Enterprise Act, 2002, whereas formerly it was under the Fair Trading Act, 1973. The EEC has replaced its Merger Regulation 4064/89 with the new Regulation (EC) No. 139/2004 of 20 January 2004, 'to meet the challenges of a more integrated market and the future enlargement of the EU'.

It is only with the passage of time and the experience gained, in working the Act in relation to the country's specific economic system, one may suggest what changes are to be made regarding the criteria and the value of assets or turnover or any other relevant factor in regulating combinations.

Endnotes

[1] The Central Government has, by its Circular No. 30/2011 dated 23-5-2011, clarified to the Regional Directors, Registrars of Companies and Official Liquidators, that after the repeal of the MRTP Act, sections 108A to 108I of the Companies Act, 1956, have become redundant and will have no legal force.

[2] (2004) 122 Comp Cas 83 SC.

[3] See *Hindustan Lever* v. *State of Maharashtra* (2003) 117 Company Cases 758 SC, upholding such a levy.

[4] (1995) 83 Comp Cas 30 Supreme Court.

[5] Paragraph 1.2.6.

[6] The Explanation to this sub-section (11) states what periods are to be excluded in determining this period of two hundred and ten days.

[7] May be browsed at the website of the Competition Commission of India: www.cci.gov.in. In addition, the Commission has also released its General Regulations—the Competition Commission of India (General) Regulations, 2009 (No. 2 of 2009) New Delhi, 21 May 2009.

[8] Section 6(1).

[9] Inquiry into combination by the Commission.

Section 20(4): For the purposes of determining whether a combination would have the effect of or is likely to have an appreciable adverse effect on competition in the relevant market, the Commission shall have due regard to all or any of the following factors, namely:— (a) actual and potential level of competition through imports in the market; (b) extent of barriers to entry into the market; (c) level of combination in the market; (d) degree of countervailing power in the market; (e) likelihood that the combination would result in the parties to the combination being able to significantly and sustainably increase prices or profit margins; (f) extent of effective competition likely to sustain in a market; (g) extent to which substitutes are available or are likely to be available in the market; (h) market share, in the relevant market, of the persons or enterprise in a combination, individually and as a combination; (i) likelihood that the combination would result in the removal of a vigorous and effective competitor or competitors in the market; (j) nature and extent of vertical integration in the market; (k) possibility of a failing business; (l) nature and extent of innovation; (m) relative advantage, by way of the contribution to the economic development, by any combination having or likely to have appreciable adverse effect on competition; (n) whether the benefits of the combination outweigh the adverse impact of the combination, if any.

[10] The substance of section 31 and other sections relating to the procedure in dealing with combination and other powers of the Commission are dealt with in the chapter on 'Enforcement'.

[11] § 7 Clayton Act, 15 U.S.C. § 18.

[12] It became applicable on 1 May 2004. It has replaced the earlier Council Regulation (EEC) No. 4064/89 of 21 December 1989 on the control of concentrations between undertakings (as amended by Regulation 1310).

[13] Article 1(2): A concentration has a Community dimension where: (a) the combined aggregate worldwide turnover of all the undertakings concerned is more than EUR 5,000 million; and (b) the aggregate Community-wide turnover of each of at least two of the undertakings concerned is more than EUR 250 million, unless each of the undertakings concerned achieves more than two-thirds of its aggregate Community-wide turnover within one and the same Member State.

Article 1(3): A concentration that does not meet the thresholds laid down in paragraph 2 has a Community dimension where: (a) the combined aggregate worldwide turnover of all the undertakings concerned is more than EUR 2,500 million; (b) in each of at least three Member States, the combined aggregate turnover of all the undertakings concerned is more than EUR 100 million; (c) in each of at least three Member States included for the purpose of point (b), the aggregate turnover of each of at least two of the undertakings concerned is more than EUR 25 million; and (d) the aggregate Community-wide turnover of each of at least two of the undertakings concerned is more than EUR 100 million, unless each of the undertakings concerned achieves more than two-thirds of its aggregate Communitywide turnover within one and the same Member State.

[14] Where the concentration consists of acquisition of parts of an undertaking, only the turnover relating to the parts which are the subject of the concentration shall be taken into account with regard to the seller or sellers Article 5(2).

[15] Article 2(3).

[16] Article 2(2).

[17] Article 3(1).

[18] Recital 22 of the Regulation.

[19] Article 3(4).

[20] Recital 20 of the Regulation.

[21] Section 22 of the Enterprise Act. Section 33 deals with the duty of the OFT to make references in relation to anticipated mergers.

[22] Section 29(r), (s) and (t) respectively.

[23] Section 20(4).

[24] Section 2(l) 'person' includes—

(i) an individual;

(ii) a Hindu undivided family;

(iii) a company;

(iv) a firm;

(v) an association of persons or a body of individuals, whether incorporated or not, in India or outside India;

(vi) any corporation established by or under any Central, State or Provincial Act or a government company as defined in section 617 of the Companies Act, 1956 (1 of 1956);

(vii) any body corporate incorporated by or under the laws of a country outside India;

(viii) a cooperative society registered under any law relating to cooperative societies;

(ix) a local authority;

(x) every artificial juridical person, not falling within any of the preceding subclauses.

[25] 193 U.S. 197 (1904).

[26] Paragraph 4.7.5.

[27] COUNCIL REGULATION (EC) No. 139/2004 of 20 January 2004 on the control of concentrations between undertakings (the EC Merger Regulation).

[28] Section 20(4)(h).

[29] Paragraph 4.7.5.

[30] Article 3(1): A concentration shall be deemed to arise where a change of control on a lasting basis results from: (a) the merger of two or more previously independent undertakings or parts of undertakings, or (b) the acquisition, by one or more persons already controlling at least one undertaking, or by one or more undertakings, whether by purchase of securities or assets, by contract or by any other means, of direct or indirect control of the whole or parts of one or more other undertakings.

[31] Article 3(2): Control shall be constituted by rights, contracts or any other means which, either separately or in combination and having regard to the considerations of fact or law involved, confer the possibility of exercising decisive influence on an undertaking, in particular by: (a) ownership or the right to use all or part of the assets of an undertaking; (b) rights or contracts which confer decisive influence on the composition, voting or decisions of the organs of an undertaking.

[32] ECSC High Authority: Decision No. 24–54 of 6 May 1954 laying down in implementation of Article 66(1) of the Treaty a regulation on what constitutes control of an undertaking, *Official Journal 009, 11/05/1954 p. 0345–0346.*

[33] Section 26(2), (3) and (4) of the Enterprise Act, 2002.

[34] 'enterprise' means a person or a department of the government, who or which is, or has been, engaged in any activity, relating to the production, storage, supply, distribution, acquisition or control of articles or goods, or the provision of services, of any kind, or in investment, or in the business of acquiring, holding, underwriting or dealing with shares, debentures or other securities of any other body corporate, either directly or through one or more of its units or divisions or subsidiaries, whether such unit or division or subsidiary is located at the same place where the enterprise is located or at a different place or at different places, but does not include any activity of the government relatable to the sovereign functions of the government including all activities carried on by the departments of the Central Government dealing with atomic energy, currency, defence and space.

Explanation—for the purposes of this clause—
(a) 'activity' includes profession or occupation;
(b) 'article' includes a new article and 'service' includes a new service;
(c) 'unit' or 'division', in relation to an enterprise, includes—
(i) a plant or factory established for the production, storage, supply, distribution, acquisition or control of any article or goods;
(ii) any branch or office established for the provision of any service.

[35] Section 19(5) for determining whether a market constitutes a 'relevant market' for the purposes of this Act, the Commission shall have due regard to the 'relevant geographic market' and 'relevant product market'; (6). The Commission shall, while determining the 'relevant geographic market', have due regard to all or any of the following factors, namely—(a) regulatory trade barriers; (b) local specification requirements; (c) national procurement policies; (d) adequate distribution facilities; (e) transport costs; (f) language; (g) consumer preferences; (h) need for secure or regular supplies or rapid after-sales services; (7). The Commission shall, while determining the 'relevant product market', have due regard to all or any of the following factors, namely—(a) physical characteristics or end-use of goods; (b) price of goods or service; (c) consumer preferences; (d) exclusion of in-house production; (e) existence of specialized producers; (f) classification of industrial products.

[36] 'Substantive assessment guidance-mergers', Office of Fair Trading, May 2003, paragraphs 4.33, 4.34.

[37] May 2003.

[38] (COM[2002], Brussels, 11.12.2002).

[39] *Anglo American Corporation/Lonrho*: 98/335/EC: Commission Decision of 23 April 1997.

[40] *Boeing/McDonnell Douglas* (*EC* Case No IV/M.877: Official Journal L 336, 08/12/1997 p. 0016–0047).

[41] *United States* v. *Alcoa* 377 US 271 (1964).

[42] *United States* v. *Columbia Steel Co.* 334 US 495 (1948).

[43] *Ford Motor Co.* v. *United States*, 405 US 562 (1972).

[44] *US* v. *United Shoe Machinery Co. of New Jersey*, 247 US 32 (1918).

[45] *International Shoe Co.* v. *Federal Trade Commission*, 280 US 291 (1930).

[46] *Timken Co.* v. *United States*, 341 US 593 (1951).

[47] *United States* v. *Penn-Olin Co.* 378 US 158 (1964).

[48] *Deutsche Telekom/BetaResearch* (Official Journal L 053, 27/02/1999 p. 0031–0045).

[49] *Brown Shoe Co. Inc.* v. *US* 370 US 294 (1962).

[50] *United States* v. *Continental Can Co.* 378 US 441 (1964).

[51] *British Telecom/MCI (II)1*–Case No IV/M.856.

[52] *WorldCom/MCI*—Official Journal L 116, 04/05/1999 p. 0001–0035.

[53] 'The absence of specific reporting obligations on ISPs in relation to Internet revenues, and the absence of consistent reporting standards for data

which is produced, means that there is no reliable publicly available estimate of the size of either the Internet sector as a whole or of any relevant sub-sector ....' paragraph 95 of the Commission's decision.

[54] Section 20(1) The Commission may, upon its own knowledge or information relating to acquisition referred to in clause (a) of section 5 or acquiring of control referred to in clause (b) of section 5 or merger or amalgamation referred to in clause (c) of that section, inquire into whether such a combination has caused or is likely to cause an appreciable adverse effect on competition in India: provided that the Commission shall not initiate any inquiry under this sub-section after the expiry of one year from the date on which such combination has taken effect. (2) The Commission shall, on receipt of a notice under sub-section (2) of section 6 inquire whether a combination referred to in that notice or reference has caused or is likely to cause an appreciable adverse effect on competition in India.

[55] On pre-notification, the Report on Competition Policy stated at paragraph 4.7.5: 'Prior approval is likely to lead to delays and unjustified bureaucratic interventions. This is likely to hamper the vital process of industrial evolution and restructuring and is, thus, not recommended. In any case, all mergers have to be approved by the high court and shareholders' interests are protected in this way. The complete absence of a pre-notification requirement could lead to more postmerger unscrambling with high social costs. For this reason, a pre-notification requirement for mergers above a certain threshold level may be considered.'

[56] Orders of Commission on certain combinations:

Section 31. (1) Where the Commission is of the opinion that any combination does not, or is not likely to, have an appreciable adverse effect on competition, it shall, by order, approve that combination including the combination in respect of which a notice has been given under sub-section (2) of section 6. (2) Where the Commission is of the opinion that the combination has, or is likely to have, an appreciable adverse effect on competition, it shall direct that the combination shall not take effect. (3) Where the Commission is of the opinion that the combination has, or is likely to have, an appreciable adverse effect on competition but such adverse effect can be eliminated by suitable modification to such combination, it may propose appropriate modification to the combination, to the parties to such combination. (4) The parties, who accept the modification proposed by the Commission under sub-section (3), shall carry out such modification within the period specified by the Commission. (5) If the parties to the combination, who have accepted the modification under sub-section (4), fail to carry out the modification within the period specified by the Commission, such combination shall be deemed to have an appreciable adverse effect on competition and the Commission shall deal with such combination in accordance with the provisions of this Act. (6) If the parties to the combination do not accept the modification proposed by the Commission under sub-section (3), such parties may, within thirty working days of the modification proposed by the Commission, submit amendment to the modification proposed by the Commission under that sub-section. (7) If the Commission agrees with the amendment submitted by the parties under sub-section (6), it shall, by order, approve the combination. (8) If the Commission does not accept the amendment submitted under sub-section (6), then, the parties shall be allowed a further period of thirty working days within which such parties shall accept the modification proposed by the Commission under sub-section (3). (9) If the parties fail to accept the modification proposed by the Commission within thirty working days referred to in sub-section (6) or within a further period of thirty working days referred to in sub-section (8), the combination shall be deemed to have an appreciable adverse effect on competition and be dealt with in accordance with the provisions of this Act. (10) Where the Commission has directed under sub-section (2) that the combination shall not take effect or the combination is deemed to have an appreciable adverse effect on competition under sub-section (9), then, without prejudice to any penalty which may be imposed or any prosecution which may be initiated under this Act, the Commission may order that – (a) the acquisition referred to in clause (a) of section 5; or (b) the acquiring of control referred to in clause (b) of section 5; or (c) the merger or amalgamation referred to in clause (c) of section 5, shall not be given effect to: Provided that the Commission may, if it considers appropriate, frame a scheme to implement its order under this sub-section. (11) If the Commission does not, on the expiry of a period of 54[two hundred and ten days from the date of notice given to the Commission under sub-section (2) of section 6], pass an order or issue direction in accordance with the provisions of sub-section (1) or sub-section (2) or sub-section (7), the combination shall be deemed to have been approved by the Commission. Explanation—For the purposes of determining the period of 55[two hundred and ten] days specified in this sub-section, the period of thirty working days specified in sub-section (6) and a further period of thirty working days specified in sub-section (8) shall be excluded. (12) Where any extension of time is sought by the parties to the combination, the period of ninety working days shall be reckoned after deducting the extended time granted at the request of the parties. (13) Where the Commission has ordered a combination to be void, the acquisition or acquiring of control or merger or amalgamation referred to in section 5, shall be dealt with by the authorities under any other law for the time being in force as if such acquisition or acquiring of control or merger or amalgamation had not taken place and the parties to the combination shall be dealt with accordingly. (14) Nothing contained in this chapter shall affect any proceeding initiated or which may be initiated under any other law for the time being in force.

[57] Sections 42–48.

[58] The Explanation to section 31 sets out the method of determining the period of two hundred ten working days.

[59] Section 31(14).

[60] The 2007 amendment omitted the provision relating to the power of the Commission to grant a temporary injunction relating to the import of any goods in contravention of the sections referred to herein.

[61] Power to issue interim orders:
Section 33. Where during an inquiry, the Commission is satisfied that an act in contravention of sub-section (1) of section 3 or sub-section (1) of section 4 or section 6 has been committed and continues to be committed or that such act is about to be committed, the Commission may, by order, temporarily restrain any party from carrying on such act until the conclusion of such inquiry or until further orders, without giving notice to such party, where it deems it necessary.

[62] *Cargill, Inc.* v. *Monfort of Colorado, Inc.* 479 US 104 (1986).

[63] *Brunswick Corp.* v. *Pueblo Bowl-O-Mat Inc.*, 429 US 477 (1977).

[64] This agreement and the related 1998 agreement are discussed in the chapter on 'Enforcement', under 'Comity'.

[65] Section 21A, introduced by the 2007 amendment.

5

Enforcement

AUTHORITIES ENFORCING THE COMPETITION ACT, 2002 AS AMENDED BY THE 2007 ACT

They are the Competition Commission established for the purposes of the Act, called the Competition Commission of India,[1] a Director-General appointed for the purpose of assisting the Competition Commission in conducting inquiry into contravention of any of the provisions of the Act, and for performing such other functions as may be provided by the Act, additional, joint, deputy, or assistant directors general or such other advisers, consultants or officers[2] and the Competition Appellate Tribunal exercising appellate powers as specified in the Act.[3] This chapter will discuss in detail their powers and functions.

Duties, Powers, and Functions of the Commission

Chapter IV of the Act makes provision for the duties, powers, and functions of the Commission.

The material provisions in this regard are: general duties[4], inquiry into certain agreements and dominant position of enterprises,[5] inquiry into combination,[6] the procedure for inquiry into anti-competitive agreements and dominant position of enterprises under s 19,[7] orders which the Commission may pass after inquiry into agreements or abuse of dominant position,[8] ordering a division of an enterprise enjoying a dominant position,[9] procedure for investigation of combinations,[10] procedure to be followed where a notice of a proposed combination has been given to the Commission under s 6[2],[11] orders which the Commission may pass on certain combinations,[12] orders which the Commission may pass relating to acts taking place outside India, but having an effect on competition in India,[13] power to issue interim orders,[14] power to regulate its own procedure,[15] rectification or orders,[16] execution of orders of Commission imposing monetary penalty.[17]

Section 18 appears to have declared somewhat widely the duties of the Commission.[18] They are:

to eliminate practices having an adverse effect on competition, promote and sustain competition, protect the interests of consumers, and ensure freedom of trade carried on by other participants, in markets in India. The Commission, as a market regulator, cannot directly eliminate anti-competitive practices, or promote, or sustain competition in India. The same would be the position relating to the protection of consumers.

Anti-competitive Agreements and Abuse of Dominance

Section 19 defines the process of making an inquiry by the Commission into alleged contraventions of section 3(1), anti-competitive agreements, and section 4(1), abuse of a dominant position. The Commission may initiate action by commencement of an inquiry on its own motion or on receipt of any information of a violation of these sections from any person, consumer or their association or a trade association or on a reference made to it by the Central Government or a State Government or a statutory authority.[19]

Under section 19[1] as it stood before the amendment, the process of inquiry by the Commission into anti-competitive agreements or abuse of a dominant position could commence on the receipt of a complaint from any person, consumer or their association or trade association; or a reference made to it by the Central Government or a State Government or a statutory authority. The amendment to this sub-section has replaced the word 'complaint' by the word information' in the part of s 19[1][a] reading 'receipt of a complaint….' In spite of the considerable debate on the effects of removing the word 'complaint', which in effect, it was contended, amounted to removing a complainant in control of his complaint, the government chose to substitute 'complaint' by 'information' as in its view, 'the ability to act on information gives CCI a better articulated regulatory role'. One of the shortcomings, pointed out, of the change to 'information' was that the person who gave the information may not be entitled to seek any relief, apart from the authenticity of the facts constituting the information remaining to be established, and enabling frivolous litigation. The government's explanation is that payment of fees in initiating the process would reduce frivolous litigation. This does not meet the point. But more than everything, the Standing Committee, after examining all representations from the members and considering the issues recommended to the government that it consult experts and reconsider the proposed change. But the government has gone ahead with its proposal.

Anti-competitive Agreements

In making the inquiry, the Commission should have due regard for all or any of the following factors: (a) creation of barriers to new entrants in the market; (b) driving existing competitors out of the market; (c) foreclosure of competition by hindering entry into the market; (d) accrual of benefits to consumers; (e) improvements in production or distribution of goods or provision of services; (f) promotion of technical, scientific and economic development by means of production or distribution of goods or provision of services.[20]

Dominant Position

In deciding upon the question if an enterprise enjoys a dominant position, the Commission should have due regard to all or any of the following factors: (a) market share of the enterprise; (b) size and resources of the enterprise; (c) size and importance of the competitors; (d) economic power of the enterprise including commercial advantages over competitors; (e) vertical integration of the enterprises or sale or service network of such enterprises; (f) dependence of consumers on the enterprise; (g) monopoly or dominant position whether acquired as a result of any statute or by virtue of being a government company or a public sector undertaking or otherwise; (h) entry barriers including barriers such as regulatory barriers, financial risk, high capital cost of entry, marketing entry barriers, technical entry barriers, economies of scale, high cost of substitutable goods or service for consumers; (i) countervailing buying power; (j) market structure and size of market; (k) social obligations and social costs; (l) relative advantage, by way of contribution to the economic development, by the enterprise enjoying a dominant position having or likely to have an appreciable adverse effect on competition; and (m) any other factor which the Commission may consider relevant for the inquiry.[21]

The Procedure

Section 26 of the Act provides for the procedure to be followed by the Commission in inquiries, under section 19, into cases of anti-competitive agreements, abuse of dominant position. The amendment has substituted the section by a new section.

The new section 26 is as follows:

Procedure for inquiry under section 19

S 19. (1) On receipt of a reference from the Central Government or a State Government or a statutory authority or on its own knowledge or information received under section 19, if the Commission is of the opinion that there exists a prima facie case, it shall direct the Director-General to cause an investigation to be made into the matter: Provided that if the subject-matter of an information received is, in the opinion of the Commission, substantially the same as or has been covered by any previous information received, then the new information may be clubbed with the previous information.

(2) Where on receipt of a reference from the Central Government or a State Government or a statutory authority or information received under section 19, the Commission is of the opinion that there exists no prima facie case, it shall close the matter forthwith and pass such orders as it deems fit and send a copy of its order to the Central Government or the State Government or the statutory authority or the parties concerned, as the case may be.

(3) The Director-General shall, on receipt of direction under sub-section (1), submit a report on his findings within such period as may be specified by the Commission.

(4) The Commission may forward a copy of the report referred to in sub-section (3) to the parties concerned: Provided that in case the investigation is caused to be made based on a reference received from the Central Government or the State Government or the statutory authority, the Commission shall forward a copy of the report referred to in sub-section (3) to the Central Government or the State Government or the statutory authority, as the case may be.

(5) If the report of the Director-General referred to in sub-section (3) recommends that there is no contravention of the provisions of this Act, the Commission shall invite objections or suggestions from the Central Government or the State Government or the statutory authority or the parties concerned, as the case may be, on such report of the Director-General.

(6) If, after consideration of the objections or suggestions referred to in sub-section (5), if any, the Commission agrees with the recommendation of the Director-General, it shall close the matter forthwith and pass such orders as it deems fit and communicate its order to the Central Government or the State Government or the statutory authority or the parties concerned, as the case may be.

(7) If, after consideration of the objections or suggestions referred to in sub-section (5), if any, the Commission is of the opinion that further investigation is called for, it may direct further investigation in the matter by the Director-General or cause further inquiry to be made in the matter or itself proceed with further inquiry in the matter in accordance with the provisions of this Act.

(8) If the report of the Director-General referred to in sub-section (3) recommends that there is contravention of any of the provisions of this Act,

and the Commission is of the opinion that further inquiry is called for, it shall inquire into such contravention in accordance with the provisions of this Act

The Changes in Section 26

The changes to the original section 26 may be noted. First, the heading of the section was 'Procedure for inquiry on complaints under section 19'. It has been changed to 'Procedure for inquiry under section 19' as now the process of inquiry may commence even on information and not necessarily pursuant to a complaint. Then, the proviso to section 26(1) is new.

Section 26(2) provides for a case where the Commission is of the opinion that there is no prima facie case. It is to the effect that the Commission shall close the matter forthwith, and pass such orders as it deems fit, and send a copy of its order to the Central Government or the state government or the statutory authority or the parties concerned, as the case may be.

The corresponding sub-section, section 26(3), before the amendment, merely stated that the Commission shall dismiss the complaint and may pass such orders as it deems fit, including imposition of costs, if necessary. The present sub-section (3) of section 26 was originally section 26(2) and there is no change.

Sub-section (4) of section 26 has been amended by substitution of the word 'may' in the place of the word 'shall'. Under the sub-section as it stood before the amendment, no discretion was left with the Commission in the matter of sending a copy of the report of the Director General on his findings on an investigation, pursuant to the direction of the Commission under section 26(1). The Commission was bound to send a copy of the report to the parties concerned or to the Central Government or the state government or the statutory authority, as the case may be. After the amendment, the Commission may send a copy of the report to the parties concerned, but shall forward a copy of the report referred to in sub-section (3) to the Central Government or the state government or the statutory authority, as the case may be, where the investigation was caused to be made based on a reference received from the Central Government or the state government or the statutory authority. The amendment does not contribute to transparency in the process, besides showing no justification for the difference in the treatment of the report.

Section 26(5): In a case where the Director-General reports that there is no contravention of the provisions of this Act, the Commission shall invite objections or suggestions from the Central Government or the state government or the statutory authority or the parties concerned, as the case may be, on such report of the Director-General. This is only an elaboration of the procedure set out in section 26(5) before the amendment, which merely required that the complainant shall be given an opportunity to rebut the findings of the Director-General.

Section 26(6): Under the original sub-section, if, after hearing the complainant, the Commission agreed with the recommendation of the Director-General, it had to dismiss the complaint. It did not provide for communicating the decision to the complainant The new sub-section (6) of section 26 is an extension of the principle and the Commission shall, in that event, viz that there is no contravention of the provisions of this Act, close the matter forthwith and pass appropriate orders and communicate them to the Central Government or the state government or the statutory authority or the parties concerned, as the case may be.

Section 26(7): The original section 26(7) provided that the Commission, where it considered that further inquiry was called for it, shall direct the complainant to proceed with the complaint. The amended section 26(7) provides that, in that case, the Commission may direct further investigation in the matter by the Director-General or cause further inquiry to be made in the matter or itself proceed with further inquiry in the matter in accordance with the provisions of this Act.

Section 26(8): The new sub-section is self-explanatory.

The Process—Section 19

To go back to the process of making the inquiry into anti-competitive agreements and dominant positions, section 19 deals with the factors that the Commission should consider while making the inquiry into these two classes.

The Commission should in, deciding what constitutes the 'relevant market' in a particular case, have due regard to the relevant 'geographic market' and the 'relevant product market'.[22]

In determining a relevant geographic market and the relevant product market, the Commission should have due regard to all or any of the following factors:

The Commission shall, while determining the 'relevant geographic market', have due regard to all or any of the following factors, namely: (a) regulatory trade barriers; (b) local specification requirements; (c) national procurement policies; (d) adequate distribution facilities; (e) transport costs; (f) language; (g) consumer preferences; and (h) need for secure or regular supplies or rapid after-sales services.

The Commission shall, while determining the 'relevant product market', have due regard to all or any of the following factors, namely: (a) physical characteristics or end-use of goods; (b) price of goods or service; (c) consumer preferences; (d) exclusion of in-house production; (e) existence of specialized producers; and (f) classification of industrial products.[23]

Orders Which may be Passed by the Commission after Inquiry into Anti-competitive Agreements or Abuse of a Dominant Position

Section 27 deals with the kinds of orders which may be passed by the Commission after inquiry into anti-competitive agreements or abuse of dominant position. The original section was amended by the 2007 amendment and the amended section provides as follows:

The Commission may pass all or any of the following orders, if after an inquiry, the Commission finds that an agreement referred to in s 3 or the action of an enterprise in a dominant position is in contravention of s 3 or s 4: [i] direct any enterprise or association of enterprises or person or association of persons involved in the agreement or abuse of the dominant position to discontinue and not to re-enter such agreement; [ii] impose such penalty, as it may deem fit which shall be not more than ten per cent of the average of the turnover for the last three preceding financial years, upon each such person or enterprises which are parties to such agreement or abuse; where the anti-competitive agreement referred to in s 3 has been entered into by a cartel, the Commission may impose upon each producer, seller, distributor, trader or service provider included in that cartel, a penalty of up to three times of its profit for each year of the continuance of such agreement or ten per cent of its turnover for each year of the continuance of such agreement, whichever is higher; [iii] the Commission may direct that the agreement shall stand modified in the manner and to the extent specified by the Commission; [iv] direct the enterprises concerned to abide by such other orders as the Commission may pass and comply with the directions, including payment of costs, if any; [v] where the Commission finds that the infringing enterprise is a member of a group, as defined under the Act, and that other members of such a group are also responsible for, or have contributed to, such a contravention, it may pass orders, under this section, against such members of the group.

There are four amendments to section 27.

(i) The first relates to the level of penalty that may be imposed on a member of a cartel, under the proviso to section 27(b). Pre-amendment, the penalty that could be imposed on a member of a cartel violating section 3 was equivalent to three times of the amount of profits made out of such agreement by the cartel or ten per cent of the average of the turnover of the cartel for the last preceding three financial years, whichever was higher.

The new proviso is as follows:

Provided that in case any agreement referred to in section 3 has been entered into by a cartel, the Commission may impose upon each producer, seller, distributor, trader or service provider included in that cartel, a penalty of up to three times of its profit for each year of the continuance of such agreement or ten per cent, of its turnover for each year of the continuance of such agreement, whichever is higher.

It may be noted that under the original proviso, a penalty equivalent to three times the amount of the profits was a fixed one, whereas under the new proviso, the penalty could be up to three times its profit, which means that this is an upper ceiling and discretion is left with the Commission. Then the profits that are to be taken into account for purposes of levying a penalty under this section are for each year of the continuance of the agreement constituting the cartel. When the existence of a cartel is rarely proved by a written agreement, the assertion is that it continues to lead to contentious defences. Under the old proviso, it was the higher of the two viz a penalty equivalent to three times the amount of profits made out of such agreement by the cartel or ten per cent of the average of the turnover of the cartel for the last preceding three financial years. Under the new proviso, the penalty would be higher by an amount up to three times of its profit for each year of the continuance of such agreement or ten per cent of its turnover for each year of the continuance of such agreement. There is no consideration of any average turnover.

(ii) The next amendment to section 27 is the omission of sub-section (c)—the power of the Commission to award compensation to parties in accordance with the provisions contained in section 34 and sub-section (f) under which the Commission may recommend to the Central Government the division of an enterprise enjoying dominant position.

The ground on which the power to award compensation has been removed from the Commission is that it was considered to be a power of an adjudicatory nature that was more properly vested in the Competition Appellate Tribunal rather than with the Commission which will only be an advisory and regulatory body. As section 28(1) has been amended to the effect that the Commission may itself direct division of an enterprise enjoying dominant position to ensure that such enterprise does not abuse its dominant position, section 27(f) was under which the Commission authorized to recommend to the Central Government, the division of an enterprise has been omitted.

(iii) Section 27(g) is a residuary clause permitting the Commission to 'pass such orders as it may think fit'. This has been amended and after amendment it reads as follows: 's 27(g): pass such other order or issue such directions as it may deem fit.'

(iv) A proviso has been added to the above mentioned section 27(g) and the entire amended sub-section with the proviso is as follows:

pass such other order or issue such directions as it may deem fit, provided that while passing orders under this section, if the Commission comes to a finding, that an enterprise in contravention to section 3 or section 4 of the Act is a Member of a group as defined in Clause (b) of the Explanation to section 5 of the Act, and other Members of such a group are also responsible for, or have contributed to, such a contravention, then it may pass orders, under this section, against such Members of the group.

Division of an Enterprise

Section 28 provides for division of any enterprise enjoying dominant position.

The amendments to this section are two: (i) one amendment empowers the Commission itself to pass an order directing division of an enterprise enjoying dominant position to ensure that such enterprise does not abuse its dominant position. Previously, it was the Central Government that may order such a division of an enterprise, but on the recommendation of the Commission; (ii) the other amendment is that section 28(2)(d) providing for an order for payment of compensation to any person who may have suffered any loss due to the dominant position of such enterprise has been omitted as, the power to order compensation now vests with the Competition Appellate Tribunal.

Inquiry into a Combination—The Procedure

Section 20 provides that, the Commission may, upon its own knowledge or on information under section 5, inquire into whether a combination has caused or is likely to cause an appreciable adverse effect on competition in India. It sets out the factors which the Commission ought to have due regard to in deciding whether or not such an effect would be caused.

Where the Commission is of the prima facie opinion that a combination is likely to cause, or has caused an appreciable adverse effect on competition within the relevant market in India, it shall issue a notice to show cause to the parties to combination calling upon them to respond within thirty days of the receipt of the notice, as to why investigation in respect of such combination should not be conducted.[24] The words 'prima facie' were introduced by the 2007 amendment and do not add anything significant to the content of the provision. After receipt of the response of the parties to the combination under subsection (1), the Commission may call for a report from the Director-General and such report shall be submitted by the Director-General within such time as the Commission may direct.[25]

If the Commission is prima facie of the opinion that the combination has or is likely to have an appreciable adverse effect on competition, it shall within seven working days from the date of the response of the parties to the combination or the receipt of the Director-General's report, whichever is later, direct the parties to the combination to publish, within ten working days of the Commission's direction, details of the combination so as to bring the combination to the knowledge or information of the public and persons affected or likely to be affected by such combination. Within prescribed periods, the Commission may invite any person affected or likely to be affected by the said combination, to file his written objections, if any, before the Commission, call for additional information from the parties to the combination, and after receipt of all information, the Commission shall proceed to deal with the case in accordance with the provisions contained in section 31.[26] The Commission shall follow the same procedure under section 29 where it has received a notice under section 6(2).[27]

Investigation of a Combination—The Procedure

Section 29 sets out the following procedure for investigation of a combination.

Where the Commission is of the prima facie opinion that a combination is likely to cause, or has caused an appreciable adverse effect on competition within the relevant market in India, it shall issue a notice to show cause to the parties to combination calling upon them to respond within thirty days of the receipt of the notice, as to why investigation in respect of such combination should not be conducted.

After receipt of the response of the parties to the combination, the Commission may call for a report from the Director-General which should be submitted by the Director-General within such time as the Commission may direct.

The Commission, if it is prima facie of the opinion that the combination has, or is likely to have, an appreciable adverse effect on competition, it shall, within seven working days from the date of receipt of the response of the parties to the combination, or the receipt of the report from Director-General, whichever is later, direct the parties to the said combination to publish details of the combination within ten working days of such direction, in such manner, as it thinks appropriate, for bringing the combination to the knowledge or information of the public and persons affected or likely to be affected by such combination.

The Commission may invite any person or member of the public, affected or likely to be affected by the said combination, to file his written objections, if any, before the Commission within fifteen working days from the date on which the details of the combination were published as directed.

Within the time periods specified in the sub-sections for each stage, the Commission may call for such additional or other information as it may deem fit from the parties to the said combination, the additional or other information shall be furnished by the parties, and after receipt of all information, the Commission shall proceed to deal with the case in accordance with the provisions contained in section 31.

The present section 29 is post-2007 amendments. There are three amendments to this section.

(i) Section 29(1) empowers the Commission, if it is of the opinion that a combination is likely to cause or has caused an appreciable adverse effect on competition within the relevant market in India, to issue a show cause notice to the parties as to why investigation in respect of such combination should not be conducted.

After the amendment the sub-section reads as follows: '(1) Where the Commission is of the *prima facie* opinion that a combination is likely to cause, or has caused an appreciable adverse effect on competition within the relevant market in India, it shall issue a notice to show cause to the parties to combination calling upon them to respond within thirty days of the receipt of the notice, as to why investigation in respect of such combination should not be conducted.' The amendment does not add anything significant to the content of the provision.

(ii) The amendment has introduced a new sub-section (1A) providing for calling for a report from the Director-General after the responses are received pursuant to the show cause notice to the parties. It is as follows: 's 29(1A): After receipt of the response of the parties to the combination under sub-section (1), the Commission may call for a report from the Director-General and such report shall be submitted by the Director-General within such time as the Commission may direct.'

(iii) The original section 29(2) provided that the Commission shall direct the parties to the combination concerned to publish details within seven working days from the date of receipt of their response. Now, after the amendment, publication of details may be ordered to be published within seven working days from the date of receipt of the response of the parties to the combination, or the receipt of the report from the Director-General called under sub-section (1A), whichever is later. The amendment follows the amendment providing for calling for a report from the Director-General under the new section 29(1A).

Notice to the Commission under Section 6(2)
of a Combination—Section 30

The 2007 amendment has substituted a new section 30 in the place of the original section. The present section 30 requires the Commission to follow the procedure set out in section 29 where it receives a notice under section 6(2).

Orders of the Commission on Certain
Combinations—Section 31[28]

The amendments in 2007 are to sub-section (11) of section 31 and the explanation relating to that sub-section. The amendment has substituted the words 'ninety working days from the date of publication referred to in sub-section (2) of section 29' by the words 'two hundred and ten days from the date of notice given to the Commission under sub-section (2) of section 6.'

After the amendment section 31(11) is as follows: '(11) If the Commission does not, on the expiry of a period of two hundred and ten days from the date of notice given to the Commission under sub-section (2) of section 6 pass an order or issue direction in accordance with the provisions of sub-section (1) or sub-section (2) or sub-section (7), the combination shall be deemed to have been approved by the Commission.' This is hardly likely that any combination may be expected in practice to be approved under this sub-section.

The sub-sections of section 31 cover: approval of the combination, directing that the combination shall not take effect where the Commission is of the opinion that any combination has or is likely to have an appreciable adverse effect on competition, approving the combination when there will be no such adverse effect on competition, accepting the amendments submitted by the parties respectively. It casts an obligation on the Commission to finally dispose of the proceedings within fixed time schedules.

In the Explanation to sub-section (11) also the period of ninety working days has been substituted by the period two hundred and ten days. The Explanation thus amended reads as follows: 'Explanation—For the purposes of determining the period of two hundred and ten working days specified in this sub-section, the period of thirty working days specified in sub-section (6) and a further period of thirty working days specified in sub-section (8) shall be excluded.'

Acts Taking Place Outside India but Having an Effect on Competition in India—Section 32

Section 32 empowers the Commission to inquire into and pass appropriate orders where anti-competitive acts are carried on by entities outside India and those anti-competitive acts have or are likely to have an appreciable adverse effect on competition in the relevant market in India. Since the section as it stood previously did not offer any indication of the type of the order which may be passed in such cases and the recommended action that would disable the person not resident in India from continuing his anti-competitive arrangement having its effect in India, the section was amended in 2007 indicating the steps that the Commission should follow in such cases.

The language of section 14 of the MRTP Act in this context may usefully be considered. It was as follows:

'Where any practice substantially falls within monopolistic, restrictive, or unfair, trade practice relating to the production, storage, supply, distribution or control of goods of any description or the provision of any services and any party to such practice does not carry on business in India, an order may be made under this Act, with respect to that part of the practice which is carried on in India.' It is well recognized that declaring unlawful any agreement or practice and restraining the local enterprise that is a party to such an agreement is sufficiently effective to make the arrangement inoperative within the country enforcing its domestic law. This is how courts have been so far aided in giving effect to the provisions of any national law in such circumstances. The *Wood Pulp* case, discussed later in this chapter established the 'effects doctrine' and showed how such activities could be dealt with.

The Amendments to Section 32

The amendments to this section clarify that in acting under this section, the Commission shall follow sections 19, 20, 26, 29, and 30 of the Act and the orders that it may pass are also to be in accordance with the provisions of the Act.

Section 32 as amended is as follows:

The Commission shall, notwithstanding that—(a) an agreement referred to in section 3 has been entered into outside India; or (b) any party to such agreement is outside India; or (c) any enterprise abusing the dominant position is outside India; or (d) a combination has taken place outside India; or (e) any party to combination is outside India; or (f) any other matter or practice or action arising out of such agreement or dominant position or combination is outside India, have power to inquire, in accordance with the provisions contained in sections 19, 20, 26, 29, and 30 of the Act into such agreement or abuse of dominant position or combination if such agreement or dominant position or combination has, or is likely to have, an appreciable adverse effect on competition in the relevant market in India and pass such orders as it may deem fit in accordance with the provisions of this Act.

Power to Issue Interim Orders[29]

Section 33, as it stood before the 2007 amendment, empowered the Commission to grant interim relief. Under this section, if during an inquiry into an anti competitive agreement or abuse of a dominant position, or a combination, the Commission was satisfied that an act in contravention of section 3(1) or section 4(1) or section 6 had been committed and continued to be committed or that such act was about to be committed, the Commission could grant a temporary injunction restraining any party from carrying on such act until the conclusion of such inquiry or until further orders, without giving notice to the opposite party, where it deems it necessary. Similarly, if the Commission was satisfied that any import of any goods was likely to contravene the above-mentioned sections, it could grant a temporary injunction restraining any party from importing such goods, until the conclusion of such inquiry or until further orders, without giving notice to the opposite party, where it deems it necessary. It should send a copy of such order granting temporary injunction to the concerned authorities. Rules 2A to 5 (both inclusive) of Order XXXIX of the First Schedule to the Code of Civil Procedure, 1908 (5 of 1908) shall, as far as may be, were to apply to a temporary injunction issued by the Commission under this Act, as applicable to a temporary injunction issued by a civil court.

Since the Commission would only be an advisory body with regulatory functions, it was considered inappropriate to vest it with adjudicatory powers exercised by a civil court to grant temporary injunctions. Therefore, retaining the substance of the original section 33, but omitting use of the words 'temporary injunction' the new section 33 substituted the original section 33.

The new section 33 is as follows:

Where during an inquiry, the Commission is satisfied that an act in contravention of sub-section (1) of section 3 or sub-section (1) of section 4 or section 6 has been committed and continues to be committed or that such act is about to be committed, the Commission may, by order, temporarily restrain any party from carrying on such act until the conclusion of such inquiry or until further orders, without giving notice to such party, where it deems it necessary.

Power to Award Compensation—Omission of Section 34

Prior to the 2007 amendment, the Commission was empowered to award compensation for loss or damage suffered by an applicant as a result of contravention of the provisions of Chapter II having been committed by an enterprise. Since this power now vests with the Competition Appellate Tribunal, section 53A(1)(b), section 34 has been omitted through the 2007 amendment.

Appearance before the Commission

Section 35 states who are allowed to appear before the Commission. The amended section is as follows: 'S 35. A person or an enterprise or the Director-General may either appear in person or authorise one or more chartered accountants or company secretaries or cost accountants or legal practitioners or any of his or its officers to present his or its case before the Commission.'

Power of the Commission to Regulate its Own Procedure—Section 36

Section 36 empowers the Commission to regulate its own procedure. The 2007 amendment has replaced the existing section by a new section 36.

The new section 36 is as follows:

S 36. Power of Commission to regulate its own procedure.

(1) In the discharge of its functions, the Commission shall be guided by the principles of natural justice and, subject to the other provisions of this Act and of any rules made by the Central Government, the Commission shall have the powers to regulate its own procedure.

(2) The Commission shall have, for the purposes of discharging its functions under this Act, the same powers as are vested in a civil court under the Code of Civil Procedure, 1908 (5 of 1908), while trying a suit, in respect of the following matters, namely: (a) summoning and enforcing the attendance of any person and examining him on oath; (b) requiring the discovery and production of documents; (c) receiving evidence on affidavit; (d) issuing commissions for the examination of witnesses or documents; (e) requisitioning, subject to the provisions of sections 123 and 124 of the Indian Evidence Act, 1872 (1 of 1872), any public record or document or copy of such record or document from any office.

(3) The Commission may call upon such experts, from the fields of economics, commerce, accountancy, international trade or from any other discipline as it deems necessary, to assist the Commission in the conduct of any inquiry by it.

(4) The Commission may direct any person—(a) to produce before the Director-General or the Secretary or an officer authorised by it, such books or other documents in the custody or under the control of such person so directed as may be specified or described in the direction, being documents relating to any trade, the examination of which may be required for the purposes of this Act; (b) to furnish to the Director-General or the Secretary or any other officer authorised by it, as respects the trade or such other information as may be in his possession in relation to the trade carried on by such person as may be required for the purposes of this Act.

The differences between the pre-amendment and the present section 36 are as follows: the declaration in the original sub-section (1) that the Commission shall not be bound by the procedure laid down by the Code of Civil Procedure has been omitted as it has no relation to the present functions of the Commission; sub-section [3] which stated that every proceeding before the Commission shall be deemed to be a judicial proceeding within the meaning of sections 193 and 228 and for the purposes of section 196 of the Indian Penal Code (45 of 1860) and the Commission shall be deemed to be a civil court for the purposes of section 195 (2 of 1974) and Chapter XXVI of the Code of Criminal Procedure, 1973 has been omitted; the new sub-section 3 enables the Commission to use the expertise of specialists in economics, commerce, accountancy, international trade or any other field in examining issues before it in any inquiry, an enabling provision.

'Principles of natural justice' require that a person, against whom an alleged violation is to be inquired into, should be given an opportunity of being heard before deciding upon the charge. It is contained in the maxim *audi alteram partem* which means that 'no man shall be condemned unheard'. The Act provides for hearing the parties as well as the public who may respond to the proposals where the Commission directs that it should be done.

Review of Orders of the Commission—Section 37

Section 37 providing for review by the Commission of its orders has been omitted by the 2007 amendment.

On more grounds than one, this omission of the provision vesting the power of review may be justified. The section did not state the grounds on which a review could be applied for. Nor was the scope of the power of review stated. But section 53O(2)(f) vests in the Competition Appellate Tribunal power to review its decisions and it will have to be in accordance with the Code of Civil Procedure, 1908 (5 of 1908).

Rectification of Orders—Section 38[30]

Section 38 empowers the Commission to rectify any mistake apparent from the record by an amendment of its order passed under the Act. The explanation to this section prohibits any amendment of the substantive part of the order. The section could have been simply worded to provide that clerical or typing mistakes may be amended as provided therein. The Commission of its own motion or at the instance of any party to the order may do the rectification.

Execution of Orders of the Commission Imposing Monetary Penalty—Section 39

Section 39 dealing with execution of orders of the Commission has been omitted by the 2007 amendment and a new section 39 has been substituted in its place. The omitted section 39 was objectionable as it provided for enforcement of any order passed by the Commission through the high court or a civil court having jurisdiction over the person or enterprise against whom it was passed.

Under the new section 39[31] any monetary penalty imposed by the Commission could be recovered under the provisions of the Income Tax Act, 1961, treating the person on whom the penalty has been imposed as an assessee in default. It is not consistent with the objectives of the Act which is regulation of the market mechanism consistent with public good and large commercial organizations will be parties. In any case, this step ought to be considered only when the person or enterprise on which the penalty has been imposed is shown to be evading the penalty and not acting bonafide. In any case, until a case is made out that evasion of such penalty is of large sums and widespread, this is not the time to introduce this section as there is a long way to go in ensuring that the rationale of the Act is absorbed in the commercial system and the system for enforcement is accepted. The Standing Committee has been told by the Ministry that the penalty would be recovered in the manner stipulated by the regulations to be made and that the method envisaged under section 39 is an additional provision that would ordinarily be used when the Commission is unable to recover the same 'using its own procedures'.

Appeals against Decision or Order of the Commission—Section 40

Section 40 which provided for an appeal being made to the Supreme Court against any decision or order of the Commission has been omitted by the 2007 amendment.

Under section 53A(1)(a) of the Act, the Competition Appellate Tribunal shall hear and dispose of appeals against any direction issued or decision made or order passed by the Commission under sub-sections 2 and 6 of sections 26, 27, 28, 31, 32, 33, 38, 39, 43, 43A, 44, 45, or 46 of the Act.

Duties of Director-General—Section 41

The duty of the Director-General (DG) is to assist the Commission to investigate into any contravention of the provisions of the Act, or any rules or regulations made hereunder. This he may do only when so directed by the Commission. For the purposes of investigation, he shall have the same powers that are conferred on the Commission under section 36(2). These powers relate to summoning and enforcing the attendance of any person and examining him on oath, requiring the discovery and production of documents, receiving evidence on affidavits, etc. In addition, he shall also have the powers under sections 240 and 240A of the Companies Act, 1956, of an inspector, investigating the affairs of a company.

Penalties

Chapter VI of the Act dealing with penalties contains sections 42 to 48. There are six amendments made in 2007 and they are as follows:

   (i) substitution of new section for section 42;
   (ii) insertion of new section 42A;
   (iii) substitution of new section for section 43;
   (iv) insertion of new section 43A;
   (v) amendment of section 45; and
   (vi) amendment of section 46.

The amendments may now be considered.

Contravention of Orders of the Commission—Section 42

The previous section 42(1) provided that the penalty for contravention of any order of the Commission or any of the conditions of its approval or sanction or direction or exemption or for failure to pay the penalty imposed under the Act was detention in civil prison for a term which may extend to one year, unless in the meantime the Commission directed his release. That person was also liable to a penalty not exceeding rupees ten lakh. The Commission was also empowered to issue directions to that person or any authority directions necessary for the proper implementation or execution of its order. Breach of that order was also punishable in the manner stated in sub-section 2 of the original section 42.

The amendment to section 42 is by way of substitution of a new section 42 for the original section 42. The new section 42 provides for the punishment for failure to comply with the orders or the directions of the Commission under specific sections stated in sub-section 2. They are: orders on agreements or abuse of dominant position section 27, division of enterprise enjoying dominant position section 28, certain combinations section 31; orders relating to acts taking place outside India but having an effect on competition in India section 32; interim orders section 33; orders relating to compensation in case of contravention of orders of Commission made under sections 27, 28, 31, 32, and 33 or any condition or restriction subject to which any approval, sanction, direction or exemption in relation to any matter has been accorded, given, made or granted under this Act or delaying in carrying out such orders or directions of the Commission (42A); penalty for non-furnishing of information on combinations (43A).[32]

Now, action relating to contravention of any order or direction of the Commission can be initiated by the Commission. Then sub-section 2 sets out the penalties for contravention of specific sections of the Act under which orders or directions were passed by the Commission. Non-compliance with any order or direction of the Commission or failure to pay the penalty imposed under section 42(2) is punishable with imprisonment for a term which may extend to three years, or with fine which may extend to rupees twenty five crores, as may be decided by the Chief Metropolitan Magistrate, Delhi, before whom proceedings will have to be brought on a complaint filed by the Commission or any of its officers authorized by it. The Chief Metropolitan Magistrate shall take cognizance only on such a duly authorized complaint. The complaint before the Magistrate is independent of any proceeding that may be brought under section 39 providing for recovery of the penalty under the Commission's Regulations or as income tax due.

Power to Award Compensation

Compensation in Case of Contravention of Orders of the Commission—Section 42A

Section 42A is a new section.[33] This section authorizes the Competition Appellate Tribunal to consider a claim for compensation for any loss or damage suffered by a person, not on account of contravention of any provision of the Act, but by the contravention of any order of the Commission by one against whom the order was made by the Commission. The substance of sections 27, 28, 31, 32, and 33 has been stated in a previous paragraph.

Penalty for Failure to Comply with Directions of the Commission and Director-General—Section 43[34]

The 2007 amendment has substituted the original section 43 by a new section, which has set a maximum limit to the fine that may be imposed under this section viz rupees one crore.

Non-furnishing of Information on Combinations—Section 43A[35]

Section 43A is a new section that empowers the Commission to impose penalty for non-furnishing of information on combinations.

Penalty for Offences in Relation to Furnishing of Information—Section 45[36]

The amendment to section 45 is by substitution of sub-section (1) by a new sub-section. That new sub-section is as follows:

(1) Without prejudice to the provisions of section 44, if a person, who furnishes or is required to furnish under this Act any particulars, documents or any information, (a) makes any statement or furnishes any document which he knows or has reason to believe to be false in any material particular; or (b) omits to state any material fact knowing it to be material; or (c) willfully alters, suppresses or destroys any document which is required to be furnished as aforesaid, such person shall be punishable with fine which may extend to rupees one crore as may be determined by the Commission.

Section 44 prescribes the penalty for making false statement or omission to furnish material information. It is that if a party to a combination makes a statement which is false in any material particular, or knowing it to be false or omits to state any material particular knowing it to be material, he shall be liable to a penalty which shall not be less than rupees fifty lakh but which may extend to rupees one crore, as may be determined by the Commission. The fine that may be imposed under section 45 is in addition to any penalty that may be imposed under section 44.

Power to Impose Lesser Penalty—Section 46

Section 46 authorizes the Commission to impose a lesser penalty in certain circumstances on a member of a cartel. The amendments to this section are: (i) substitution of the first proviso by a new proviso; (ii) substitution of the word 'first' in the second proviso by the word 'has'; (iii) insertion, after the second proviso, of another proviso, providing another condition for imposing a lesser penalty.

S 46. The Commission may, if it is satisfied that any producer, seller, distributor, trader or service provider included in any cartel, which is alleged to have violated section 3, has made a full and true disclosure in respect of the alleged violations and such disclosure is vital, impose upon such producer, seller, distributor, trader or service provider a lesser penalty as it may deem fit, than leviable under this Act or the rules or the regulations:

Provided that lesser penalty shall not be imposed by the Commission in cases where the report of investigation directed under section 26 has been received before making of such disclosure.

Provided further that lesser penalty shall be imposed by the Commission only in respect of a producer, seller, distributor, trader or service provider included in the cartel, who [has] made the full, true and vital disclosures under this section.

Provided also that lesser penalty shall not be imposed by the Commission if the person making the disclosure does not continue to cooperate with the Commission till the completion of the proceedings before the Commission.

Provided also that the Commission may, if it is satisfied that such producer, seller, distributor, trader or service provider included in the cartel had in the course of proceedings,—(a) not complied with the condition on which the lesser penalty was imposed by the Commission; or (b) had given false evidence; or (c) the disclosure made is not vital, and thereupon such producer, seller, distributor, trader or service provider may be tried for the offence with respect to which the lesser penalty was imposed and shall also be liable to the imposition of penalty to which such person has been liable, had lesser penalty not been imposed.

The first amendment is the substitution of the original first proviso with the present proviso. Under the original proviso, lesser penalty shall not be imposed where the disclosure by the member of the cartel is made after proceedings for violation of the Act, rules or regulations have been instituted or any investigation under section 26 by the Director-General has been directed. Under the new proviso lesser penalty shall not be imposed by the Commission in cases where the report of investigation directed under section 26 has been received before making of such disclosure. The next amendment is the substitution of the word 'has' in the second proviso in the place of the word 'first'. The effect is that the disclosure should be made and not restricted to the person making the disclosure first. Then the penultimate proviso has been introduced declaring that the lesser penalty shall not be imposed if the person making the disclosure does not continue to cooperate with the Commission till the completion of the proceedings before the Commission.

Section 46 authorizes the Commission to impose, on a member of a cartel, a lesser penalty than what would be leviable under the Act or the rules or the regulations, if the conditions stated in the section are met by any member of a cartel.

The conditions are: (i) the member of the cartel, alleged to have violated section 3, should have made a full and true disclosure in respect of the alleged violations and such disclosure is vital; (ii) the disclosure should have been made before the receipt of the report of investigation by the Director General directed to be made by the Commission, under section 26, in an inquiry into an anti-competitive agreement; (iii) the lesser penalty shall be imposed only in respect of the member of the cartel who has made the full, true and vital disclosures under section 46; (iv) the lesser penalty shall not be imposed on the member of the cartel making the disclosure does not continue to co-operate with the Commission till the completion of the proceedings before the Commission; (v) the Commission may, if it is satisfied that such member of the cartel, had in the course of proceedings, (a) not complied with the condition on which the lesser penalty was imposed by the Commission; or (b) had given false evidence; or (c) the disclosure made is not vital, that member of the cartel may be tried for the offence with respect to which the lesser penalty was imposed and shall also be liable to the imposition of penalty to which such person has been liable, had lesser penalty not been imposed.

The object of such a provision is to induce a member of a cartel to give to the Commission complete information of the other members of the cartel, how and from where they operate, and their objectives. Such important information would be difficult to obtain through an investigation by an outside agency, particularly where the members of the cartel operate from different countries and as should be expected, many of their transactions would not be reduced into writing.

It should also be noted that there is no total immunity, as in the EC[37] but only lesser penalty than what would be leviable. Section 27(b) states what would be the penalty that would be 'leviable'. It shall be not more than ten per cent of the average of the turnover for the last three preceding financial years, upon each of such person or enterprises which are parties to such agreements or abuse, as the Commission may consider fit. In the case of a member of a cartel, alleged to have violated section 3, the penalty that may be imposed on each member is a penalty of up to three times of its profit for each year of the continuance of such agreement or ten per cent of its turnover for each year of the continuance of such agreement, whichever is higher.

The determination of the amount of lesser penalty would inevitably be a subjective one, but one aspect that should be considered is the benefit to the enterprise viz the difference between the penalty leviable and the actual lesser penalty.

Penalty—UK

In the UK the Director of Fair Trading must prepare and publish guidance as to the appropriate amount of any penalty. The guidance should have been approved by the Secretary of State.[38] A financial penalty imposed by the Office of Fair Trading, UK under section 36 of the Competition Act will be calculated following a five step approach: calculation of the starting point having regard to the seriousness of the infringement and the relevant turnover of the undertaking, adjustment for duration, adjustment for other factors, adjustment for further aggravating or mitigating factors, and adjustment if the maximum penalty of ten per cent of the worldwide turnover of the undertaking is exceeded and to avoid double jeopardy.[39] The guidance states that the relevant turnover is the turnover of the undertaking in the relevant product market and relevant geographic market affected by the infringement in the undertaking's last business year and that it would be calculated after deduction of sales rebates, values added tax, and other taxes directly related to turnover. In this context the definition of 'turnover', under the Competition Act, 2002, as including the value of goods or services is too general.

Contravention by Companies—Section 48[40]

Section 48 is the standard provision dealing with the liability of a company and its officers for offences committed by that company. Where a contravention of any provision of the Act, rule, regulation, order, direction under the Act is by a company, the company and every person who, at the time the contravention was committed, was in charge of, and was responsible to the company for the conduct of the business of the company, will be deemed to be guilty of the contravention and liable to punishment. It provides a defence to a person charged with the violation to show by proof that the contravention was committed without his knowledge or that he had exercised all due diligence to prevent the commission of such contravention. Due diligence is a question of fact to be established by the steps taken by the person to instal a system which would ensure the prevention of contraventions.

The Competition Appellate Tribunal

Procedure and Powers of the Appellate Tribunal—Section 53O

The powers and procedure of the Competition Appellate Tribunal are set out in section 53O. The substance is that it shall not be bound by the procedure laid down in the Code of Civil Procedure, 1908 (5 of 1908), but shall be guided by the principles of natural justice and, subject to the other provisions of this Act and of any rules made by the Central Government, the Competition Appellate Tribunal shall have power to regulate its own procedure including the places at which they shall have their sittings. This only deals with the procedure it may establish for exercising its functions. There is nothing in the section about the grounds of appeal. Therefore, an appeal may be made to the Competition Appellate Tribunal on a question of fact or of law. In any case, even otherwise, this is permitted in first appeals.

Adjudication on Claims for Compensation

The power to award compensation towards loss or damage suffered by any person or enterprise arising out of the violation of any of the provisions of the Act has been taken away from the Commission, which, after the amendments, is only a regulatory and an advisory body functioning with experts, and that power now vests with the Competition Appellate Tribunal a quasi-judicial body.

Before the 2007 amendments, the power to award compensation was vested with the Commission, under section 34 of the Act, and section 34 has been omitted by the amendments. The reason for the omission is that this power is more appropriately vested with the Competition Appellate Tribunal, a quasi-judicial body rather than the Commission which will only perform regulatory functions. After the amendments, the issue of compensation arising out of contravention of any of the provisions of the Act is governed by section 53A(1)(b). This section provides that the Competition Appellate Tribunal may adjudicate on a claim for compensation in the following cases: (i) a claim that may arise from the findings of the Commission or the orders of the Appellate Tribunal in an appeal against any finding of the Commission or (ii) under section 42A—a claim in case of contravention of any order of the Commission or [iii] a claim under section 53Q(2)—contravention, without any reasonable ground, of any order of the Appellate Tribunal or delaying in carrying out such orders of the Appellate Tribunal. Section 53N states the procedure for ordering the recovery of compensation under of this Act.

At first, it is to be noted that direct effect of the amendments is that the focus on the liability to pay compensation, under section 34 has been lost. Under that section, the principle was stated simply and in an understandable manner. Section 34(1) stated it thus: 'Without prejudice to any other provisions contained in this Act, any person may make an application to the Commission for an order for the recovery of compensation from any enterprise for any loss or damage shown to have been suffered, by such person as a result of any contravention of the provisions of Chapter II, having been committed by such enterprise'. The principle under competition law is that anyone suffering a loss or damage as a direct result of the contravention of the Act is eligible to show a case for compensation from the person or enterprise having contravened the Act, the condition being that it should be what is recognized as anti-trust injury, not any injury.

The need to provide for compensation for contraventions of the orders of the Commission and the Competition Appellate Tribunal is not clear. In fact, any injury that will provide a cause of action will be only that injury that arises directly from the breach of any provision of the Act. Under the amended Act, this would be decided by the Competition Appellate Tribunal based on the findings of the Commission or in appeals before it by the Tribunal itself. If there is a further breach by not complying with the any order of the Commission or the Competition Appellate Tribunal, it is a matter for further action by those bodies and it cannot form a basis for compensation. At best the compensation for breach of the Act may be determined appropriately, if it is a continuing offence. Penalties of the nature provided by section 43, section 43A, and section 53Q(1) would be appropriate.

Awarding Compensation—Section 53N

S 53N. (1) Without prejudice to any other provisions contained in this Act, the Central Government or a State Government or a local authority or any enterprise or any person may make an application to the Appellate Tribunal to adjudicate on claim for compensation that may arise from the findings of the Commission or the orders of the Appellate Tribunal in an appeal against any findings of the Commission or under section 42A or under sub-section 2 of section 53Q of the Act, and to pass an order for the recovery of compensation from any enterprise for any loss or damage shown to have been suffered, by the Central Government or a State Government or a local authority or any enterprise or any person as a result of any contravention of the provisions of Chapter II, having been committed by the enterprise.

(2) Every application made under sub-section (1) shall be accompanied by the findings of the Commission, if any, and also be accompanied with such fees as may be prescribed.

(3) The Appellate Tribunal may, after an inquiry made into the allegations mentioned in the application made under sub-section (1), pass an order directing

the enterprise to make payment to the applicant, of the amount determined by it as realizable from the enterprise as compensation for the loss or damage caused to the applicant as a result of any contravention of the provisions of Chapter II having been committed by such enterprise:

provided that the Appellate Tribunal may obtain the recommendations of the Commission before passing an order of compensation.

(4) Where any loss or damage referred to in sub-section (1) is caused to numerous persons having the same interest, one or more of such persons may, with the permission of the Appellate Tribunal, make an application under that sub-section for and on behalf of, or for the benefit of, the persons so interested, and thereupon, the provisions of rule 8 of Order 1 of the First Schedule to the Code of Civil Procedure, 1908 (5 of 1908), shall apply subject to the modification that every reference therein to a suit or decree shall be construed as a reference to the application before the Appellate Tribunal and the order of the Appellate Tribunal thereon.

Explanation—For the removal of doubts, it is hereby declared that

(a) an application may be made for compensation before the Appellate Tribunal only after either the Commission or the Appellate Tribunal on appeal under clause a of sub-section 1 of section 53A of the Act, has determined in a proceeding before it that violation of the provisions of the Act has taken place, or if provisions of section 42A or sub-section 2 of section 53Q of the Act are attracted;

(b) enquiry to be conducted under sub-section (3) shall be for the purpose of determining the eligibility and quantum of compensation due to a person applying for the same, and not for examining afresh the findings of the Commission or the Appellate Tribunal on whether any violation of the Act has taken place.

Section 53N is clearly a wider section than section 34 which has been omitted. Section 34(1) permitted *any person* to make an application to the Commission 'for an order for the recovery of compensation from any enterprise for any loss or damage shown to have been suffered, by such person as a result of any contravention of the provisions of Chapter II, having been committed by such enterprise'. It could be a person who initiated action before the Commission leading to a decision that an enterprise had contravened any provision of the Act or any third party establishing that he had suffered loss or damage by reason of that contravention. Section 53N has widened the category of persons who may now make an application for compensation for any loss or damage arising out of the contravention. It could be the Central Government or a state government or a local authority or any enterprise or any person claiming to have suffered loss or damage as stated.

Under section 53N compensation may be claimed not only on account of loss or damage suffered by any person as a result of a contravention of any of the provisions of Chapter II, but on other grounds also, as permitted under section 42A or section 53Q(2).

Section 42A dealing with compensation in case of contravention of orders of the Commission was considered earlier in this chapter. A claim under section 42A for recovery of compensation from any enterprise for any loss or damage may be made if it can be shown that it was suffered, by such person as a result of the said enterprise violating directions issued by the Commission or that person contravening, without any reasonable ground, any decision or order of the Commission issued under sections 27, 28, 31, 32, and 33 or any condition or restriction subject to which any approval, sanction, direction, or exemption in relation to any matter has been accorded, given, made, or granted under this Act or his delaying in carrying out such orders or directions of the Commission.

Section 53Q(2) is a similar provision, but in respect of contravention of any order of the Competition Appellate Tribunal. Section 53Q(1) deals with the penalty for contravention of any order of the Competition Appellate Tribunal.

The whole section 53Q is as follows:

Contravention of orders of Appellate Tribunal

S 53Q. (1) Without prejudice to the provisions of this Act, if any person contravenes, without any reasonable ground, any order of the Appellate Tribunal, he shall be liable for a penalty of not exceeding rupees one crore or imprisonment for a term up to three years or with both as the Chief Metropolitan Magistrate, Delhi may deem fit:

provided that the Chief Metropolitan Magistrate, Delhi shall not take cognizance of any offence punishable under this sub-section, save on a complaint made by an officer authorized by the Appellate Tribunal.

(2) Without prejudice to the provisions of this Act, any person may make an application to the Appellate Tribunal for an order for the recovery of compensation from any enterprise for any loss or damage shown to have been suffered, by such person as a result of the said enterprise contravening, without any reasonable ground, any order of the Appellate Tribunal or delaying in carrying out such orders of the Appellate Tribunal.

The Procedure for Adjudicating a Claim for Compensation

It should be noted that, under section 53N, where the application is not under section 42A or section 53Q(2), the basic requisite is that there shall be a finding by the Commission or the Tribunal, in appeal proceedings, of a contravention of a provision of Chapter II of the Act. It is a decision on a question of fact which is the starting point for making a claim. The obvious reason is that, where the contravention is not the subject of an appeal, it is not for the Competition Appellate Tribunal to make an inquiry into whether there has been a contravention. The Tribunal will make the inquiry before passing an order for recovery of compensation, and also seek the recommendations of the Commission before making its order. The expression used in sub-section (3) of section 53N in indicating the quantum of compensation is not satisfactory. It is that the Tribunal may order payment to the applicant of an amount determined by it as 'realizable' from the enterprise as compensation for the loss or damage caused to the applicant as a result of any contravention of the provisions of Chapter II having been committed by such enterprise. By any standard, compensation should be related to the extent of the loss or damage that has been shown and whether the act complained of was intentional or not negligent. Excepting in unusual cases, the question of ability to pay the compensation should not be allowed to be pressed in defence. In the first place, 'realizable' is very vague and the Tribunal should not be left with the task of determining what amounts are 'realizable' from an enterprise as compensation. Then, the more important objection is that compensation cannot be determined on the basis of what can be realized. It is an unrelated factor.

Provision for Representative Actions

Sub-section (4) of section 53N provides for applications on behalf of a number of persons who have suffered any loss or damage, and they have the same interest. In such a case, one of them may make the application on behalf of all of them, with the permission of the Tribunal, for recovery of compensation. Consumers of a product or service in question are one example. Permission of the Tribunal is necessary as it will have to be shown that all of them have a common interest in the subject of the application.

The Explanation (a) to section 53N states, by way of emphasis, that an application for recovery of compensation may made to the Competition Appellate Tribunal only after either the Commission, in proceedings before it, or the Competition Appellate Tribunal, in an appeal before it under section 53A(1)(a), has determined that violation of the provisions of the Act has taken place or where compensation is claimed for contravention of the orders of the Commission or the Appellate Tribunal, the provisions of section 42A or section 53Q(2) are attracted. Explanation (b) to s 53N is also clarificatory. It states that the enquiry to be conducted on an application for recovery of compensation shall be for the purpose of determining the eligibility and quantum of compensation due to a person applying for the same, and not for examining afresh the findings of the Commission or the Appellate Tribunal on whether any violation of the Act has taken place.

Execution of Orders of Appellate Tribunal—Section 53P

S 53P. (1) Every order made by the Appellate Tribunal shall be enforced by it in the same manner as if it were a decree made by a court in a suit pending therein, and it shall be lawful for the Appellate Tribunal to send, in case of its inability to execute such order, to the court within the local limits of whose jurisdiction,— (a) in the case of an order against a company, the registered office of the company is situated; or (b) in the case of an order against any other person, place where the person concerned voluntarily resides or carries on business or personally works for gain, is situated.

(2) Notwithstanding anything contained in sub-section (1), the Appellate Tribunal may transmit any order made by it to a civil court having local jurisdiction and such civil court shall execute the order as if it were a decree made by that court.

This section has made the enforcement of an order of the Appellate Tribunal clear and it should be free from objection on the ground of any conflict with the principle of separation of powers of the executive and the judiciary. The order may be executed either by court having jurisdiction, in the case of a company, over the place where the registered office of the company is situated, and in other cases, over the place where the person against whom the order is to be executed voluntarily resides or carries on business or personally works for gain. Under sub-section (2) the Appellate Tribunal may transmit its order, for execution, to a civil court having local jurisdiction, which is one having jurisdiction over the place where the damage or loss was caused.

Comparative Law

Enforcement—EEC Provisions

EEC Council Regulation No. 17 First Regulation dated 6 February 1962, implementing Articles 81 and 82 of the Treaty, amended by Council

Regulation (EC) No. 1216/1999 of 10 June 1999, set out the provisions for enforcement of Articles 81 and 82 dealing with anti-competitive agreements, decisions, etc., and abuse of a dominant position respectively. The European Commission's powers are given below.

Negative Clearance

Article 2 of this Regulation authorizes the Commission to issue negative clearances to the effect that, on the basis of the facts in its possession, there are no grounds under Article 81(1) or Article 82, for action on its part in respect of an agreement, decision or practice. A negative clearance will be considered on the application of an undertaking or associations of undertakings.

Infringements of Article 81 or 82

Where on application or on its own knowledge, the Commission finds that there has been an infringement of any of these two Articles, it may by decision require the undertakings or associations of undertakings concerned, to bring such infringement to an end. An application for such a decision may be made by any member state, or any natural or legal persons who claim a legitimate interest. The Commission may, before making a decision requiring the undertaking or associations of undertakings to bring the infringement to an end, make recommendations to them for termination of the infringement.[41]

Seeking Exemptions

Undertakings seeking exemption under Article 81(3) relating to agreements, decisions and concerted practices falling under Article 81(1) are to notify them to the Commission, and until they are so notified no decision on the application of Article 81(3) will be taken. Exempted from this requirement to notify the Commission are: where the parties operate only in one member state and the agreements, decisions or practices do not relate either to imports or to exports between member states; vertical restraints; certain conditions of licenses of intellectual property; agreements that have as their sole object the development or uniform application of standards or types or joint research for improvement of techniques, provided the results are accessible to all parties thereto and may be used by each of them.[42] An exemption is granted for a specific period and subject to conditions and may be revoked if the conditions are breached.[43] The Commission has the sole power, subject to review by the

Court of Justice, to declare Article 81(1) inapplicable pursuant to Article 81(3).[44] The Commission has the power to apply Articles 81(1) and 82.[45]

The Commission is required to act in constant liaison with competent authorities of the member states and prior to taking any decision, in granting negative clearances, exemptions or renewal, amendment or revocation of any exemption. While applying Articles 81(1) and 82, the Commission should consult an Advisory Committee on Restrictive Practices and Monopolies, which will be composed of officials competent in the matter of restrictive practices and monopolies.[46]

Investigations

In making any investigation of a violation of Article 81 or Article 82, the officials authorized by the Commission are empowered: (*a*) to examine the books and other business records; (*b*) to take copies of or extracts from the books and business records; (*c*) to ask for oral explanations on the spot; and (*d*) to enter any premises; land and means of transport of undertakings.[47]

Fines

Fines may be levied, depending upon the gravity and the duration of the breach, of up to 10 per cent of the turnover in the preceding business year of each of the undertakings participating in the infringement where, either intentionally or negligently: (*a*) they infringe Article 81(1) or Article 82; or (*b*) they commit a breach of any of the conditions subject to which an exemption under Article 81(3) was given.[48] In addition, the Commission may impose on undertakings or associations of undertakings periodic penalties in order to compel them: (*a*) to put an end to an infringement of Article 81 or 82 determined by the Commission; (*b*) to refrain from any act prohibited by an order granting exemption under Article 81(3); (*c*) to supply complete and correct information which was requested; and (*d*.) to submit to an investigation ordered by the Commission.[49] The Court of Justice has unlimited authority to review decisions of the Commission fixing a fine or periodic penalty payment. It may cancel, reduce or increase the fine or periodic penalty payment imposed.[50]

Setting Fines—EC

In this context, the 'Guidelines on the method of setting fines imposed pursuant to Article 23(2)(a) of Regulation No 1/2003'[51] issued by the

European Commission is relevant. The basic principle stated is that to achieve a deterring effect on the actual infringers and potential infringers, the Commission should refer to the value of the sales of goods or services to which the infringement relates as a basis for setting the fine and that the duration of the infringement should also play a significant role in the setting of the appropriate amount of the fine. It necessarily has an impact on the potential consequences of the infringement on the market. It is therefore considered important that the fine should also reflect the number of years during which an undertaking participated in the infringement.

The following elaboration of the principle is most noteworthy:

> The combination of the value of sales to which the infringement relates and of the duration of the infringement is regarded as providing an appropriate proxy to reflect the economic importance of the infringement as well as the relative weight of each undertaking in the infringement. Reference to these factors provides a good indication of the order of magnitude of the fine and should not be regarded as the basis for an automatic and arithmetical calculation method.

Professional Secrecy

Information obtained during the investigation shall be used only for the purposes of investigation. Also, the Commission or any of its officials and other servants shall not disclose information covered by obligations of professional secrecy. However, publication of general information or surveys that do not contain information of undertakings is not prohibited.[52]

Special Study of Sectors

It is to be noted that the Commission has been specially authorized to examine any sector of the economy showing indications of price movements, inflexibility of prices or other circumstances suggesting that in the economic sector concerned, competition is being restricted or distorted within the common market. In that event, the Commission may decide to conduct a general inquiry into that sector and towards that purpose it may request undertakings in the sector concerned to supply the information necessary for giving effect to the principles formulated in Articles 81 and 82 and for carrying out the duties entrusted to it. It may also ask the undertaking or associations of undertakings in the sector to communicate to it all agreements, decisions and concerted practices exempted from notification. In cases where it appears that, by reason of their size, undertakings or groups of undertakings could be occupying a dominant position, the Commission could ask for particulars of the structure of the undertakings and of their behaviour as are requisite to an appraisal of their position in relation to Article 82.[53]

The Competition Commission, UK

Section 45 of the Competition Act, 1998, UK, provides for the establishment of the Commission. It is to have such functions as are conferred on it by or as a result of this Act. The Act dissolved the Monopolies and Mergers Commission and its functions were transferred to this Commission. Schedule 7 to the Act makes further provisions relating to the Commission. In indicating the Commission's powers, Paragraph 8 of this Schedule states that, subject to the provisions of the Act, the Commission has power to do anything (except borrow money): (*a*) calculated to facilitate the discharge of its functions; or (*b*) incidental or conducive to the discharge of its functions.

Paragraph 2(1) of Part I of Schedule 7 states that the Competition Commission is to consist of members appointed by the Secretary of State to form panels for the purposes of the Commission's functions in relation to: (*a*) appeals; (*b*) the Commission's general functions;[54] (*c*) newspaper merger references; and (*d*.) sectors such as electricity, water, and telecommunications.

Paragraph 3(1) provides that the Commission is to have a chairman appointed by the Secretary of State from among the reporting panel members. Reporting panel members are those appointed to form a panel for the purposes of the Commission's general functions. Paragraph 4 requires that the Secretary of State must appoint one of the appeal panel members to preside over the discharge of the Commission's functions in relation to appeals.

In the UK, the institutional mechanism relating to competition and consumer issues is as follows.[55]

The Department of Trade and Industry sets the overall policy and legal framework for competition and consumer issues in the UK. The Secretary of State is responsible specifically for the appointment of Members of the Commission, for the provision and monitoring of its funding and for assessing the Commission's contribution towards agreed targets.

The Commission has statutory powers and responsibilities covering competition issues. It conducts in-depth inquiries into mergers and markets. It makes decisions against the competition tests set out in the Enterprise Act, 2002. In the event of adverse findings, it decides on appropriate remedies. It also investigates references on the regulated sectors of the economy.

Each year, its Council of the Commission, using key performance indicators, will monitor the performance of the Commission in achieving high skills and expertise of staff and members.

The constitution and composition of the Commission is as follows.[56] The Secretary of State for Trade and Industry appoints members for an eight-year term following an open competition. They are appointed for their individual experience, ability and diversity of background, not as representatives of particular organizations, interests or political parties. There are usually about 50 members and except for the chairman, they work part-time.

There are specialist panels for utilities, telecommunications, water and newspapers. The utilities panel is the specialist panel for gas and electricity inquiries. The Commission's staff, of about 150, include administrators; professionals (accountants, economists, business advisers, and lawyers); and support staff, such as information services, finance and human resources. About two-thirds are direct employees; the remainder are on temporary contract or on loan from government departments.

Enforcement of the Competition Act, 1998, UK

The powers of investigation and enforcement under the Act conferred on the Director-General of Fair Trading (Director) are contained in sections 25–41 of Chapter III of that Act. They are in relation to the Chapter I prohibition, viz. anti-competitive agreements, etc., and the Chapter II prohibition, viz. abuse of a dominant position. The Director may conduct an investigation if there are reasonable grounds for suspecting that the Chapter I prohibition has been infringed; or that the Chapter II prohibition has been infringed.[57] During the course of the investigation he may require by a notice in writing any person to produce to him a specified document, or to provide him with specified information, which he considers relates to any matter relevant to the investigation. The notice should also state the subject matter and purpose of the investigation; and the nature of the offences created by sections 42 to 44.[58]

Interim Measures

Section 35 empowers the Director to issue interim directions, during his investigation, when he has a reasonable suspicion that the Chapter I prohibition, or that the Chapter II prohibition has been infringed. He may act under this section only when he considers that it is a matter of urgency for him to act for preventing serious, irreparable damage to a particular person or category of person, or of protecting the public interest. Directions as interim measures can be appealed to the Competition Appeal Tribunal (the CAT).

Where he decides that there has been an infringement of the Chapter I prohibition or Chapter II prohibition, he may require the party to bring the infringement to an end.[59] If a person fails without reasonable excuse to comply with the directions of the Director, he may apply to the court for an appropriate order to secure compliance with the direction by the defaulter.[60]

Penalties may be levied by the Director for infringements, but they are leviable only if he is satisfied that the infringement has been committed intentionally or negligently by the undertaking.[61]

No penalty fixed by the Director under this section may exceed 10 per cent of the turnover of the undertaking.[62] In the case of a violation of Chapter I prohibition, the power to levy a penalty is subject to section 39 and does not apply if the Director is satisfied that the undertaking acted on the reasonable assumption that that section gave it immunity in respect of the agreement.

Section 39 provides immunity from penalty to a 'small agreement', which is not a price-fixing agreement but one satisfying the criteria of combined turnover of the parties to the agreement, the share of the market affected by the agreement, as may be prescribed. This immunity may be withdrawn, if the Director considers that the agreement is likely to infringe the Chapter I prohibition.

Similarly, section 40 provides limited immunity in relation to Chapter II prohibition regarding 'conduct of minor significance'. It means conduct that falls within prescribed category and the criteria for prescribing that category would be the turnover of the person whose conduct it is and the share of the market affected by the conduct. This immunity may also be withdrawn if the Director considers that the conduct may violate Chapter II prohibition.

The OFT's 'Draft competition law guideline for consultation' on enforcement[63] states: 'The immunity applies only to financial penalties.

An anti-competitive agreement or abusive conduct by such undertakings is still an infringement, and consequently the OFT may take other enforcement action, and the immunity does not prevent third parties from claiming damages for the loss caused by such an agreement or conduct.'

Binding Commitments[64]

Under section 31A(2) of the Competition Act, UK, the OFT may, instead of continuing with an investigation into an alleged infringement of Article 81, Article 82, the Chapter I and/or Chapter II prohibitions of the Act, and for the purposes of addressing the competition concerns it has identified, accept such binding commitments offered to it by a person or persons as it considers appropriate. Under section 31A(4)(b) of the Act, the OFT may release binding commitments.

Commitments are obligations of a person undertaking to cease or modify his conduct in a particular area, terminating an exclusive arrangement, removing a particular clause from an agreement, withdrawing from a particular activity, licensing specific assets or even divesting itself of a part of its business.

Binding commitments are likely to be accepted where competition concerns are readily identifiable, the competition concerns are fully addressed by the commitments offered, and the proposed commitments are capable of being implemented effectively and, if necessary, within a short period of time. Binding commitments will not be accepted where compliance with and the effectiveness of any binding commitments would be difficult to discern, and/or where the OFT considers that not to complete its investigation and make a decision would undermine deterrence. Cases involving serious abuse of a dominant position would also not be considered.

They will not also be accepted in cases involving secret cartels between competitors, which include: price-fixing, bid-rigging (collusive tendering) establishing output restrictions or quotas, sharing markets, and/or dividing markets. But even in such cases, binding commitments may be accepted if the 'administrative cost involved in continuing the investigation and proceeding to a final decision would outweigh the benefits'.

Whilst binding commitments are in force, the OFT may review their effectiveness and take such action as regards variation or release as it deems appropriate.

'Privileged Communication'—During Investigation

Section 30 of the Competition Act, UK, protects certain types of communications made during the Director's investigation as privileged communication that a person cannot be compelled to produce or disclose.

Section '"Privileged communication" means a communication (a) between a professional legal adviser and his client, or (b) made in connection with, or in contemplation of, legal proceedings and for the purposes of those proceedings, which in proceedings in the high court would be protected from disclosure on grounds of legal professional privilege.'

US—Enforcement

The Department of Justice (DOJ) and the Federal Trade Commission (FTC) are the agencies that enforce the antitrust laws of the US. The principal enactments are: the Sherman Act, 1890, the Clayton Act, 1914 and the Federal Trade Commission Act 1914.

Violations of the Sherman Act may be prosecuted as civil or criminal offences. The department has sole responsibility for the criminal enforcement of the Sherman Act. In a civil proceeding the department may obtain an injunction against prohibited practices. The Attorney General and the FTC are authorized to seek a court order enjoining consummation of a merger that would violate section 7 of the Clayton Act.

Under the FTC Act rendering unlawful 'unfair methods of competition in or affecting commerce, and unfair or deceptive acts or practices in or affecting commerce', the FTC is authorized to take administrative action against conduct that violates the Sherman Act and the Clayton Act, as well as anti-competitive practices that do not fall within the scope of the Sherman or Clayton Act.

Having considered, at the beginning of this chapter, the law and the mechanism for enforcing the provisions of the Act, we may now consider some other specific provisions of the 2002 Act under the heading 'Miscellaneous' in Chapter IX of the Act.

Exemptions

Section 54 empowers the Central Government to exempt, by notification, from the application of the Act or any provision thereof and for specific periods, the following: (*a*) any class of enterprises if such exemption is necessary in the interest of security of the state or public interest; (*b*) any practice or agreement arising out of and in accordance with any obligation assumed by India under any treaty, agreement or convention with any other country or countries; or (*c*) any enterprise which performs a sovereign function on behalf of the Central Government or a state government but where such an enterprise is engaged in any activity including the activity relatable to the sovereign functions of the government, the exemption should be granted only in respect of the activity relatable to the sovereign functions.

Under the first sub-clause, exemption may be granted only to a class of enterprises and not to any individual enterprise.

Interests of security may arise in contracts for the supply of defence equipment, etc. The Defense Production Act of 1950, US, provides for exemption covering voluntary agreements among various approved industry groups for the development of preparedness programmes to meet potential national emergencies. Persons participating in such agreements are 'immunized from the operation of the antitrust laws with respect to good faith activities undertaken to fulfill their responsibilities under the agreement.'

The US has granted immunity of varying extent from antitrust laws to a number of businesses. They range from agricultural and fishermen's marketing agencies to joint operating arrangements between newspapers for sharing production facilities, joint programme of research and development by small business, etc. Section 6 of the Clayton Act declares that antitrust laws are not applicable to labour unions.[65] The US Webb-Pomerene Act provides a limited antitrust exemption for the formation and operation of associations of otherwise competing businesses to engage in collective export sales. The exemption applies only to the export of 'goods, wares, or merchandise.' It does not apply to conduct that has an anti-competitive effect in the US, or that injures domestic competitors of the members of an export association. Nor does it provide any immunity from prosecution under foreign antitrust laws. Associations seeking an exemption under the Webb-Pomerene Act must file their articles of agreement and annual reports with the Commission, but pre-formation approval from the Commission is not required.[66]

As already noted, by virtue of section 3(5)(ii) of the Competition Act, section 3 dealing with anti-competitive agreements will not apply to any agreement relating to the supply of goods for export.

The term 'public interest' is wide and any exemption on this ground should establish a reasonable justification and the public interest sought to be protected.

Under the second sub-clause, exemption may be granted by the Central Government to any practice or agreement arising out of any treaty or convention. But this could have been limited to state that such exemption ought not to conflict with any of the provisions of the Act or its objective. Article 234 of the EEC Treaty is an example. It states that agreements entered into between member states and between any member state and any third party before the Treaty entered into force shall not be affected but if any agreement is not compatible with the Treaty, the member state or states concerned shall take all appropriate steps to eliminate the incompatibilities established.

The last sub-clause is self-explanatory and does not need any specific comment.

Non-disclosure of Information

Though the Act does not use the concept of a privileged communication, in the context of any inquiry or investigation, Section 57 provides for some protection against disclosure of information relating to an enterprise that has been obtained by or on behalf of the Commission or the Appellate Tribunal[67] for the purposes of the Act. Such information shall not, without the previous permission in writing of the enterprise, be disclosed otherwise than in compliance with or for the purposes of this Act, or any other law for the time being in force.

Overriding Effect

Section 60 is to the effect that this Act shall 'have overriding effect' which means that the Act shall have effect even though it may be inconsistent with any other law for the time being in force. This has to be read along with section 62 that declares that this Act will be in addition to, and not in derogation of, any other law for the time being in force.

Jurisdiction of Civil Courts Excluded

S 61 provides for the exclusion of the jurisdiction of civil courts. The pre-amendment s 61 only excluded any matter which the Commission was empowered to determine under the Act. The amendment has included any matter that may be determined by the Competition Appellate Tribunal also within the prohibition of s 61.

Repeal of the MRTP Act—Section 66

Section 66 provides for the repeal of the MRTP Act. In sum, it provides for consequential action to be taken in the interregnum relating to matters pending under the MRTP Act. We may consider the material sub-sections in so far as they are of concern to the general public, as the section deals with a number actions relating to the staff of the MRTP Commission on its dissolution and such matters.

Section 66 as amended by the 2009 Act[68] provides for the following: (i) the repeal of the MRTP Act, 1969; (ii) the consequent dissolution of the MRTP Commission established under that Act; (iii) the repeal will not affect any previous liability incurred in that Act or affect any penalty or punishment incurred in respect of any contravention under that Act; (iv) all cases pertaining to monopolistic trade practices or restrictive trade practices pending (including such cases, in which any unfair trade practice has also been alleged), before the MRTP Commission shall, on the commencement of the Competition Amendment Act, 2009 stand transferred to the Appellate Tribunal and shall be adjudicated by the Appellate Tribunal in accordance with the provisions of the MRTP Act as if that Act had not been repealed;

(v) subject to the previous provision, all cases, including applications for loss or damages under the MRTP Act, pertaining to unfair trade practices other than those referred to in clause (x) of sub-section(1) of section 36A of the Monopolies and Restrictive Trade Practices Act, 1969 (54 of 1969) and pending before the Monopolies and Restrictive Trade Practices Commission [immediately before the commencement of the Competition (Amendment) Act, 2009 shall, on such commencement], shall, stand transferred to the National Commission constituted under the Consumer Protection Act, 1986 (68 of 1986) and the National Commission shall dispose of such cases as if they were cases filed under that Act and the National Commission may transfer any such case to the appropriate State Commission; it should be noted that such cases are to be disposed of under the MRTP Act, as if that Act had not been repealed;

(vi) all the cases relating to unfair trade practices pending, before the National Commission under this sub-section, on or before the date on which the competition (Amendment) Bill, 2009 receives the assent of the President, shall, on and from that date, stand transferred to the Appellate Tribunal and be adjudicated by the Appellate Tribunal in accordance with the provisions of the repealed Act as if that Act had not been repealed;

(vii) unfair trade practices referred to in clause (x) of sub-section (1) of section 36A of the Monopolies and Restrictive Trade Practices Act, 1969 and pending before the Monopolies and Restrictive Trade Practices Commission shall, 'on the commencement of the Competition (Amendment) Act, 2009' stand transferred to the Appellate Tribunal and the Appellate Tribunal shall dispose of such cases as if they were cases filed under that Act;

(viii) investigations or proceedings, other than those relating to unfair trade practices, pending before the Director-General of Investigation and Registration on or before the commencement of this Act shall, on such commencement, stand transferred to the Competition Commission of India, and the Competition Commission of India may conduct or order for conduct of such investigation or proceedings in the manner as it deems fit;

(ix) investigations or proceedings, relating to unfair trade practices, other than those referred to in clause (x) of sub-section (1) of section 36A of the Monopolies and Restrictive Trade Practices Act, 1969 (54 of 1969) and pending before the Director-General of Investigation and Registration on or before the commencement of this Act shall, on such commencement, stand transferred to the National Commission constituted under the Consumer Protection Act, 1986 (68 of 1986) and the National Commission may conduct or order for conduct of such investigation or proceedings in the manner as it deems fit;

(x) investigations or proceedings, relating to unfair trade practices pending before the National Commission, on or before the date on which the Competition (Amendment) Bill, 2009 receives the assent of the President shall, on and from that date, stand transferred to the Appellate Tribunal and the Appellate Tribunal may conduct or order for conduct of such investigation or proceedings in the manner as it deems fit;

(xi) investigations or proceedings relating to unfair trade practices referred to in clause (x) of sub-section (1) of section 36A of the Monopolies and Restrictive Trade Practices Act, 1969 (54 of 1969), and pending before the Director-General of Investigation and Registration on or before the commencement of this Act shall, on such commencement, stand transferred to the Competition Commission of India and the Competition Commission of India may conduct or order for conduct of such investigation in the manner as it deems fit; (xi) other cases shall abate.

Cross-border Issues and Competition

So far we have discussed the mechanism for controlling anti-competitive acts carried on by persons having the location of their operations at some place in India and, therefore, directly subject to the territorial jurisdiction of Indian courts and tribunals. It is possible for enterprises without having a fixed place of business in India to control the operations of any enterprise in India in a manner injuring the process of competition in India. Share-holding is not necessary for this purpose and it could be through a distribution agreement, price-fixing arrangement, or exclusive dealing agreements that have as their object the elimination of a competitor or partitioning the market. There are overseas cartels operating from different countries and engaged in conspiracies to carry out such anti-competitive practices that are the serious concern of industrially advanced countries and they are grappling with the problem of methods of cooperation in rendering these cartels ineffective, as it is well understood that domestic legislation has only territorial effect.

The position under section 32 has been discussed earlier.

It is well recognized that declaring unlawful any agreement or practice and restraining the local enterprise that is a party to such an agreement is sufficiently effective to make the arrangement inoperative within the country enforcing its domestic law. This is how courts have been so far aided in giving effect to the provisions of any national law in such circumstances.

'Wood Pulp' Case[69]

This was a case where the EC had imposed fines on certain enterprises, having their registered offices outside the EC, for violation of Article 81. The charges against them were that they fixed, in concert, prices to customers in the EC, provided exchange of individualized data concerning prices with certain other wood pulp producers, and made price recommendations through the trade association. The appellants, producers of wood pulp and two associations of wood pulp producers challenged that decision in an appeal to the European Court of Justice.

The Commission had based its decision on the ground that all the addressees of the decision were either exporting directly to purchasers within the Community, or were doing business within the Community through branches, subsidiaries, agencies or other establishments in the Community and that the action in concert applied to the vast majority of the sales of those undertakings to and in the Community. The Commission concluded: 'The effect of the agreements and practices on prices announced and/or charged to customers and on resale of pulp within the EEC was therefore not only substantial but intended, and was the primary and direct result of the agreements and practices.'

The jurisdiction of the Commission to apply its competition rules to them was challenged by some of the appellants. The argument was that conduct outside the Community could not be sought to be regulated merely because the repercussions of that conduct were felt within the Community. Meeting that objection, the Court held:

> Where wood pulp producers established in those countries sell directly to purchasers established in the Community and engage in price competition in order to win orders from those customers that constitute competition within the common market. It follows that where those producers concert on the prices to be charged to their customers in the Community and put that concertation into effect by selling at prices which are actually coordinated, they are taking part in concertation which has the object and effect of restricting competition within the common market within the meaning of Article 85 of the Treaty.

The Court pointed out that such conduct had two elements, one relating to the formation of the agreement or decision and the other, the implementation and that the place of implementation was the decisive factor. Holding that in as much as the place of implementation was within the Community, 'the Community's jurisdiction to apply its competition rules to such conduct is covered by the territoriality principle as universally recognized in public international law', the Court added that when the overseas enterprises implemented their decisions within the Community, it was immaterial whether or not they had recourse to subsidiaries, agents, sub-agents, or branches within the Community in order to make their contacts with purchasers within the Community.

Multilateral Framework on Competition Policy

The efforts at the WTO in evolving a multilateral framework on competition policy are summarized below.

WTO and competition policy

The Singapore Ministerial Conference held in 1996, decided to establish a working group to study issues raised by members relating to the interaction between trade and competition policy, including anti-competitive practices, in order to identify any areas that may merit further consideration in the WTO framework. This working group was to work in cooperation with the other working group established at the same Conference on the relationship between trade and investment and also with the United Nations Conference on Trade and Development, UNCTAD, and other intergovernmental fora as considered necessary. It was expressly stated that future negotiations, if any, regarding multilateral disciplines in these areas, would take place only after an explicit consensus decision among WTO members regarding such negotiations.

The Working Group on trade and competition policy met in 1997. It noted that approximately 80 WTO member countries, including some 50 developing and transition countries, had adopted competition laws, also known as 'antitrust' or 'anti-monopoly' laws. In considering the inter-action between trade and competition policy, the Working Group studied the following: the impact of anti-competitive practices of enterprises and associations on international trade; the impact of state monopolies, exclusive rights and regulatory policies on competition and international trade; the relationship between the trade-related aspects of intellectual property rights and competition policy; the relationship between investment and competition policy; and the impact of trade policy on competition.

The Group issued in 1998 a report on its deliberations. At its meetings in 1999, the Group found a divergence of opinion among the members on the need for action at the level of the WTO to enhance the relevance of competition policy to the multilateral trading system. While some expressed support for a multilateral framework on competition policy in the WTO, others preferred bilateral agreements towards effective implementation of competition policies in their respective regions. The issue was left to be considered at the Seattle Conference, but the Working Group found that the objections to a multilateral framework were continued.

The direction of the Doha Ministerial Conference in 2001 to the Working Group on the Interaction between Trade and Competition Policy was 'to focus on the clarification of: core principles, including transparency, non-discrimination and procedural fairness, and provisions on hardcore cartels; modalities for voluntary cooperation; and support for progressive reinforcement of competition institutions in developing countries through capacity building'.

As of now, there has been little progress and any consensus on a multilateral framework on competition policy for the members of the

WTO is a remote theoretical goal. Till something approximating to that end can be identified as acceptable, the next practicable option would be for countries to enter into bilateral agreements with their trading partners on some agreed modes of dealing with competition issues arising out of their trade, whether it is the investigation of any antitrust conduct beyond the territory of one of them, or dealing with the effects of that conduct in the territory of another.

The Report of the International Competition Policy Advisory Committee, US, 2000

One of the mandates of this Committee was to study future directions in enforcement cooperation between US antitrust authorities and their counterparts around the world, particularly in their anti-cartel prosecution efforts.

Role for WTO

On the role of international organizations in dealing with competition issues arising out of international trade, this Committee stated: 'Specifically, this Advisory Committee sees efforts at developing a harmonized and comprehensive multilateral antitrust code administered by a new supranational competition authority or the WTO as both unrealistic and unwise.' The Committee considered that the role for WTO would be in developing a common understanding of the issues surrounding the intersection of trade and competition policy but that it should concentrate on governmental restraints, which according to the Committee was the area of WTO's 'core competence'. Referring to the work of the Working Group of the WTO on Interaction between Trade and Competition Policy, the Committee recommended that the WTO undertake these 'illustrative and largely educative steps' to make the WTO a more 'competition policy friendly' environment. But the Committee was against the WTO developing new competition rules under the WTO umbrella.

The Committee recommended that governments think of creating a new venue where government officials, private firms, non-governmental organizations and other bodies may exchange ideas and work towards solutions for competition law and policy problems.

The Committee felt that bilateral agreements were a desirable alternative till international agreements could be developed and agreed upon. On agreements providing for comity, the Committee states: 'to be truly effective, positive comity requires correspondence between the parties' antitrust laws and enforcement commitment'. This is pursuant to the experience with some countries that are slow to act under such agreements, when the actions of the domestic enterprise had weakened the competitive ability of the overseas enterprise.

Cooperation Agreements Among States—Bilateral Agreements

The effective enforcement of a country's antitrust law against offenders who do not have establishments there, but operate from overseas, raise problems of jurisdiction, conflict in the relevant laws, manner of enforcement and related matters. All these cannot be resolved by any central legislation applicable to all countries. It is a matter to be resolved largely by bilateral and where workable, by multilateral agreements. The objective of such agreements would be cooperation among states in investigating, collecting information, and assistance in prosecuting offenders shown to be residing or carrying on business in a particular country, outside the country seeking investigation into breaches of its antitrust legislation.

US

The International Antitrust Enforcement Assistance Act of 1994 authorizes the Department of Justice and the Federal Trade Commission to enter into antitrust mutual assistance agreements with other countries, in accordance with this legislation, in investigating in the US and collecting evidence relating to a violation of an antitrust law of a foreign country. For example, they should ensure that the overseas antitrust authority requesting an investigation in the US, assures them of reciprocal assistance, maintains confidentiality of the evidence collected, etc.

US and EC

The US has entered into bilateral agreements and mutual legal assistance treaties with a number of countries. The basic bilateral agreement of 23 September 1991, between the US and the European Communities covers the application of their competition laws. The purpose of this agreement is to promote cooperation and coordination between the US and the European Communities and lessen the possibility or impact of differences between them in the application of their competition laws.

This 1991 agreement has been supplemented by another agreement of 1998 to specify the application of comity principles in the enforcement of their competition laws. The important provisions of the second agreement are stated in the paragraph dealing with comity. The mutual legal assistance treaties are treaties of general application pursuant to which the US and the foreign country agree to assist one another in criminal law enforcement matters.

The 1991 Agreement between the US and the EC—Important Clauses

Under this agreement of 1991, each party should notify the other whenever its competition authorities become aware that their enforcement activities may affect important interests of the other. They should share information of the following nature: information that will: (*a*) facilitate effective application of their respective competition laws; or (*b*) promote better understanding by them of economic conditions and theories relevant to their competition authorities' enforcement activities. The agreement provides for periodic meetings of competition authorities from each party for exchanging information on their current enforcement activities and priorities, and information on economic sectors of common interest, discussing policy changes which they are considering and other matters of mutual interest relating to the application of competition laws.

Towards cooperation and coordination in enforcement activities, the competition authorities of each party should also render assistance to the competition authorities of the other in their enforcement activities, to the extent compatible with the assisting party's laws and important interests, and within its reasonably available resources. The competition authorities of either party may, after giving appropriate notice to the other party, limit or terminate their participation in a coordination arrangement and pursue their enforcement activities independently.[70]

Article V of this agreement dealing with cooperation regarding anti-competitive activities in the territory of one party that adversely affect the interests of the other party is the crucial provision. This provides a procedure for notification and initiation of enforcement activity, where one party believes that anti-competitive activities carried out on the territory of the other party are adversely affecting its important interests. In such an event, the first party may notify the other party and may request that the other party's competition authorities initiate appropriate enforcement activities. It is for the notified party to take the final decision that shall be communicated to the notifying party, who should have the freedom to take such action as appropriate against the anti-competitive activities it complained about.

Neither party is bound to disclose to the other party any information, the disclosure of which is prohibited by the law governing the party in possession of that information or would be incompatible with important interests of the party possessing the information.[71]

In the case of *Boeing/McDonnell Douglas* discussed in the chapter on 'Combinations', a case with a community dimension and the geographic market being the whole world, the EC, before making a final decision consulted, under this bilateral agreement of 1991, the US authorities and 'asked the Federal Trade Commission to take account of the European Union's important interests in safeguarding competition in the market for large civil aircraft'. The US Department of Defence and Department of Justice, on behalf of the US government, informed the European Commission that, among other objections, a decision prohibiting the proposed merger could harm important US defence interests.

Since it was not established that a dominant position would be strengthened or created in the defence sector as a result of the proposed concentration, the Commission limited the scope of its action to the civil side of the operation. This was only one aspect of the case and ultimately, the concentration was approved, on the undertakings given by Boeing.

Comity

The word 'comity' is of Latin origin and means courtesy. *Wharton's Law Lexicon* (fourteenth edition), explaining the meaning of the phrase 'comity of nations' states: 'the most appropriate phrase to express the true foundation and extent of the obligation of the laws of one nation within the territories of another. It is derived from the voluntary consent of the latter, and is inadmissible when it is contrary to its known policy or prejudicial to its interests.'

Antitrust Enforcement Guidelines for International Operations issued by the US Department of Justice and the Federal Trade Commission in April, 1995, explains 'comity' as 'a broad concept of respect among co-equal sovereign nations', and continues stating that in determining whether to assert jurisdiction to investigate or bring an action, or to seek particular remedies in a given case, the consideration would be whether significant interests of any foreign sovereign would be affected.

Agreement between the European Communities and
the Government of the United States of America on
the application of positive comity principles in the
enforcement of their competition laws (1998)

By way of elaborating the principles of positive comity and towards increasing the effectiveness of the 1991 bilateral agreement, the US and the EC entered into a supplementary agreement, which is called the 'positive comity' agreement.

Some salient features of this agreement between the US and the EU on the application of comity principles in the enforcement of their competition laws may be noted.[72]

The scope of the agreement is to make provision for dealing with anti-competitive activities taking place in the country of one of the parties adversely affecting the interests of the other party, and where such activities are not permissible according to the competition law of the country in which the activities occur. The purpose of the agreement is to ensure that trade and investment flows between the two parties and competition and consumer welfare are not impeded by anti-competitive activities for which one or both the parties may provide a remedy.[73] The objective is to 'establish cooperative procedures to achieve the most effective and efficient enforcement of competition law'. This means that where anti-competitive activities occur principally in and are directed principally towards one party's territory, the other party will leave it to the competition authorities of the first party, where they are able to take effective action.

Article III of this agreement defines 'positive comity'. It provides for the competition authorities of one party requesting the competition authorities of the other party to investigate and, if warranted, to remedy anti-competitive activities in accordance with the other party's competition laws. Such a request may be made regardless of whether the activities also violate the first party's competition laws, and regardless of whether the competition authorities of the first party have commenced or contemplate taking enforcement activities under their own competition laws.[74] It may be agreed between the parties that the first party, viz. the requesting party will defer or suspend pending or contemplated enforcement activities during the pendency of enforcement activities of the other party.

Normally, enforcement activities will be suspended when the anti-competitive activities at issue do not have a direct, substantial and reasonably foreseeable impact on consumers in the first party's territory, or where they do have such an impact but they occur principally in and are directed principally towards the other party's territory, or when the adverse effects of such activities in the first party's territory may be effectively dealt with and adequately remedied by the other party. However, the first party suspending action may at a later stage initiate action itself and inform the other party. If the other party intends to continue its action, both the parties may coordinate their investigations as provided in the earlier agreement entered into in 1991, to which the present agreement will be supplementary.[75]

Similarly the US and the EU have entered into an arrangement to ensure that when both review a merger situation, both jurisdictions reach, as far as possible, consistent, or at least non-conflicting, outcomes. This is set out in the US–EU Merger Working Group's document entitled '*Best Practices on Cooperation in Merger Investigations*'.[76] It provides for coordination in timing in investigation, collection and evaluation of evidence, advice to the parties on studying the remedy proposals so that inconsistent results or difficulties in implementation are avoided. The document states: 'It is intended to set forth an advisory framework for interagency cooperation. The agencies reserve their full discretion in the implementation of these best practices and nothing in this document is intended to create any enforceable rights.'

The future

After some time in the light of its experience in implementing the Competition Act, 2002, India should assess how best it can draw upon the experience of other countries that have enforced antitrust legislation for longer periods. It would then be in a portion to determine the legislative model appropriate to the country's business structure and economic programmes.

***

Endnotes

[1] Section 7.

[2] Section 16.

[3] Chapter VIIIA, introduced by the 2007 amendment, containing sections 53A to 53U deals with their appointment, powers etc.; the new sub-section, section 2(ba) defines the 'Appellate Tribunal' as "Appellate Tribunal" means the Competition Appellate Tribunal established under sub-section (1) of Section 53A.

[4] Section 18.
[5] Section 19.
[6] Section 20.
[7] Section 26.
[8] Section 27.
[9] Section 28.
[10] Section 29.
[11] Section 30.
[12] Section 31.
[13] Section 32.
[14] Section 33.
[15] Section 36.
[16] Section 38.
[17] Section 39.
[18] Section 18. Subject to the provisions of this Act, it shall be the duty of the Commission to eliminate practices having adverse effect on competition, promote and sustain competition, protect the interests of consumers and ensure freedom of trade carried on by other participants, in markets in India: Provided that the Commission may, for the purpose of discharging its duties or performing its functions under this Act, enter into any memorandum or arrangement with the prior approval of the Central Government, with any agency of any foreign country.

[19] References by a statutory authority and the Commission between themselves are covered by section 21 and section 21A, and have been referred to in the chapter on 'Combination'.

[20] Section 19(3).

[21] Section 19(4).

[22] Section 19(5). The 'relevant market', means 'the relevant geographic market', and 'the relevant product market', which have been discussed in the chapters on 'Anti-competitive Agreements' and 'Abuse of a Dominant Position'.

[23] Section 19(6) and (7).

[24] Section 29(1).

[25] Section 29(1A.)

[26] Section 29(2)–(6).

[27] Section 30.

[28] Section 31. '(1) Where the Commission is of the opinion that any combination does not, or is not likely to, have an appreciable adverse effect on competition, it shall, by order, approve that combination including the combination in respect of which a notice has been given under sub-section (2) of section 6.

(2) Where the Commission is of the opinion that the combination has, or is likely to have, an appreciable adverse effect on competition, it shall direct that the combination shall not take effect.

(3) Where the Commission is of the opinion that the combination has, or is likely to have, an appreciable adverse effect on competition but such adverse

effect can be eliminated by suitable modification to such combination; it may propose appropriate modification to the combination, to the parties to such combination.

(4) The parties, who accept the modification proposed by the Commission under sub-section (3), shall carry out such modification within the period specified by the Commission.

(5) If the parties to the combination, who have accepted the modification under sub-section (4), fail to carry out the modification within the period specified by the Commission, such combination shall be deemed to have an appreciable adverse effect on competition and the Commission shall deal with such combination in accordance with the provisions of this Act.

(6) If the parties to the combination do not accept the modification proposed by the Commission under sub-section (3), such parties may, within thirty working days of the modification proposed by the Commission, submit amendment to the modification proposed by the Commission under that sub-section.

(7) If the Commission agrees with the amendment submitted by the parties under sub-section (6), it shall, by order, approve the combination.

(8) If the Commission does not accept the amendment submitted under sub-section (6), then, the parties shall be allowed a further period of thirty working days within which such parties shall accept the modification proposed by the Commission under sub-section (3).

(9) If the parties fail to accept the modification proposed by the Commission within thirty working days referred to in sub-section (6) or within a further period of thirty working days referred to in sub-section (8), the combination shall be deemed to have an appreciable adverse effect on competition and be dealt with in accordance with the provisions of this Act.

(10) Where the Commission has directed under sub-section (2) that the combination shall not take effect or the combination is deemed to have an appreciable adverse effect on competition under sub-section (9), then, without prejudice to any penalty which may be imposed or any prosecution which may be initiated under this Act, the Commission may order that—(a) the acquisition referred to in clause (a) of section 5; or (b) the acquiring of control referred to in clause (b) of section 5; or (c) the merger or amalgamation referred to in clause (c) of section 5, shall not be given effect to: Provided that the Commission may, if it considers appropriate, frame a scheme to implement its order under this sub-section.

(11) If the Commission does not, on the expiry of a period of two hundred and ten days from the date of notice given to the Commission under sub-section (2) of section 6, pass an order or issue direction in accordance with the provisions of sub-section (1) or sub-section (2) or sub-section (7), the combination shall be deemed to have been approved by the Commission.

Explanation—For the purposes of determining the period of two hundred and ten days specified in this sub-section, the period of thirty working days specified in sub-section (6) and a further period of thirty working days specified in sub-section (8) shall be excluded.

(12) Where any extension of time is sought by the parties to the combination, the period of ninety working days shall be reckoned after deducting the extended time granted at the request of the parties.

(13) Where the Commission has ordered a combination to be void, the acquisition or acquiring of control or merger or amalgamation referred to in section 5, shall be dealt with by the authorities under any other law for the time being in force as if such acquisition or acquiring of control or merger or amalgamation had not taken place and the parties to the combination shall be dealt with accordingly.

(14) Nothing contained in this chapter shall affect any proceeding initiated or which may be initiated under any other law for the time being in force.'

[29] Section 33.

[30] Section 38. '(1) With a view to rectifying any mistake apparent from the record, the Commission may amend any order passed by it under the provisions of this Act. (2) Subject to the other provisions of this Act, the Commission may make—(a) an amendment under sub-section (1) of its own motion; (b) an amendment for rectifying any such mistake which has been brought to its notice by any party to the order.

Explanation—For the removal of doubts, it is hereby declared that the Commission shall not, while rectifying any mistake apparent from record, amend substantive part of its order passed under the provisions of this Act.'

[31] Section 39(1). 'If a person fails to pay any monetary penalty imposed on him under this Act, the Commission shall proceed to recover such penalty in such manner as may be specified by the regulations. (2) In a case where the Commission is of the opinion that it would be expedient to recover the penalty imposed under this Act in accordance with the provisions of the Income Tax Act, 1961 (43 of 1961), it may make a reference to this effect to the concerned income-tax authority under that Act for recovery of the penalty as tax due under the said Act. (3) Where a reference has been made by the Commission under sub-section (2) for recovery of penalty, the person upon whom the penalty has been imposed shall be deemed to be the assessee in default under the Income Tax Act, 1961 (43 of 1961), and the provisions contained in sections 221 to 227, 228A, 229, 231 and 232 of the said Act and the Second Schedule to that Act and any rules made thereunder shall, in so far as may be, apply as if the said provisions were the provisions of this Act and referred to sums by way of penalty imposed under this Act instead of to income-tax and sums imposed by way of penalty, fine and interest under the Income Tax Act, 1961, and to the Commission instead of the Assessing Officer.

Explanation 1—Any reference to sub-section (2) or sub-section (6) of section 220 of the Income Tax Act, 1961 (43 of 1961), in the said provisions of that Act or the rules made thereunder shall be construed as references to sections 43 to 45 of this Act.

Explanation 2—The Tax Recovery Commissioner and the Tax Recovery Officer referred to in the Income Tax Act, 1961 (43 of 1961), shall be deemed to be the Tax Recovery Commissioner and the Tax Recovery Officer for the purposes of recovery of sums imposed by way of penalty under this Act and reference made by the Commission under sub-section (2) would amount to drawing of a certificate by the Tax Recovery Officer as far as demand relating to penalty under this Act.

Explanation 3—Any reference to appeal in Chapter XVII-D and the Second Schedule of the Income Tax Act, 1961 (43 of 1961), shall be construed as a reference to appeal before the Competition Appellate Tribunal under section 53B of this Act.

[32] Section 42. Contravention of orders of Commission (1) The Commission may cause an inquiry to be made into compliance of its orders or directions made in exercise of its powers under the Act.

(2) If any person, without reasonable cause, fails to comply with the orders or directions of the Commission issued under sections 27, 28, 31, 32, 33, 42A and 43A of the Act, he shall be punishable with fine which may extend to rupees one lakh for each day during which such non-compliance occurs, subject to a maximum of rupees ten crore, as the Commission may determine.

(3) If any person does not comply with the orders or directions issued, or fails to pay the fine imposed under sub-section (2), he shall, without prejudice to any proceeding under section 39, be punishable with imprisonment for a term which may extend to three years, or with fine which may extend to rupees twenty-five crore, or with both, as the Chief Metropolitan Magistrate, Delhi, may deem fit: Provided that the Chief Metropolitan Magistrate, Delhi, shall not take cognizance of any offence under this section save on a complaint filed by the Commission or any of its officers authorized by it.

[33] Section 42A. Compensation in case of contravention of orders of Commission.

Without prejudice to the provisions of this Act, any person may make an application to the Appellate Tribunal for an order for the recovery of compensation from any enterprise for any loss or damage shown to have been suffered, by such person as a result of the said enterprise violating directions issued by the Commission or contravening, without any reasonable ground, any decision or order of the Commission issued under sections 27, 28, 31, 32 and 33 or any condition or restriction subject to which any approval, sanction, direction or exemption in relation to any matter has been accorded, given, made or granted under this Act or delaying in carrying out such orders or directions of the Commission.

[34] Section 43. Penalty for failure to comply with directions of Commission and Director-General.

If any person fails to comply, without reasonable cause, with a direction given by: (a) the Commission under sub-sections (2) and (4) of section 36; or (b) the Director-General while exercising powers referred to in sub-section (2) of section 41, such person shall be punishable with fine which may extend to rupees one lakh for each day during which such failure continues subject to a maximum of rupees one crore, as may be determined by the Commission.

[35] Section 43A. If any person or enterprise who fails to give notice to the Commission under sub-section (2) of section 6, the Commission shall impose on such person or enterprise a penalty which may extend to one per cent of the total turnover or the assets, whichever is higher, of such a combination.

[36] Section 45. (1) Without prejudice to the provisions of section 44, if a person, who furnishes or is required to furnish under this Act any particulars, documents or any information—(a) makes any statement or furnishes any document which he knows or has reason to believe to be false in any material particular; or (b) omits to state any material fact knowing it to be material; or (c) willfully alters, suppresses or destroys any document which is required to be furnished as aforesaid, such person shall be punishable with fine which may extend to rupees one crore as may be determined by the Commission. (2) Without prejudice to the provisions of sub-section (1), the Commission may also pass such other order as it deems fit.

[37] See Commission Notice on immunity from fines and reduction of fines in cartel cases (Text with EEA relevance) of 8/12/2006 discussed in Chapter 2.

[38] The Director must prepare and publish guidance as to the appropriate amount of any penalty—section 38 of the Competition Act, 1998.

[39] OFT's guidance as to the appropriate amount of a penalty, 2004.

[40] Section 48. (1) Where a person committing contravention of any of the provisions of this Act or of any rule, regulation, order made or direction issued thereunder is a company, every person who, at the time the contravention was committed, was in charge of, and was responsible to the company for the conduct of the business of the company, as well as the company, shall be deemed to be guilty of the contravention and shall be liable to be proceeded against and punished accordingly: Provided that nothing contained in this sub-section shall render any such person liable to any punishment if he proves that the contravention was committed without his knowledge or that he had exercised all due diligence to prevent the commission of such contravention. (2) Notwithstanding anything contained in sub-section (1), where a contravention of any of the provisions of this Act or of any rule, regulation, order made or direction issued thereunder has been committed by a company and it is proved that the contravention has taken place with the consent or connivance of, or is attributable to any neglect on the part of, any director, manager, secretary or other officer of the company, such director, manager, secretary or other officer shall also be deemed to be guilty of that contravention and shall be liable to be proceeded against and punished accordingly.

Explanation—For the purposes of this section (a) "company" means a body corporate and includes a firm or other association of individuals; and (b) "director", in relation to a firm, means a partner in the firm.

[41] Article 3.
[42] Article 4.
[43] Article 8.
[44] Article 9(1).
[45] Article 9(2).
[46] Article 10.
[47] Article 14.
[48] Article 15.
[49] Article 16.
[50] Article 17.
[51] Date of document: 01/09/2006.
[52] Article 20.
[53] Article 12.
[54] 'General functions' means functions other than those relating to appeals and the functions of the Council of the Commission. The Council referred to is the management board of the Commission called Competition Commission Council.
[55] 'The Roles of the Competition Commission and the Department of Trade and Industry in Promoting Competition', Competition Commission press release of June 2003.
[56] Source: Competition Commission's press release 'What is the Competition Commission?'
[57] Section 25.
[58] Section 26; sections 42–44 make failure to produce a document, during investigation, inspection of the premises, etc., offences.
[59] Sections 32, 33.
[60] Section 34.
[61] Section 36.
[62] Section 36(8).
[63] OFT 407a, April 2004, paragraph 5.19.
[64] The OFT's Guidance as to the Circumstances in Which It may be Appropriate to Accept Commitments—ANNEXE A to 'Enforcement' Draft Competition Law Guideline for Consultation, OFT407a, April 2004.
[65] Section 6 of the Clayton Act: Antitrust Laws Not Applicable to Labor Organizations.

The labor of a human being is not a commodity or article of commerce. Nothing contained in the antitrust laws shall be construed to forbid the existence and operation of labor, agricultural, or horticultural organizations, instituted for the purposes of mutual help, and not having capital stock or conducted for profit, or to forbid or restrain individual members of such organizations from lawfully carrying out the legitimate objects thereof; nor shall such organizations, or the members thereof, be held or construed to be illegal combinations or conspiracies in restraint of trade, under the antitrust laws.

[66] 'Antitrust Enforcement Guidelines for International Operations'—Issued by the US Department of Justice and the Federal Trade Commission, April 1995.

[67] Added by the 2007 amendment.

[68] Section 66. (1) The Monopolies and Restrictive Trade Practices Act, 1969 (54 of 1969) is hereby repealed and the Monopolies and Restrictive Trade Practices Commission established under sub-section (1) of section 5 of the said Act (hereinafter referred to as the repealed Act) shall stand dissolved.

(1A) The repeal of the Monopolies and Restrictive Trade Practices Act, 1969 (54 of 1969) shall, however, not affect—a) the previous operation of the Act so repealed or anything duly done or suffered thereunder; or b) any right, privilege, obligation or liability acquired, accrued or incurred under the Act so repealed; or c) any penalty, confiscation or punishment incurred in respect of any contravention under the Act so repealed; or d) any proceeding or remedy in respect of any such right, privilege, obligation, liability, penalty, confiscation or punishment as aforesaid, and any such proceeding or remedy may be instituted, continued or enforced, and any such penalty, confiscation or punishment may be imposed or made as if that Act had not been repealed.

2) On the dissolution of the Monopolies and Restrictive Trade Practices Commission, the person appointed as the chairman of the Monopolies and Restrictive Trade Practices Commission and every other person appointed as member and Director-General of Investigation and Registration, Additional, Joint, Deputy, or Assistant Directors-General of Investigation and Registration and any officer and other employee of that Commission and holding office as such immediately before such dissolution shall vacate their respective offices and such chairman and other members shall be entitled to claim compensation not exceeding three months' pay and allowances for the premature termination of term of their office or of any contract of service.

Provided that the Director-General of Investigation and Registration, Additional, Joint, Deputy or Assistant Directors-General of Investigation and Registration or any officer or other employee who has been, immediately before the dissolution of the Monopolies and Restrictive Trade Practices Commission appointed on deputation basis to the Monopolies and Restrictive Trade Practices Commission, shall, on such dissolution, stand reverted to his parent cadre, Ministry or Department, as the case may be:

Provided further that the Director-General of Investigation and Registration, Additional, Joint, Deputy or Assistant Directors-General of Investigation and Registration or any officer or other employee who has been, immediately before the dissolution of the Monopolies and Restrictive Trade Practices Commission, employed on regular basis by the Monopolies and Restrictive Trade Practices Commission, shall become, on and from such dissolution, the officer and employee, respectively, of the Competition Commission of India or the Appellate Tribunal, in such manner as may be specified by the Central Government, with the same rights and privileges as to pension, gratuity and other like matters as would have been admissible to him if the rights in relation to such Monopolies and Restrictive Trade Practices Commission had not been transferred to, and vested in, the Competition Commission of India or the Appellate Tribunal, as the case may be, and shall continue to do so unless and until his employment in the Competition Commission of India or the Appellate Tribunal, as the case may be, is duly terminated or until his remuneration, terms and conditions of employment are duly altered by the Competition Commission of India or the Appellate Tribunal, as the case may be:

Provided also that notwithstanding anything contained in the Industrial Disputes Act, 1947 (14 of 1947), or in any other law for the time being in force, the transfer of the services of any Director-General of Investigation and Registration, Additional, Joint, Deputy or Assistant Directors-General of Investigation and Registration or any officer or other employee, employed in the Monopolies and Restrictive Trade Practices Commission, to [the Competition Commission of India or the Appellate Tribunal], as the case may be, shall not entitle such Director-General of Investigation and Registration, Additional, Joint, Deputy or Assistant Directors-General of Investigation and Registration or any officer or other employee any compensation under this Act or any other law for the time being in force and no such claim shall be entertained by any court, tribunal or other authority:

Provided also that where the Monopolies and Restrictive Trade Practices Commission has established a provident fund, superannuation, welfare or other fund for the benefit of the Director-General of Investigation and Registration, Additional, Joint, Deputy or Assistant Directors-General of Investigation and Registration or the officers and other employees employed in the Monopolies and Restrictive Trade Practices Commission, the monies relatable to the officers and other employees whose services have been transferred by or under this Act to [the Competition Commission of India or the Appellate Tribunal, as the case may be, shall, out of the monies standing] on the dissolution of the Monopolies and Restrictive Trade Practices Commission to the credit of such provident fund, superannuation, welfare or other fund, stand transferred to, and vest in, [the Competition Commission of India or the Appellate Tribunal as the case may be, and such monies which stand so transferred shall be dealt with by the said Commission or the Tribunal, as the case may be, in such manner as may be prescribed.]

(3) All cases pertaining to monopolistic trade practices or restrictive trade practices pending (including such cases, in which any unfair trade practice has also been alleged), before the Monopolies and Restrictive Trade Practices Commission shall, on the commencement of the competition Amendment Act, 2009 stand transferred to the Appellate Tribunal and shall be adjudicated by the Appellate Tribunal in accordance with the provisions of the repealed Act as if that Act had not been repealed.

Explanation—For the removal of doubts, it is hereby declared that all cases referred to in this sub-section, sub-section(4) and sub-section(5) shall be deemed to include all applications made for the losses or damages under section 12(B) of the Monopolies and Restrictive Trade Practices Act,1969 (54 of 1969) as it stood before its repeal;

4) Subject to the provisions of sub-section(3), all cases pertaining to unfair trade practices other than those referred to in clause (x) of sub-section(1) of section 36A of the Monopolies and Restrictive Trade Practices Act, 1969 (54 of 1969) and pending before the Monopolies and Restrictive Trade Practices Commission [immediately before the commencement of the Competition (Amendment) Act, 2009 shall, on such commencement], shall, stand transferred to the National Commission constituted under the Consumer Protection Act, 1986 (68 of 1986) and the National Commission shall dispose of such cases as if they were cases filed under that Act:

Provided that the National Commission may, if it considers appropriate, transfer any case transferred to it under this sub-section, to the concerned State Commission established under section 9 of the Consumer Protection Act, 1986 (68 of 1986) and that State Commission shall dispose of such case as if it was filed under that Act.

Provided further that all the cases relating to the unfair trade practices pending before the National Commission under this sub-section, on or before the date on which the competition (Amendment) Bill, 2009 receives the assent of the President, shall, on and from that date, stand transferred to the Appellate Tribunal and be adjudicated by the Appellate Tribunal in accordance with the provisions of the repealed Act as if that Act had not been repealed.

5) [All cases pertaining to unfair trade practices referred to in clause (x) of sub-section (1) of section 36A of the Monopolies and Restrictive Trade Practices Act, 1969 and pending before the Monopolies and Restrictive Trade Practices Commission shall, "on the commencement of the Competition (Amendment) Act, 2009" stand transferred to the Appellate Tribunal and the Appellate Tribunal shall dispose of such cases as if they were cases filed under that Act.]

6) All investigations or proceedings, other than those relating to unfair trade practices, pending before the Director-General of Investigation and Registration on or before the commencement of this Act shall, on such commencement, stand transferred to the Competition Commission of India, and the Competition Commission of India may conduct or order for conduct of such investigation or proceedings in the manner as it deems fit.

7) All investigations or proceedings, relating to unfair trade practices, other than those referred to in clause (x) of sub-section (1) of section 36A of the Monopolies and Restrictive Trade Practices Act, 1969 (54 of 1969) and pending before the Director-General of Investigation and Registration on or before the commencement of this Act shall, on such commencement, stand transferred to the National Commission constituted under the Consumer Protection Act,

1986 (68 of 1986) and the National Commission may conduct or order for conduct of such investigation or proceedings in the manner as it deems fit.

Provided that all investigations or proceedings, relating to unfair trade practices pending before the National Commission, on or before the date on which the Competition (Amendment) Bill, 2009 receives the assent of the President shall, on and from that date, stand transferred to the Appellate Tribunal and the Appellate Tribunal may conduct or order for conduct of such investigation or proceedings in the manner as it deems fit.

8) All investigations or proceedings relating to unfair trade practices referred to in clause (x) of sub-section (1) of section 36A of the Monopolies and Restrictive Trade Practices Act, 1969 (54 of 1969), and pending before the Director-General of Investigation and Registration on or before the commencement of this Act shall, on such commencement, stand transferred to the Competition Commission of India and the Competition Commission of India may conduct or order for conduct of such investigation in the manner as it deems fit.

9) Save as otherwise provided under sub-sections (3) to (8), all cases or proceedings pending before the Monopolies and Restrictive Trade Practices Commission shall abate.

10) The mention of the particular matters referred to in sub-sections (3) to (8) shall not be held to prejudice or affect the general application of section 6 of the General Clauses Act, 1897 (10 of 1897) with regard to the effect of repeal.

[69] *A. Ahlström Osakeyhtiö and Others* v. *Commission of the European Communities*, Judgement of the European Court of Justice of 27 September 1988.

[70] Article IV.

[71] Article VIII.

[72] 21998A0618(01). Agreement between the European Communities and the Government of the United States of America on the application of positive comity principles in the enforcement of their competition laws *Official Journal L 173, 18/06/1998* p. 0028–0031.

[73] Article I.

[74] Article III.

[75] Article IV.

[76] Discussed in the previous chapter.

Epilogue

The Competition Act, 2002, has been in force for about a decade; and much needs to be done so that the regulatory impact is felt by all the sections of the society viz the business enterprises, traders and consumers. Some of the areas that need attention may be recapitulated.

PROFESSIONAL SERVICES

Competition among the learned professions and the role of the governing bodies of the respective professions—law, medicine, accountancy and such other professions is one that needs immediate steps. For example in the case of the legal profession, the question is now mixed up with the right of foreign law firms to offer their services in India. The Competition Act is intended to preserve competition, which includes protecting the ability of individuals and enterprises to compete. As matters stand now, the regulatory bodies of the professions mentioned above extend their authority over the members of the respective professions beyond their legitimate areas of control viz., prescribing qualifications for entry into the profession, regulating that entry by ensuring that qualifications are met, and disciplinary action in the case of misconduct. This seriously limits the ability of the members to compete. The right to inform the clients of the practitioner's area of experience, the fixing of fees by the practitioner with the client and other terms are not matters for regulation by these bodies.

There is no argument where a member's own conduct in entering into agreements with others or an association offends section 3 as an anti-competitive agreement. The more important question now is the legality, with the Competition Act in force, of the rules of the professional bodies imposing restraints on a member in the matter of advertisement of his carrying on the profession, the fee he may charge, the number of clients he may have and such conditions that go beyond the purpose for which the regulatory body has been established. Such restraints imposed by these bodies would not be caught by section 3(1) as it refers only to *agreements between association of enterprises or association of persons* and not to 'decisions of associations of persons'. Section 3(3)(b) dealing with a decision made by an association of persons which 'limits or controls production, supply, markets, technical development, investment or provision of services' is much too general and not specific to cover these professional regulatory bodies. The Act should be amended to include decisions of associations of persons so that the rules of the regulatory bodies relating to professional services could be made to comply with the Competition Act and do not limit the ability of the members of these bodies to compete.

It is notorious that the client is at a serious disadvantage by reason of the asymmetry of information regarding the practitioner's actual experience in the area in which the client requires professional services. When he has no information about others with the necessary experience available, which would enable him to choose his adviser, he cannot make any sensible choice. In this situation, prohibition of advertisements by practitioners about their actual, verifiable experience would only render his helplessness acute.

The High Level Committee on Competition Policy and Law had highlighted this issue in the chapter on 'Competition Policy and Professional Services' stating that 'Regulations which disallow normal promotional activity, which deny the consumers the benefit of full unrestricted and informed profile about professional firms and deny the consumers of the choice of firms, should have no place.'

Fixing of remuneration is a matter that should be determined by the conditions in the market for services, by the law of supply and demand and information in the possession of the person paying for those services. It cannot be a matter for legislation, particularly as it would deprive the consumers of the benefits of free competition.

MERGERS

There should be an express provision in the Companies Act, 1956 providing for a declaration by the parties before the high court that the provisions of the Competition Act, 2002 are not applicable to the scheme or arrangement so that the court or tribunal may decide on the application without further verification. If the declaration is that the Competition Act applies to the scheme, the court or tribunal may postpone decision till it is cleared by the Commission. The time to do this is now.

MULTIDISCIPLINARY PARTNERSHIPS

The legality of such arrangements does not appear to have been studied in depth, apart from the fact that it has not been established that there is any great demand in the market for services through such arrangements.

CARTELS

It is well to recognize that in fighting cartels, what is important is strong investigative machinery, supported by mutual assistance agreements with other countries in investigating such organizations and sharing information of the operations of cartels. The European Community is a good example in combating cartels through, among other tools, severe fines.

It is well known that there are a number of cartels in certain industries in India, and breaking them down according to law needs attention.

Benefits to the Consumer

Does the consumer pay only reasonable charges, which free and fair competition would ensure, and is he served efficiently? There is little transparency in the terms and conditions of the service providers in the telecom business, especially those providing service relating to mobile telephones. It is well known that as far as the consumer is concerned, there is no freedom of contract. The fact that there is a separate regulator for this business is no bar for the Commission to initiate action, as the consumers have been suffering from unreasonable charges, in addition to poor 'customer care'. Similarly, there have been wide complaints against service by insurance companies, particularly those providing health insurance services.

Appendix

List of sections of the Competition Act, 2002 amended by the Competition (Amendment) Act, 2007 (Act No. 39 of 2007) and the Competition (Amendment) Act, 2009 (Act No. 39) of 2009.

(a) Sections covered by the Amendment Act 2007:

sections 2, 4, 5, 6(2), 6(2A), 8, 9,10,12, 13, 16, 17, 19, 20, 21, section 21A (new section), sections 22 to 25, sections 26 to 37, section 39, sections 40 to 42, 42A (new section), 43, 43A (new section), sections 45, 46, 49, section 51(1), section 52, introduction of chapter VIIIA, containing sections 53A to 53U, providing for the establishment of the Competition Appellate Tribunal and connected matters, sections 57, 58, 59, 61, 63, 64, and section 66 providing for a time-frame for dissolution of the MRTP Commission on the repeal of the MRTP Act and for the transfer after the expiry of this period of pending cases under that Act to the Appellate Tribunal and the National Commission constituted under the Consumer Protection Act, 1986 and connected matters.

(b) Section covered by the Amendment Act 2009:

section 66 providing for the transfer of cases pending before the MRTP Commission on the commencement of the Competition Amendment Act, 2009 Act to the Appellate Tribunal and the National Commission constituted under the Consumer Protection Act, 1986 and connected matters.

Bibliography

Chapter 1

Report of the High Level Committee on Competition Policy and Law, 2000.

General Agreement on Tariffs and Trade, 1994 (GATT 1994).

General Agreement on Trade in Service (GATS).

Trade Related Aspects of Intellectual Property Rights (TRIPS).

'Report on Competition in Professional Services' European Commission, *Communication From The Commission COM (2004) 83 Final*, Brussels, 9 February 2004.

Office of Fair Trading, UK (OFT) document 'Services of general economic interest exclusion'—Draft competition law guideline for consultation, April 2004.

European Commission's 'Notice on immunity from fines and reduction of fines in cartel cases' (2002/C 45/03), European Commission Directive 2002/77/EC of 16 September 2002 on competition in the markets for electronic communications networks and services.

Chapter 2

'Draft competition law guideline on Article 81 and the Chapter I prohibition', April 2004 Office of Fair Trading, UK—(OFT 401).

'European Union XXXIInd Report on Competition Policy 2002'.

'Price Fixing, Bid Rigging, and Market Allocation Schemes: An Antitrust Primer'—The US Department of Justice, 2 January 2001, revised 28 September 2005.

'Cartels—Detection and Remedies, a guide for purchasers', Office of Fair Trading, UK.

'Antitrust Guidelines for the Licensing of Intellectual Property' 1995—Department of Justice and the Federal Trade Commission, US.

Chapter 3

'Article 82 and the Chapter II prohibition'—Draft competition law guideline for consultation, Office of Fair Trading, UK (OFT 402—April 2004).

Chapter 4

'Substantive Assessment Guidance-Mergers', Office of Fair Trading, May 2003.

The Horizontal Merger Guidelines 1992 as amended on 8 April 1997, issued by the US Department of Justice and the Federal Trade Commission.

Council Regulation (EC) No. 139/2004 of 20 January 2004 on the control of concentrations between undertakings (the EC Merger Regulation).

The European Commission's Notice of 9 December 1997, on the definition of the relevant market for the purposes of Community Competition Law.

Securities and Exchange Board of India (Substantial Acquisition of Shares and Takeovers) Regulations, 1997.

US–EC Merger Working Group's document entitled 'US–EU Merger Working Group—Best Practices on Cooperation in Merger Investigations.'

The 'Antitrust Guidelines for Collaborations Among Competitors', issued by the Federal Trade Commission and the US Department of Justice in April 2000.

The Final Report to the Attorney General and Assistant Attorney General for Antitrust, 2000, of the International Competition Policy Advisory Committee of the Department of Justice, USA.

Chapter 5

EEC Council Regulation No. 17, first regulation dated 6 February 1962 implementing Articles 81 and 82 of the Treaty, amended by Council Regulation (EC) No. 1216/1999 of 10 June 1999 setting out the provisions for enforcement of the Articles 81 and

82 dealing with anti-competitive agreements, decisions, etc., and abuse of a dominant position respectively.

The Report of the International Competition Policy Advisory Committee, USA, 2000.

Antitrust Enforcement Guidelines for International Operations issued by the US Department of Justice and the Federal Trade Commission in April, 1995.

Agreement between the Government of the United States of America and the Commission of the European Communities regarding the application of their competition laws—Exchange of interpretative letters with the Government of the United States of America—1991.

Agreement between the European Communities and the Government of the United States of America on the application of positive comity principles in the enforcement of their competition laws—1998.

The International Antitrust Enforcement Assistance Act of 1994, US.

Webb–Pomerene Act, 1918, US.

The Defense Production Act of 1950, US.

Case Index

A. Ahlström Osakeyhito and Others v. *European Communities*, Judgement of the European Court of Justice of 27 September 1988	335
AKZO Chemie BV v. *Commission of the European Communities*, Case C-62, Judgement of the Court (Fifth Chamber) of 3 July 1991	185
Albrecht v. *Herald Co.*, 390 US 145 (1968)	128
Alsatel v. *SA Novasam*, Case 247/86, European Court (Reports 1988, Page 05987)	50
Anglo American Corporation/Lonrho: 98/335/EC: Commission Decision of 23 April 1997	236
Arizona v. *Maricopa County Medical Society*, 457 US 332 (1982)	108
Board of Trade of City of Chicago v. *United States,* 246 US 231 [1918]	23, 93
Boeing/McDonnell Douglas (*EC* Case No IV/M.877: Official Journal L 336, 08/12/1997, p. 0016–0047)	237
British Telecom/MCI (II)—Case No IV/M.(856)	255
Brooke Group Ltd v. *Brown & Williamson Tobacco Corp.*, 509 US 209 (1993)	183
Brown Shoe Co. Inc. v. *United States*, 370 US 294 (1962)	91, 252
Brunswick Corp. v. *Pueblo Bowl-O-Mat Inc.*, 429 US 477 (1977)	142
Business Electronics v. *Sharp Electronics*, 485 US 717 (1988)	102, 127
Cargill, Inc. v. *Monfort of Colorado, Inc.*, 479 US 104 (1986)	261
CBEM Case 311/84 European Court (Reports 1985, Page 03261)	46
Christie's and Sotheby's—EC Press Release DN: IP/02/1585, 'Commission rules against collusive behaviour of Christie's and Sotheby's', 30 October 2002	107

Compagnie Maritime Belge Transports SA and Others v. *Commission of the European Communities in Brussels* in Joined Cases C-395/96 P and C-396/96 P, Judgement of the European Court (Fifth Chamber), 16 March 2000	171
Continental T.V., Inc. v. *Gte Sylvania Inc.*, 433 US 36 (1977)	102
Deutsche Telekom/BetaResearch (Official Journal L 053, 27/02/1999)	227, 251
Dr Miles Medical Co. v. *John D. Park & Sons Co.*, 220 US 373 (1911)	100
Eastman Kodak Co. v. *ImageTech. Svcs*, 504 US 451 (1992)	124
Europemballage Corporation and Continental Can Company Inc. v. *Commission of the European Communities*, Case 6–72 Judgement of the Court of 21 February 1973	172
Fashion Originators' Guild v. *Federal Trade Commission*, 312 US 457	94
Federal Trade Commission v. *Morton Salt Co.*, 334 US 37 (1948)	178
Flat Glass Cartel- EU	111
Ford Motor Co. v. *United States*, 405 US 562 (1972)	99, 244
FTC v. *Indiana Federation of Dentists*, 476 US 447 (1986)	87
General Motors Continental NV v. *Commission of the European Communities*, Case 26–75 Judgement of the Court of 13 November 1975	177
Goldfarb v. *Virginia State Bar*, 421 US 773 (1975)	54, 88
Hartford-Empire Co. v. *United States*, 323 US 386 (1945)	134
Hindustan Lever Employees Union v. *Hindustan Lever Ltd and Others*, (1995) 83 Comp Cas	206
Hoffmann-La Roche & Co. Ag, Basle v. *Commission of the European Communities*, Case 85/76	169
International Salt Co. v. *United States*, 332 US 392 (1947)	94, 122
International Shoe Co. v. *Federal Trade Commission*, 280 US 291 (1930)	246
Istituto Chemioterapico Italiano S.p.A. et Commercial Solvents Corporation v. *Commission of the European Communities*, Joined Cases 6 and 7/73R	192
Italy v. *Commission*—Case 41/83 (1985, ECR 880)	46
Jefferson Parish Hospital Dist. No. 2 v. *Hyde*, 466 US 2 (1984)	123
Lombard Club—EC press release	106

Case Index

Lift and Escalator Cartels	112
Manuele Arduino—Case C-35/99	84
Matsushita Elec. Industrial Co. and Others v. *Zenith Radio Corp. and Others*, 475 US 574 (1986)	182
Northern Pac. R. Co. v. *United States*, 356 US 1	94
Northern Securities Co. v. *United States*, 193 US 197 (1904)	220
NV Nederlandsche Banden Industrie Michelin v. *Commission of the European Communities*, Judgement of the Court of 9 November 1983, Case 322/81	176
Parker v. *Brown*, 317 US 341 (1943)	88
Plasterboard cartel—Commission imposes heavy fines on four companies involved in plasterboard cartel—EC press release	107
Radio Telefis Eireann (RTE) and Independent Television Publications Ltd. (ITP) v. *Commission of the European Communities*, Joined Cases C-241/91 P and C-242/91 P, Judgement of the Court of 6 April 1995	193
SACCHI—Case 155/73 (1974, ECR 409)	46
Sarabhai Chemicals P. Ltd and Another, in re, (1979) 49 Company Cases 145 MRTP Commission	109
Standard Oil Co. of California v. *United States*, 337 US 293 (1949)	125
Standard Oil Co. of New Jersey v. *United States*, 221 US 1 (1910)	99
Standard Oil co. v. *Trade Comm'n.*, 340 US 231 (1951)	179, 188
State Oil Co. v. *Khan, No. 96–871*	128
Swedish Match and Another v. *Securities Exchange Board of India and Another*	203
Tampa Electric Co. v. *Nashville Co.*, 365 US 320 (1961)	125
Tata Engineering and Locomotive Co. Ltd v. *Registrar of Restrictive Trade Agreements* (1977), 47 Comp Cas 520 Supreme Court	96
Tetra Pak International SA v. *Commission of the European Communities*, Case C-333/94 P, Judgement of the Court (Fifth Chamber) of 14 November 1996	173, 187
Timken Co. v. *United States*, 341 US 593 (1951)	110
UK Agricultural Tractor Registration Exchange (Official Journal L 06, 13/03/1992, p. 0019–0033)	80

United Brands Company and United Brands Continentaal BV v. Commission of the European Communities, Case 27/76, Judgement of the Court of 14 February 1978	190, 191
United States v. Addyston Pipe & Steel Co., 85 F.271, aff'd	94
United States v. Alcoa, 377 US 271 (1964)	241
United States v. Columbia Steel Co., 334 US 495 (1948)	241
United States v. Continental Can Co., 378 US 441 (1964)	254
United States v. Du Pont & Co., 351 US 377 (1956)	91
United States v. General Electric Co., 272 US 476 (1926)	132
United States v. General Motors, 384 US 127 (1966)	127
United States v. Masonite Corporation, 316 US 265 (1942)	135
United States v. New Wrinkle, Inc., 342 US 371 (1952)	134
United States v. Paramount Pictures, 334 US 131	244
United States v. Penn-Olin Co., 378 US 158 (1964)	249
United States v. Socony-Vacuum Oil Co., 310 US 150 (1940)	94, 108
United States v. Trenton Potteries Co. et al., 273 US 392	105
United States v. Univis Lens Co., 316 US 241 (1942)	133
United States v. United Shoe Machinery Co. of New Jersey, 247 US 32 (1918)	245
Utah Pie Co. v. Continental Baking and Others, 386 US 685 (1967)	180
Wanadoo Interactive—Extract from the European Commission Press Release IP/03/1025, Brussels, 16 July 2003	188
White Motor Co. v. United States, 372 US 253 (1963)	189
Wood Pulp case—*A. Ahlström Osakeyhtiö and Others v. Commission of the European Communities*, Judgement of the European Court of Justice of 27 September 1988	317
WorldCom/MCI—*Official Journal L 116*, 04/05/1999 (p. 0001–0035)	256
Wouters, Case C-309/99, Judgement of the Court of 19 February 2002	55, 85

General Index

abuse by holder of exclusive right conferred by state 177
abuse of a dominant position 6, 25, 161, 167
abusive conduct outside the dominated market 173
acquiring machinery for standardization 245
acquisition 222
acquisition/control 236
acquisition of assets 244
acquisition of shares 202
acquisition/merger 208
acts in bonafide competition excepted 159
acts of persons from abroad affecting competition in India 58
acts taking place outside India but having an effect on competition in India—Section 32 287
adequacy of section 3(5) 136
adjudication on claims for compensation 299
agreement 68, 78
agreement for exchange of information 79
agreement restricting buying from certain classes of sellers 127
agreement to sell at fixed minimum prices 100

air cargo carriers—price fixing cartel 111
amendments to section 27 281
amendments to section 4 158
anti-competitive agreements 5, 21, 67, 277
anti-competitive agreements and abuse of dominance 276
anti-competitive agreements, abuse of a dominant position, orders which may be passed by the Commission 281
antitrust injury 142, 261
antitrust issues 2
appeal to the Supreme Court 42
appeals against decision or order of the Commission—Section 40 292
appeals to Competition Appellate Tribunal 40
appearance before the Commission 289
appreciable adverse effect on competition 230
areas needing further consideration 49
ascertaining the dominant position—statutory guides under the Competition Act, 2002 164
assessing dominant position 169
assets 224

association of persons—professions 70
auction houses 107
authorities enforcing the Competition Act, 2002 as amended by the 2007 Act 275
authorities enforcing the Competition Act, 2002, 26
awarding compensation 260
awarding compensation—section 53n 300

background setting leading to the act 7
benefits that may flow from an agreement 102
bid rigging 112
bilateral agreements 265
binding commitments 311
business practices 12

cartel 69
cartel cases 105
cartels 23
causing another company to become a subsidiary 237
causing entry barriers 99
ceasing to be distinct enterprises 218
changes in section 26 279
collective dominance—sharing the market on a geographical basis 171
combination 219
combination/acquisition 6, 25
combination—the legal framework 208
comity 323
committee's assessment 8
companies incorporated outside India 71

comparative law 214, 304, 162, 75, 196
compensation for loss or damage 142
compensation in case of contravention of orders of the Commission—section 42A 302
Competition Act—Overview 21
Competition Act, 1998, UK 163
Competition Act, 2002 1
competition advocacy 34, 35
Competition Appellate Tribunal 39, 40
Competition Commission 27
competition in professional services 57
competition issues in telecommunication services 50
competition law of the EEC 75
competition law of the US 77
concentrated industry 241
concentration of economic power 15
concentration—definition 216
condition in license agreement fixing prices 132
conspiracy to sell at predatory prices 182
contravention by companies—section 48 143, 298
contravention of orders of appellate tribunal
contravention of orders of the Commission—section 42 293
contravention of the orders of the Commission—section 42 143
control 225
control of anti-competitive combinations 230
cooperation agreements among states—bilateral agreements 321

coverage of the act: the new regulatory system 3
cross-border issues and competition 317
cross-licensing of patents among competitors 134

dealing with cartels—penalty 116
dealing with cartels—the purchasers 120
decisions' of associations of persons—professional rules—India 81
definitions under the Competition Act, 2002 219
determining the relevant market 89
director-general 38
discontinuance of abuse/penalties 196
discontinuing sale of raw material 192
discriminatory pricing 178
division of an enterprise 283
division of the enterprise 197
domestic regulation 11
dominant position 277
dominant position—definition 159
dominant position—elaboration 160
dominant position—relevant market 165
draft national competition policy 36
duties of director general—section 41 292
duties, powers, and functions of the Commission 275

EC position 185
effect on competition 91
eliminating competition 99
enforcement—some issues 42
enforcement 26

enforcement against those not carrying on business in India—section 32 144
enforcement authorities 18
enforcement of the Competition Act, 1998, UK 309
enforcement provisions 141
enforcement—EEC provisions 304
enterprise 69, 229
entry barriers 190
European Union—liberal professions 83
evaluating a combination 231
evaluating appreciable adverse effect on competition within India relevant market 89
evaluating technology transfer agreements under competition law—US, EU 138
exchange of price information, non-price information 79
exclusive distribution agreements 127
exclusive supply agreements 125
execution of orders of appellate tribunal—section 53p 304
execution of orders of the Commission imposing monetary penalty—section 39 291
exemptions 312
exercise of intellectual property rights and competition—section 3[5] 131

factors to be considered in determining the geographic and product market 167
fines 306
fixing prices for product processed by a licensee 133
fixing prices—*del credere* agent 135

flat glass cartel—eu 111
FTC v. *Indiana Federation of Dentists* 87
functions of TRAI—aligning with the Competition Commission 51

GATS 10
goods 71
government 72
government companies 72
group 229
guidelines for evaluating effects of a merger on competition—US, UK 235

immunity from fine 118
immunity under the EC law—cartels 117
implementation of the MRTP Act 19
industrial policy – small-scale industry 45
infringements of article 81 or 82 305
inquiry into a combination—procedure 283
interchangeability of a product—the cellophane case 91
interim measures 310
interim orders—section 33 142, 197, 260
internet access services 256
investigation of a combination—procedure 284
investigations 306

joint control—shareholding and restructuring agreement 251
joint ventures 247
jurisdiction of civil courts excluded 314

law relating to competition 21
legitimate competition 188
lift and escalator cartels 112
limiting production, technical development, etc. 109
merger eliminating a competitor 252
merger or amalgamation 229
mergers 217
mergers—the Companies Act, 1956 203
minimizing conflict 262
minimum fees—*Goldfarb* v. *Virginia State Bar* 88
modernizing legislation—EEC 76
monopolies and exclusive service suppliers 11
monopolies created by the state—EU 46
monopolistic trade practices 16
MRTP Act 201
multidisciplinary partnerships 54
multijurisdiction mergers 261
multilateral framework on competition policy 318

need for control of mergers and acquisitions 207
need to review section 3(5) 140
negative clearance 305
non-disclosure of information 314
non-furnishing of information on combinations—section 43A 295
notice to the Commission under section 6(2) of a combination—section 30 286

obligation under TRIPS 137
OFT on price fixing 101

General Index

orders of the Commission on certain combinations—section 31   286
orders that may be passed by the Competition Commission   141, 195
overriding effect   314

parties to an agreement   69
patents   132
penalties   293
penalties under the act   43
penalty for offences in relation to furnishing of information—section 45   295
penalty—UK   297
per se rule   93
person   70
plasterboard cartel   107
pooling of patents and price-fixing   134
positive comity, enforcement of competition laws—1998 agreement between the EC and the USA   324
potential competition—section 7 of the Clayton Act   249
potential for conflict   44
power of the commission to regulate its own procedure—section 36   290
power to award compensation   289, 294
power to impose lesser penalty—section 46   295
power to issue interim orders   288
power to make regulations, sections 63 and 64   37
power to punish for contempt   42
practice   72
predatory price   160
predatory pricing   180

predatory pricing—internet access services   188
price   72
prior notification   264
privileged communication'—during investigation   312
procedure and powers of the appellate tribunal—section 53O   298
procedure for inquiry under section 19   278
process of dealing with abuse of a dominant position   195
pro-competitive benefits of vertical restraints   129
product market, end-uses   254
professional secrecy   307
professional services   53
provision for representative actions   303

rectification of orders—section 38   291
reduction of fine   119
refusal to deal   127
refusal to licence copyright material   193
refusal to supply   191
registrable agreements relating to restrictive trade practices   18
regulation of combinations under the competition act—the process   258
regulation of combinations—section 6   218
regulations setting out the procedure applicable to combinations   214
relevant geographic market   90, 166, 167
relevant product market   90, 166, 167

reliefs 260
repeal of the MRTP Act—
  section 66   315
report on competition in
  professional services, European
  Commission   57
resale price maintenance   128
restraint on competition outside the
  country through combination
  and a joint venture   248
restriction of territory of sale,
  persons, etc   189
restriction on employment,
  Chairperson and Members of
  Competition Commission   33
restriction on employment of
  chairman and other members
  of the Competition Appellate
  Tribunal   41
restrictive trade practice   17
review of orders of the
  Commission—section 37   291
review of the provisions of the
  Act   266
role for WTO   320
rule of reason   93
rule of reason—section 3(1)   95
rules for determining effect on
  competition   93

section 3—substance   73
secretary to the Commission,
  experts, professionals to assist the
  Commission   48
section 27   196
section 3(1)—appreciable adverse
  effect on competition within
  India   78
section 3(2)   104
section 3(3) cartels and similar
  groups   104

section 3—the elements   78
section 4—dominant position:
  abuse   157
seeking exemptions   305
selection of Chairperson and
  Members, Competition
  Commission   28
selling at a lower price   179
service   73
setting fines—EC   306
shares in a competing company
  246
sharing the market   110
skill and knowledge
  requirements   30
special study of sectors   307
specialization agreements   114
state monopolies   46
sub-markets   91
subsidiary's conduct attributed to
  holding company   172
substance of the articles of GATS   11

Telecom Regulatory Authority of
  India Act [TRAI], 1997   51
telecommunication services   255
telecommunications   49
term of office section 10,
  Chairperson and Members of
  Competition Commission   33
termination of a dealer's appointment
  by a manufacturer   102
territory restriction, franchisee   102
the 1991 agreement between the
  US and the EC—important
  clauses   322
the 2002 Act   236
the amendments to section 32   288
the Clayton Act—USA   214
the Companies Act, 1956   202
the Competition Act, 1998, UK   77

General Index

the Competition Act, UK—
professional services 82
the Competition Appellate
Tribunal 298
the Competition Commission,
UK 308
the courts' approach 205
the EC merger regulation 215
the Enterprise Act, 2002—UK 217
the Lombard Club 106
the material provisions of the law 15
the new competition law— repealing
the MRTP Act 13
the procedure—section 26 277
the procedure for adjudicating a
claim for compensation 302
the process—section 19 280
the proviso to section 3(3) 114
the Report of the International
Competition Policy Advisory
Committee, US, 2000 320
the scheme of the MRTP Act 15
the Securities and Exchange Board of
India (SEBI) 202
the substance of the agreement 266
the two rules under the competition
act 94
threshold levels 264
tie-in 121
trade 73
transaction costs 263

treatment of vertical restraints 129
TRIPS 12
turnover 229
tying-in—necessary market
power 123

UK 235
UK Agricultural Tractor Registration
Exchange 80
UK—cartels, leniency
programme 119
unfair trade practices 18
unfair trading conditions 176
US—enforcement 312
US–EU merger working group—
best practices on cooperation in
merger investigations 266

vertical integration 241
vertical restraints—section 3(4) 120
volume rebates 183
what is a cartel? 104
why a merger 204

Wood Pulp case 317
Wouters—multidisciplinary
partnerships 85
WTO agreements and the act 13
WTO and competition policy 318
WTO obligations 10

About the Author

T. Ramappa, a lawyer based in Chennai, is a legal consultant with a deep and long experience in company law and corporate commercial matters such as mergers, joint ventures, technology transfer agreements, equipment purchase contracts, licensing of intellectual property rights, their infringements, and arbitration. His articles on some of these subjects have been published in leading journals and newspapers in India. Some of his earlier published books include *Intellectual Property Rights under WTO: Tasks before India* (Wheeler Publishing: 2000), *Legal Issues in Electronic Commerce* (Macmillan India: 2002), and *Intellectual Property Rights Law in India* (Asia Law House: 2011). He has also been, for a long time, an associate member of the Institute of Company Secretaries of India (ICSI).